1 Jewish orphanages in Dutch society

Abstract

There were seven Jewish orphanages in the Netherlands before 1890: two Sephardic (boys/girls) and two Ashkenazi (boys/girls) homes in Amsterdam, and three "general" (co-educational) orphanages in The Hague, Rotterdam and in Utrecht. The Jewish orphanage in Leiden was established in 1890 specifically for children who were too young to be admitted to any of these pre-existing Jewish orphanages. Indeed, about half the children who were included in this study entered the orphanage in Leiden being less than six years old, including 25 two-year-old children, and seven toddlers who were just one year old.

Keywords: Jewish orphanages, Netherlands, pillarized society, social institutions, nineteenth century

Although small in size (barely 112,000 in a total population of just under 8 million in 1930; Table 1.1), the pre-war Jewish community in Holland maintained its own social institutions, including orphanages, hospitals (such as the *Joodse Invalide*), old-age homes, and even a mental institution (*Het Apeldoornse Bos*). This was entirely in line with the way Dutch society was organized before the Second World War, and in fact until the 1970s. Protestants and Catholics, making up 81% of the population in 1930 (Table 1.1), also had their own social institutions, including orphanages. Between so many Protestant, Catholic, and civil or "public" (i.e. non-religious or non-denominational) social institutions, the Jewish orphanages did not draw particular attention. Providing social care was not seen as a government responsibility before the war. It was very much left to each social group to look after their own.

This "vertical" affiliation was not limited to Protestants and Catholics. Socialists and Liberals also maintained their own organizations. These covered every aspect of society: political party, professional societies, trade unions, newspaper, broadcasting (radio) corporation, social institutions, and so on. The Dutch use the word *verzuild* for this organization, a *zuil* being a pillar supporting a roof or building. Although there was competition and animosity between the pillars, there was a strong feeling that each of the pillars had a shared responsibility towards supporting Dutch society as a whole.

Focke, Jaap W., *Machseh Lajesoumim: A Jewish Orphanage in the City of Leiden, 1890-1943*.
Taylor & Francis Group, 2021
DOI: 10.5117/9789463726955_ch01

Table 1.1 **The very nature of a "verzuilde" ("pillarized") society: The Netherlands according to the National Census of 1930 (the last one before the war)**

Denomination	Netherlands	%	Amsterdam	%	Leiden	%
Nederduits Hervormd	2.732.333	34,4	160.913	21,2	29.837	42,1
Waalsch Hervormd	6.358		1.865		249	
Remonstrants	29.719		4.004		1.090	
Christelijk gereformeerd	50.230		2.911		531	
Doopsgezind	62.012		9.054		514	
Evangelisch Luthers	78.330		24.941		1.050	
Hersteld Evangelisch Luthers	11.937		8.024		87	
Gereformeerde Kerken	638.372		30.266		4.568	
total Protestant:	3.602.933	45,4	241.978	31,9	37.926	53,5
Roomsch Katholiek	2.890.022		166.526		17.625	
Oud Roomsch	10.182		621		77	
total Roman Catholic:	2.900.204	36,5	167.147	22,1	17.702	25,0
Nederlands Israëlitisch	106.723		60.976		314	
Portugeesch Israëlitisch	5.194		4.547		5	
total Israelite:	111.917	1,4	65.523	8,7	319	0,5
Other denominations	169.575	2,1	18.735	2,5	1.841	2,6
Not religeous (secular)	1.144.393	14,4	263.991	34,9	13.037	18,4
Unknown	185	-	12	-	0	-
Grand total respondents:	7.935.565	100	757.386	100	70.825	100
1930	Netherlands		Amsterdam		Leiden	

With universal suffrage since 1919, general elections based on candidate lists prepared by political parties, proportional representation in parliament, and a very low electoral threshold (0.67%), no party can ever hope to gain a ruling majority, and no government has ever been possible without coalitions, collaboration, and compromises. It gave rise to the Dutch *polder model* of politics, whereby, instead of an elected government deciding solely based on "winner takes all", parties involved sit around the table until a mutually agreed compromise is reached. This model, based on creating consensus, outlasted the *verzuiling* by many decades, but it has become under pressure with the further political fragmentation[1] and the rise of populist parties in recent decades.

---

1   No less than 23 political parties were admitted to the 2017 general elections, thirteen of which achieved representation in parliament (including, for the first time, an Islamic party). When this book went to press, 37 parties were admitted to the general election of March 2021.

Protestants, having achieved hard-won independence from Catholic Spain, dominated the country from the early days of the Dutch Republic and the "Golden Age" which followed. Holland was considered a Protestant country. Catholics formed the largest minority, without equal rights until their emancipation during and after the French occupation (1795-1813).

The Catholic pillar was more homogenous, in line with its more centralist organization, than the Protestant pillar. The 1930 census recognized no less than eight different Protestant congregations (Table 1.1), and many more if small church groups and sects are included. Many of these not only maintained their own church, but also separate social organizations, schools, and in some cases even a political party. It was not until 1977 that the Catholic People's Party (*Katholieke Volkspartij*) and the two largest Protestant parties merged into what is now a Christian-democrat political party, Christian Democratic Appeal (*Christen-Democratisch Appèl*). Some smaller Christian parties remain independent to this day.

The emancipation of Jews in Holland (not unlike the emancipation of Catholics) was a gradual process dating back to 1796 during the French period, when their full civic rights were enshrined by the parliament of the Batavian Republic. The Jewish clergy and establishment were not altogether happy with the emancipation, because it signified the end of their power to settle legal affairs within their own community. There is extensive literature on the history of the Jewish community in the Netherlands. For further reading, see Michman et al., *Pinkas* (1999), in Dutch and Hebrew, as well as a host of (English-language) articles in the published proceedings of the International Symposia on the History of the Jews in the Netherlands (particularly Brasz & Kaplan, 2001; Kaplan, 2008), and Blom et al. (2002, 2017, 2021).

Sephardic Jews had come to the Netherlands from Spain and Portugal in the sixteenth century, either directly, or via other Mediterranean countries, to escape repression by the Almohad caliphs, or later by the Catholic rulers of the Iberian Peninsula. When the Sephardic Jews arrived, the Dutch Republic had entered *"a spectacularly creative episode"* (Jonathan Israel, 1995; also in Blom et al., 2017) and they quickly formed a relatively affluent community.

Ashkenazi Jews arrived in the Netherlands much later, particularly during the last decades of the nineteenth century, fleeing repression and pogroms in Eastern Europe and Russia, but also from Germany. They arrived generally penniless and in greater numbers at a time when the Republic had declined and fallen back to a monarchy. They had a much harder struggle to lift themselves from poverty.

There were some 5000 Sephardim and 106,000 Ashkenazi Jews in the Netherlands (Table 1.1; Census 1930). Sephardic Jews are usually called *"Portugees"*, while for Ashkenazi, most of whom spoke Yiddish when they arrived, the words *"Hoogduits"* or *"Nederlands Israëlitisch"* are used. Thus, the two great synagogues of Amsterdam are the *Portugese* and the *Hoogduitse* synagogues (the latter is now the *Joods Historisch Museum*), standing opposite each other on the Jonas Daniël Meijer Square.

The Jewish Quarter in Amsterdam, which was in fact a mixed Jewish/non-Jewish neighbourhood, harboured an impoverished population. These Jews were in general far more interested in improving their economic fortunes, if necessary by adapting to Dutch culture, than in forming an independent Jewish pillar in society. Their preferred affiliation was politically left, rather than religious. State and religion were formally separated in Holland in 1848, and gradually many people became more secular. For Jews as well as for Protestants and (possibly to a lesser degree) Catholics, it became acceptable to find their own personal balance between maintaining their religious identity and affiliation, and the wish to integrate in Dutch society (Blom & Cahen, 2017). The development of the Socialist pillar was a gradual process during the nineteenth and twentieth centuries, coinciding with development of a labour movement. Economic development accelerated from approximately 1870, and the growing proletariat started to gain influence. The Liberal pillar developed later and became attractive to the growing group of Dutch Jews who had outgrown poverty and gained firm positions in Dutch society.

"Jewish" shops, industries and businesses developed. Jews were also increasingly achieving positions in academia, finance, law, medicine, and other professions. Only in agriculture and technical professions did they remain underrepresented (ibidem). The relatively mild form of anti-Semitism in pre-war Holland, and the relatively weak attraction of Zionism to Dutch Jews (compared to Eastern Europe) had much to do with the above-mentioned developments. Salemink (2001) claims that Dutch Catholics by 1930 still formed a segregated sub-society, more so than the Dutch Jews, who appeared to be more assimilated than the Catholics (ibid., p. 108) at the time.[2] Some Jewish Dutchmen declared that they were hardly conscious of their Jewish roots until they were brutally confronted with that fact by the Nazis. But despite significant secularization and acculturation, even assimilation, many Jews maintained their affiliation with Jewish culture and history, the lasting impact of 2700 years of repeated expulsions and ever-changing diaspora. Quite different to Christians or Muslims, who do not share such exclusive history, Jews who gave up their religion were often still Jews in their own eyes. The Dutch model was certainly not ideal, or without conflicts and frictions between the various groups. Anti-Semitism and discrimination also occurred.

---

2   Clearly in some circles anti-Catholic sentiment was stronger than any such feelings towards the Jews. No doubt the fact that the Dutch Catholics became politically powerful following their emancipation played a role. The phrase *"Liever Turks dan Paaps"* ("I'd rather suffer Turks [Muslims], than Catholics") never entirely lost its bite in the Protestant part of the Netherlands.

Although the Jewish Dutch maintained their own religious and social institutions, these are generally not considered to represent a fully-fledged pillar (Blom & Cahen, 2017; Happe, 2017, 2018). It was too small, and some important aspects of a pillar, such as a Jewish political party, never developed. The great majority of Jewish children attended common "public" (i.e. non-denominational) Dutch schools. Zionism exerted great fascination, but until the arrival of refugees from 1933 it had very few real followers in Holland compared to countries in the East. The vast majority of Jews in the Netherlands were Dutch citizens, in sharp contrast with Belgium and France where most were aliens. It is fascinating[3] to review the hundreds of intrinsically Dutch family names which the Ashkenazi Jews adopted when civil registration was implemented during the French period.

Amongst the many Protestant, Catholic, and non-religious orphanages which existed between 1850 and 1940, the eight Jewish orphanages (Table 1.2) did not stand out. Providing social care was largely left to private initiatives. Funding had to come from within each community, and every denominational group was expected to look after their own. The increasing need for social care was driven by industrial development, poverty, and large families.

The first two (Sephardic) orphanages were established in Amsterdam in 1648 (for boys) and 1734 (for girls), followed by the two Ashkenazi orphanages in 1738 (boys) and 1761 (girls). Rotterdam and The Hague followed in 1833 and 1849. These two cities had the largest Jewish communities after Amsterdam, but not large enough to justify more than one orphanage, so they accepted Sephardic and Ashkenazi children, and girls as well as boys. The "Central" orphanage in Utrecht was established in 1871 to cater for children from the – often very small – Jewish communities outside Amsterdam, Rotterdam and The Hague, and the countryside in general. The orphanage in Leiden was the last one to open its doors, in 1890 (Ch. 2). Table 1.2 summarizes the basic information about the eight orphanages mainly from Metz (2005), and from other sources quoted in the text.

Apart from these "regular" eight orphanages, three other Jewish institutions need to be mentioned (Table 1.3) which also provided dedicated child's care. The Bergstichting in Laren took in children who were judicially removed from their parental home, amongst others. The Rudelsheimstichting in Hilversum took care of Jewish mentally handicapped children. Paedagogium Achisomov developed as a stand-alone children's ward of Het Apeldoornse Bos, a Jewish psychiatric institution.

There were contacts and connections between these eleven institutions, which were complimentary to each other in more than one way. The Jewish congregation in Leiden financially supported both the local orphanage, and the Rudelsheimstichting, until 1942 when the Jewish institutions were stripped of control over

---

3   See, for example, www.joods.nl/ or search on: Joodse achternamen.

Table 1.2   The Jewish orphanages in The Netherlands, summarized from Metz (2005) and other sources

City & Name	Established Denomination Boys/Girls	Capacity (appr. year)	Additional information New = new purpose-built home	Orphanage liquidated on:	No people deported incl. staff
Amsterdam Aby Yethomiem[1]	1648 Sephardic Boys from age 5	? (1717) 22 (1850) 18 (1943)	1717 Acquired first building[2] Year unknown Jodenbreestr. no. 87 Year unknown Plantage Middenlaan no. 80[3]	10th February 1943	18 (?)
Amsterdam Mazon Habanoth[4]	1743 Sephardic Girls from age 5	19 (1750) 3 (1860) 18 (1943)	1741-1787 Zwanenburgerstraat 1787-1868 Nieuwe Herengracht no. 121 1868-1943 N. Prinsengracht no. 17 Gedenkboek 1934[5]	10th February 1943[6]	14 (?)
Amsterdam Megadle Jethomim[7]	1738 Ashkenazi Boys from age 5	25 (1836) 45 (1865) 100 (1943)	1836 Zwanenburgerstraat (25 boys) 1865-1943 Amstel no. 21 (10?) (new) Gedenkboek 1938	10th February 1943	>50[8] (?)
Amsterdam Mangasiem Toviem Magadle Jethomiem[9]	1761 Ashkenazi Girls from age 5	14 (1842) 34 (1861) 80 (1915) 103 (1943)	Possible precursor in 1734 1861 Rapenburgerstraat no. 171 1889 Rapenburgerstr. no. 169 (addition)	10th February 1943	70
Rotterdam Megaddelee[10] Jethomiem	1833 Mixed From age 5	30 (1889) 50-60 (1933)	1848-1851 Boompjes/ Kwakernaat 1851-1898 Oppert no. 243 1898-1943 Matenesselaan no. 208 (new) Gedenkboek 1933	26th February 1943	55[11] (?)
The Hague Ezer Hathom[12]	1849 Mixed From age 5	20 (1851) 35 (1889) 42 (1932)	1849-1880 Stille Veerkade no. 20 1880-1932 Raamstraat no. 45 1932-1943 Pletterijstraat no. 66 (new)	6th March 1943	51[13]

City & Name	Established Denomination Boys/Girls	Capacity (appr. year)	Additional information New = new purpose-built home	Orphanage liquidated on:	No people deported incl. staff
Utrecht Miflat Jatom[14]	1871 Central[15] Mixed From age 5-6	45 (1871) 54 (1942)	1871-1942 Nieuwegracht 92 (1938-1939 Baarnseweg Den Dolder[16]) 1942-1943 Geld.kade 67-71 (A'dam)	15th October 1942 > February 10th, 1943[17]	52[18]
Leiden Machseh Lajesoumim[19]	1890 Central Mixed No lower age restriction	30 (1891) 58 (1929)	1890 Nieuwsteeg no. 4. 1891-1929 Stille Rijn no. 4 1929-1943 Roodenburger-str. no. 1a (new) Gedenkboek 1929	17th March 1943	59[20]

1 Padre de los Huerfanos (Father of Orphans).
2 Location unknown.
3 It had a capacity of sixteen, but there was limited demand from this community, and only ten places were occupied.
4 Bringing up Daughters (Opvoeding der Dochteren).
5 Mendes-da Costa, 1934.
6 Metz (2005, p. 54): "The building on the Nieuwe Prinsengracht was renovated in 1926, and a memorial book issued in 1934. We know very little about circumstances during the German occupation. There probably were fourteen girls living there at the time. The children and their caretakers were all taken away and deported in February 1943."
7 Bringing up Orphans (Opvoeding der Wezen).
8 The Joods Monument lists 68 victims, but some of them left the orphanage before 10th February 1943.
9 Taking care of orphaned girls is charitable work indeed (Tot goede werken behoort opvoeding van weesmeisjes).
10 Bringing up Orphans (Opvoeding van Wezen); Originally Ezrath Jethomiem (Assistance to Orphans).
11 On the same day the children of the Jewish orphanage, the patients of the Jewish hospital, and those of the Oudeliedengesticht (the old age home, zoek beter woord) were taken away and deported to Westerbork, in total some 250 people (Metz, 2005). The Joods Monument lists 55 child victims as wards of the orphanage.
12 Assistence to Orphans.
13 The Joods Monument lists 60 victims; some of them had left the orphanage before 6th March 1943.
14 Home for Children.
15 "Central" means that children were accepted from anywhere in the country (and from other countries during refugee crises), and from both Ashkenazi and Sephardic backgrounds. However, a lower age limit applied in Utrecht of five to six years, and the need to accept babies when necessary, was the primary reason to establish the Leiden orphanage.
16 The summer villa of the Utrecht orphanage was used to house 56 refugee children from Germany (Crone, 2005) following the Kristallnacht.
17 The home in Utrecht was liquidated in October 1942, and the children and staff were "evacuated" to Amsterdam. Most were deported to Westerbork on 10th February 1943.
18 This is made up of 33 refugees and 22 Dutch children, total 55 of which 8 or 9 survived. Excluding 8 (?) staff members and the 2 young children of Director Themans. Note: figures may vary depending on how and on which date a count is made. The Joods Monument lists 56 victims (November 2017).
19 Machasee la-Jethomiem (Refuge for Orphans).
20 This is made up of 7 staff and 52 children, including the 2 children of Director Italie; 2 children were released, and 2 children survived deportation (Table 7.1, pp. 178-179).

Table 1.3

City Name	Established Denomination (target group)	Capacity (appr. year)	Additional information	Orphanage liquidated on:	No people deported (appr.)
Laren Berg Stichting	1911 *Inter alia* Judicial out of home placements	40 (1920) 80 (1935) 104 (1940)	Doodweg no. 2 (Laren) -- 1942 Rapenburg nos. 92-96 (A'dam)	5th Dec. 1942	36[1]
Hilversum Rudelsheim Stichting	1925 Mentally handicapped	30 (1925) 88 (1938)	1925 Verdilaan no. 10 1942 Soestdijkerstraatweg[2] no. 151	16th April 1942/7th April 1943	79[3]
Apeldoorn Paedagogium Achisomog	1933 Mentally handicapped	7 (1925) 72 (1933)	This was initially the children's ward of Apeldoornse Bos	22nd Jan. 1943	94[4]

1   The director saved 70 out of 106 of his children from deportation.
2   The building on Verdilaan was confiscated by the Wehrmacht on 16th April 1942.
3   Ten staff and 69 children were taken to Amsterdam, then to Westerbork before being deported to Sobibor (Staal, 2008).
4   A list of the names of 1069 deported patients and staff of Apeldoornse Bos was published in *De Stentor* on 21st January 2013; see also Westerbork and the Joods Monument.

Table 1.3. Dedicated institutional childcare was also provided by the Rudelsheim and Berg Foundations, and by Achisomov, the children's ward of the Apeldoornse Bos mental institution. They accepted children who could not be properly cared for by the "regular" Jewish orphanages.

their own finances. On occasion, children were transferred from one institution to another. Several children from the orphanage in Leiden were transferred to the Rudelsheimstichting, including Maurits Levie, Barend Ritmeester and Isidoor Wegloop, or to Achisomov (including Barend Bora Kool, Levie van der Pool, and Maurits Alvares Vega). Note that the numbers of children quoted in Tables 1.2 and 1.3 cannot be established with accuracy. From 1933, as war was approaching, the number of residents (including refugees) changed with increasing frequency, particularly in Utrecht where the Jewish orphanage took in more refugees than any of the others. The number of children in Achisomov increased from 7 in 1925 to 74 in 1939 and continued to increase during the first years of the occupation. Presser (1965, p. 322) estimated that by late 1942 there were at least 94 children in Achisomov (see also Ch. 7.3). The *Joods Monument* lists[4] 58 victims from the

4   As per September 2018. The lists on the Joods Monument may not be inclusive, and they may also include children who had left before the orphanage in question was liquidated.

Rudelsheimstichting, and 46 victims from the Bergstichting. Both the Berg and Rudelsheim Foundations served as a home for Jewish war orphans after May 1945 (van der Eerden, 2014; Staal, 2008, 2015).

Because the orphanage in Utrecht was taking care of children outside the reach of the pre-existing institutions, the establishment of yet another Jewish orphanage was not a self-evident necessity, nor was Leiden an obvious choice for its location. Leiden is an old city in the western part of Holland, just 35 km south-west of Amsterdam, and 15 km north-east of The Hague. It proudly features a grand fair on the 2nd and 3rd of October every year, to celebrate the delivery from the Spanish army in 1574. In the whole of the Netherlands, only the schoolchildren in the Leiden region have that day off. Following a period of economic prosperity, it entered a long period of decline in the eighteenth and nineteenth centuries. By the early twentieth century, the central part of the city, it was said, was even more impoverished than the centre of Amsterdam.

From the late eighteenth century, Leiden had a small Jewish community within its walls, which slowly grew to 319 souls in 1930, less than 0.5% of the Leiden population (Table 1.1). This Jewish community was also relatively affluent compared to the Jewish population in Amsterdam. Thus, there was no need for a Jewish orphanage within the city. Instead, the new orphanage was designed for a national function: to cater for children in need who were too young (less than five to six years) for the other orphanages, or who did not fulfil other requirements to be admitted. The initiative to establish this orphanage in Leiden came from A.I. Kiek. He was concerned that, as a result of the above-mentioned restrictions (including those applicable to his own orphanage, he was director of the Jewish orphanage in Rotterdam), too many very young children were left in the country without proper care.

The history of the early years is given by Leman (1929) and is summarized in the next chapter. The new orphanage was called *Machseh Lajesoumim* (Refuge for Orphans). Its official name was *Centraal Israëlitisch Wees- en Doorgangshuis* (Central [i.e. *nation-wide*] Jewish Orphanage and Transit Home). It was intended from the start as a place where any Jewish child, no matter the age or gender, whether Sephardic or Ashkenazi, or of whatever background, would be catered for. In addition, it was less strict with respect to Jewish law and tradition when it came to admitting children (Metz, 2005). Most importantly, children in need, for whom it was not clear who the father was, were also welcome in Leiden. These factors probably formed the basis for the rather easy-going and liberal nature of this – otherwise orthodox – institution, particularly after the move to the new building in 1929.

Including the words "transit home" in the name reflects the initial idea that children who were taken in because they were too young, would transfer to the orphanage in which they "belonged" as soon as they reached the required age. An Ashkenazi boy from Amsterdam would go the orphanage on the Amstel, upon reaching age five or six. A Jewish child from The Hague would move there if he still had family in The Hague, or, if they were Sephardic, he or she could move to the Sephardic boys' or girls' home in Amsterdam. Indeed, such transfers took place in the first 39 years of the orphanage (van Zegveld, 1993). Given the difficult conditions in the Leiden orphanage in that period (next chapter), that was probably very appropriate. But from 1929 onwards an increasing number of children did not leave when they could have transferred. The wonderful new building will certainly have played a role in as far as children themselves preferred to stay in Leiden. But the orphanages in Amsterdam, Rotterdam and The Hague also had modern, well-equipped buildings, so the building in Leiden in itself does not explain why children did not transfer when reaching the appropriate age. Several witness accounts suggest how strong the feeling was among the children in Leiden of belonging to a family as they grew older. Precisely the fact that many children arrived at much younger age in Leiden (some under two) meant that they spent their most formative years in Leiden. Sally Montezinos (Chs. 2.3, 7.2, 8.5) is a good example. The older children and adolescents also played a role, certainly in a social sense, in taking care of the young ones. A great number of group photographs, taken by one of the older children, also include some of the much younger children. Lastly, but this is speculation, the director and his staff probably had no desire to encourage children to transfer as long as they could continue to accept new applications of very young ones. Of course, the war made everything which occurred *before* the war look more positive than it was in reality. Nevertheless, there is ample contemporary evidence, some of it included in the following chapters, to support the idea that the Leiden orphanage, from the summer of 1929, was in many respects a happy place.

The number of "real" orphans was very small in all these institutions. Most or even all children still had at least one parent, usually the mother. Fathers were supposed to support the families, and it was therefore often the death of the father or his inability to provide support for other reasons, which caused children to be taken into institutional care. If the mother died, children often stayed with the father while the older girls in the family took over the role of the mother. Families were large, poor, and often unstable, parents died, or divorced, remarried someone who also had children from a previous marriage, and so on. The case of Barend Bora Kool (Ch. 8.2) provides a good illustration. Contact between the orphanage children and parents was highly variable. Piet de Vries (Ch. 5.3) spent many summer holidays with his mother, away from Leiden. Others received regular visits in Leiden. The mother of Mieke Dagloonder is said to have never visited her daughter in Leiden.

Several books tell us about life in these Jewish orphanages. Leman (1929) issued a memorial book for the Leiden orphanage. Daan Choekat (1986) gives us an inside view of the Ashkenazi boys' home in Amsterdam. An official memorial publication to celebrate the 200th birthday of this orphanage on the Amstel River (Asscher et al., 1938) contains unique photographs. Lea Appel (1982) provides a rare view of the Ashkenazi girls' home on Rapenburgerstraat in Amsterdam, also with many photographs, but without identifying the children. Other memorial books were issued for the Jewish orphanage in Rotterdam (Wijsenbeek, 1933) and the Portuguese Jewish girls' orphanage in Amsterdam (Mendes da Costa, 1934). Much information about the orphanage in Utrecht is given by Crone (2005).

The first 39 years of the orphanage in Leiden were difficult in many ways. But on 18th June 1929, the Jewish orphanage in Leiden moved into a brand-new building at Roodenburgerstraat no. 1a, in what was planned to become a new, south-east, extension of the city. The plot to build on was purchased in 1903, but it took a quarter of a century to raise the funds to start building in 1928. The new building was inaugurated in 1929. This book focuses on the period from 1929 to 1943, supported by an overwhelming amount of information, photographs, and surviving stories, but also because it represents a time of relative happiness and stability, which lasted not even fourteen years before it came to an unimaginably brutal end.

References

Appel, Lea, 1982; *"Het brood der doden. Geschiedenis en ondergang van een joods meisjes-weeshuis"*. Baarn, Bosch & Keuning, ISBN 9024644275. [An illustrated history of the Ashkenazi girls' home in Amsterdam. For a description of the Ashkenazi boys' home in Amsterdam, See Choekat, 1986, and references in Ch. 1.]

Asscher, E., Ph. Coppenhagen, B.P. Gomperts & J.M. Lob, 1938; *"Gedenkboek ter gelegenheid van het 200-jarig bestaan van het Nederlandsch Israëlitisch Jongensweeshuis Megadlé Jethomim te Amsterdam"* [Commemorative book on the occasion of the 200th anniversary of the Dutch Israelite Boys' Orphanage Megadlé Jethomim in Amsterdam (in Dutch)]. Published by the Board of Governors. See also Choekat, 1986, and Appel, 1982.

Blom, J.C.H., 1989b; *"Nederland in de jaren dertig: een 'burgerlijk-verzuilde' maatschappij in een crisisperiode"*. In: Blom, 1989a, pp. 1-27.

Blom, J.C.H. & J.J. Cahen, 2017; *"Joodse Nederlanders, Nederlandse joden en joden in Nederland (1870-1940)"*. In: Blom et al., 2017, pp. 275-359.

Blom, J.C.H., D.J. Wertheim, H. Berg & B.T. Wallet (eds), 2021; *"Reappraising the history of the Jews in the Netherlands"*. Trans. by David McKay. London, Littman Library of Jewish Civilization, ISBN 9781786941879. [In press.]

Blom, J.C.H., H. Berg, B. Wallet & D. Wertheim (eds), 2017; *"Geschiedenis van de Joden in Nederland"*. Balans, ISBN 9789460034374. [The English edition, not used in preparing this book, is in press with Littmann Library, see Blom et al., 2021.]

Blom, J.C.H., R.G. Fuks-Mansfeld & I. Schöffer (eds), 2002; *"The history of the Jews in the Netherlands"*. Oxford, The Littman Library of Jewish Civilization, ISBN 9781904113553 or 9781874774518.

Brasz, Chaya & Yosef Kaplan (eds), 2001; *"Dutch Jews as perceived by themselves and by others: The proceedings of the eighth International Symposium on the History of the Jews in the Netherlands"*. Leiden, Brill, ISBN 9004120386. [This volume contains English-language articles on many aspects of Jewish life and history in the Netherlands.] See also Kaplan, 2008.

Census (the Netherlands), 1930 and other years. Available at www.volkstellingen.nl.

Choekat, Daan, 1986; *"Daantjes jeugdjaren in het Joodse Jongensweeshuis"*. Bne Brak, Daan Choekat & Sons, ISBN 9652220841. [An insider's view of the Ashkenazi boys' home on the Amstel, Amsterdam]. See also Asscher et al., 1938, and Appel, 1982.

Crone, F., 2005; *"Voorbijgaand verblijf. Joodse weeskinderen in oorlogstijd"*. Amsterdam, De Prom, ISBN 9068011162. [Focused on refugees from Germany and the Jewish orphanage in Utrecht.]

Eerden, E. van der, 2014; *"De Berg-Stichting: 'oase in harde en desillusioneerende maatschappij'"*. *Contactblad '40-'45*, pp. 4-7. ISSN 1569-1209.

Happe, Katja, 2017; *"Viele falsche Hoffnungen: Judenverfolgung in den Niederlanden 1940-1945"*. Paderborn, Ferdinand Schöningh Verlag, ISBN-13 9783506784247. [A Dutch translation was published in 2018: *"Veel valse hoop. De jodenvervolging in Nederland 1940-1945"*. Atlas Contact, ISBN 9789045035888.]

Israel, Jonathan I., 1998; *"The Dutch Republic: Its rise, greatness, and fall, 1477-1806"*. Oxford, Clarendon Press, ISBN 0198730721/8207344.

Kaplan, Yosef (ed.), 2008; *"The Dutch intersection: The Jews and the Netherlands in modern history"*. Leiden, Brill. Available online (from some universities) at EBSCOhost Academic Collection – World Wide. [This volume contains English-language articles on many aspects of Jewish life and history in the Netherlands.] See also Brasz & Kaplan, 2001.

Leman, IS, (5689) 1929; *"Het Centraal Israelitisch Wees- en Doorgangshuis te Leiden in woord en beeld (1890-1929)"*. Title on the cover: *"Uit de geschiedenis van een nuttige instelling"*. Den Haag, Drukkerij Levisson, with contributions by J.L. Palache.

Mendes da Costa, Joseph, 1934; *"Het Portugeesch-Israëlitisch Meisjesweeshuis 'Mazon Habanoth' Amsterdam 5495 (1734) 6 Sebath, 5694 (1934): uitgegeven ter gelegenheid van zijn tweehonderd jarig bestaan"*. [Memorial book, 200 years of the Sephardic girls' orphanage in Amsterdam; rare copy in JHM (JCK), Amsterdam.]

Metz, Daniël, 2005; *"Een historisch overzicht van acht joodse weeshuizen in Nederland"*. *Misjpoge, tijdschrift van de Nederlandse Kring voor Joodse Genealogie* 2005-2.

Michman, Dan, 1989; *"Migration versus 'Species Hollandia Judaica': The role of migration in the nineteenth and twentieth centuries in preserving ties between Dutch and World Jewry"*. *Studia Rosenthaliana* 23, 54-76.

Michman, Jozeph, Hartog Beem & Dan Michman, 1999; *"Pinkas. Geschiedenis van de joodse gemeenschap in Nederland"*. Incorporating research by Victor Brilleman. Amsterdam, Uitgeverij Contact & NIK, ISBN 9025495133. [The original text of this comprehensive history of the Jews in the Netherlands is also available in Hebrew, Yad Vashem, Holocaust Martyrs' and Heroes Remembrance Authority, Jerusalem, 1985.]

Presser, J., 1965; *"Ondergang. De vervolging en verdelging van het Nederlandse Jodendom, 1940-1945"*. 's-Gravenhage, Staatsuitgeverij/Martinus Nijhoff. [The entire Dutch text is available online (with search facility) at http://www.dbnl.org. Although written more than half a century ago, the book is still very readable and impressive today.] An English translation was pulished by E.P. Dutton & Co. in 1969 (ASIN B000LD8D7S), and again in 1988 under the title *"Ashes in the wind: The destruction of Dutch Jewry"* by Wayne State University Press; re-issued in 2010, ISBN 9780285638136.

Salemink, Theo, 2001; *"Strangers in a strange country: Catholic views of Jews in the Netherlands, 1918-1945"*. In: Brasz & Kaplan, 2001, pp. 107-123.

Staal, Philip, 2008; *"Roestvrijstaal. Speurtocht naar de erfenis van Joodse oorlogswezen"*. Delft, Eburon, ISBN 9789059722712. English edition: Staal, 2015.

Staal, Philip, 2015; *"Settling the account (Mijn erfenis)"*. Bloomington, iUniverse, ISBN 9781491751664/51657.

Wijsenbeek, S.S., 1933; *"Gedenkboek 100 jaar Joods Weeshuis Rotterdam"* [Memorial book: 100 years of the Jewish orphanage in Rotterdam]. [A rare copy at Rotterdam Gemeentearchief, no. 1174.]

Zegveld, W.F. van, 1993; *"Joods Wees- en Doorgangshuis Leiden, bewoners 1890-1951"*. Originally in: *"De Joden van Leiden"*. Unpublished; 4 volumes. [Several copies were made, available (i.a.) at Erfgoed Leiden (ELO) and the Joods Historisch Museum, Amsterdam. The results of his painstaking research have served as a basis for subsequent investigations. Note that his report is an important source of information on children and staff in the Leiden orphanage who are not included in this book because they had left before the move to the new building in 1929, as well as Jewish citizens of the Leiden region who were not connected to the orphanage.]

2   1890 to 1929: A long and difficult period

Abstract

The 300-year-old building was entirely unsuitable as a children's care home. It had no facilities, and it was so dilapidated that it could not be restored. Year by year, the governors discussed possible solutions. In 1903 they acquired a plot of land on the outskirts of Leiden, in the Rodenburger Polder. But lack of funds kept building plans in limbo until a new and expanded board of governors, now also including women, decided to make a commitment despite the economic uncertainties at the time. Building started in June 1928, made possible by active fundraising and supported by Protestant and Catholic organizations, civil authorities, and the community in Leiden as a whole.

Keywords: Jewish orphanage, 1890-1929

2.1   Making do at Stille Rijn no. 4

The Leiden orphanage was opened on 19th May 1890 in a temporary building at Nieuwsteeg no. 4 in Leiden. A year later, on 7th July 1891, it moved into a building at Nieuwe Rijn no. 4 (Figs. 2.1 and 2.2). The building, a former wool warehouse, was a gift, and as such it was gratefully accepted by the board of governors, but it was wholly inadequate as a home for children. It was very old (it had served as a beer brewery in 1578) and badly maintained. Only gas lighting was available. There was constant fear of a fire in this building with its timber interior. There was no facility to take care of the sick, no adequate playground, there were holes in the floor, and during storms pieces of the roof were blown away. Thousands of florins were spent on repairs, money which the governors would have much preferred to go into the building fund (Leman, 1929). Yet they managed with what they had (Figs. 2.3 and 2.4) for 39 years[1] without a major accident. The two cases of children dying in the orphanage occurred in the early years: Amalia van den Berg on 8th May 1893 and Rebecca Kades on 31st December 1895, both as a result of illness (van Zegveld 1993, p. 170).

---

1   Including the year at Nieuwe Rijn.

Focke, Jaap W., *Machseh Lajesoumim: A Jewish Orphanage in the City of Leiden, 1890-1943*.
Taylor & Francis Group, 2021
DOI: 10.5117/9789463726955_CH02

Figure 2.1: Stille Rijn no. 4, early twentieth century. The signs left and right of the door, behind the trees, read: "Centraal Isr. Kinder en Doorgangsweeshuis"; the sign above the first floor: "Toevlucht voor Weezen" (in Hebrew: Machseh Lajesoumim) (see text).

From the beginning, the governors in Leiden had in mind to build a new home, if ever the necessary funds could be raised. They will have looked with some envy at the Ashkenazi *boys'* home in Amsterdam (Megadle Jethomim, see Table 1.2) which, 25 years earlier (1865), had moved, with some 45 boys, into a newly built home, beautiful and well equipped, on the banks of the Amstel River (see Asscher et al., 1938). That building was demolished after the war, together with almost the entire Jewish Quarter of Amsterdam, but the outline is marked by granite stones, partly covered by the *Muziektheater.*[2] It was more than double the size, and it had, within the building, a synagogue, playrooms, sick bay, teaching rooms, and even

2   https://jck.nl/nl/node/1783 and https://www.joodsamsterdam.nl/joods-jongensweeshuis-megadle-jethomim/.

Figure 2.2: The old orphanage at Stille Rijn no. 4 is the first building on the left. Photo probably taken around 1905, looking east towards the oldest part of the city. *"Stille"* or "silent" means this body of water is no longer a flowing river. In Roman times, however, this was an active branch of the Rhine River, and part of the Limes, the frontier between the Roman Empire (on the right) and the barbarians. A rich collection of Roman artefacts has been discovered along the Dutch Limes in recent decades.

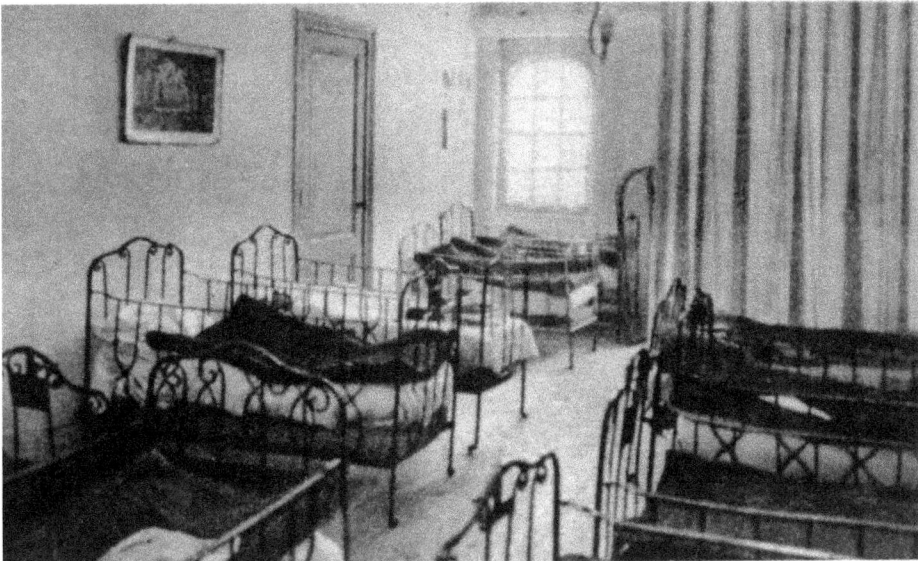

Figure 2.3: One of the bedrooms in the old orphanage.

Figure 2.4: From 1890 to 1929, this was the only room available for some 30 children for dining, playing and doing homework. From Leman, 1929.

a sukkah to celebrate the Feast of Tabernacles while being able to look at the sky (Asscher et al., 1938). It would continue to grow until it housed some 100 boys in 1943. In Rotterdam, a new building was inaugurated in 1898 at Matenesselaan no. 208 (Wijsenbeek, 1933). The Ashkenazi *girls'* home in Amsterdam had solved its most pressing space problems in 1889 (Metz, 2005) by acquiring the building at Rapenburgerstraat no. 169, adjacent to the existing one at no. 171 (Appel, 1982). In The Hague they had also decided that a new building was required at the beginning of the twentieth century, but as was the case in Leiden, it took almost 30 years for the plan to come to fruition. They moved to Pletterijstraat no. 66 in 1932, three years after the new orphanage in Leiden was inaugurated (van Creveld, 2001, 2004).

Financial realities about building a new home forced the governors in Leiden to consider other options as well, such as renovating the building on Stille Rijn, or extending it by buying the adjacent building, or buying an altogether different pre-existing building and adapting it to the needs of an orphanage. Even merging with one of the other orphanages was looked at, but without positive result: the differences in styles, regulations, and philosophy were too great. A "construction committee" had been convened in 1898 to consider building a new orphanage. It failed to achieve anything. A second committee in 1902 was more successful, and in 1903 a plot of land was purchased in what is known today as the *Profburgwijk*,[3] the *Professors' and Burgomasters' Quarter*, which itself was also new and still under construction in 1929. It is characterized by rows of brick townhouses which remain highly in demand to this day (van Duin & van Ommen, 2000).

In March 1906 the decision to build was reconfirmed; but in January 1907 it was postponed again. Then the governors tried to sell the building plot, but the market was not favourable, and architect W.C. Mulder, the erstwhile owner, raised objections, saying he sold the plot conditionally for the specific purpose of building a new orphanage. Twenty years later the governors were probably grateful that he helped to stop the sale of the plot. By that time, the new city quarter had begun to take shape and the value of the plot, acquired for 3000 florins in 1903,[4] had significantly increased (Leman, 1929).

But the building plans remained in limbo until 1919, when the board was completely overhauled. Nine of the sixteen governors resigned. They were replaced by eighteen new governors, including – for the first time – nine women. The new chairman was Ernst Loeb, an immigrant from Germany and a prominent member of the Jewish community in Leiden.[5] The new board quickly brought about important changes in the way the orphanage was run. Children with some income from work no longer had to give up part of their earnings to the orphanage. Whereas the boys in the Amsterdam orphanage continued to wear their uniforms until the end in 1943, uniforms were abolished in Leiden in November 1919, another sign of modernization as more liberal ideas were gaining ground. Corporal punishment had never been allowed in the orphanage in Leiden, although surely some of the staff had "loose hands" according to some witnesses. A yearly holiday was organized on the North Sea coast for those children who did not spend the holiday with family.

Renewed efforts were made to put the building plans into effect, but economics after the First World War were difficult. An effective propaganda machine was created, throughout the Netherlands, to raise funds by means of sponsorships, donations, lotteries, and so on. Yet it seemed that it would take many more years to get enough capital to start building. In 1927 another committee, arguing that

3   Streets are named after prominent professors at Leiden University, or burgomasters (mayors) of the city. It attracted many relatively affluent citizens from other parts of Leiden, as well as quite a few Jewish families, many of them refugees, if they had been able to bring their previous trade or craft from Germany.

4   The cost of the new building, without internal outfitting, was estimated at 40,000 florins. Thirty years later the actual costs would amount to 90,000 florins.

5   He ran a fashion and furniture shop at Breestraat 161 from 1912. The shop was confiscated by the Germans in 1942, Loeb was deported, and he died at Auschwitz on 31st August 1942. Four *Stolpersteine* were laid for Loeb, his wife, and two of his children in front of Breestraat 161 in 2010 (Siebelt, *Onderduikers* website, 2011).

continuing in the building on Stille Rijn was not an option anymore, gave the governors three choices: move to Amsterdam or Haarlem, merge with the orphanage in The Hague, or build a new home in Leiden. Somewhat surprisingly, given that not enough funds were available, the latter option was chosen. The wish to remain independent and to stay in Leiden seems to have prevailed.

The feeling was apparently mutual: the municipality of Leiden was keen to keep the orphanage within the city, even though the Jewish community in the city did not need it. Once the decision was taken to start building, a pamphlet was issued *"to all citizens of Leiden"* expressing satisfaction, and calling for donations with *"the intention to present as a gift of the citizens of Leiden the furniture and internal fittings, to be made in Leiden workshops, for one or more of the halls and rooms in the new building, because the orphanage decided to stay here and therefore will remain a Leiden institution"* (bold printed words as shown in the pamphlet). It went on to state that *"as our Israelite countrymen have never failed to answer calls to all citizens to contribute to good causes of any kind, we should all come to their aid in allowing the new orphanage to be properly furnished"*. The *executive* committee in support of the building initiative consisted of prominent Jewish citizens of the city of Leiden. The *honorary* committee[6] supporting the initiative and putting their name (and social position) to it, was headed by the mayor of Leiden (with the archetypal Dutch name *Adriaan van de Sande Bakhuyzen*), and 30 other dignitaries from every denomination of Leiden society: four aldermen of the municipal government, the rector of the university, a Catholic dean, a vicar and a minister of the two main Protestant communities, to name a few. As strong as the *verzuiling* in Dutch society may have been, and notwithstanding frequent expressions of mutual antipathy and interparochial fighting, it did not prevent active cooperation and mutual support between the various denominations.

The decision in 1927 to commit to building was based on the optimistic perseverance of some of the committee members who simply promised the more sceptical members that *"the money would be there"* when needed. And, in the end, it was. The photograph in Figure 2.5 was included by Leman (1929) evidently in view of the great significance of what the governors had done. It is the only such photograph I know of. It shows 21 people, including eleven women.

Suddenly everything moved fast. On 18th June 1928, the four cornerstones were laid by the children of four members of the building committee (Fig. 2.6). From the smiles on the faces of Levi Levisson and particularly of Director Italie (first and second from left in Fig. 2.7) we may read the joy in anticipation of the problems at the Stille Rijn being almost a thing of the past. Exactly one year later, on 18th

---

6   Nothing ever happens in Holland without a committee, an indispensable implement of a pillarized society.

Figure 2.5: The very last meeting of the board of governors in the "Regentenkamer" of the old orphanage.

Figure 2.6: Heskelientje Levisson places the first of the four cornerstones on Monday, 18th June 1928. The photograph appeared on the front page of the *Leidsch Dagblad*, 18th June 1928. JHM Photo F431.

Figure 2.7: Group photo after the cornerstone ceremony, 18th June 1928. Back row from left: Levi Levisson (head of the building committee, and probably the most influential governor), Nathan Italie (the director of the orphanage since 1921), Is Leman, E. Viskoper Szn (treasurer), Mr. and Mrs. Heilbut. The children in front from left: Hetty Hertzberger, Heskeline Levisson, Rudie Viskoper, Harry Heilbut. JHM Photo F000806.

June 1929, the new orphanage was officially opened, ending 39 relatively difficult years. The move of 1929 was in many ways a new beginning, and the effect was enormous, as suggested by the following chapters.

2.2   The children of the Stille Rijn

At the start of the orphanage in 1890, some seven to nine children were cared for; the youngest, Levie de Jong, was just one and a half years old. Initially, the idea was to provide childcare free of charge, but financial difficulties made it necessary to ask for contributions from the families. This was not self-evident: poverty and family social problems were the main causes for children, being Jewish or of other denomination, being taken into orphanages in the nineteenth and the first half of the twentieth centuries. In his memorial book (1929) on the occasion of leaving the Stille Rijn home, secretary of the orphanage Leman (Fig. 2.7, third from left) proudly reports that *"we never refused to accept a child because the family could not pay the fee"*. At the same time, he rails against *"philanthropic parasites and scroungers"* (*"klaploopers"*, he calls them), families whom he considered quite capable of making contributions, but who refused to do so. But no child was ever refused for that reason.

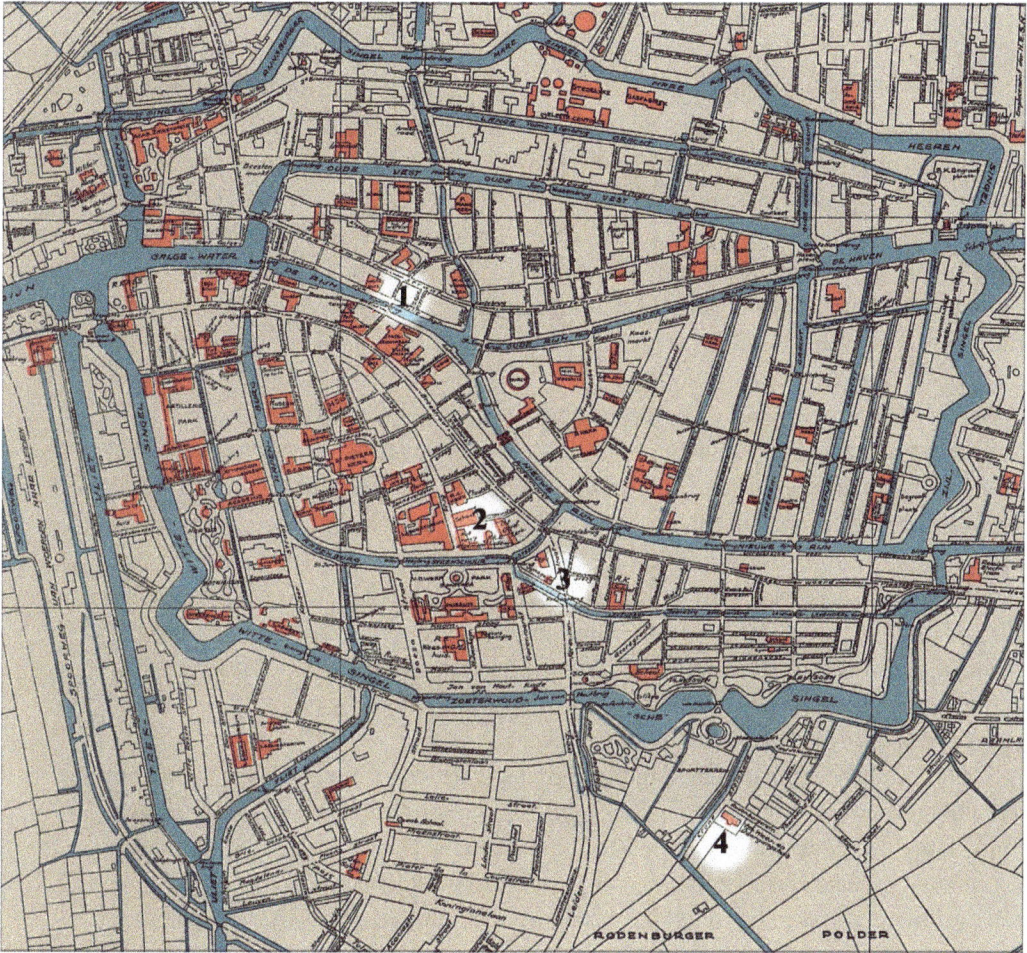

Map of Leiden (1929) showing the medieval city centre with many canals, surrounded by the zigzagging canals called *singels*. Until the twelfth century, the Rhine River flowed through Leiden (from right to left on the map) to Katwijk on the coast. Courtesy Erfgoed Leiden (ELO LEI001019900, detail). Width of the map is approximately 2 km.
1: The old Jewish orphanage (1891-1929)
2: Langebrug elementary schools
3: The synagogue
4: The new Jewish orphanage (1929-1943)

The Rodenburger Polder (bottom right) was still under development at this time, but the new orphanage (4), inaugurated in the same year the map was issued (1929), is already shown on this map. This area would become known as the *Professoren- en Burgemeesterswijk* (van Duin & van Ommen, 2000).

and private archives during this study, has been preserved. Documentary evidence which could not be included in the book, has been placed in individual dossiers.

Foreign readers may not be familiar with the history of the Netherlands before or during the war. For their benefit, some "historical context" is included, so that the events may be better understood. Many wartime events raise difficult and controversial questions which are still hotly debated in the Netherlands today. Some of these issues are mentioned in the text or in the notes, but only very briefly, in order not to hinder the primary objectives of this book. References are listed at the end of each chapter in line with current practice. An extended bibliography (English texts where possible) is provided at the end of the book to suggest further reading on these subjects.

Many survivors or their descendants have been of invaluable assistance in making this book. The survivors are almost always excluded from genealogical sites and Holocaust websites and monuments, which is unfortunate. Indeed, both USHMM in Washington, DC, and Yad Vashem in Jerusalem have begun to make (more) survivor information available to family members and researchers or the general public. All known survivors are included in the list at the end of the book. Nine individual survivor stories are included in Chapter 9. They can be read as stand-alone stories, but the different ways in which they survived may provide valuable context to the other chapters in this book. For many people, the war did not end in May 1945, as discussed in Chapter 10.

When I first became involved in these investigations, a long time ago, I may not have been fully aware of what the Holocaust had done to those who had survived. I may have confronted them with direct questions without realizing which doors inside their memory I was trying to open, and the devastating effect that could have. I have done my best to be much more sensitive in later stages of the investigation and while preparing this book, and I hope that the stories in the following chapters, and the way they are told, will be taken in that spirit.

I welcome comments, corrections, or complementary information.

Jaap W. Focke
Leiden, 28th February 2021

and retrieving information about their lives in the orphanage, building on the work done by my predecessors[2] and trying to add *"a face to each name"* was a primary objective of this study. The list at the end of the book is as accurate and complete as could be achieved with the available data. Retrieving and preserving testimonial and documentary evidence became an important secondary objective of this study, particularly with respect to the period of the German occupation.

Including all the names is a fundamental aspect of this book. I believe it is also in accordance with the spirit of Yad Vashem[3] as explained in the Epilogue. But it presented me with two problems: 1) the reader may be overwhelmed by the large number of names mentioned in the text, and 2) it proved difficult to reconcile individual stories with the chronology. For example, the story of Sally Montezinos (Ch. 2.3) who arrived in 1926 and never really left the orphanage, unfolds gradually over Chapters 2 to 8.

I have tried to circumvent both problems by introducing a limited number of children who carry the story of the orphanage through time (see Table of Contents). Once they are introduced in a first paragraph, like Sally in Chapter 2.3, they will "return" in subsequent chapters to continue the story. In a similar way the stories of Lotte Adler, Betsy Wolff, Piet de Vries, Hans Kloosterman and a few others unfold over several chapters. Other, younger children will be mentioned "on the way" and they can be found in the text through the Persons Index. This should significantly reduce the number of names which must be remembered to follow the story of the orphanage. It should also be possible to read individual stories without reading the book from cover to cover. The compromise between following the chronology and the individual stories may lead to some duplication.

Many children and staff could be identified in at least one photograph in this book, which may therefore also serve as a monument to its inhabitants. Naturally, a lot more is known about some of the older children compared to the very young ones, those who perished in the Holocaust. The youngest of all was Louis Bobbe, who entered the orphanage in November 1942 when he was just one year and eight months old, and who was killed half a year later in Sobibor in German-occupied Poland together with his four-year-old brother, Benjamin.

Wherever possible, the facts and stories that are presented in this book have been checked for accuracy. The tremendous proliferation of data available on the internet, and the increasing occurrence of incorrect statements, often copied from one website to another without verification, made this more important than expected. All corroborative evidence, particularly documents retrieved from public

2   See Acknowledgements.
3   Yad vaShem means "a Hand [a 'monument'] and a Name".

Preface

The presence (1890-1943) of a Jewish orphanage in Leiden, an old city in the western part of Holland, raises many questions. *What kind of institution was this? Why was it established, given the fact that there were already many Jewish childcare institutions in the Netherlands, and why in Leiden, which had only a small Jewish community? What made this institution different from the others? Who were the children, and why were they brought to an orphanage in the first place since most of them still had one or even two parents? What kind of life did they have before the war, and what happened to the children and the staff after the German invasion of Holland in May 1940? Who survived the war and how did they survive? What happened when the war was over?*

This book is chronologically structured. Following the shortest possible introduction (Chapter 1), the first period from establishment in 1890 to the inauguration of a new building in 1929 (shown on the front cover) is covered in Chapters 2 and 3. Information about that period is relatively sparse. But from 1929 the surviving stories and photographs are so abundant that this book only contains a selection. The period from 1929 to 1940 (Chapters 4 and 5) was by all accounts the happiest period in the history of this institution. It is broken into two parts, because events in Germany began to cast a shadow when Hitler took power in 1933, even as life in Holland continued much as before.

The focus of this study was strongly on the people and life in the orphanage from 1929 onwards, *before* the war. But the German invasion in May 1940, the ensuing occupation (Chapter 6), and the liquidation of the orphanage (the *ontruiming*[1]) in March 1943 (Chapter 7), inevitably constitute an important and dominating part of this book. Chapter 8 is dedicated to those who left the orphanage before the liquidation in March 1943 and shows how terribly effective the final stages of the Holocaust were in the Netherlands. Chapter 9 includes survivor stories and Chapter 10 covers the period after liberation in 1945.

Because of the lack of data from before the inauguration of the new building, the book concentrates on the (some 168) children who lived in the orphanage for at least two to three months from 1929, including those 25 who lived in the old building and moved to the new one. Establishing the identity of these 168 children

---

[1] For Dutch or German words used in the text, see list and explanation at the back.

Focke, Jaap W., *Machseh Lajesoumim: A Jewish Orphanage in the City of Leiden, 1890-1943.*
Taylor & Francis Group, 2021
DOI: 10.5117/9789463726955_PREFACE

and the website created by Frans Hoek[4] proved to be useful to unearth hitherto unknown material, such as photographs submitted by Mrs. M. Gilliamse, allowing the identification of Debora Sanders, and Mrs. Henny Schippers, who found a photograph of Philip Poons. I thank Mr. A. Stofkooper for his support concerning his father; Mr. R. Bosten for his information concerning Alexander Lipschits; Mr. F. Wolters with respect to his mother Els van Santen and her brothers Karel and Philip; Mrs. Pauline Jonkers-Stroink and Mr. A. de Bruin for information about Etty Heerma van Voss; Mr. A. van Straten with respect to his parents, who sheltered Aron Wolff.

I received generous support and research assistance from Michiel Schwarzenberg and Raymond Schütz of the Red Cross in The Hague; Guido Abuys of the Memorial Centre Kamp Westerbork; Sierk Plantinga of the National Archives in The Hague; Laurence Schram, Alexandra Matagne and Dorien Vyzel of Kazerne Dossin in Mechelen; Filip Strubbe of the Algemene Rijksarchief in Brussels; Beth Dotan and Zwi Oren of the Ghetto Fighters' House museum in Israel; Annemiek Gringold, Peter Buys and Anton Kras of the Jewish Historical Museum (JCK) in Amsterdam; Mrs. Katharina Kniefacz and staff of the Gedenkstätte Mauthausen; Thomas Rahe and Jens Brunner of the Gedenkstätte Bergen-Belsen; Alexander Avram, Director of the Hall of Names and the Central Database of Shoah Victims' Names in Yad Vashem; Hartmut Peters (Gröschler Haus, Jever); Miriam Keesing (DOKIN); Monica Kingreen (Fritz Bauer Institut, Frankfurt a/M); Petra van den Boomgaard (NIOD); and Leo Levie, Secretary of the Jewish Community in Leiden at the time of the investigations.

I am most indebted to Hans Blom, Professor Emeritus of History at the University of Amsterdam and former Director of the Netherlands Institute for War Documentation (NIOD) in Amsterdam, who reviewed the manuscript, and who provided repeated support and critical advice during the last few years.

I also gratefully acknowledge the willingness to provide critical comments of Prof. Dan Michman, Director of Yad Vashem's International Institute for Holocaust Research; Havi Dreifuss, Professor of History at Tel Aviv University; Hans de Vries, Senior Researcher at NIOD in Amsterdam; and Barbera Bikker (Stichting Herdenking Jodenvervolging Leiden).

Last but not least, I am proud of the students of the Erasmus College in Zoetermeer, and their teachers Hans Wolf, Tibo van Wingen and Bert Schut, who have come to Leiden in their own after-school time every year without fail since 2007 until 2020 (when it was interrupted by the Corona crisis), to read out the names of the 55 children and staff who did not return from deportation, in the large hall of their erstwhile home from which they were forcefully taken on the eve of 17th March 1943, or in the garden at the back, which once was their playground.

---

4   Frans died on 12th November 2019. The website is now defunct. Information about the Jewish orphanage in Leiden can also be found on the site www.herdenkingleiden.nl/.

Acknowledgements

When Mr. F.J.M. Smits in The Hague commissioned two journalists of Q-Productions, Gerard Kerkvliet and Martin Uitvlugt (probably in 1971), to investigate what happened to the Jewish orphanage in Leiden in March 1943, he truly laid the first stone for this book.[1] Their interviews with Hijme Stoffels and Emilie Stoffels-van Brussel, which eventually also led to the recovery of the Stoffels' wartime archive, as well as with Piet de Vries and other survivors of the war, were instrumental in preserving the memory of the orphanage and its inhabitants. Cor van Zegveld[2] initiated serious academic studies about the Jewish population in Leiden, until he had to pass on the work to Leonard Kasteleyn in the late 1990s, who spent another twelve years searching archives and interviewing survivors. Most importantly, he established or confirmed the identity of almost all the children and the staff of the orphanage in the many extant photographs. The present author became involved in 2006. Leonard passed on the work and part of his research results to me in 2014. When speaking in this book about "we" or "us", it is intended to include the author as well as his predecessors, although I remain solely responsible for any errors or shortcomings.

Without the willingness of survivors to talk to us, this book could not have been written. Many contributions by Mimi de Wind-Weiman, Piet de Vries, Hans Kloosterman, the families Klein and Philipson-Armon, Mary Vromen-de Raay and her daughter Shifrah Romano, Roni Maor (Aron Wolff), and Kurt and Helga Gottschalk are gratefully acknowledged.

I also thank Jopie Schröder-Vos and Mien Stam-van der Staay, the friends of Lotte Adler; Mr. L. Brussé and his sisters for their account of Sally Montezinos; Johanna and Marij van der Kroft for the stories about their mother, Betsy Wolff; Marianne Kroese, the daughter of Piet de Vries; Deborah Shelton and Hanna Sherak, daughters of Eva and Ruth Herskovits; Miriam Spziro-Baitalmy concerning the children of the SS *Bodegraven*; and the families of Emilie and Hijme Stoffels. Peter de Jong, Mieke Vink, Ab van Brussel and Frits Stoffels all shared their memories and allowed the author access to the war archive of Hijme and Emilie. The "Joods Monument"[3]

---

1   Smits lived in the neighbourhood, until he was arrested by (or by order of) the German police. After the war, when he asked about what happened to the people who lived there, he did not get clear answers, until he asked Gerard Uitvlugt to investigate. It is significant (see Ch. 10) that he took inquisitive action some 25 years after the war. *Leids Dagblad*, 25th April 1984.

2   Cor died on 30th May 2006, aged 86.

3   www.joodsmonument.nl/.

[Dan Michman was born in Amsterdam in 1947 and came to Israel as a child in 1957, when his father, Jozeph Melkman (Michman), was appointed General Director of Yad Vashem. After his military service, he studied Jewish history and Hebrew linguistics at the Hebrew University of Jerusalem, where he earned his doctorate in 1978 by writing a dissertation on *"Jewish Refugees from Germany in the Netherlands, 1933-1940"*. In 1976 he joined the faculty of the Department of Jewish History at Bar-Ilan University, teaching and researching in the field of modern Jewish history in general and in the Shoah in particular. He has been involved with Yad Vashem's scholarly and educational activities since the early 1980s and served as Chief Historian from 2000 till 2011. He has published books and articles in a variety of languages on the history of Dutch and Belgian Jewry, Israeli society, and mostly on various aspects of the Shoah – historiography, ghettos, *Judenräte* and Jewish leadership, Jewish religious life, problems of Jewish refugees and migration, resistance, Western Europe, the survivors, the impact of the Shoah on Israeli society and religious Jewry, and more.]

widow.[3] These teachings were taken care of in Diaspora Jewry in the Middle Ages and the Early Modern period by what we would call today non-profit organizations (in traditional terms: *Chevrot Kadisha*). In the modern period in the Netherlands, this tradition was integrated into the local system of social organizations that were run by the various segments (*zuilen*) of Dutch society, which included orphanages. This is the general Dutch-Jewish background of the *Machseh Lajesoumim* orphanage of Leiden described in this detailed and moving study.

Shortly after the occupation of the Netherlands in May 1940, the persecution of the Jews started, and it encompassed all levels of Jewish life. The lethal phase of these persecutions was the so-called "Final Solution of the Jewish Question." This phase, which was the ultimate realization of the Nazi enterprise, targeted Jews in the most remote places (such as the islands of Rhodes and Kos in the Mediterranean) and all of them – whether old or young. Thus came also the end to the *Machseh Lajesoumim* orphanage of Leiden.

To what extent is a detailed study of one, relatively small, institution in a tiny Jewish community of importance? Due to my position as Head of the Yad Vashem International Institute for Holocaust Research people often ask me: After so many years of research – is there still anything new to learn? I respond by saying, that when I entered the field of Holocaust research in the first half of the 1970s, I never thought that this field would expand and intensify so much as we experience today. But it did. And the reason is that the Holocaust was a watershed event in European and global history. In spite of the fact that the Holocaust was a relatively short historical event – twelve years and 98 days – it affected many countries and societies, and had long-term reverberations regarding ideologies, concepts of life and morality, academic standards, education and more. In this context, it is important not to talk about the Holocaust in vague, generalizing terms but to get acquainted with the specifics, even with minuscule acts. The study presented in this book contributes precisely to that. Moreover, the acts of memorization of the victims who perished and the describing of the rehabilitation of the few who survived are a contribution to the needed rebuilding of the concept of human dignity. The author, Jaap Focke, took it upon himself to carry out this job and dedicated many years to painstaking research that would enable him to reconstruct the history of *Machseh Lajesoumim* and its orphans, situate the institution's fate in the proper context and reconstruct the human image of the orphans. The result is a study that should be used in Holocaust education; through this one example, the encounter with the enormity of the Holocaust can be better understood.

Rosh Hodesh Av 5780/22nd July 2020

---

3 Deuteronomy 24:21 and many more places.

Foreword

Professor Dan Michman

Head, The International Institute for Holocaust Research; and Incumbent of the John Najmann Chair of Holocaust Studies, Yad Vashem, Jerusalem

Professor (Emeritus) of Modern Jewish History, The Israel and Golda Koschitzky Department of Jewish History and Contemporary Jewry; and former (1983-2018) Chair of The Arnold and Leona Finkler Institute of Holocaust Research and Incumbent of the Abe and Edita Spiegel Family Chair of Holocaust Research, Bar-Ilan University

The Nazi German anti-Jewish enterprise, commonly called "the Holocaust" or "Shoah", which was aimed at eradicating the *jüdischen Geist* ("Jewish spirit") and its racial carriers "the Jews", engulfed Europe between 1933 and 1945. It resulted not only in close to six million murdered Jewish souls but also in the almost total destruction throughout Europe of Jewish life as it had developed over many centuries.

Jewish society everywhere, including in the Netherlands, changed dramatically in the nineteenth and twentieth centuries due to emancipation, integration, secularization, politicization, economic diversification, and emigration. However, various Jewish traditional customs and social features which had been central to Jewish social existence since antiquity, continued – even if in forms adapted to modern standards. Two of these features were education and caring for the weak, especially orphans. These features were anchored in biblical teachings: regarding education – *"Hear, my son, the instruction of thy father, and forsake not the teaching of thy mother"*[1] and *"train up a child in the way he should go, and even when he is old, he will not depart from it"*[2]; and regarding the obligation to care for orphans – the recurring instruction to not forget and to defend *"the stranger, the fatherless, and the*

---

1   Proverbs 1:8.
2   Proverbs 22:6.

Focke, Jaap W., *Machseh Lajesoumim: A Jewish Orphanage in the City of Leiden, 1890-1943*.
Taylor & Francis Group, 2021
DOI: 10.5117/9789463726955_FOREWORD

Table of Contents

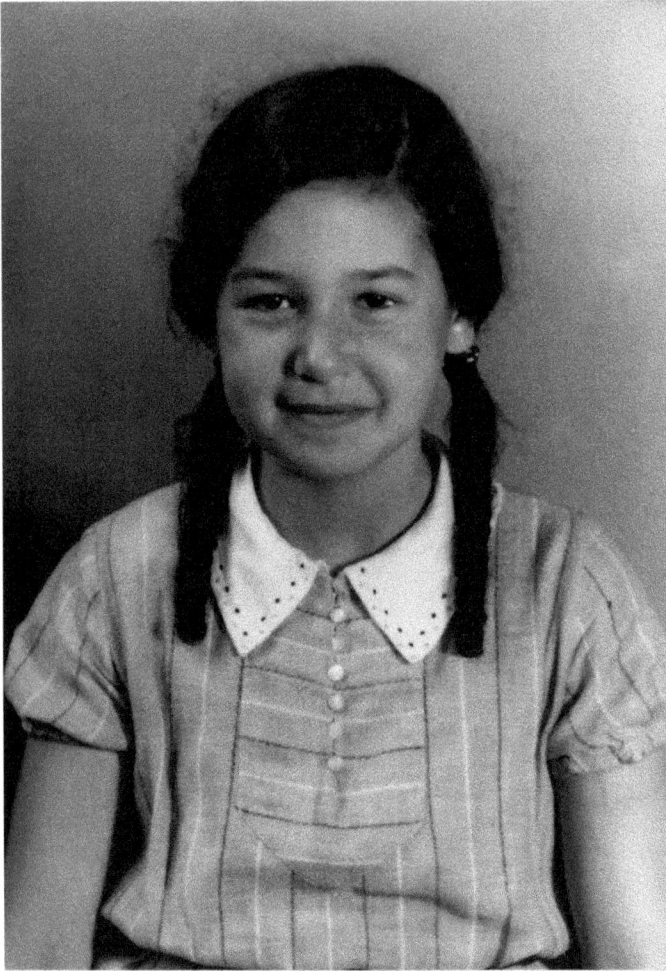

Lotte Adler
Frankfurt, 8th February 1925-Sobibor, 26th March 1943
Photograph taken in Frankfurt am Main (Germany) in 1937 when she was
12 years old

Lotte's father was arrested in 1937 and killed in KL Buchenwald on 3rd
July 1938. After *Kristallnacht* (9th/10th November 1938) her mother sent
Lotte and her younger sister Henny to safety in Holland by train with the
Kindertransport of 22nd November 1938. They were taken in by the orphanage
in Leiden that same night.
But the Germans caught up with them when they invaded Holland in May 1940.

Machseh Lajesoumim (Refuge for orphans) was the name shown on the new building, above the front doors, partly visible on the photograph on the back cover. Its official name, which adorned the old building on Stille Rijn (Fig. 2.1), was *"Centraal Israëlitisch Wees- en Doorgangshuis"*, that is, National Jewish Orphanage and Transit Home.

This book is dedicated to the memory of the children and stafff of the Jewish Orphanage in Leiden who perished in the Holocaust.

Alleenlijk wacht u, en bewaart uw ziel wel, dat gij niet vergeet de dingen, die uw ogen gezien hebben; en dat zij niet van uw hart wijken, al de dagen uws levens; en gij zult ze aan uw kinderen en uw kindskinderen bekend maken.[1]

Only take heed to thyself, and keep thy soul diligently, lest thou forget the things which thine eyes have seen, and lest they depart from thy heart all the days of thy life: but teach them thy sons, and thy sons' sons.[2]

Deut. 4:9

[1] Statenvertaling.
[2] King James.

This publication was made possible with support from the Vereniging Centraal Israëlitisch Wees- en Doorgangshuis Machseh Lajesoumiem.

First published in 2021 by Amsterdam University Press Ltd.

Published 2025 by Routledge
4 Park Square, Milton Park, Abingdon, Oxon OX14 4RN
605 Third Avenue, New York, NY 10158

Routledge is an imprint of the Taylor & Francis Group, an informa business

ISBN: 9789463726955 (hbk)
ISBN: 9781041182276 (pbk)
ISBN: 9781003699071 (ebk)
NUR   688

Cover design: Coördesign, Leiden

DOI   10.5117/9789463726955

For Product Safety Concerns and Information please contact our EU representative:
GPSR@taylorandfrancis.com
Taylor & Francis Verlag GmbH, Kaufingerstraße 24, 80331 München, Germany

Machseh Lajesoumim

A Jewish Orphanage in the City of Leiden
1890-1943

Jaap W. Focke

Foreword by Prof. Dan Michman
Head of the International Institute for Holocaust Research
at Yad Vashem, Jerusalem

Incorporating unpublished data provided by W.F. van Zegveld (†)
and L.P. Kasteleyn
Photographic restoration by F. Hoek (†)

Routledge
Taylor & Francis Group
LONDON AND NEW YORK

Table 2.1   The 25 children who moved from the old orphanage building to the new one in June, 1929

Name	Arrival date in orphanage	Age at arrival (y)	Departure date	Years in Orphanage
Muller, Frits	10-2-1917	5,0	14-2-1930	13,0
Muller, Marianne (Jannie)	31-5-1917	3,4	4-9-1930	13,3
Reeder, Hartog Samuel (Harry) de	25-9-1918	4,1	9-8-1932	13,9
Kloos, Ludwig	16-10-1920	4,3	17-11-1932	12,1
Vries, Harry de	30-3-1921	7,8	9-8-1932	11,4
Vries, Jacob (Jaap) de	30-3-1921	3,9	30-8-1935	14,4
Pool, Mozes (Max) van der	27-9-1922	6,6	13-10-1930	8,0
Worms, Jozeph (Joop)	16-1-1923	2,9	29-4-1940	17,3
Santen, Esther (Esje) van	5-2-1923	2,7	31-3-1939	16,2
Veltein, Hijman	19-5-1923	7,1	15-7-1930	7,2
Santen, Jansje (Jenny) van	16-6-1924	10,3	25-4-1932	7,9
Pront, Judith (Jupie)	11-9-1924	8,5	11-11-1935	11,2
Leeda, Rachel (Chelly)	25-9-1924	2,7	6-9-1933	8,9
Spiro, Sientje	4-3-1926	9,9	24-9-1935	9,6
Spiro, Abraham (Bram)	4-3-1926	8,8	24-9-1935	9,6
Montezinos, Salomon Levie (Sally)	21-12-1926	2,6	17-3-1943	16,2
Santen, Karel van	21-12-1926	8,3	2-7-1940	13,5
West, Adriana van	28-12-1926	6,0	27-11-1929	2,9
Weiman, Mietje (Mimi)	14-1-1927	9,5	30-4-1935	8,3
Blik, Nathan	12-2-1927	3,0	10-5-1932	5,2
Segal, Reina	28-12-1927	3,0	17-3-1943	15,2
Witteboon, Jaques Maurice	28-12-1927	9,7	10-11-1936	8,9
Bobbe, Jetje (Jetty)	24-5-1928	4,1	17-3-1943	14,8
Spier, Henry (Harry)	24-5-1928	3,0	17-3-1943	14,8
Weiman, Samuel Salomon (Sal)	11-2-1929	10,0	29-4-1936	7,2

The orphanage had been rather unlucky in the choice of directors (always a married childless couple) who served as "parents". Until 1921 their titles were indeed *father* and *mother*. Six couples had come and gone since 1890 before the arrival, in late 1921, of Nathan Italie (Fig. 2.7, second from left) and his wife, Sara Schaap. Nathan would remain director for almost 22 years, until the end in 1943.

Since establishment in 1890, until the move in 1929, 142 children were cared for, 91 boys and 51 girls (Leman, 1929; van Zegveld 1993). Not much is known about the children from the early years of the orphanage, compared to the vast amount of information about the period from 1929. If photos of the children existed from before 1929, I have not been able to locate them. But some "Stille Rijn" children, arriving as they did at a very young age, were still there when the new building was inaugurated (Table 2.1). Some of them, like Jetty Bobbe, Sally Montezinos and Harry

Spier, also stayed until the end in 1943. Sally, Harry and Mimi Weiman are the first to carry the story of this book, reconstructing life at the Roodenburgerstraat, and helping to preserve the memory of all the children who lived there.

2.3   1926: Sally Montezinos arrives, two and a half years old

Salomon Levie (Sally) Montezinos was born on 6th May 1924 in The Hague into a family which already had eight children aged fourteen to two (see also Ch. 8.5).

The family (see Ch. 8.5) had moved from Amsterdam to The Hague in 1911. Upon the death of their father in September 1926, the eldest three, Branca (then seventeen), Jacob (fifteen) and Grietje (fourteen), stayed at home. Of the other six, Bilha (ten) and Eva (nine) had been taken in by family some time before the death of the father. In November both went to the orphanage in The Hague, together with Anna (twelve) and Abraham (seven). The remaining two, Josefina (four) and Sally (two), were too young to join them, and they stayed at home in the care of their older sisters. It was probably a stressful situation, and late December 1926, Sally was accepted in Leiden, while Josefina was taken in by the Portuguese-Israelite girls' home in Amsterdam in early 1927. She was the only one of this Sephardic family to go to a "Portuguese" Jewish orphanage. For Sally to go to Leiden was probably the best available option: the Leiden orphanage was specifically established to cater for Jewish children of either denomination, and well positioned to deal with the very young. It was also not far from their hometown The Hague. Six other Sephardic children had been taken into the Leiden orphanage before him, but only one was still there when Sally arrived: Jacob Nabarro (van Zegveld, 1993). When Jacob became six years old, he transferred to the Sephardic boys' home in Amsterdam, as had his brother Salomon some time before. From that time on, Sally would be the only Sephardic boy in Leiden until the arrival of the four Alvares Vega children in 1941. The other children noticed that Sally pronounced his prayers differently, in the Sephardic tradition.

He was five years old in the summer of 1929 when he moved with everybody else who lived in the orphanage at the time to the brand-new building on Roodenburgerstraat. In 1932 Anna, Bilha, Eva and Abraham moved to the equally impressive new home of the orphanage in The Hague at Pletterijstraat 66 (van Creveld, 2001, 2004). In 1930 Sally became six years old; theoretically he could have gone to The

Figure 2.8: Probably the oldest extant picture of Sally; from the group photograph taken in 1932 in the new building (Figure 4.14).

Hague to join his four siblings, or to the Sephardic boys' orphanage in Amsterdam, Josephine being in Amsterdam as well. But he stayed in Leiden (Fig. 2.8). Possibly there was no immediate vacancy in The Hague, but I suspect, in view of what we know about Sally that his preference to stay in Leiden, which he expressed so forcefully in later years (Ch. 7.2), may have developed early on.

Sally's story continues in the following chapters. He never really left the orphanage; when the end came in 1943, he had lived there for more than sixteen years (Chs. 7.2, 7.8, 8.5).

2.4   1927-1928: Mimi Weiman (nine), Reina Segal (three), and Harry Spier (three) arrive

About three weeks after Sally's arrival, on 14th January 1927, Mimi Weiman[7] arrived in the orphanage on Stille Rijn. She was, at nine and a half years, old enough to remember her first two and a half years at Stille Rijn. She would spend more than seven years in the orphanage, witness the move to the new building, and survive the war. She shared her memories with Leonard Kasteleyn, part of which was passed on to the present author. She also contributed to the identification of people on the many extant photographs, and thus became an important contributor to this book. She remembered the poverty of the Stille Rijn period, and students from Leiden University occasionally bringing presents for the children to cheer them up.

On 28th December 1927, another young child was registered: Reina Segal, just a week before her third birthday. Reina was born in Amsterdam on 5th January 1925, the last of seven children. Her father, Abraham, ran a market stall along the Zwanenburgwal in Amsterdam. Her brother Salomon died in 1916 at age two, and two other siblings also died at young age, probably before Reina was born. Her mother, Leentje van Sijs, died on 26th January 1927 at age 38, leaving Abraham with four[8] children aged thirteen, ten, five and two. Clearly the family had been in difficult circumstance for some time. Reina had been lodged in the non-Jewish *"Hulp voor Onbehuisden"* care home[9] for six weeks in the summer of 1926, and – that time with her sister Betje – for another five weeks in November, before the death of her mother. During the second half of 1927, her uncle, Lion Winnik, took care of her, before she was brought to the Jewish orphanage in Leiden on 28th December 1927. Her sister Betje was lodged in the only other *"Central"* Jewish orphanage, in Utrecht (see Table 1.1). Five months later, on 23rd

---

7   Later Mrs. de Wind; she died in Scheveningen in 2005.
8   Assuming that the many other siblings were old enough to look after themselves.
9   Shelter for the homeless; 2[de] Constantijn Huygensstraat, Amsterdam.

May 1928, Abraham married Elisabeth Visser and on 1st May 1929 a daughter was born: Klaartje, who died in infancy. Reina regularly went to Amsterdam to visit her father and stepmother.

Harry Spier was almost three years old when he arrived at the Stille Rijn home on 24th May 1928. Like Sally, Reina and Harry would spend the rest of their lives, just about fifteen years, in the orphanage. We will hear more about them in the following chapters. Harry was a funny character. He is the one who unwittingly provided the title to the first post-war report about the orphanage (Kerkvliet & Uitvlugt, 1974) by writing to the Stoffels from Westerbork and asking Betsy Wolff, who had moved in with them the week before the liquidation of the orphanage, to send him, of all things, a pot piccalilli (Fig. 7.14).

The long period on the Stille Rijn must have been traumatic for staff and governors, as is evident from the ever-changing, frantic efforts to leave the place: making building plans, buying land, wanting to sell it again, looking at large vacant buildings in Leiden as a possible alternative home, looking into buying the building next door on Stille Rijn, closing down the place altogether and merging with one of the other orphanages. Every year, the annual report contained a list of problems. They left the Stille Rijn building with a sigh of relief, not only grateful that no major disaster had ever happened in the rickety building (Leman, 1929), but also in anticipation of moving to a brand-new home.

References

Appel, Lea, 1982; *"Het brood der doden. Geschiedenis en ondergang van een joods meisjesweeshuis"*. Baarn, Bosch & Keuning, ISBN 9024644275. [An illustrated history of the Ashkenazi girls' home in Amsterdam. For a description of the Ashkenazi boys' home in Amsterdam, See Choekat, 1986, and references in Ch. 1.]

Asscher, E., Ph. Coppenhagen, B.P. Gomperts & J.M. Lob, 1938; *"Gedenkboek ter gelegenheid van het 200-jarig bestaan van het Nederlandsch Israëlitisch Jongensweeshuis Megadlé Jethomim te Amsterdam"* [Commemorative book on the occasion of the 200th anniversary of the Dutch Israelite Boys' Orphanage Megadlé Jethomim in Amsterdam (in Dutch)]. Published by the Board of Governors. See also Choekat, 1986, and Appel, 1982.

Creveld, I.B. van, 2001; *"Het wezen van wezen. Joodse wezen in Den Haag 1850-1943. Een monument"*. De Nieuwe Haagsche, ISBN 9077032096. [Describes the history of the Jewish orphanage in The Hague and its liquidation in 1943.]

Creveld, I.B. van, 2004; *"Hulp aan wezen in oorlogstijd"*. De Nieuwe Haagsche, ISBN 9077032711. [Reports on new information about the orphanage in The Hague based on the orphanage's archives, upon their recovery and return from Russia.]

Duin, Th. van & K. van Ommen, 2000; *"Van stadspolder tot beschermd stadsgezicht. Het ontstaan en de groei van de Professoren- en Burgemeesterswijk en Rijndijkbuurt"*. Leiden, Vereniging Professoren- en Burgemeesterswijk, ISBN 909014174X.

Kerkvliet, G. & M. Uitvlugt, 1974; *"De vernietiging van het Joodse Weeshuis te Leiden tijdens de Duitse bezetting"*. *Studia Rosenthaliana* 8, 268-299. [An abbreviated version was published as G. Kerkvliet & M. Uitvlugt, 1988; *"Een pot piccalilly voor Westerbork. Verslag van de vernietiging van het Joodse weeshuis te Leiden"*. *Jaarboekje voor Geschiedenis en Oudheidkunde van Leiden en omstreken* 80, 147-180.]

Leman, IS, (5689) 1929; *"Het Centraal Israelitisch Wees- en Doorgangshuis te Leiden in woord en beeld (1890-1929)"*. Title on the cover: *"Uit de geschiedenis van een nuttige instelling"*. Den Haag, Drukkerij Levisson, with contributions by J.L Palache.

Metz, Daniël, 2005; *"Een historisch overzicht van acht joodse weeshuizen in Nederland"*. *Misjpoge, tijdschrift van de Nederlandse Kring voor Joodse Genealogie* 2005-2.

Wijsenbeek, S.S., 1933; *"Gedenkboek 100 jaar Joods Weeshuis Rotterdam"* [Memorial book: 100 years of the Jewish orphanage in Rotterdam]. [A rare copy at Rotterdam Gemeentearchief, no. 1174.]

Zegveld, W.F. van, 1993; *"Joods Wees- en Doorgangshuis Leiden, bewoners 1890-1951"*. Originally in: *"De Joden van Leiden"*. Unpublished; 4 volumes. [Several copies were made, available (i.a.) at Erfgoed Leiden (ELO) and the Joods Historisch Museum, Amsterdam. The results of his painstaking research have served as a basis for subsequent investigations. Note that his report is an important source of information on children and staff in the Leiden orphanage who are not included in this book because they had left before the move to the new building in 1929, as well as Jewish citizens of the Leiden region who were not connected to the orphanage.]

3   1929: A magnificent new home

Abstract

In June 1928 building started on the plot of land acquired in 1903. The new orphanage was opened in June 1929. It turned out to be an astounding improvement with two dormitories for boys, two for girls, two kitchens, offices, washrooms, private rooms for the director and his wife, rooms for resident staff, a sickbay, a large playroom which also served as sukkah, and a large playground in the garden. Little is known about the children who lived in the orphanage in its early years. But many stories and photographs have survived about the 25 children and the staff members who moved into the new building in 1929, and the 143 children who entered the orphanage subsequently.

Keywords: Non-Jewish school, Zionism, *Betsalel Youth Weekly*, Meyer de Hond

The new building at the corner of Roodenburgerstraat/Cronesteinkade was in almost every aspect the opposite compared to the building on Stille Rijn. It was large, stylish, modern, well-built and sturdy; it had central heating, a garden and playground, four large dormitories, a sickbay for boys, and one for girls, and plenty of washrooms, rooms for the director and the resident staff, and so on. This was a watershed in the history of the Leiden orphanage. After 39 years in a makeshift rickety building, the five permanent staff and 25 children moved into a building which must have looked to them like a palace from a fairy tale. It was difficult to construct a coherent story about the years from 1890 to 1929. But from the end of 1929 onwards, so many stories have been found, news items, photographs, documents, letters to Jewish periodicals, that it was difficult to decide what to include in this book and what to leave out.

W.C. Mulder, the architect who had sold the building plot to the corporation in 1903, had died in December 1920, after which the governors worked with another architect, Bernard Buurman. Very appropriately, Buurman, whose name means *"neighbour"*, lived on Roodenburgerstraat opposite the reserved building plot, overlooking the construction of the building he himself designed. Buurman co-opted another architect, M. Oesterman, who knew how to incorporate Jewish

Focke, Jaap W., *Machseh Lajesoumim: A Jewish Orphanage in the City of Leiden, 1890-1943*.
Taylor & Francis Group, 2021
DOI: 10.5117/9789463726955_CH03

Bij de opening van het Israëlietische Weeshuis te Leiden nam onze fotograaf bovenstaande groep officieele personen, waaronder voorkomen de heeren burgemeester v. d. Sande Bakhuyzen, prof. dr. J. L. Palache, L. Levisson, wethouder Goslinga, architect Buurman en mr. dr. van Strijen, gemeente-secretaris.

Figure 3.1: Newspaper coverage (*Leidsch Dagblad*) of the official opening on 18th June 1929. The guests are seated in the annex, in the half-circled playroom which also served as a "desert hut" during Sukkot (*Loofhuttenfeest*, the Feast of Tabernacles). See Figures 3.3 and 3.7.

religious and cultural constraints into the design of the building. They were told *"to keep the design simple and straightforward"*, which they did. Yellow Frisian brick was used, with modest relief and protrusions built into the walls to produce a building which despite the simplicity is considered unique in Leiden up to this day.

Additional funds were raised during building, and gifts were received from various sources. A lady from Arnhem[10] donated the beautiful cast-iron double doors for the front entrance; the doors, with a prominent Star of David, survived an attempt in the 1970s to replace them with modern doors. The dining hall was furnished by the above-mentioned committee of Leiden citizens (Ch. 2), and a similar committee from The Hague furnished another hall. The Leiden branch of the National Horticulture Society sponsored the development of the garden.

10   Mrs. Hertogs-Hijman, fide P.J.M. de Baar, *Leidsch Dagblad*, 21st September 1992.

Figure 3.2: The front side of the new building, probably 1930-1931 (see text and design drawings).

A year, to the day, after the laying of the cornerstones the building was officially opened, with the usual presence of dignitaries from the Leiden establishment (Fig. 3.1), including some who had put their signature to the call for help to the Leiden citizens. Mimi Weiman, then twelve years old, remembered being in a choir that sang to them during the opening ceremony.

The exterior of the building today remains almost entirely intact, as it was designed in 1927. The interior, however, was converted several times after the war. But the floor plans, as designed in 1928, have been preserved and there are descriptions from several of the surviving children. Figure 3.2, probably from 1930 or 1931, shows the central three-story block, flanked by two wings. A protrusion separates the central block from each of the wings: behind each is a staircase. Above the main entrance, the words: "Machseh Lajesoumim"; directly above the name, behind three windows, are the private rooms of Director Italie, and on the third floor of the central block are service rooms.

The design drawing of the ground floor (Fig. 3.3) shows the vestibule (A) with a small room on either side for tutoring boys (B1) and girls (B2), the central hall (C), and behind it the huge playroom (D) for the smaller children. It included the half-round annex which is visible on many photographs. The dignitaries in Figure 3.1 are seated within that half-round annex.

The left (south-east) wing, on the ground floor, housed the kosher kitchens (E1, E2) and the main dining hall (F), which also was planned to serve as boys' dayroom. The right (north-west) wing ground floor of the building had the dayroom for the

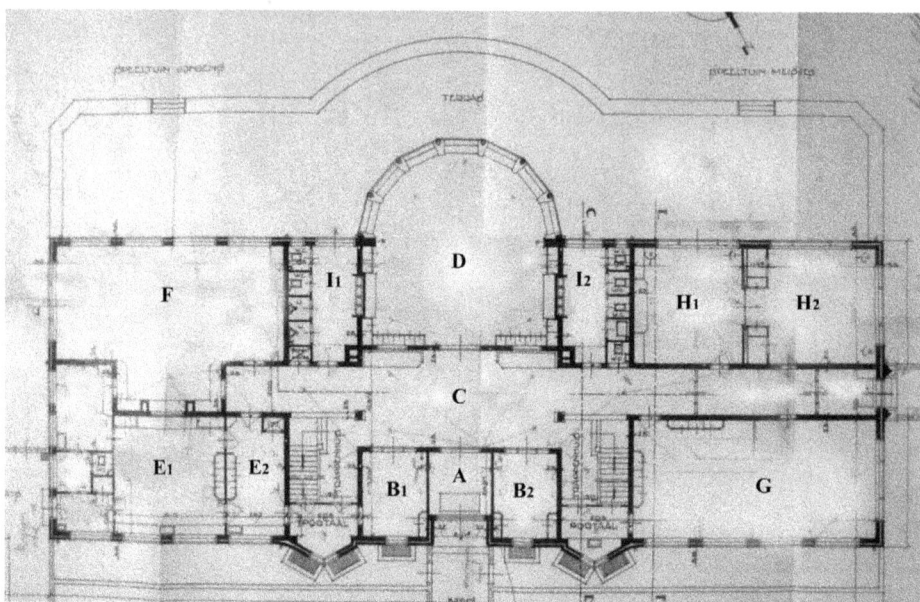

Figure 3.3: Ground floor design plan (1927), signed by Buurman, the architect.

girls (G) on the front side, and the office (H1) and dayroom (H2) of the director on the back side. Jacob Philipson, the *administrateur* of the orphanage, probably had his desk (Fig. 6.18) in room H1 or H2.

Behind the terrace, in the garden at the back, the plan had a boys' playground on the left (as seen from the main front entrance), and one for girls on the right. At least, such was the plan in 1928. In effect, apart from the dormitories and the washrooms/cloakrooms, the planned separation between boys' and girls' rooms was never implemented. Dining room F was not convenient as a dayroom for boys, and the planned girls' dayroom (G) became a living room for both girls and boys. *"There were books, lots of them, behind glass. You had to ask Ms. Klein to borrow one. There was a radio and a piano. It was always cosy. The room could be divided into a larger and a smaller room. We [the older children] usually got together in the smaller room."*[11] Some other rooms were also put to different use, for example, when a bedroom was created on the second floor for the children of the director (Ch. 5.5).

The building had four entrances. The front entrance served as a nice background for the photograph of Figure 3.8, but the children usually entered the building from the terrace through cloakrooms I1 and I2. Figure 4.1 shows the staff on the back terrace, in front of the open doors of the director's office (H). Figure 4.2 shows the

11   Piet de Vries; see interview notes in his dossier.

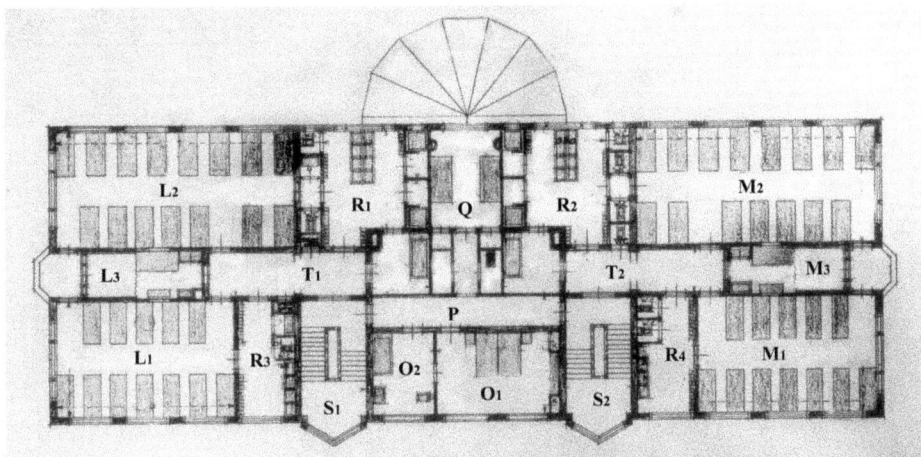

Figure 3.4: Design plan (1927) of the second floor (i.e. the first floor above the ground floor).

back terrace on the other side, with the annex and the boys' back entrance (I1). The boys' and girls' entrances (I1 and I2) connected directly[12] to the boys' and girls' staircases, and their respective bedrooms.

The second floor (Fig. 3.4) had the bedrooms for older boys (L1) and for older girls (M1) on the front side of the building, and the bedrooms for the younger boys (L2) and girls (M2) on the back side. Each wing had a room (L3, M3, more a small suite with a bedroom, a living room and a balcony) between the two bedrooms. probably for the senior nannies. The central part shows the bedroom (O) and bathroom of the director and his wife, a corridor (P) and a room (Q) called *isoleerkamer*, presumably intended for cases of contagious illness. This room was later converted to a bedroom for the children of the director and his wife. Separate washrooms/wardrobes (R1-4) served the boys' and girls' dormitories, respectively. S1 and S2 are the boys' and girls' staircases.

The third floor (Fig. 3.5) had a large room to handle laundry (U) and a small kitchen (V) on the front side, a sickbay for boys (W1) on the left and for girls (W2) at the right side, separated by a room for a nanny or nurse (X), and a large attic on each of the wings of the building (Y1 and Y2). Each attic had two rooms (Z1-4) to accommodate resident staff. These rooms were under the sloping roof, but they had dormers to allow for proper windows (see Fig. 3.6; the windows of room Z1 are open). The dormers may have been a late addition since they are not indicated on the design plans. There was additional storage space, and the boys used to practice boxing in the attic (Kerkvliet & Uitvlugt, 1973).

---

12 Some post-war witness accounts confuse "left" and "right" wing parts of the building (such as the two staircases), depending on the point of view.

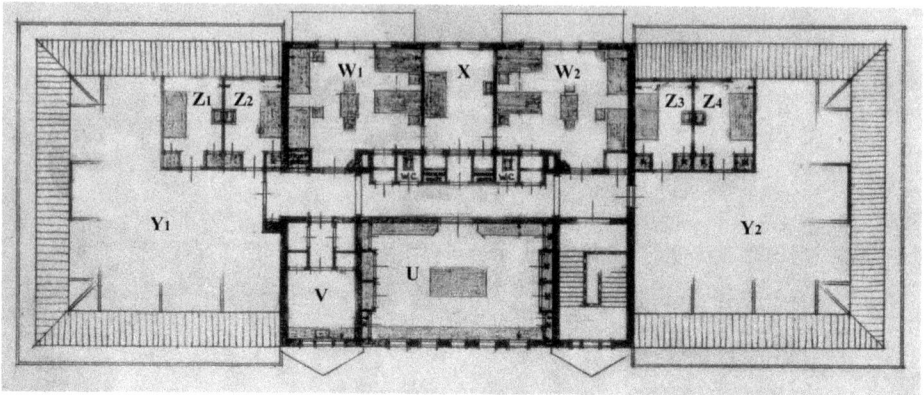

Figure 3.5: Design drawing (1927) of the third floor, and the attic of the left and right wing.

It is very unfortunate that two ugly extensions were added to the building by the municipality after the war, preventing people passing by along the Cronesteinkade to see the back side of the building as shown on the photograph of Figure 3.6.

The drawings suggest that 54 children could be accommodated in the four bedrooms. But it seems the actual capacity was higher. Piet remembered that as the need arose, additional beds were put in the bedrooms, or wherever space was available on the second or third floor, but that the rooms were rarely ever fully occupied. Of course, the numbers of each category did not always match, so the age border between "older" and "younger" may have varied with time. More of a nuisance was a mismatch between the total number of boys (often too many) and the number of girls (not to capacity), and it is possible that on occasion small boys were placed in the small girls' bedroom. Over the period 1929-1943, the orphanage housed 91 boys and 77 girls for any period of at least two months. This is a somewhat arbitrary cut-off which allows refugee children who were transferred to another institution after two to three months to be included, but not temporary guests, who were not genuine residents.

The boys and girls were not supposed to mix during the night. Each dormitory wing had its own stairwell (S1 and S2 on Fig. 3.4). To get from one dormitory to the other, they had to pass from their own corridor (T1 or T2) through corridor O in the director's wing, or down one staircase, through the central hall, and up the other stairs; a risky business. The new Jewish orphanage in The Hague, completed in 1932, also had separate staircases, but in addition the dormitories were on different floors: the boys' stairwell led to the second floor, while the stairwell for girls led directly to the third floor, supposedly creating a more effective separation.

The gender separation was in any case not so strict in Leiden. The division of the large playground which was planned on the architect's drawing was never

Figure 3.6: The backside of the building in 1929; photographed about a week after the inauguration in June 1929. On the left of the photo what is called the "right wing", as seen standing in front of the building in Roodenburgerstraat. On the ground floor, left: the director's offices under the striped awnings. On the second floor, left: the four windows of the small girls' dormitory. On the third floor, centre: the windows of the two sickbays (with balconies) and in between the room of a nanny or nurse. Under the sloping roof: the two attics with the rooms for resident staff (with dormers).

implemented. Figure 4.4 shows that the dining room was not well-suited to also serve as a boys' living room, and the girls' dayroom soon became the living room for boys as well. On each side of the main entrance there was a small study room, one for boys, the other for girls, with a table and straight chairs. Recalled Piet de Vries: *"We boys could also be found in the girls' study room".* The elementary (primary) schools attended by the orphanage children were also co-educational (see Ch. 4.4). However, secondary schools in Holland, particularly if they had a significant vocational component, were often gender segregated, which meant that boys and girls in the orphanage who were used to co-educational circumstances were separated after completing elementary school, usually at age twelve. Piet found it ridiculous and annoying. He had a girlfriend in the orphanage: Fanny Günsberg. He remembered that there were four large tables in the dining room: two for the smaller children, mixed, and one each for the older boys and the older girls (see Fig. 4.4). However, in the few available photographs the older children are mixed, while the small boys in front are flocked together, evidently because that is what they preferred.

Figure 3.7: The back side, just after completion in 1929, showing the annex and the two cables by which the roof could be elevated during Sukkot.

Note that on Figure 3.6 the left part of the photo is what is called the "right wing" (or northeast wing) in this chapter, as seen standing in front of the building on Roodenburgerstraat. It shows the two director's offices under the striped awnings on the ground floor, and the four windows of the dormitory for the young girls on the second floor. On the third floor the windows of the two sickbays (with balconies) and in between the room for a nanny or nurse. Under the sloping roof: the two attics with the rooms for resident staff (with dormers). The Leiden newspapers published the photo and commented: *"Last week [i.e. 18th June 1929] the new building of the Central Jewish Orphanage and Transit Home was officially inaugurated. This photograph clearly shows how very pleasant and spacious the new building turns out to be."* Figure 3.7 also dates from 1929 and shows the two cables by which the roof of the annex could be opened, transforming the playroom into a sukkah from which the sky could be seen, during *Loofhuttenfeest*, the Feast of Tabernacles.

Since 1903, when the plot was part of a largely empty polder landscape, the first streets and rows of houses had appeared, and what is now known as the *Profburgwijk* was beginning to take shape (van Duin & van Ommen, 2000), new streets being named after a mayor of Leiden, or a famous professor at Leiden University, such as Lorentz, Buys Ballot, Zeeman, Hugo de Vries, van het Hoff, Kamerlingh Onnes and van der Waals. The district was immediately popular and has remained so to this day. Like Amsterdam, the medieval inner city of Leiden was very impoverished and overpopulated at the close of the nineteenth century, and it took the municipality of Leiden more than half a century to build enough new townships surrounding the old city, and decades more to restore and upgrade the inner city. The new quarter attracted many old and new citizens, including well-known Leiden Jewish families such as Mok, Philipson, Bloemkoper and van Kleef, to name a few (see Siebelt, 2011b). In this respect the Profburgwijk shows similarity, on a much smaller scale,[13] to the Rivierenbuurt (streets named after rivers) in Amsterdam, which attracted people who could afford to escape the inner city, as well as some of the more affluent refugees from Germany, such as the family of Anne Frank.

---

13   By 1940, some 17,000 Jews lived in the Rivierenbuurt, i.e. some 40% of Amsterdam's Jewish population.

Figure 3.8: Probably early 1930. Children on the way to school, posing at the main entrance, in front of the cast-iron double doors with the Jewish star. Shown are: Annie Simons (1), Mien Beem (number on her grey cap) (2), Juul Beem (white cap) (3), Mimi Weiman (black cap) (4), Esther Appel (5), Harry de Reeder (6), Joop Worms (7), Bram Spiro (8), David Beem (9), Leo Auerhaan(10), and Sal Weiman (11).

The move to the new building heralded a new period for the orphanage. Figure 3.8 shows a group of smiling children, boys and girls and of various ages, photographed at the main entrance, apparently on the way to school. The photograph was probably taken in early 1930, soon after the building was completed. The children only rarely, if ever, passed through these doors, using instead the entrances on the back of the building.

Figure 3.8 is the first extant photograph of its kind. Since Kerkvliet and Uitvlugt (1973) initiated interest in the history of the orphanage a great number of such photographs have been uncovered. They form an important part of the following chapters, making it possible to *"put a face to the name"* for many of the 168 children who lived here since the summer of 1929.

References

Duin, Th. van & K. van Ommen, 2000; *"Van stadspolder tot beschermd stadsgezicht. Het ontstaan en de groei van de Professoren- en Burgemeesterswijk en Rijndijkbuurt"*. Leiden, Vereniging Professoren- en Burgemeesterswijk, ISBN 909014174X.
Kerkvliet, G. & M. Uitvlugt, 1973; *"Een pot picalilly voor Westerbork. Journalistiek verslag over de vernietiging van het joodse weeshuis in Leiden"*. Den Haag, Q-Producties. Author's collection. [The original stencilled report, containing verbatim quotes from interviews with the Stoffels, Geertje Gebert, and Piet de Vries.] See also Kerkvliet & Uitvlugt, 1974.
Siebelt, Alphons, 2011b; *"Gids voor Leiden in de Tweede Wereldoorlog. Beschreven in 650 adressen"* [Guide to Leiden in the Second World War, described in 650 addresses]. Leiden, Ginkgo.

4   1929 to 1933: Happy years

Abstract

The inauguration of the new building in June 1929 allowed a significant increase in activity. By the end of 1929 the number of children had increased from 25 to 40. The building had a large playground for the younger children, the older children had a living room with radio and books, there was room for them to exercise and they could practice boxing in the attic. Although the institution was religiously orthodox, the director maintained a remarkably liberal attitude. Children attended non-religious Dutch schools, friends could visit them in the orphanage, and they could visit them in their homes in return. Compared to the previous 39 years, this was a happy period. It was only marred by the death of the director's wife, and financial problems caused by malpractice by the treasurer.

Keywords: Langebrug School, Zionism in the Netherlands

4.1   The new building

Apart from Director Italie, his wife, Sara Schaap, and the staff ladies Gobes, Bierschenk and de Leeuw, 25 children moved to the new building in 1929 after spending many years in the old building on Stille Rijn (Table 2.1). All testimonies indicate that they were very pleased with the new building. It is also remarkable that we have not a single photo of any of the children in the orphanage[1] from the 39 years between 1890 and 1929, while the number of photographs from 1929 to 1942 is overwhelming. It has been pointed out that, in the minds of the survivors, and in the light of the war and the Holocaust, the pre-war years looked much happier than they were. That will almost certainly also apply to what is described in this book, and surely there were also less positive experiences in the orphanage. Some children did not want to leave, while Mimi Weiman declared she would never want to come back (Ch. 5). But the contrast between the period before and after 1929 was not affected by later events, and there is convincing contemporaneous evidence to

---

[1]   Not counting the picture in Leman (1929) of two anonymous children showing their orphan's uniform.

Focke, Jaap W., *Machseh Lajesoumim: A Jewish Orphanage in the City of Leiden, 1890-1943*.
Taylor & Francis Group, 2021
DOI: 10.5117/9789463726955_CH04

Figure 4.1: The "permanent" staff on the terrace behind the building, 1930. From left: Mien Gobes, Nathan Italie, his first wife, Sara Italie-Schaap, Rachel Bierschenk, Jet de Leeuw. Left: a dark view into Nathan's office (H1 on Figure 3.3), behind Rachel and Jet: the annex. In the corner, hardly visible but the doors are open, the girls' entrance.

support the view that this was a relatively happy period for the resident children: letters to *Betsalel*, contact with non-Jewish friends (for example, the friends of Lotte Adler: Jopie Vos and Mien van der Staay, Ch. 5.7), the many photographs, the fact that children who were supposed to transfer out, often preferred to stay in Leiden, such as Sally Montezinos, who told his employer (Ch. 7.2) that the orphanage was both his home and his family. The photographs are probably the most informative. Many group photos were initiated by the (older) children (Lotte Adler and Mimi Weiman had their own camera) and they include children from every age group, apparently keen to be included. The prints were shared between them, and the same photo may appear in the albums of Lotte Adler, Piet de Vries, Betsy Wolff, and even the album of Director Nathan Italie.

Staff meetings could now comfortably take place inside in the director's dayroom, which also served as his office or on the terrace in front (Fig. 4.1). Social functions, such as celebrating Nathan's birthday, were held there as well, if the weather allowed it. In the corner between office and the annex, behind the staff on Figure 4.2 the open double doors can just be seen. It gave access to the boys'[2] cloakroom and lavatories (I1 in Fig. 3.3).

2   In some reports, the boys' and girls' entrances/staircases are mistakenly switched.

Figure 4.2: Children playing on the terrace behind the building, the other side of the annex compared to Figure 4.1. In the corner, double doors open, is the boys' entrance. On the right, the windows of the dining room.

Nathan and Sarah Italie, seen in Figure 4.1 with three women of the resident staff, did not have children of their own, and Sara was said to have had a very warm heart for the children in their care. While the staff was having their meetings on one side of the annex (as seen from the garden), children might be playing on the other side (Fig. 4.2). The architect's drawing had planned separate boys' and girls' playgrounds in front, as well as at the back of the building, but this gender separation was never implemented.

As explained in Chapter 1, the orphanages were primarily a social institution to take care of children if the parents were separated, or if the father had died, or if the parents were sick or otherwise incapacitated and not able to care for their children. It was a period of great poverty, and the economic crisis of 1929 made it worse. There was no effective birth control and no comprehensive state-provided welfare. Consequently, there was no lack of demand for the increased capacity of the new orphanage and its hugely improved facilities. Among the new arrivals in the second half of 1929 were Hans Kloosterman, and a little girl who would quickly become his friend: Mieke Dagloonder.

4.2   1929: Hans Kloosterman and Mieke Dagloonder arrive, two years old

Hans was born in Amsterdam on 19th February 1927 and arrived in Leiden on 2nd December 1929. His mother, Eva Turfkruijer, sent him to foster care when he was seventeen months old. After living a few months in the *Janna Children's Home*,[3] his foster mother brought him to Leiden. His father was Catholic and separated from his mother before Hans was born. Little is known about Hans' father; but Hijme Stoffels (the neighbour who played an important role during the war) tracked him down in October 1943 to tell him, not too gently, to take over responsibility for Hans (which he did, but it did not work out well: see Dossier Kloosterman).

For Hans, who arrived so young and with preciously few memories of a previous family life, the orphanage was everything: it was his home and he regarded the other children as *"my brothers and sisters"*, much more than for some others who arrived later in their lives.

The same probably applied to Mieke Dagloonder, who arrived two weeks after Hans, on 18th December 1929, also just two years old. On the 1932 photograph (Fig. 4.3) Mieke stands first from left. Hans told us that Mieke and he became inseparable very quickly. Mieke's mother, Esther de Rosa, was only sixteen when Mieke was born. Mieke's father Joseph died six weeks later. Her mother never paid her a visit in Leiden, which was noticed by the other children. Sitting on the bench second from left is – unmistakably conspicuous – Bram Degen (Chs. 7.4 and 9.5). On the far right (with a toy car) is Harrie Spier (see Ch. 7.8). Two boys in Figure 4.3 remain unidentified; there were six boys of about the same age (five years) in 1932. The two unidentified boys could be Hijman Cohen and/or Isidoor Wegloop. The date is probably around summer 1932; Betsy, the last of the eight identified children to come to Leiden, arrived on 11th January 1932.

Figure 4.4 shows the dining room from the inside, probably in the winter of 1929/1930, given the age of the children who have been recognized in this photo (see caption). The dining room had four big tables, and a table for the staff, who usually had their meals after the children. Each table was designed to have fourteen chairs, for 56 children in total. It would have been crowded if all children and all the staff were there, e.g. during Shabbat or the high religious days of observance, but normally the small children had their meals separately from the older ones.

---

3   The *Jannahuis* was established on the Middenweg in East Amsterdam in 1923 for children of unmarried women.

Figure 4.3: Summer 1932: Sitting in front: unidentified, Bram Degen, Hans Kloosterman, Harry Spier with car; standing from left: Mieke Dagloonder, Didia Klein, Charles Kirschenbaum, Jopie Beem, unidentified, Betsy Wolff. Uniforms had been abolished in 1919, but the children often wore dusters when playing.

Director Italie and his first wife, Sara, might have taken their meals privately or in the dining room. After Sara's death in 1932 and his second marriage in 1934, he and his family (his children were born in 1935 and 1937) had their meals in their private quarters, except on Shabbat, when they joined staff and children to celebrate the special meal together, staff putting their chairs at the head of each table. The tables were laid by the children. The tablecloth on weekdays was an easily washable plastic, removed after dinner. Piet de Vries was expert in rolling it out on the tables in one smooth movement. On Shabbat a real white cloth was laid on the tables.

Hans Kloosterman[4] recalls about his years in the orphanage as a toddler:

The smaller children only got up after the older ones [six years and older] had left for school. The nanny handled the small boys. Miss Altenberg or the Jewish teacher

4   Letter to L.P. Kasteleyn, 20th November 2000, translated.

Figure 4.4: The dining hall, summer 1935. Front row third from left: possibly Max Konijn; fifth (at the corner) Herman Rozeveld. Middle table, facing us from left Corrie Frenkel, Paula Jacobsohn, Mieke Dagloonder, and (the small boy) possibly Willem van Weddingen. Back row facing us from left: Lodi Cohen; right behind Mieke: Jopie Beem; below the large picture (showing the Leiden Community Hall, the sponsor of the room's furniture) Jupie Pront. The big boy in front of her on the third table and covering part of Jupie's face on the photo could be her friend, Herman Stofkooper. Identifications courtesy Leonard Kasteleyn. Source: Levisson Album.

came to get the small girls out of bed. After washing and dressing, we assembled in the dining room for breakfast. We all got porridge (oatmeal or semolina, bread pudding, or – after Pesach – porridge made from matzes), and we could always come back for a second helping. Prayer, of course, before and after the meal. Then bathroom visits, and off to the playroom. The playroom was fantastic, with lots of things to play with. [...] One of my earliest memories of the orphanage is sitting in the playroom on the lap of a nanny at a hexagonal table with a light-blue linoleum top. The floor was covered in the same material. [...] Later, I discovered that there were cupboards all along the outer walls of the playroom. Our nanny stored our toys in there at the end of the day, to take them out again next morning.

The increased capacity offered by the new building was quickly used: the second half of 1929 saw the arrival of thirteen children.[5]

---

5   Mien Beem and her siblings Juul, David and Josef, Leo Auerhaan, Jacques Overste and his brother Adolf Maurits, Samuel Engelschman and his brother Barend, Hans Kloosterman, Esther Appel, Herman Stofkooper, and Mieke Dagloonder.

Figure 4.5: The large playroom in the annex, probably from the same period ad Fig. 4.4.

In the whole year of 1929, there were seventeen arrivals, compared to only two departures, a net influx of fifteen children. It is not known how the staff handled it since the records of the orphanage were lost during the war. Probably one or two additional nannies were hired.

Figure 4.5 shows the large playroom mentioned by Hans, within the half-round annex.

4.3   Mimi Weiman and her friends; the "new" orphanage has landed

By 1932, the new home had clearly come into its own. No doubt there will have been some problems, and quarrels as in any normal family, but the children played together, boys and girls, old and young, and often made friends. There was strong familiarity. There are five *"hands on shoulders"* in Figure 4.6, and Ies Cohen on the far right is holding the hand of the small boy next to him. That may be Hans Kloosterman (his friend Mieke is also on the picture). Ies Cohen is twelve years old on this photograph, if the picture was taken in 1932. He had arrived with his older brother Lodi (Ch. 9.6) in April 1930. The young women on the left holding Mieke Dagloonder is a German Christian nanny, probably Hedwig Helman, or otherwise her sister Elfride.

The photos in Figures 4.6 and 4.7 were taken with the camera of Mimi Weiman. Her arrival on 14th January 1927 when she was nine and a half years old was

Figure 4.6: In the back garden, probably 1932. Front row from left: Didia Klein, Hans Porcelijn, Betsy Wolff, Chellie Leeda, unknown, Sally Montezinos, David Beem, Hans Kloosterman (?), Ies Cohen. Back row from left: a nanny with Mieke Dagloonder on her shoulder, Harry and Jacob de Vries, Mimi Weiman, Sientje Spiro with hand on Ies' shoulder.

mentioned in Chapter 2.3. She left the orphanage on 30th April 1935 when she was almost 18. The camera was a present at her brother Sal's bar mitzvah in February 1932. She shared her vivid memories of her eight years in the orphanage and helped to identify the children on her photographs as well as those from other sources (Kasteleyn, personal communication, 2012). She often asked someone else to take the photo, so that she appears in the photos herself. She could develop and print the photos herself in a dark room in the orphanage.

4.4   Going to school

The toddlers had more than enough to do inside the new building, and in the large garden and playground. The small children, from age six, had two major external activities during the week: attending the two Saturday services in the synagogue, and going to elementary school at the Langebrug. They walked, under the guidance of Mien Gobes, along Cronesteinkade, across Singel through the park, to Levendaal/ Garenmarkt. Figure 4.8 shows the Levendaal Canal as it was until 1935, when the canal on the viewers side of the bridge was filled in. They then walked past the

Figure 4.7: Another of Mimi's group photos in the back garden of the orphanage. Probably 1933. Names: see below.
The children on Figure 4.7:

1	Mirjam Frenkel	9	Annie Simons	18	Juul Beem (?)
2	Mimi Weiman	10	Sal Porcelijn (?)	19	Bram Degen
3	Mieke Dagloonder	11	Louis Limburg	20	Barend Ritmeester
4	Hettie de Jong	12	Leo Auerhaan (?)	21	Hans Kloosterman
5	Didia Klein	13	Jopie Beem	22	Henny Jansen
6	Corrie Frenkel	14	Jettie Bobbe	23	Charles Kirschenbaum
7	Ies Cohen	15	unidentified	24	Frieda Lichtenbaum
8	Harrie Spier	16	Hans Porcelijn (?)	25	Salomon Ritmeester
		17	Sallie Montezinos	26	unidentified

synagogue (the square grey building behind the right-hand side of the bridge, marked S) and across Steenschuur to Langebrug. In 1969 the Korte Levendaal (Fig. 4.9), behind the bridge and in front of the synagogue, was filled in to make way for the ugliest possible parking lot. Since that time the substructure of the old Barbara Bridge was buried in the ground under Korevaarstraat. It had to be dug up in 2017 and removed, as part of the city's plan to build an underground car park under the Garenmarkt.

The small Jewish community in Leiden – about 125 souls in 1737 (Kasteleyn, 2003) – did not boast its own school, until schoolmaster David Haagens moved into

Figure 4.8: Leiden, before 1923. View of Levendaal, with Zijdegracht from the left, the Barbara Bridge, and Jodenkerksteeg (literary: "Jewish Church Alley") to the right; a tramline was laid across the bridge in 1923. The Levendaal Canal on the viewer's side of the bridge was filled in 1935, and Zijdegracht/Jodenkerksteeg widened and renamed Korevaarstraat. The canal behind the bridge ends in the distance at Rapenburg and Steenschuur, with the Langebrug schools behind. One can see the Lodewijks Church just above the trees on the right-hand side. In 1969 this part of the canal was filled in. The squarish building marked S, behind the bridge, is the synagogue. Figure 4.9 shows the route as seen in the opposite direction, from the Lodewijks Church. Photo courtesy ELO Leiden.

a rented house along Langebrug in 1805 and started teaching at his home. Two years later, the entire neighbourhood was destroyed when a gunpowder ship exploded in the Steenschuur, killing ten out of eighteen pupils of the Jewish school.[6] Master Haagen, who had lost his wife and four children in the disaster, left the city. This was during the French occupation (1795-1813), when the "United Provinces" became a much more centralized state, governed by national laws, and strongly influenced by the ideals emanating from the French Revolution and the Enlightenment, including the strict separation between church and state. No attempt was made to start a Jewish school again in Leiden.

The French domination had a huge and lasting influence on Dutch society, but when it was over there was almost immediate resistance against the secularization of the education system, both in the predominantly Protestant Northern, and the predominantly Roman Catholic Southern Netherlands. The constitution of 1848 reinstated the freedom to organize schools based on religion, or any other philosophy,

6   Mrs. J.L. Ponsen, Museum *Het Wevershuis*, Leiden (personal communication, 2016).

Figure 4.9: The same view as Figure 4.8, but looking in the opposite direction, from the top of the Lodewijks Church in 1957. It shows the route the children took (towards the photographer) from the orphanage (O) in the distance, passing the synagogue (the roof marked by an S), along the Kort Levendaal (kLD, the canal with the sharp bend), over the Groenebrug crossing the Steenschuur, and turning left towards the Langebrug schools. Photo courtesy ELO Leiden.

realm of thought or educational principles. From this time, there were *openbare* (public[7]) schools, under the aegis of the municipality, and overall quality control by the national government, and *Bijzondere* (special, private and/or denominational) schools, set up by institutions, church organizations, or groups of parents, being Protestant or Catholic, or believing in a particular education philosophy such as Montessori or Dalton, and so on. In short, the Dutch school system began to reflect the *verzuiling* as described in Chapter 1. But the law of 1848 did not result in a significant increase in Jewish schools (Braber, 2013). After another 70 years of "education wars" following the initial victory of 1848, a new law was introduced in 1917 stipulating that *all* schools, both public and denominational, would be funded in the same manner by the central government, as is still the situation at present. But even then, the number of Jewish schools did not dramatically increase. From the

7   Public meaning non-denominational; not to be confused with what is called a "public school" in the UK.

Figure 4.10: Grade 6 of the bovenschool at Langebrug, probably in school year 1929/1930. Most of the children will have been eleven or twelve years old. Jan Koolhaas (1) had three Jewish classmates, all three from the orphanage: Herman Stofkooper (2) (Ch. 9.8), Karel van Santen (3) (Ch. 8.1) and Jacob (Jaap) de Vries (4). Photo courtesy Jan Koolhaas.

1920s some Jewish schools were set up in the urban centres, but by far not enough to cater for the Jewish community at that time. Even in Amsterdam, which had a Jewish population of at least 66,000 souls (out of a total Amsterdam population of 766,000 in 1930), only some 800 pupils attended Jewish schools (see references in Braber, 2013). The paucity of Jewish schools reflects the secularization of the Jewish bourgeoisie (Blom & Cahen, 2017) and their wish to integrate or assimilate in Dutch society.[8] They chose to send their children to secular, non-denominational schools with conviction (ibidem). As pointed out before, however, most did not relinquish their Jewish identity. Jewish religious and cultural education was provided by the Jewish congregation itself, after school hours.

There is no indication that Director Italie ever desired to have a Jewish school resurrected in Leiden, and the children of the Leiden orphanage attended non-Jewish schools, with children from many different backgrounds, for as long as the

---

8   It should be noted that until the influx of refugees from the East from 1933, the vast majority of Jews in the Netherlands had Dutch citizenship, a situation that was quite different from that in Belgium and France.

orphanage existed. He also was keen to distribute the children over the two schools at Langebrug (the "upper" and the "lower" school) to prevent too large a group from the orphanage from being in any one class. Children from Jewish families elsewhere in Leiden also attended the Langebrug school, such as Meijer and Tobias Mendelson, the sons of the sexton of the synagogue.

Figure 4.10 shows a class at the Langebrug *bovenschool* (upper school), 25 children, three of whom were from the orphanage. Six years later (Fig. 5.8), the practice to send the children to the *"openbare"* school, and, if possible, to limit the number of orphanage children in each class, was still adhered to. At the orphanage, Jewish religious and cultural education was provided by in-house staff, such as Esther Klein (Fig. 6.17), as well as by the director himself, supplemented with lessons by external teachers, such as Victor Bloemkoper, who also lived in the Profburgwijk. From the many, diverse,

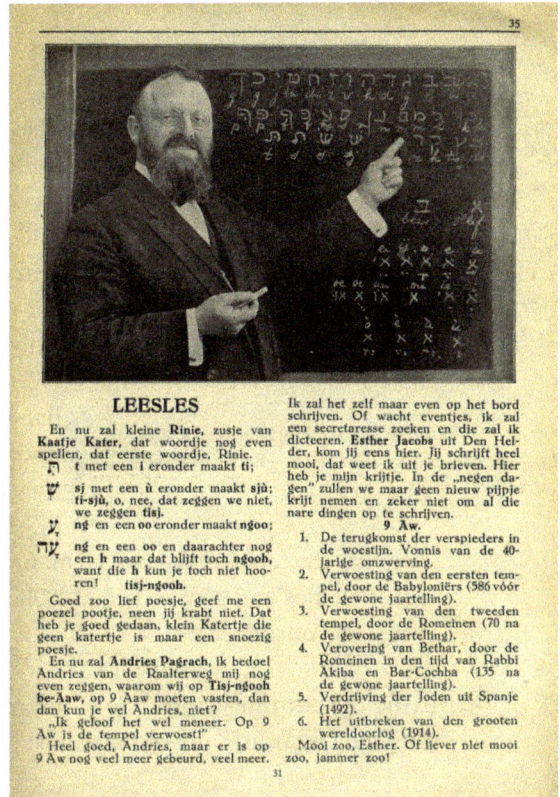

Figure 4.11: Rabbi de Hond replying to letters by Esther Appel and Esther van Santen and using the opportunity to give a Hebrew reading lesson.

pre-war organizations which aimed to complement the general education with Jewish religious and cultural teachings, Rebbe Meyer de Hond stands out, as founder (in 1913) and moderator of the Betsalel Youth Organization, and particularly the establishment of the *Betsalel Joodsche Jeugdkrant*, a weekly youth journal. Being aware, of course, that most of his readers did not attend Jewish schools, he made a strong effort to add educational content to his weekly journal, such as Hebrew language lessons (Fig. 4.11).

The teenagers in the Leiden orphanage were avid readers, as shown by the many letters they submitted to *Betsalel* during the short period (between 1928 and 1935) of its existence. As the chief editor of *Betsalel*, de Hond discussed the letters he had received from Jewish children from all over the country, and replied to them in his peculiar, somewhat childish style, which probably was not regarded as inappropriate at the time. An example is shown in Figure 4.12, his reply to a letter which was signed by no less than nineteen children from the orphanage in Leiden.

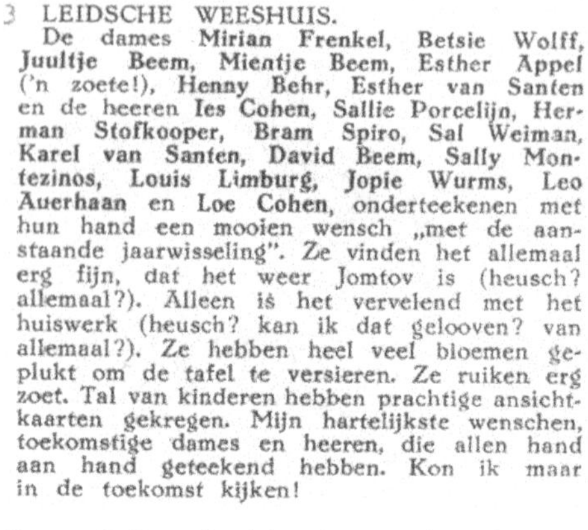

3 LEIDSCHE WEESHUIS.
De dames Mirian Frenkel, Betsie Wolff,
Juultje Beem, Mientje Beem, Esther Appel
('n zoete!), Henny Behr, Esther van Santen
en de heeren Ies Cohen, Sallie Porcelijn, Herman Stofkooper, Bram Spiro, Sal Weiman,
Karel van Santen, David Beem, Sally Montezinos, Louis Limburg, Jopie Wurms, Leo
Auerhaan en Loe Cohen, onderteekenen met
hun hand een mooien wensch „met de aan-
staande jaarwisseling". Ze vinden het allemaal
erg fijn, dat het weer Jomtov is (heusch?
allemaal?). Alleen is het vervelend met het
huiswerk (heusch? kan ik dat gelooven? van
allemaal?). Ze hebben heel veel bloemen ge-
plukt om de tafel te versieren. Ze ruiken erg
zoet. Tal van kinderen hebben prachtige ansicht-
kaarten gekregen. Mijn hartelijkste wenschen,
toekomstige dames en heeren, die allen hand
aan hand geteekend hebben. Kon ik maar
in de toekomst kijken!

Figure 4.12: Example of the editor's reply to a letter from the orphanage, 1934. (Henny Behr = Henny Jansen).

Freely translated, part of it reads:

LEIDEN ORPHANAGE

The [young] ladies Mirian Frenkel, Betsy Wolff, Juultje Beem, Mientje Beem, Esther Appel (a sweet one!), Henny Behr, Esther van Santen, and the young gentlemen Ies Cohen, Sallie Porcelijn, Herman Stofkooper, Bram Spiro, Sal Weiman, Karel van Santen, David Beem, Sally Montezinos, Louis Limburg, Jopie Wurms [Worms], Leo Auerhaan and Loe [Lodi] Cohen, hand-sign their letter with best wishes 'for the upcoming turn of the year'. They enjoy (do they really?) celebrating yet another yom tov. [...] They plucked sweet-smelling flowers to beautify the tables and received many postcards. My heartfelt congratulations, future ladies and gentlemen. [...] Oh, if only I could see what the future may bring for you all!

During the summer of 1934 de Hond reports that he has received – for the first time – a letter from Sally Montezinos:

> The brother of Josie[9] [who is] well known to us here. [...] They hey had a nice holiday together in The Hague, ate grapes and tomatoes in the Westland, went to Kijkduin, and back to The Hague before going home. [...] He is ten years old, in grade 5. Welcome new friend, give my regards to the children, the ladies [of the staff], and Mijnheer en Mevrouw [Mr and Mrs, i.e. Director Italie and his wife].

He hopes that from now on, Sally will write to him every week, just like his sister in Amsterdam.

The Betsalel Weekly ceased to exist in 1935, hit by financial problems and the difficult economy, while dark clouds were gathering over Europe (Ch. 5). From his days as a student de Hond was given a difficult time by some of the religious leadership in the Netherlands. He had to go into exile to Berlin to obtain his certificate as a rabbi. When he returned to the Netherlands, his German certificate was not recognized. But his many contributions to Jewish cultural life, and his deep commitment to the fate of the Jewish paupers in Amsterdam, are beyond dispute. De Hond was one of those who – without knowing what was going to happen – had prescience; when

---

9   That is Josefina, who lived in the Portuguese Girls' Orphanage in Amsterdam.

Figure 4.13: April 1933. Far left upright on her knees: Annie Simons. Front row: Mimi Weiman, Jupie Pront, Hettie de Jong (with glasses), Els van Santen. Back row from left: Eljakim's mother, Eljakim Schaap (on Jupie's back), Ms. Mien Gobes.

he boarded the train to Sobibor on 20th July 1943, he reputedly called out *"Hineni, Hineni…"*.[10] He was killed three days later.

4.5   A small boy from Palestine

The Zionist movement was by far not as strong in the Netherlands as it was in Germany and Eastern Europe, but it certainly contributed to the self-consciousness of Dutch Jewry in the twentieth century. No doubt the Pesach prayers in the orphanage ended with the ever-repeated hopeful wish *"Next year in Jerusalem"*, like everywhere else in the diaspora. Even though only a small minority considered themselves true Zionist, the fascination with the Jewish return to *Eretz Yisrael*, and rebuilding what for more than two millennia had been regarded as their homeland, was enormous. Indeed, the visit of a *"small boy from Palestine"* in April 1932 caused great excitement in the orphanage. It was Eljakim Schaap, family of Sara Italie-Schaap, and the senior girls made sure he was included in Mimi's photographs (Fig. 4.13). Several of the

10   *"I am ready, my Lord"* (as translated by Leonard Cohen in his last song, *"You want it darker"*, October 2016).

girls wrote enthusiastically to *Betsalel* about the two-year-old visitor, complaining that they could not talk to him because *"de jongen spreekt alleen Joods"* ("the boy only speaks Jewish").

It is remarkable that Mien Gobes, as senior staff member, appears in photographs (such as Fig. 4.13). She was 33 at the time and had joined the orphanage in March 1923. She must have had a good relationship with the older girls. The younger children, of whom she was formally in charge, regarded her as strict, and having "loose hands", the Dutch expression to indicate that if you irritated her, you could expect a box on the ears.

4.6   1932: A ceremonial photograph

For the group photo of Figure 4.14, taken in November 1932, the orphanage assembled in the great hall. The photograph shows 44 children and five staff, including a non-resident nanny (no. 33), who is the only one who could not be identified.

Director Italie and his wife, Sara, are not present on the photograph. Sara was seriously ill at the time. She died on 7th December 1932, just weeks after this picture was taken. Also missing is Chellie Leeda, who was ten years at the time. Sara and Maurits Levie are present on the photo; they had arrived at 2nd November, which helped in dating the picture. Ludwig Kloos is not present; he left on 17th November. Two years later, another assembly photograph was taken, now with Nathan Italie present, and sitting proudly in the centre (Fig. 5.4).

Shortly after the funeral of Sara, another disaster struck the orphanage when it transpired (December 1932) that the treasurer of the board of governors had embezzled some 110,000 florins from the reserves of the orphanage. Elias Viskoper Szn (Fig. 2.7; b.1884, not to be confused with his nephew: Elias Viskoper Jzn, b.1878) was the owner of the renowned Astoria Cinema in Dordrecht, and the Apollo Cinema in The Hague. It is difficult not to feel sorry for him, as the global economic crisis took effect, and his financial difficulties became worse during the early 1930s. The deficit of the Apollo Cinema grew to some *fl* 400,000, and it was later calculated that he owed *fl* 764,985 to 40 creditors.[11] By December 1932 he had resigned all his public positions. He was arrested on 27th December 1932 for fraud and embezzlement and was declared bankrupt on 12th January 1933. Viskoper was sentenced to two years in prison.[12] Elias, his wife Rosa and their son Rudi (Fig. 2.7) perished in Auschwitz; two other children survived the war.

---

11   *Het Vaderland*, 20th October 1933.
12   *Leidsche Courant*, 21st January 1933. I could not find out how much of the sentence he served.

Figure 4.14: November 1932. Formal group photo in the great hall of the orphanage. Names: see below.

1	Juultje Beem	18	Hans Porcelijn	35	Louis Limburg
2	Esje van Santen	19	David Beem	36	Hans Kloosterman
3	Mien Beem	20	Ies Cohen	37	Salomon Ritmeester
4	Joop Worms	21	Jac. Witteboon	38	Charles Kirschenbaum
5	Lodi Cohen	22	Leo Auerhaan	39	Betsy Wolff
6	Bram Spiro	23	Jopie Beem	40	Sally Montezinos
7	Mimi Weiman	24	Isidoor Wegloop	41	Mirjam Frenkel
8	Sal Porcelijn	25	Flo Altenberg	42	Barend Ritmeester
9	Karel van Santen	26	Didia Klein	43	Sientje Spiro
10	Jaap de Vries	27	Rachel Bierschenk	44	Corrie Frenkel
11	Sal Weiman	28	Jet de Leeuw	45	Mieke Dagloonder
12	Esther Appel	29	Mien Gobes	46	Harrie Spier
13	Hetty de Jong	30	Bram Degen	47	Jettie Bobbe
14	Jupie Pront	31	Sara Levie	48	Frieda Lichtenbaum
15	Herman Stofkooper	32	Hijman Cohen	49	Reina Segal
16	Henny Jansen (Behr)	33	unidentified nanny		
17	Annie Simons	34	Maurits Levie		

In a special meeting of the board of governors on Sunday, 15th January 1933, the chairman, Professor J.L. Palache, complained about a host of sensational rumours which was circulating about the situation, and which had led to Viskoper's arrest. The board had not intended to involve the judiciary in the case. He stressed that

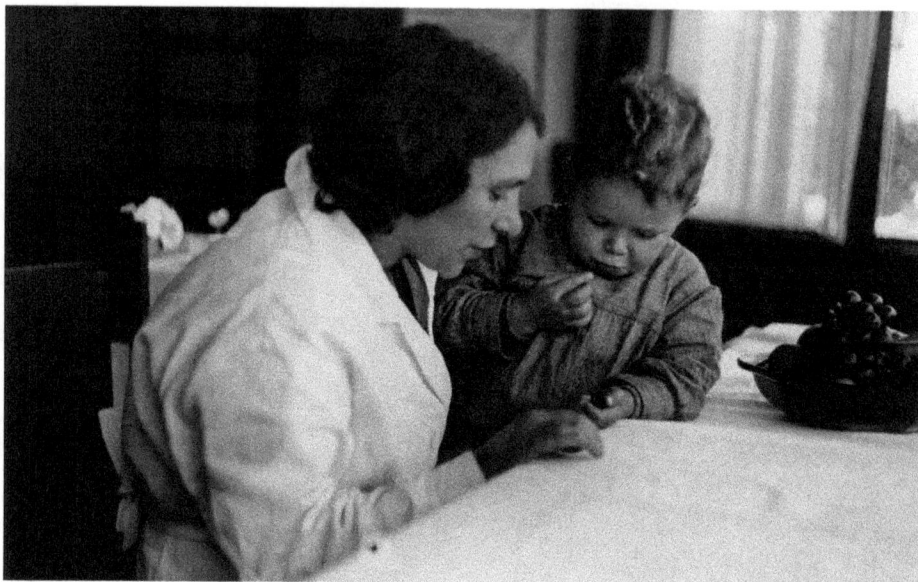

Figure 4.15: January 1933. Mien Gobes with Herman Rozeveld, who had arrived on 5th January 1930, just two years old.

"whatever the implications [...] the beautiful building stands in Leiden, not burdened by debt or mortgage, and the care for the children had not suffered in any way".[13] He also mentioned the failure of the external accountant to do his duty, and cautioned against passing too harsh a judgement on the ex-treasurer.

The Leiden newspapers contain a great number of articles[14] and calls for action, to raise money in support of the Jewish orphanage when it was being built (Ch. 2), and this continued after its completion. Following the financial disaster of 1932, support came from all over the country, and from people of different religions and political denominations. Within a few years the financial health of the orphanage was restored.

Reaching the end of this chapter does not imply that the relatively happy years had come to an end after only four years. On the contrary, in many ways, for another seven years, life in the orphanage continued very much as before. But the outside world started to change in 1933, and even the Leiden orphanage was confronted with the growing tensions. With hindsight the changes of 1933 were far more significant than even pessimistic observers thought at the time, reason to dedicate a separate

---

13 *"de kinderen hebben er tot heden geen boterham minder om gegeten"*, *Leidsch Dagblad*, 16th January 1933.
14 All articles concerning the Leiden orphanage which were printed in the *Leids Dagblad* and the *Leidse Courant* between 1880 and 1947 have been collected: see Dossier Leidse Krantenartikelen.

chapter to the period from 1933 to 1939. But the children, even the older ones, were apparently hardly touched by political developments.

Most of the surviving photographs were taken according to some plan: usually the children consciously pose for and look into the camera, even if they were called together by someone, often one of the older girls, on the spur of the moment. Figure 4.15 is one of the few pictures with a more impromptu nature. It was taken in January 1933, when the skies over Germany were rapidly darkening.

References

Blom, J.C.H. & J.J. Cahen, 2017; *"Joodse Nederlanders, Nederlandse joden en joden in Nederland (1870-1940)"*. In: Blom et al., 2017, pp. 275-359.

Blom, J.C.H., D.J. Wertheim, H. Berg & B.T. Wallet (eds), 2021; *"Reappraising the history of the Jews in the Netherlands"*. Trans. by David McKay. London, Littman Library of Jewish Civilization, ISBN 9781786941879. [In press.]

Blom, J.C.H., H. Berg, B. Wallet & D. Wertheim (eds), 2017; *"Geschiedenis van de Joden in Nederland"*. Balans, ISBN 9789460034374. [The English edition, not used in preparing this book, is in press with Littmann Library, see Blom et al., 2021.]

Braber, Ben, 2013; *"This cannot happen here: Integration and Jewish resistance in the Netherlands 1940-1945"*. Amsterdam, Amsterdam University Press, ISBN 9789089645838. Available online at www.oapen.org. [This book addresses the question whether and how the integration of Jews into Dutch society influenced their resistance to persecution during the German occupation of the Netherlands in the Second World War.]

Kasteleyn, L.P., 2003; *"Vervolging en bescherming, joden in Leiden 1933-1945"*. Leiden, Museum de Lakenhal.

5   1933 to 1939: Clouds over Europe

Abstract

The Nazi takeover in Germany in early 1933 and the ever-worsening anti-Jewish campaign caused anxiety in Holland. Jewish and other (political) refugees tried to get asylum in Holland or enter the country illegally. Many assumed that Germany would not violate Holland's neutrality. The first Jewish refugee children arrived at the orphanage in Leiden in April 1933. In total some 30 refugee children were taken in by the orphanage in Leiden between 1933 and 1940. Those refugees who were still in Holland on 15th March 1940 found themselves caught under the same Nazi regime they had tried to escape from.

Keywords: Nazi takeover of Germany, Kristallnacht, refugees, Kindertransport, Truus Wiijsmuller

5.1   1933: **Adolf Hitler becomes Chancellor of Germany**

Hitler rose to power on the back of frustration and anger following the German defeat in the First World War, the intolerable burden of debt and imposed penalties, the economic crisis in 1929, failing democracy of the Weimar Republic, and the fear of communism as unemployment rose and benefits were cut. The Nazi Party (National Socialist German Workers' Party, *Nationalsozialistische Deutsche Arbeiterpartei*) grew from 107 seats in parliament to 230 seats (out of 608) in 1932. Having gained legitimate power in 1933, Hitler quickly converted his position into a dictatorship, using the various institutions of the Nazi Party built up over the preceding fourteen years. All the members of his powerful inner circle, such as Joseph Goebbels, Hermann Goering, and Heinrich Himmler, were already at his side.

The new regime moved fast. The Dachau and the Oranienburg concentration camps, the first such camps in Germany, were operational in March 1933, barely two months after the Nazis took power. Ever larger numbers of real and perceived opponents were locked up in camps all over Germany, usually without due process. As early as 1920, the Nazi Party had included in its programme the intention to

Focke, Jaap W., *Machseh Lajesoumim: A Jewish Orphanage in the City of Leiden, 1890-1943*.
Taylor & Francis Group, 2021
DOI: 10.5117/9789463726955_CH05

isolate and remove the Jews from German society. They set about implementing this programme without delay or hesitation. On 7th April 1933, a law came into effect to exclude Jewish and other *"politically unreliable"* civil servants and employees from state service. The law had a strong racial basis. For good measure, another law was issued in Hitler's name on 15th September 1933 to *"protect German [i.e. Aryan] blood and German honour".* Jewish enrolment in schools and colleges was restricted and Jewish participation in the medical and legal professions was curtailed. More than 400 such laws[1] were issued between 1933 and the outbreak of the war in 1939, many of them not issued by Hitler, but by lower level and local administrations which took their cue from him, without having to be told. The city of Berlin forbade Jewish lawyers and notaries from working on legal matters, the mayor of Munich disallowed Jewish doctors from treating non-Jewish patients, and the Bavarian Interior Ministry denied admission of Jewish students to medical school. Within a year of Hitler coming to power, it had become virtually impossible for Jews to earn a living from professional activities in Germany. By the end of 1933, some 40,000 Jews had left Germany, of which some 4000 had emigrated to the Netherlands.

In 1935 and 1937, German Jews had to declare all assets, at home or abroad: properties, savings, investments – a clear indication that the government was planning to expropriate them. Many Jews saw the signs on the wall and left the country, but at lower levels than in 1933 (on average around 25,000 per year from 1933 to 1937, with another peak after the introduction of the Nuremberg racial legislation in September 1935). Life for Jews had become *"difficult, but not impossible"* (J. Michman, 1987). But in 1938, after the *Anschluss* of Austria and the increasing occurrence of pogroms in Germany, emigration numbers started to rise again, particularly after *Kristallnacht* (Ch. 5.6). The cumulative effect was enormous (USHMM website). The number of Jews in Germany declined from some 523,000 in 1933 to 202,000 in 1939, a decrease of no less than 60%, and to 163,000 by October 1941, when emigration of Jews from Germany was no longer possible. Those who did not leave Germany may have been too old to do so. Others may have been reluctant to be uprooted, and leave their relatives or their possessions behind, believing it could not possibly get much worse, that it would eventually blow over, or they lacked the money, the knowledge, or the required presence of mind to emigrate. However, the most important and sinister barrier before one could leave was the need for an *entry permit to another country.* Many countries restricted the number of refugees they allowed in. Even the USA, being a pre-eminent immigration country, limited access for Jewish refugees from Europe, against overwhelming demand: in June 1939, 27,000 available places under the US

---

1   US Holocaust Memorial Museum (USHMM), Washington, DC.

quota system attracted 309,000 applications from Jews in Germany, Austria and (occupied) Czechoslovakia.[2]

In the Netherlands, the government also maintained a restrictive policy, quoting fears about unemployment and social disturbance as a reason. Nevertheless, from 1933 onwards a few thousand Jewish refugees had been allowed entry if they had valid papers and enough means of existence. Others, such as the family Gottschalk and the parents of Mindel Färber (Chs. 9.1 and 9.2) arrived by illegally crossing the border between Germany and the Netherlands. Gertrude van Tijn, who played an active role in assisting the refugees, concluded (Wasserstein, 2014) that compared to other Western European countries and the USA, the admission policy in Holland was surprisingly liberal until 1938 (Ch. 5.6). It was the last country to allow Jewish refugees to enter without visa. Between March 1933 and the end of 1937 some 22,000 Jews had moved to Holland, out of 127,000 registered Jewish emigrants (ibidem).

Catering for the needs of refugees, regardless of their denomination or status (legal or illegal), was not seen at the time as government business, but as the responsibility of private relief organizations, usually within the framework of the pillarized society. Several committees and other private initiatives to support Jewish refugees from Germany were established in the Netherlands as early as March 1933. The most important were the *Comité Bijzondere Joodsche Belangen* (Committee for Special Jewish Interests, CBJB), which was chaired by Abraham Asscher, a well-known diamond tycoon from Amsterdam,[3] and the subordinate *Comité voor Joodsche Vluchtelingen* (Committee for Jewish Refugees, CJV), which was chaired by David Cohen, who was professor of classical languages and history first at Leiden and later at the University of Amsterdam. Both gentlemen were very keen to remain in good standing with the government and worked strictly within its constraints and policies, including the condition that the committee would arrange all funding required to take care of the refugees. Also part of the committee was L.E. Visser, who had been on the Dutch Supreme Court from 1915, becoming its president in 1939. During the German occupation, Asscher and Cohen would become co-chairmen of the *Joodse Raad*, the Jewish Council, which was established in February 1941 by order of the German administration. In that capacity they would maintain their reluctance to do anything which would upset the authorities, whether Dutch or German. It should be noted that such an attitude was displayed by the Dutch bourgeoisie in general, regardless of denomination or religion. But Visser took a

2   USHMM, see at https://encyclopedia.ushmm.org the articles "german-jewish-refugees-1933-1939" and "united-states-immigration-and-refugee-law-1921-1980".
3   Abraham and Joseph Asscher came over to the UK at the behest of King Eward VII to take charge of the cutting of the 3106 carat Cullinan diamond. Abraham reputedly carried the raw stone in his pocket when they returned to Holland on the ferry.

more independent and courageous stand, as is evident from his communications with David Cohen (J. Melkman, 1974).

5.2   The first refugee children from the East arrive in Leiden

Among the refugees were also unaccompanied children. Many of these children had family or friends in Holland willing to take children into their homes. The Dutch government discouraged that, however, preferring the unaccompanied children to be taken in by institutions such as orphanages and children's homes in order to prevent the refugees from integrating into Dutch society, and hoping that most of the refugees would eventually move on to other countries. Thus, the Jewish and some non-Jewish orphanages in the Netherlands became involved with these refugee children. Moreover, the ministry often transferred the children from one institution to another after just about three months, thus uprooting them before they would be able to settle down.

The Jewish orphanages in the Netherlands provided care for orphans or half-orphans, or children in need of care for other reasons, from a socio-economic perspective. It was not considered self-evident that they would accept children who were fleeing Germany for political reasons, and who often had relatively affluent parents. But inevitably, as the persecution of Jews in Germany intensified, the number of refugee children which were taken into the care of Dutch Jewish institutions increased. The archives of the Jewish orphanage in The Hague show[4] that the CJV was approached by the Jewish orphanage in Frankfurt am Main in the course of 1933, which asked whether the orphanages in the Netherlands would also accept children who were not orphans but refugees. When the CJV asked the orphanage in The Hague, it replied positively, and many refugee children arrived in The Hague for shorter or longer periods from 1933 onwards. Additional beds were acquired, the attic at the Pletterijstraat was transformed into a hall, and some children were housed with foster families. The largest number of refugee children were taken in by the Central Jewish Orphanage in Utrecht. This orphanage did not have space for so many children, but they had a villa available in nearby Den Dolder, which was used during the holidays. This villa was converted to accommodate the refugees (Crone, 2005).

Table 5.1 lists the refugee children who were taken in by the Jewish orphanage in Leiden.[5] The children who left Holland before the war were not the focus of this

4   Haags Gemeentearchief, 0194-01; courtesy Miriam Keesing. The archives of the Jewish orphanage in The Hague were found in Moscow and returned to the Netherlands in 2003 (van Crefeld, 2004).
5   From March 1933; to the best of my knowledge.

Figure 5.1: April-June 1933. Marga Gurfinkel, the small girl on a tricycle, just three years old, and one of the first German refugee children to be accommodated by the orphanage in Leiden. From left: Mirjam Frenkel, Sally Montezinos (with autoped), Chellie Leeda, Corrie Frenkel (behind her), Esje van Santen, David Beem, unknown, Esther Appel holding Marga Gurfinkel, Annie Simons (back), and Betsy Wolff (front). Someone is looking out of a dining room window.

study, but information which was available at the time of writing is summarized below. Scope remains for further research.

The first refugees arrived on 6th April 1933, a month after the Nazi takeover in Germany. They were three Gurfinkel children: Rudi, Make and Benjamin, from Köln (Cologne), fourteen, twelve and eleven years old. They were followed ten days later by their three sisters, Esther (ten), Ida (eight) and Marga (three), who was included in a photograph (Fig. 5.1) shortly after arrival. The six Gurfinkels left again on 23rd June 1933 and (officially) became residents of Palestine on 24th December 1934.

Helga and Kurt Gottschalk were transferred from Leiden to the *Burgerweeshuis* in Amsterdam on 10th July 1939. They were still in Amsterdam on the day the Germans invaded, but they escaped four days later on the SS *Bodegraven* and survived the war. Their story is told in Chapter 9.1.

Inge Preuss may have survived the war. Ruth Familier had come to Holland from Spain, which in 1939 was devastated by the Civil War. Her brother Ernst also spent a short time in the Leiden orphanage. They returned to Spain before the German invasion of the Netherlands. Egon Lapidas returned to Germany with his family. He

Table 5.1 Refugee children taken in by the Jewish Orphanage in Leiden, 1933-1943. Listed by date of arrival in Leiden The list is probably not complete.

Name	Date of birth	Place of birth	Leiden Orphanage		Comments
			Arrival	years	
Gurfinkel, Rudi	04-03-1919	Hanau	06-04-1933	0.2	Survived
Gurfinkel, Make	03-09-1920	Köln	06-04-1933	0.2	Survived
Gurfinkel, Benjamin	26-10-1921	Köln	06-04-1933	0.2	Survived
Schipper, Heinrich	30-03-1921	Ex Köln	08-04-1933	0.2	15-9-1942, Auschwitz
Schipper, Klara	09-01-1925	Ex Köln	08-04-1933	0.2	Survived > USA
Schipper, Leon	20-10-1928	Ex Köln	08-04-1933	0.2	Survived > USA
Gurfinkel, Esther	01-05-1923	Köln	16-04-1933	0.2	Survived
Gurfinkel, Ida	28-08-1925	Köln	16-04-1933	0.2	Survived
Gurfinkel, Marga	28-01-1930	Köln	16-04-1933	0.2	Survived
Preuss, Inge	26-02-1928	Berlin	04-10-1933	0.9	Survived
Lapidas, Egon	13-01-1924	Treuburg	15-11-1933	0.2	5-12-1942, Łódź
Jacobsohn, Paula	03-04-1925	Hamburg	17-05-1934	2.5	28-2-1945, Stutthof
Brink, Inho ten	22-09-1932	Lingen	02-03-1936	6.4	6-10-1944 Auschwitz
Wygoda, Israel	25-10-1922	Fulda	13-09-1936	4.5	Survived > France
Protter, Ralph	10-05-1930	Köln	12-04-1937	5.9	26-03-1943, Sobibor
Günsberg, Fanny	15-01-1927	Gelsenkirchen	05-01-1938	5.2	26-03-1943, Sobibor
Günsberg, Lothar	22-04-1928	Gelsenkirchen	24-10-1938	4.4	26-03-1943, Sobibor
Familier, Ruth	08-12-1929	Köln	01-08-1939	0.5	Survived > Spain 1939
Kristallnacht 9th/10th November 1938					
Adler, Lotte	08-02-1925	Frankfurt a/M	22-11-1938	4.3	26-03-1943, Sobibor
Adler, Henny	23-07-1930	Frankfurt a/M	22-11-1938	4.3	26-03-1943, Sobibor
Strauss, Edith	03-06-1930	Buchen	22-11-1938	0.9	Survived > USA 1939
Liffmann, Ruth	16-11-1934	Beckrath?	?-04-1939	?	Survived >Belgium
Gottschalk, Helga	18-11-1932	Geilenkirchen	20-04-1939	0.2	Escaped SS Bodegraven
Gottschalk, Kurt	15-07-1937	Geilenkirchen	20-04-1939	0.2	Escaped SS Bodegraven
David, Bermann	09-05-1937	Köln	20-04-1939	0.2	17-09-1943, Auschwitz
Schlesinger, Anni	05-02-1934	Vienna	20-04-1939	0.2	06-10-1944, Auschwitz
Goldenberg, Greta	24-01-1936	Amsterdam	04-12-1939	2.3	05-03-1943, Sobibor
Färber, Mindel	05-04-1939	Düsseldorf	08-01-1941	2.2	Survived Palestine
Herskovits, Eva	08-03-1928	Hanover	18-06-1941	0.4	Survived > USA
Wahrhaftig, Gusta	31-10-1940	Den Haag	12-1-1943	?	30-3-1943 Sobibor

Total: 30

Figure 5.2: Heinrich Schipper in Belgium, c. 1940? Courtesy Alg. Rijksarchief Brussels/ Dienst Archief Oorlogsslachtoffers.

was deported on 24th October 1941 from Berlin to Łódź (Litzmannstadt), where he was killed, probably on or around 5th December 1942.

On 6th April 1933, three Schipper children arrived: Heinrich (twelve), Klara (eight), and Leon (four). They left Leiden after three months. They were stateless. At some stage, the family moved to Belgium. Heinrich was registered in the *Jodenregister* of Antwerp on 19th December 1940, the day after a German decree ordered Jews to register themselves. Contrary to Dutch Civil Registry, recording faith was unconstitutional in Belgium. Heinrich (Fig. 5.2) was caught in a razzia and incarcerated in Kazerne Dossin (see Ch. 8.4), his parents were arrested one and two weeks later. They were deported from Kazerne Dossin and killed in Auschwitz on 14th and 28th September[6]. Klara (Claire) survived in onderduik. Leon was arrested but released from Dossin together with the other arrested children from the Wezembeek Orphanage near Brussels, following intervention by the Queen Mother Elizabeth[7]. Leon passed away on 16th January 2015, Claire on 3rd January 2018.

Bermann David (David is his family name), Anni Schlesinger, and Ruth Liffmann, had come from the Jewish orphanage in Rotterdam, and were transferred together to the orphanage in Leiden. Bermann and Anni spent the months of April to July 1939 in Leiden, just as Helga and Kurt Gottschalk, before being transferred to the *Burgerweeshuis* in Amsterdam.[8] Anni and Bermann were transferred to Westerbork, respectively a month and just a week before the escape of so many *Burgerweeshuis* children on the SS *Bodegraven*, mentioned above and described in Chapter 9.1. Ruth Liffman joined her father in Brussels on 13th June 1939. Being four years old, she had to be accompanied on the train. Following some discussion with the Interior Ministry about who should pay the costs, the Vereeniging Centraal Israëlitisch Wees- en Doorgangshuis "Machseh Lajesoumiem" (the foundation behind the Jewish Ophanage in Leiden) covered the expense. The father came to Essen on the Dutch-Belgian border to collect his daughter.

6   Courtesy Mr. Gunter Vandeplas, Algemeen Rijksarchief Brussels.
7   Courtesy Mrs. B. Bikker. On Wezembeek: see Jacques Wynants in: Revue belge de philologie et d'histoire, tome 77, fasc. 4, 1999, and Schram & Styvel (www.vrt.be 25-8-2019).
8   See Dokin.nl.

Figure 5.3: Ruth (left) and Eva (right) Herskovits with parents and older sister Grete in Hanover, on 3rd January 1939, the day before the two girls were sent to Holland. Photo enhanced by K.J. Dijkstra; private collection Herskovits family, by permission.

Some others, like Ralph Protter and Fanny and Lothar Günsberg, remained in Leiden until the liquidation of the orphanage on 17th March 1943 (Ch. 7). It is not clear at this time why some refugees were kept on the move, while others were not.

The family of Eva Herskovits and her twin sister, Ruth, lived in Hanover, Germany. Ruth published an extensive biography of the family in German (2003) and English: *"A final reckoning: A Hannover family's life and death in the Shoah"* (Herskovits, 2002; Gutmann, 2013[9]). The parents, Samuel Herskovits and Helene Kiss, hoped to move to Britain. Leaving Germany became urgent after Kristallnacht (9th/10th November 1938). They decided to send the two girls to Holland on the *Kindertransport* of 4th January 1939, much against Eva's wish. A family photograph was taken (Fig. 5.3) the day before departure.

---

9   I am grateful to Mrs. B. Bikker *Stichting Herdenking Jodenvervolging Leiden,* who drew my attention to this book, shortly before the manuscript was finalized. It was too late to move this text to Chapter 9, where it would be better positioned. A Dutch summary of Ruth's book is available on www.herdenkingleiden. nl/.More information about the children mentioned in this chapter will be included in this website.

Ruth (Gutmann, 2013) recalled:

On January 3, 1939, our parents took Grete, Eva, and me to the photographer on Goethestrasse to document what would be our final day together. The next day we assembled with the other children at the railroad station. We joined a transport from Berlin. This was nothing like the vacation trips we used to take with our parents. The railroad station had lost its air of pleasurable anticipation. It was merely grimy and deserted that morning. Eva's protests had been to no avail. She and I were setting out alone. [...] I can still see their faces, especially my mother's. Her tears streamed down her face, but she made no effort to stop crying and to wipe them away. [...] Within days [after arrival in Holland] the first letter from our parents arrived. They sent us the photograph of our family taken the last day we were together. Eva's unhappiness, much more vocal than mine, was somewhat assuaged when she held the picture in her hands. It hurt me to see the grave expression in the eyes of Father and Grete. Our mother even sadder and resigned looked into the camera. Eva insisted that the picture be kept under her pillow, and she was relieved when I agreed to her demand. All I had to do to remember their faces was to close my eyes. Every night before I went to sleep, I saw them as clearly as if they were standing before me.

After quarantine they were initially placed in the *Emmahuis* in Beverwijk (on the coast), then in the *Burgerweeshuis* in Amsterdam.

Mid-May their sister Grete, then seventeen years old, passed by on her way to Britain with bad news. Ruth recalled:

Mrs. Wijsmuller, a senior official of the Refugee Committee who with her husband's occasional assistance supervised our group home, had arranged to give us a few hours of complete privacy for our reunion with Grete. We went to her home, located in a beautiful old house on Nassaugracht, one of the streets bordering on a canal. Her housekeeper, whom we also knew from her visits to the Burgerweeshuis, showed us into a dark, though highly polished, dining room. Lunch, set on a table by the window overlooking the water, consisted of white bread with chocolate spread, a favourite treat in Holland. As soon as we were alone, we began to question Grete about our mother. Haltingly she told us what had actually happened at home in Hannover. Our mother had died, [...] probably of pneumonia. The notes Father sent us from her were written in preparation for her stay in the hospital. By the time Father finally told us that she had undergone an operation, she was no longer alive.

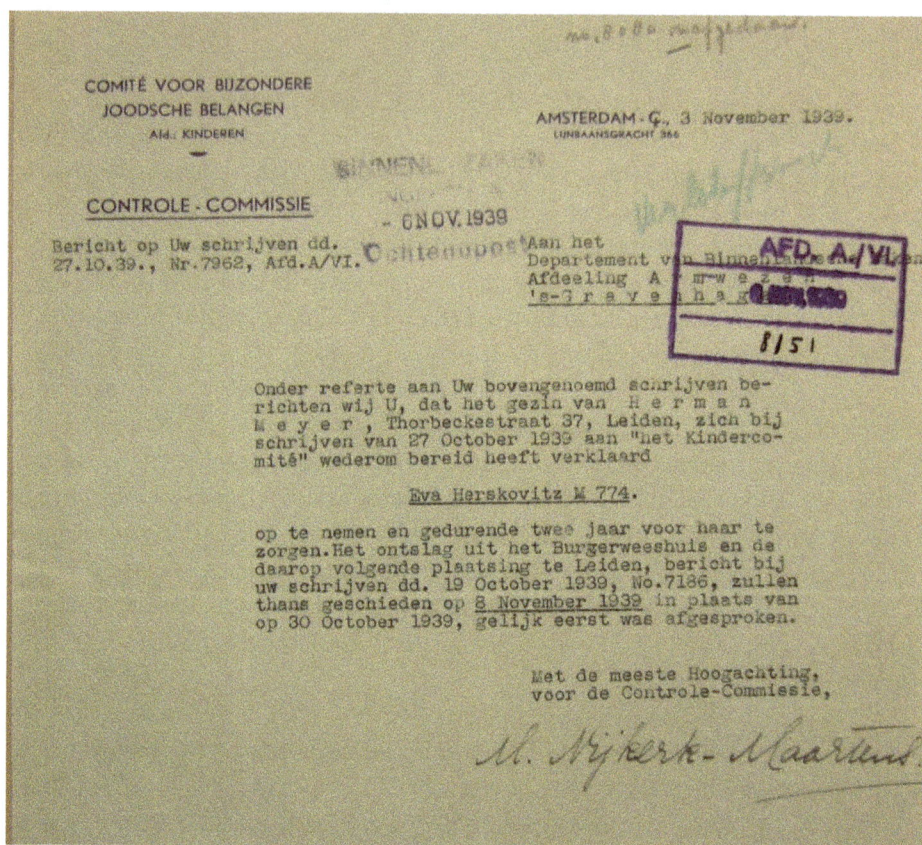

Figure 5.4: From CBJB to Interior Ministry, 3rd November 1939, confirming that Mr. Herman Meyer is prepared to accept Eva Herskovits in foster care for the coming two years, and that Eva can therefore be released by the Burgerweeshuis in Amsterdam as per 8th November 1939. Source: Dokin.nl, courtesy M. Keesing, 2016.

The preference of the Dutch government to place refugee children in institutions rather than with families was not an ironclad policy. Where possible the CBJB arranged for refugee children to transfer to foster families. They kept lists of families willing to accept refugee children throughout the country but needed to obtain permission from the Interior Ministry to place them. The CBJB tried to place Eva and Ruth as closely together as possible. In July 1939 they had found two foster families living close to each other in The Hague. But when one of these addresses, originally intended for Ruth, had to be allocated to another child, the CBJB cancelled the placement of Eva to prevent the girls being separated. Three months later, two new addresses were found, in Leiden, in the same street.

In November 1939 Eva was transferred (Fig. 5.4) from the *Burgerweeshuis* to the family of Herman Meijer, Thorbeckestraat no. 37, who had committed himself to take care of her for two years. At the same time Ruth was going to the family of Victor Bloemkoper, Thorbeckestraat no. 17, no more than 200 metres away. There were other Jewish families living in this neighbourhood, and the Jewish orphanage was just another 170 metres away, around the corner. Everybody knew each other, playing in the streets, attending the same elementary school, going to the synagogue. But Eva was not happy with her foster family.[10] The family Meijer had a very different background[11] compared with Ruth's foster family (Bloemkoper). They were above-average wary and assertive, and not easily intimidated by the German oppression. Daughter Gerda was active in the resistance (Meijer-Wijler, 1993), together with Emilie and Hijme Stoffels, who came to live in same neighbourhood in early 1942 (Ch. 6.5). The entire Meijer family survived the war in *onderduik*.

Eva left the Meijer family and was registered as resident of the Jewish orphanage on 18th June 1941.[12] Ruth stayed with the family Bloemkoper during this time. In late October 1941 the girls were unexpectedly ordered by their father to return to Hanover, and they joined their family again on 7th November 1941. His original idea had been that in Holland the girls would be *"closer to England"*, and Grete had in fact emigrated to Britain just weeks after Ruth and Eva went Holland, as mentioned above. But from September 1939 England had been at war with Germany and moving to the UK was no longer feasible. Instead, Samuel had been working on going to Cuba. But he was obviously not aware that the Nazis had decided, just about the time he recalled the girls to disallow Jews from leaving the Reich altogether (RSHA decree of 23rd October 1941), and they found themselves stuck in Hanover.

In 1944 the family was deported to Theresienstadt, and from there to Auschwitz where Eva and Ruth escaped death when they were selected by Joseph Mengele for his so called *"twin research"*. They were liberated in May 1945 after going through several other concentration camps and emigrated to the USA. But the war traumas did not leave Eva; she took her own life on 12th July 1973. Eva's daughter to Barbera Bikker,[13] personal communication, 2020):

On the anniversary of her father's death at the hands of the Nazis in Auschwitz, I think it is important to tell the truth, even when it is sad. So many survivors were

---

10 There is no suggestion that the family Meijer was to blame for this.

11 There were many families Meijer in Leiden, three of which had been cattle dealers in Vlagtwedde in the far north-eastern part of the Netherlands. This may lead to confusion.

12 Ruth writes that Eva had moved to the orphanage before May 1940, but the move was only registered on 18th June 1941. It is highly unlikely that the orphanage would have failed to register her (with the town hall and the alien police) within a few days of her moving in.

13 Stichting Herdenking Jodenvervolging Leiden.

so wounded by the traumas they lived through that they eventually took their own
lives. Unfortunately, my mother was one of those people.

The last pre-war national census (1930) registered 111,917 Jewish Dutchmen. The
vast majority was born in the Netherlands, and practically all of them were Dutch
citizens. By 1940, their number had increased by some 20,000 Jewish refugees from
the East (de Jong, 1969-1994, vol. 5, p. 496; Presser, 1965, p. 418). Since the number of
refugees which were allowed entry is estimated at approximately 40,000,[14] it implies
that about half of the immigrants moved on to other countries before the war, as
the Dutch government had hoped. The attitude[15] of the Dutch government may
unwittingly have saved the lives of an unknown number of them, if they succeeded
in leaving continental Europe in time. The refugees in Table 5.1 who were allowed
to stay in Holland, such as Lotte and Henny Adler (Ch. 5.7), were overtaken by the
German onslaught and found themselves caught again under the same Nazi regime
which they tried to escape from when coming to Holland.

As mentioned above, Truus Wijsmuller facilitated the meeting of Ruth and Eva
Herskovits with their sister Grete. Among the non-Jewish people who supported
the refugees seeking to enter Holland, Truus (née Meijers, 1896-1978) stands out.
She came from a liberal Protestant family in Alkmaar and became involved in
refugee work soon after the First World War. After first engaging herself with aid
for children in need in defeated Austria, she realized the growing predicament
of Jews in Germany as early as 1933, becoming active in the relief activities for
Jewish refugees. She made several trips to Germany to collect relatives of Jews in
Holland and bring them safely across the border. She became well known to the
members of the above-mentioned Jewish relief committees (particularly Gertrude
van Tijn of the CJV), and their counterparts in the UK. When the British government
agreed, after Kristallnacht (Ch. 5.6), to waive the most restrictive visa requirements
for an unspecified number of Jewish children seeking asylum, the British relief
organizations were at a loss how to put it into effect, and Truus was asked to assist
in organizing an emigration programme. She travelled to Vienna in December 1938
to facilitate the release of children who could qualify for these special UK entry
papers (Keesing, 2013). She managed to talk directly to Adolf Eichmann,[16] who was

---

14 *Andere Tijden*, 7th October 2015; it is not clear if all illegal immigrants are included in this figure.
15 It should be noted that by 1939 there were also some 25,000 non-Jewish refugees in Holland, resulting
from Nazi persecution of communists and other unwanted political movements (http://www.volkstellingen.
nl). The Dutch government was not particularly happy to harbour too many of these refugees either.
16 Eichmann joined the SD HQ in Berlin in 1934, and played a role chasing many Jews out of Germany,
and out of Austria after 1938 (where Truus met him). He became head of Section IVB4 in the RSHA in
Berlin, where he was responsible for the efficient technical and logistical implementation of the "Final

stationed in Vienna at that time and was in charge of "Jewish Affairs" (Austria had become part of the German Reich due to the *Anschluss* in March 1938). Eichmann told her that she could take away 600 Jewish children *if she could do that within five days*. Reputedly, he did not expect her to achieve that. But she did, and on 10th December 1938 a train left Vienna with 600 children to Holland. Most of the children proceeded to the UK via Hoek van Holland, while some 100 remained in the Netherlands (ibidem). It was not the first, nor the last of her exceptional achievements. Her successful attempt to let some 74 refugee children (including Kurt and Helga Gottschalk) escape to the UK on the last day of the German invasion, one hour before the Dutch army capitulated on 14th May 1940 and while Rotterdam was burning, stands out as much as the deal she made with Eichmann. This part of the story is told in Chapter 9.1.

5.3   1934: Life goes on; another ceremonial photograph

Life in the orphanage in Leiden continued after 1933 much as before. More photographs were taken (Fig. 5.5). Most of the refugees (nine out of eleven) who had arrived in Leiden in 1933 had been transferred out again by the end of that year. After the initial peak in 1933, the number of Jewish refugees arriving in Holland from Germany remained relatively stable until 1938. In that same period seven new refugees were accepted by the orphanage in Leiden (Table 5.1). Five of those would become "permanent" residents in the orphanage: Inho ten Brink, Israel Wygoda, Ralph Protter, and Fanny and Lothar Günsberg.

Paula Jacobsohn (Fig. 5.5, no. 11) stayed in Leiden for two and a half years and moved to the orphanage in Utrecht in November 1936 (Crone, 2005). In February 1942 the refugee children in Utrecht were deported to Westerbork (see Ch. 7.2). She was deported to Theresienstadt on 18th January 1944, and from there to Auschwitz and Stutthof (near Danzig). She did not survive.

Herman Stofkooper and Lodi Cohen, also in Figure 5.5 (nos. 2 and 3), were related: Herman's mother was Sophia Cohen, family of Lodi as well as Lies Cohen, the second wife of Director Italie.

In April 1934 another assembly photograph of all the orphanage inhabitants was taken (Fig. 5.6) just like the one from 1932 (Fig. 4.14). These two pictures are the only such photos known to date. No fewer than 49 people (out of 53) could be identified with confidence.

Solution" throughout occupied Europe. His capture and subsequent trial in Jerusalem (1960-1962) opened the eyes of the world to the immensity of the Holocaust.

Figure 5.5: Summer 1934. Photo taken by Mimi Weiman at the back of the building, in front of the half-round annex.

1	Sientje Spiro	8	Annie Simons ?	15	Reina Segal
2	Herman Stofkooper	9	Mirjam Frenkel	16	Jet van den Berg
3	Lodi Cohen	10	Sal Porcelijn	17	Corrie Frenkel
4	Ies Cohen	11	Paula Jacobsohn	18	Jetty Bobbe
5	Esther Appel	12	Leo Auerhaan	19	Louis Limburg
6	Joop Worms	13	Marie van den Berg	20	Harry Spier
7	Henny Jansen (Behr)	14	Didia Klein	21	unidentified

It may have irked Nathan Italie that he was not present for the first photo, due to his wife, Sara Schaap, being ill and her death just a few weeks later. That may have prompted him to order another one to be taken so soon after the first one. Nathan, now 44, had decided to marry again: with Lies Cohen (Ch. 5.5). The marriage took place on 23rd July 1934, three months after this photograph was taken. Two people (no. 12 and no. 40) remain unidentified, while no. 31 is probably Maurits Levie, and no. 46 may be Victor Wittenburg, but their identification could not be independently confirmed.

The orphanage in Leiden was a "transit institution", and indeed from time to time children who reached age five or six were transferred to another orphanage. Some children were transferred to one of the institutions for special care (Table 1.3): Bergstichting in Laren, Rudelsheim in Hilversum, or Achisomov in Apeldoorn. Some

Figure 5.6: Assembly photograph, April 1934, photo taken by Mimi Weiman at the back of the building, in front of the half-round annex.

1	Bram Spiro	15	Ies Cohen	29	Rachel Bierschenk	43	Mieke Dagloonder
2	Jacq. Witteboom	16	Henny Jansen	30	Henriette van Pels	44	Sally Montezinos
3	Karel van Santen	17	David Beem	31	Maurits Levie (?)	45	Reina Segal
4	Jaap de Vries	18	Esther Appel	32	Louis Limburg	46	Victor Wittenburg (?)
5	Mimi Weiman	19	Joop Worms	33	Inge Preuss	47	Frieda Lichtenbaum
6	Herman Stofkooper	20	Judith Pront	34	Charles Kirchenbaum	48	Herman Rozeveld
7	Mien Beem	21	Leo Auerhaan	35	Mirjam Frenkel	49	Barend Ritmeester
8	Esther van Santen	22	Sientje Spiro	36	Jettie Bobbe	50	Salomon Ritmeester
9	Floor Altenberg	23	Betsie Wolff	37	Bram Degen	51	Harry Spier
10	Lodie Cohen	24	Mien Gobes	38	Marie van den Berg	52	Hans Porcelijn
11	Sal Porcelijn	25	Didia Klein	39	Jopie Beem	53	Hans Kloosterman
12	?	26	Jet de Leeuw	40	unidentified nanny		
13	Sal Weiman	27	Nathan Italie	41	Corrie Frenkel		
14	Hetty de Jong	28	Jet van den Berg	42	Hijman Cohen		

witness accounts suggest that one or two children were expelled for misconduct. But a surprising number of children never left the orphanage until they reached the regulatory maximum age of eighteen years. During the German occupation the rule became meaningless because Jews were not allowed to change their residence.

Mimi Weiman (Fig. 5.7) left the orphanage on 30th April 1935, two months before her eighteenth birthday. In her extensive interviews with L.P. Kasteleyn she tempered the rosy view one may have had about the orphanage. Her grandmother

Fig 5.7: Mimi Weiman, April 1935.

had brought her in January 1927 when she was nine years old. Upon arrival she had to relinquish her personal possessions: an earring and a gold watch which her grandmother had given her. She only got them back upon departure eight years later. After elementary school, she attended the *huishoudschool*, the standard vocational school for girls who were regarded as "future wives". Ms. Bierschenk assisted her in using a sewing machine, Ms. de Leeuw with learning how to cook. For years Mimi did duty in the linen room on the top floor.

We lived in a straitjacket, had no say in anything. Degrading punishments were meted out, and – worse – often without any reasonable justification. Cancelling the holiday in case progress at school was deemed insufficient; being locked up alone in a small room, physical punishment.

Upon leaving, she received an outfit: underwear, two dresses, aprons, and a nurse's uniform because she was going to work at a convalescence home on the coast (*JoZeBeKo*[17]). But she was not happy there and soon left. Returning to the orphanage was apparently a possibility, but she found the idea to go back *"abhorrent"*.

Schooling in this period also continued as before. Most children from age six attended one of the two Langebrug elementary schools (Fig. 5.8). From age twelve (if they had not repeated classes) they attended an intermediate-level secondary school, or a vocational training institute. Herman Stofkooper and Lodi Cohen were, by exception, attending higher secondary education. That privilege was not granted to Fanny Günsberg, Piet de Vries' girlfriend, although Piet was certain that she would have done well. There may have been more pupils who would have done well in higher education, if they had been given the opportunity.

17   Joodsche Zee en Bosch Kolonie.

Figure 5.8: April 1936, grade 5, Langebrug bovenschool. Jan Voogt (1) had three Jewish classmates, all three from the orphanage: Jettie Bobbe (2), Jet van den Berg (3), and Louis Limburg (4, at the back). Photograph provided by Jan Voogt.

5.4   1935: **Piet de Vries arrives, ten years old**

Piet was born on 12th March 1925 in the *Nederlands Israëlitisch Ziekenhuis*, a Jewish hospital on the Nieuwe Keizersgracht 100-114 in Amsterdam. He was the son of a Jewish mother, Rebecca Franschman. His non-Jewish father, Wouter de Vries, was a *"bierbottelaars knecht"*, a worker in a beer bottling factory, who died on 21st February 1934, at age 33.

For Hans Kloosterman, who arrived at age two, the orphanage was everything, his home and his family; he had little else. He described his years in the orphanage as "the best of my life". He emigrated to Australia after the war. Once contact with "Holland" was established in 2000 (arranged by L.P. Kasteleyn), he was very keen to also contact Piet de Vries and Bram Degen.

Piet (Fig. 5.9), who arrived in Leiden at age ten, and who maintained close contact with his mother, had a more distant view with respect to the orphanage. Nevertheless, even he, who had lived in Amsterdam under dreadful circumstances before coming to Leiden, concluded that: *"going home to our families, we fell from heaven to earth. Everything we needed was provided for [in Leiden] and we were free as birds in the sky."* At the same time, the regime was not soft: *"If one the children*

Figure 5.9: November 1937. Piet de Vries (12) in front with the ball; his soccer friends behind him from left: Hans Porcelijn (12), Leo Auerhaan (15), Bram van Stratum (13) and Louis Limburg (14). Behind them the windows of the dining hall.

Figure 5.10: Hans Kloosterman, summer holiday, 1937. Behind him from left: Corrie Frenkel, Esther Appel, and Frieda Lichtenbaum. Esther had left the orphanage in 1936 when she was eighteen.

in the room began to cry at night, before you could do anything, half of them were crying as well. No staff came to have a look."

Children who still had family (most of them had one or even both parents) spent two weeks of the summer holiday with them, although in some cases the parent did not maintain contact with their child. Piet usually spent the summer holiday with his mother in Amsterdam. Having lived much of his early years in Amsterdam,

Figure 5.11: This photograph, taken in the early summer of 1936, only came to light in 2020. We could identify 18 (out of 25) people with certainty (courtesy Leonard and Martine Kasteleyn); the identity of 5 others is qualified by "probably" or "possibly". These relaxed, impromptu group photographs tell us something about the special character of the Leiden orphanage: the mixture of children of all ages, the laughing faces, the many "hands-on-shoulders" (as noticed already in Ch. 4.3). Some children were barely two years old when they arrived, and many children spent an extraordinary long time together in the orphanage. As Hans Kloosterman wrote, "they were my brothers and sisters". Photograph JHM F1635-6, courtesy Jewish Historical Museum, Amsterdam.

1. Jettie Bobbe
2. Louis Limburg
3. Mirjam Frenkel
4. *probably* Mary Konijn
5. Sally Montezinos
6. Frieda Lichtenbaum
7. *possibly* Max Konijn
8. *possibly* Willy Blog
9. Joop de Vries

10. Hans Porcelijn
11. Lenie (nanny)
12. *probably* Willem v. Weddingen *(Semmie)*
13. Esther Appel
14. *probably* Francina van Weddingen
15. Herman Rozeveld *(Dikkie)*
16. unidentified
17. Juul Beem
18. Reina Segal

19. Rita Arndt
20. Betsy Wolff
21. Piet de Vries
22. Corrie Frenkel
23. Paula Jacobsohn
24. Hennie Feniger
25. unidentified

he was a "native" of the city. His girlfriend in the orphanage during his final years there, Fanny Günsberg (she arrived in January 1938), usually spent the summer with her father in Weert (Limburg).

Children who had no family to go to, like Hans Kloosterman (Fig. 5.10; but his mother visited him in Leiden every few weeks), were entertained in Katwijk, or elsewhere on the North Sea coast not far from Leiden, for a summer holiday. The picture was probably taken at *"JoZeBoKo"*, a Jewish convalescence and holiday

Figure 5.12: Ms. Rachel Bierschenk in the dunes with some members of her "young ladies" social club. From left: Sientje Spiro, an unidentified nanny, behind her Jupie Pront, Mimi Weiman, Rachel Bierschenk, Esther van Santen, unidentified lady, Annie Simons (?).

institute in Wijk aan Zee. Esther Appel, in uniform, worked there. She had left the orphanage in September 1936 when she was eighteen years old. The four knew each other well; they had spent many years together in the orphanage in Leiden. Hans had been there for a week when Esther arrived on 10th December 1929.

Upon his arrival in Leiden, Ms. de Leeuw decided to give Piet a more Jewish-sounding name and called him Daniel. But he himself reverted to his original name soon after he was taken from Leiden to Westerbork in March 1943.

Director Italie maintained the basic orthodox religious rules and regulations. But he was remarkably liberal in many other aspects. The children, from age thirteen, were allowed to visit friends elsewhere in Leiden in the evening; friends were also welcome in the orphanage, which must have been a nice place to visit after 1929. Leiden before the war was not an affluent city,[18] and for some visiting children the new orphanage was probably a place of unparalleled luxury. The liberty to make gentile friends suited some of the older children very well, such as Lotte Adler (Ch. 5.6).

Piet remembers the evenings in the orphanage as almost always enjoyable and cosy. That is to say: until Friday afternoon, when it was all over, and the religious

18 On the contrary, Leiden was reputed to be the second most impoverished city in Holland after Amsterdam.

norms were strictly imposed. Saturday morning the entire orphanage attended Sabbath service from 7:30 to 9:30 am, before taking breakfast. Another service was attended, by all, in the afternoon, and yet another in the evening. Two more visits to the synagogue had to be made during weekdays. Years later, Piet provoked the director's ire by shaving on sabbath. Perhaps surprisingly given his background, he was a member of a Zionist youth organization.[19]

Piet had arrived in Leiden with his brother Joop, who was two years younger (Fig. 5.11). He also had a sister, Marietje, who was born 2nd January 1924 and thus a year older than Piet. She was placed in the Ashkenazi girls' orphanage in Amsterdam. After leaving the orphanage she went to work at Het Apeldoornse Bos, a Jewish psychiatric institution. She wrote to Piet in Leiden; two important letters from 1943, the last ones she wrote, have been preserved (Ch. 7.3).

The photo in Figure 5.12 dates from 1934. All these years, Ms. Rachel Bierschenk (Fig. 6.16) ran a small social club in the orphanage. Members were asked to pay a minimal contribution. Her central position at the back and her smile seem to reflect her sense of proud ownership of the little club. The woman in the dark dress second from right may be the mother of the unidentified nanny, who probably was German.

In the previous chapter (Fig. 4.13) it was noted that the women of the "permanent staff", in this case Ms. Mien Gobes, appear on some of the photographs taken by (and with) the older girls. Ms. Gobes also appears in Figure 5.15.

5.5   The family of Director Italie

Nathan Italie became director of the Jewish orphanage in Leiden in 1922. He and Sara Schaap had no children of their own, which was in accordance with the regulations of the orphanage, which stipulated that the *"father and mother of the house, must be a properly married man and wife, without children of their own, of upright religious standing, and well versed in the demands of a strict Jewish orthodox household and the education of Israelite children".* Sara's family had a butcher's shop in Rotterdam; when during the war, some ten years after Sara's death, it became virtually impossible to obtain kosher meat in Leiden, the orphanage was provisioned by Sara's family.

Nathan came from an orthodox family; he was the eldest of four boys and one girl. His brother Gabriel was teaching classical languages at the Tweede Stedelijk Gymnasium (later Maerlant Lyceum) in The Hague. He survived the war, the only one of the five siblings, in Theresienstadt, and left us a valuable daily journal covering his entire war period experiences (published by W.M. de Lang, 2009). Their brother Arthur had a son, Elchanan, who also survived the war, with the help of Hijme Stoffels (Ch. 9.9).

---

19   They had an assembly place behind Breestraat, along or close to Mosterdsteeg.

Figure 5.13: Nathan and Lies Italie-Cohen with Hanna and Elchanan, c. 1938, in the director's living quarters, also his office, on the ground floor.

Nathan had been in charge of a deaf-mute institution, before joining the or-phanage in Leiden, and he could read lips. The children were aware of that, and watched their words, even if they were outside and the director was looking at them through the windows. He had a natural authority, without being an authoritarian: *"he was much too cultured to ever raise his voice".* He also had a particular, solemn style in addressing the older children; letters arriving in Leiden from Piet's mother were handed down to him by the director with the words: *"Mister de Vries, here is a letter from Madame your Mother."*

After Sara had died in late 1932, aged 35, Nathan married again, on 23rd July 1934, with Elizabeth ("Lies") Cohen, the daughter of Hartog Cohen, who had been chazzan in Leiden until his death in 1930[20] and who lived on Wasstraat, just a few blocks away from the orphanage. On 11th May 1935, a daughter was born, Hanna Sara, and on 8th February 1937, a son, Elchanan Tsewie (Fig. 5.13). This event was of course not foreseen in the 1927 building plans, but a room on the first floor, above the large extension and playroom, was converted into a bedroom for the two children. The governors were very satisfied with Nathan being director and if they had any objection to the director having his own children in the orphanage, they were apparently not

20   His death probably caused Lodi and Izak (Ies) Cohen to end up in the orphanage in April 1930; see Chapter 9.6.

prepared to lose him for such a reason. Many photographs have survived showing one or both children together with other orphanage children. Clearly, they were accepted by them as part of the "family", even though they had their own bedroom and took their meals in the director's quarters (except on special occasions).

These years, 1935 to 1939, despite the ever-darkening clouds over Europe, may have been the happiest in Nathan's life, not in the least because of the blessing of having his own children. He was equally dedicated to his wards in the orphanage, he had a strong staff team at his disposal, and a modern, well-equipped, building. With the memories of Stille Rijn behind him, he was probably well aware of his good fortune (Fig. 5.13).

5.6   1938: Kristallnacht (9th/10th November) and the Kindertransports

In early 1938 the refugee admission policy in the Netherlands (with respect to Jewish and other refugees) had become more restrictive. Carel Goseling, minister of justice (1937-1939) and a member of the Catholic State Party (*Roomsch-Katholieke Staatspartij*), purportedly concerned that immigrants would compete on the labour market, kept the border practically closed to refugees, unless they could prove that they would move on to another country. But moving on was very difficult because all other obvious countries to go to were also restricting immigration, even the USA. It should be noted that by 1939 there were also some 25,000 non-Jewish refugees in Holland, resulting from Nazi persecution of communists and members of other unwanted political movements. In one of his memos, Goseling described refugees from Germany as potentially *"undesirable elements"*. On 17th October 1938, his ministry issued instructions to the border police that refugees without valid papers should not be permitted to enter at all. This was a very cynical decision since it was known that many Jews in Germany were stateless or had lost their German citizenship and thus their papers. As a result, people smugglers were active getting refugees across the border illegally, and the border police did their best to catch them. Interestingly, however, as the situation in Germany worsened, Dutch public opinion became more sympathetic to the plight of the refugees, putting the government under pressure to relent.

Just before the border became practically closed to refugees, two more children were taken in by the orphanage in Leiden: Fanny (15th January 1927) and Lothar Günsberg (22nd April 1928); they were born in Gelsenkirchen (Germany). Fanny arrived in Leiden on 5th January, and Lothar on 24th October 1938.

A few weeks after Lothar's arrival, on the night 9th to 10th November 1938, Jews and Jewish shops were attacked by organized mobs throughout Germany and Austria. Some 90 Jews were murdered and more than 200 synagogues went up in flames throughout the German Reich. Countless Jewish-owned shops had their windows smashed and their interiors looted. In Vienna alone, some 4000 Jewish shops were destroyed. The many smashed shop windows gave rise to the name: Kristallnacht, the night of the [shattered] glass. Even the most optimistic person must have realized that there was no future for Jews in Germany, to say the least. Following 5 five years of relatively modest Jewish emigration from Germany, many more people tried to escape, if they had the necessary funds, contacts, entry visa to another country, family abroad, or the ability to illegally cross the border to a neighbouring country.

Under growing public pressure[21] after Kristallnacht, the Dutch government relaxed its asylum policy. Between November 1938 and March 1939, some 8000 Jewish refugees from Germany were admitted into the country. A special category of immigrants were children who arrived in Holland by train, without their parents, by Kindertransport. Not much is known about these transports since few documents exist. Both Gertude van Tijn of the CJV and Truus Wijsmuller were involved in these transports. They predated the Kindertransports to the UK, which have been much better documented, and which were made possible when the UK government, provided between 9000 and 10,000 special entry visas (for the children, not for their parents). The earlier transports to Holland seem to have been mostly private initiatives, such as the one of 22nd November (Crone, 2005; Stam-van der Staay, 2003) which carried Lotte and Henny Adler and Edith Strauss from Frankfurt am Main to Amsterdam, and from there to the Leiden orphanage. In the UK as well as in the Netherlands, the government yielded to pressure from public opinion, but without much goodwill. In the UK, after September 1939, many refugee children of fifteen years and above were interned as enemy aliens. Some of them were deported (the term was actually used at the time) to Australia (papers in Hammel & Lewkowicz, 2012), where many were again interned as enemy aliens, even after the British government had realized the injustice of their deportation and asked the Australian government to release them.

The history of the Frankfurt Kindertransport of 22nd November goes back to early 1938, when the Jewish orphanage in Frankfurt discussed with the CJV the possibility of sending a number of its children to Holland. The exchanges between German and Dutch orphanages and/or the CJV illustrates how desperate the situation had become. The minutes of a meeting, on 17th November 1938, in the N.I. Boys' Orphanage in Amsterdam, has been preserved in the Rotterdam Municipal Archives (courtesy Miriam Keesing, 2016). All the eight Jewish orphanages and the Bergstichting (Tables 1.1 and 1.2) had sent a representative. After lobbying, Minister of Justice C. Goseling agreed to allow 24 (sic!) children to enter the country on 2nd November. Despite his consent,

---

21   The Dutch daily *Het Volksdagblad* argued on 17th November 1938 that the Dutch government should allow many more refugees from Germany entry into the Netherlands. It printed *"De grens moet open"* ("Open the border"). On 3rd December 1938 a national collection was held in aid of refugees. The prime minister publicly contributed but he did not change his mind.

his department staff[22] raised further objections, and demanded that for each individual child an admission request would be submitted. In the meantime, Kristallnacht had changed the situation, and the orphanage in Frankfurt reported that the number of children in their care had increased almost overnight from 70 to 135. On 15th November, the Dutch orphanages considered taking more than the requested 24 children from Frankfurt, but after contact with David Cohen (chairman of the CJV) this proposal did not come to fruition. On 15th November lists of names were received, while the orphanage in Frankfurt reported that they were in serious difficulty because all the male personnel had been arrested and taken away. The Amsterdam meeting wanted to speed up the evacuation of the selected children, but they failed to reach the relevant civil servant to authorize their crossing the Dutch border. They considered requesting an audience with Justice Minister Goseling, by telegram to indicate the urgency of the matter. Other delegates were in favour of leaving it to the CJV, whose member R. Eitje was going to visit The Hague the following day. Most, but not all, of the delegates were aware that many children up for transport to Holland were not so much orphans but rather political refugees, from families which would not normally rely on social institutions for assistance. The delegates continued to deliberate over how to get the transport on the rails as quickly as possible. However, being aware of David Cohen's attitude, they were keen to prevent upsetting the government, a recurring theme in this book before the war, as well as during the occupation. Even a proposal to publish the proceedings of this meeting in the newspapers was rejected, because doing that could be regarded as an attempt to *"effect [...] pressure on the government"*, something to be prevented at all costs.

Unfortunately, many archives have been lost, and no lists with names have been found of these early transports to Holland. But they can be partly reconstructed (Keesing, 2013; Keesing et al., 2019) from data in the Netherlands, such as card indexes at the Civil Registry, or the records of the Dutch alien police where all refugees had to report within 24 hours of arrival.

More transports took place from Berlin and other German cities in the week of 23rd November 1938 (Crone, 2005). The Kindertransports to the UK also began around that time (Harris & Oppenheimer, 2000; Fast, 2011; Hodge, 2011); the first arrived in Harwich on 2nd December 1938 with 196 children. Some of the children on these transports stayed in the Netherlands. Estimates of the number of unaccompanied refugee children who received asylum in Holland after Kristallnacht vary from 1500 (Crone, 2005) to 2000.[23]

In Berlin, at Friedrichstrasse railway station, a monument (*Züge in das Leben; Züge in den Tod*) commemorates the Kindertransports.[24] It is hard to fathom the tragedy of

---

22 The head of the border police and alien registration.

23 H. Goekoop, *"De vlucht na Kristallnacht"*, *Andere Tijden*, 24th April 2014.

24 "Trains to life; trains to death". Similar monuments exist in Hoek van Holland and Harwich, and some other cities.

parents who had the foresight and the courage to send away their children in those circumstances, or the loneliness of the children who may not have understood why they were abandoned by their own parents. It is estimated (Hammel & Lewkowicz, 2012) that more than half the number of children who survived the war thanks to a Kindertransport never saw their parents again.

However important the Kindertransports may have been, probably no more than some 12,000 children were able to escape continental Europe in this manner, less than 1% of the number of children who were murdered in the Holocaust. Crone (2005) provides a sad review of the unwillingness of governments to reach out to them, not to speak of the moral implications of helping the children to escape, but not allowing their parents to join them.[25]

5.7   1938: Henny and Lotte Adler arrive, eight and thirteen years old

In the year 1938 Lotte (8th February 1925; see frontispiece) and Henny (23rd July 1930) Adler lived with their mother, Clara Braun, at Dominikanerplatz 12 in Frankfurt am Main (Fig. 5.14). Elsa Strauss and her daughter Edith were living in with them. Henny and Edith were about the same age. Before 1937, the two mothers and three girls at least once spent a summer holiday in Holland, on the beach at Zandvoort, while Her-

Figure 5.14: Lotte and Henny Adler in Frankfurt am Main, Germany, 1935.

man Adler stayed behind in Frankfurt. When the situation for Jews deteriorated, the Adler's considered emigrating to America, where they had family, but Herman was arrested in 1937 on some pretext and incarcerated in Buchenwald concentration camp, near Weimar, where he perished on 3rd July 1938.

Lotte remembered Kristallnacht very well, she often talked about the frightening noises from marching and singing men in the street, and the sound of shattering glass (Stam-van der Staay, 2003).

On 20th November, their Uncle Louis came by to tell them that he had managed to include the three girls in a Kindertransport to Holland. This was, with reasonable certainty,[26] the transport

25 See the website of the Kindertransports: http://www.kindertransport.org/history.htm.
26 Both Mien van der Staay and Jopie Vos related in great detail what Lotte told them about the train journey, and Lotte was their only source of information on this subject.

Figure 5.15: Older and younger girls, and staff members, join for a photograph, first half of 1939. Front row from left: Henny Adler, Edith Strauss, Henny Feniger, unknown; middle row: Frieda Lichtenbaum (arms aside) and Mieke Dagloonder; back row from left: Reina Segal, Betsy Wolff, unidentified nanny, Didia Klein, chief nanny Mien Gobes, Corrie Frenkel, Jettie Bobbe. Photo from Lotte's own photo album, courtesy Mrs. Schröder-Vos.

of children from the Frankfurt orphanage described above. The mothers promised the girls they would collect them in Holland as soon as they received entry visas to the USA for the girls. Lotte's story of the train journey is identical to what survivors who were on this transport remembered. Mozes Frank, who was, like Lotte, thirteen years old, was also on that train. He remembered (Crone, 2005, p. 63) how the train was held up for hours at the German-Dutch border by German police and military: *"They were clearly trying to scare us, stamping through the train with their heavy boots. Most children, ten to fourteen years old, were crying."*

Lotte told her friend Mien that there were also dogs, and that they had to wait endlessly at the border, before the train moved on to Amsterdam. The children were distributed over several orphanages. Mozes went to Utrecht. Lotte, Henny and Edith to Leiden. They arrived at night and were received by Nathan Italie (who spoke to them in fluent German), and Jet de Leeuw. Once in bed in the dormitory, Lotte became acutely aware that from now on she was responsible for Henny, as she had promised her mother before leaving Frankfurt.

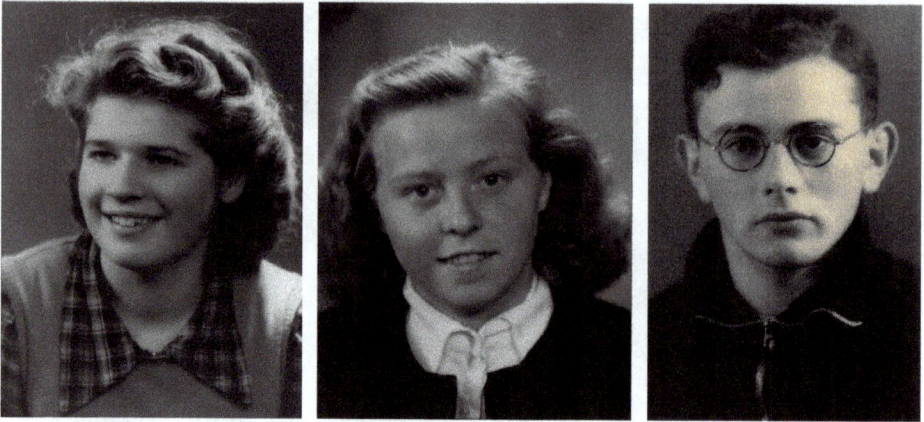

Figure 5.16: From left: Jopie Vos (later Mrs. Schröder), Mien van der Staay (later Mrs. Stam), and Israel Wygoda. Photos of Lotte's three best friends from her own photo album. Jopie and Mien were her classmates at the Haanstra school. Israel Wygoda lived with her in the orphanage. Photo's courtesy Mrs. Schröder-Vos.

A few weeks later, mothers Adler and Strauss received their papers and travelled to the USA, leaving the girls in the Leiden orphanage with a view to get them over to the USA as quickly as possible. Edith Strauss received her papers on 19th December 1938; she left the orphanage on her way to America on 27th October 1939. The papers for Lotte and Henny were not yet forthcoming (Ch. 10.1).

Lotte had to get used to sleeping in a dormitory, but she was happy with the positive atmosphere in the orphanage. It was *"gezellig"*, another archetypal Dutch word combining cosy, pleasant, relaxed, easy going (Fig. 5.15). When walking with Ms. Gobes to the alien police in Leiden the next day, Lotte realized they could walk through the Plantsoen (a city park) without being stopped by signs prohibiting Jews to enter. Little did she realize that these same signs would appear in occupied Holland just two years later.

Lotte entered the Haanstra Kweekschool (a teacher training college) on the Rapenburg/Vliet in November 1938. She became friends with Mien van der Staay (later Stam) and Jopie Vos (later Schröder), who both lived in Leiden (Fig. 5.16). Mien published a memorial booklet for Lotte (Stam-van der Staay, 2003), while Jopie shared her memories of Lotte when the documentary *"Bagage van Leiden"* was made (NMG Productions, 2010). Most importantly, Jopie preserved the photo album which Lotte left with her for safekeeping in March 1943. Lotte had a natural affinity for small children and loved the practical lessons (Fig. 5.17) which were part of the curriculum. Many photos in this book came from her own photo album, which now resides at the Westerbork Memorial site.

Many questions remain unanswered. How did Uncle Louis manage to get the three girls on this train, while there were so many children in the Frankfurt

Figure 5.17: Lotte (left-centre) during her period at the Haanstra vocational institute in Leiden.

orphanage who were not allowed to join this transport? Why were the mothers granted entry visas to the USA without simultaneously receiving visas for their children? Why did Else Strauss obtain a visa for Edith so much earlier (late 1938) than Clara Adler, who obtained visas for Lotte and Henny only in 1941? Why were the three children allowed to settle in the orphanage, while other refugee minors (such as Kurt and Helga Gottschalk) were moved around?

In the archives of the (USA-based) *German-Jewish Children's Aid Foundation*, now included in the archives of the Joint Distribution Committee,[27] are the letters sent by Gertrude van Tijn of the Committee for Jewish Refugees[28] (CJV) in November 1940 (i.e. well into the German occupation of Holland) with lists of German refugee children in Holland with US family connections. The CJV urged them to expedite the paperwork necessary to send the children to the USA (which was still a neutral country at that time). The lists contain the names of 272 children, divided in six categories. Lotte and Henny are not included in these lists, although both would have been in the first category, with the best chances of gaining entry to the USA because their mother was already there.

27 Search https://archives.jdc.org/.
28 Gertrude van Tijn-Cohn played a key role in the committee as well as in the Joodse Raad (Wasserstein, 2014). She escaped in 1944 to Palestine via Bergen-Belsen on the same train as Mindel Färber (Ch. 9.3), and Serina de Paauw, the mother of Aron Wolff (Ch. 9.4).

Figure 5.18: Probably 1940; back row from left to right: Benno Redish held by Mieke Dagloonder, Hanna and Elchanan Italie, and Lotte Adler. In front: the Fleurima twins. Note the sticky tape on the windows. From Lotte Adler's album, 1940. Courtesy Mrs. Schröder-Vos, 2009.

I do not know why they were not included in this list. The attempt was in any case not successful. The bureaucracy took too long, it rapidly became more difficult and then impossible for Jews to leave occupied Holland, and in December 1941 the USA was drawn into the war, losing its status as a neutral country. For many children who escaped from Germany by Kindertransport, applications for a US visa had been made prior to their departure from Germany. Some had to wait for ten years before such a visa was approved (Hammel & Lewkowicz, 2012). Probably (subject to further research) very few of the children (if any) on van Tijn's list did indeed escape to the USA.

5.8   1938: A photo album for Governor Levisson

On the occasion of the 60th birthday of L. Levisson, the prominent administrator in the "1919" board of governors (Fig. 2.7) of the orphanage, an album was prepared for him with photographs and personal messages from the staff and those children who could write. Most if not all of the photos were taken specifically for this album and

Figure 5.19: Selected photographs from the Levisson Album, 1938. Names: see next page.

Names by row, from top-left to lowest-right:

Rita Arndt	Leo Auerhaan	Juul Beem	Jettie Bobbe	Frieda Lichtenbaum
Ies Cohen	Hans Porcelijn	Bram Degen	Sam. Engelschman	Ch. Kirschenbaum
Herman Rozeveld	Reina Segal	Harry Spier	Joop Worms	Didia Klein
Louis Limburg	Sally Montezinos	Ralph Protter	Salomon Ritmeester	Fanny Günsberg
Betsy Wolff	Israel Wygoda	Hans Kloosterman	Mieke Dagloonder	Corrie & Mirjam Frenkel
Piet & Joop de Vries	Max & Bram v Stratum		Joop & David Beem	Harry & Henny Feniger

have the same style and background, so that both the identity of the children and the date of the photograph is beyond doubt. Thus, the photographs in the album helped to confirm the identity of children in the many other photographs that have survived. The photos in Figure 5.19 are a selection; for some (such as Rita Arndt), the photograph in the album is the only one of reasonable quality that exists. For others, it fills an age gap – for example, in 1938 Herman Rozeveld was five years older than he was in his other photograph, from 1933 (Fig. 4.15). Brothers and sisters posed together for this occasion. All the children who could write added a note to congratulate Levisson. Fanny Günsberg apologized that she could not write it in Dutch yet; she had arrived just three months before. Many wished him a long and happy life and health. Rita Arndt, Bram Degen, Joop de Vries, and Mieke Dagloonder wished him above all *"lots of presents"*.

Figure 5.20: Ms. Broeksema with six unidentified children. Levisson album, 1938.

Ms. B. Broeksema, who worked as a nanny in the orphanage in 1938, wrote a congratulatory note on behalf of six small children who could not yet write. She probably was not Jewish (van Zegveld, 1993). She added a photograph (Fig. 5.20), but unfortunately without mentioning the names of the children, who could not be identified. It was also not possible to select a group of children who could be in this photograph on the basis of their age in 1938 (by selecting children born after 1932 who were in the orphanage during 1937-1938). It is therefore possible that the list (at the end of the book) is not complete.

The tableau of children and staff as contained in the Levisson album serves as a landmark before we turn to the next chapter. Not long after Levisson celebrated his 60th birthday, the political situation in Europe became worse. German military power was growing for everybody to see. In September 1938 the Sudetenland was given to Hitler, who soon thereafter proceeded to annex the rest of Czechoslovakia against the agreement he made with the UK and France; attacks against the Jews culminated in Kristallnacht; German rhetoric against Poland forbode a future attack.

Holland mobilized at the end of August 1939, a week before the German invasion of Poland. Some of the older boys from the orphanage, such as Karel van Santen (Ch. 8.1) and Herman Stofkooper (Ch. 9.7), appeared in Leiden in uniform as tensions increased. Figure 5.18 shows the windows of the dining room being taped, to prevent the glass from shattering during a possible bombardment, either during the German invasion in May 1940, or more likely during the Blitz on London later that year.

More than once, the Dutch government was warned that a German invasion was imminent in late 1939 and early 1940. But each time it did not happen, as we now know because Hitler decided to postpone the attack. As a result, some people assumed that the warnings were not based on a real threat.

On 8th April 1940, Germany invaded Denmark and Norway; in Holland, people were holding their breath.

References

Census (the Netherlands), 1930 and other years. Available at www.volkstellingen.nl.

Creveld, I.B. van, 2001; *"Het wezen van wezen. Joodse wezen in Den Haag 1850-1943. Een monument"*. De Nieuwe Haagsche, ISBN 9077032096. [Describes the history of the Jewish orphanage in The Hague and its liquidation in 1943.]

Creveld, I.B. van, 2004; *"Hulp aan wezen in oorlogstijd"*. De Nieuwe Haagsche, ISBN 9077032711. [Reports on new information about the orphanage in The Hague based on the orphanage's archives, upon their recovery and return from Russia.]

Crone, F., 2005; *"Voorbijgaand verblijf. Joodse weeskinderen in oorlogstijd"*. Amsterdam, De Prom, ISBN 9068011162. [Focused on refugees from Germany and the Jewish orphanage in Utrecht.]

Fast, Vera, 2011; *"Children's exodus: A history of the Kindertransport"*. London, Tauris, ISBN 9781848855373. See also Harris & Oppenheimer, 2000.

Gutmann, Ruth, 2013; *"A final reckoning: A Hannover family's life and death in the Shoah"*. Tuscaloosa, University of Alabama Press, ISBN 9780817387181. Available on Scribd.com. Original German edition: Herskovits-Gutmann, 2002.

Hammel, A. & B. Lewkowicz (eds), (2012); *"The Kindertransport to Britain 1938/39: New perspectives"*. Amsterdam, Brill/Rodopi, ISBN 9789042036154. [This book offers different or complementary views compared to Harris & Oppenheimer, 2000, or Fast, 2011.]

Harris, M.J. & D. Oppenheimer, 2000; *"Into the arms of strangers: Stories of the Kindertransport"*. London, Bloomsbury, ISBN 158234101X. http://www.kindertransport.org/history. htm. See also: Fast, 2011, and Hammel & Lewkowicz, 2012.

Herskovits-Gutmann, Ruth, 2002; *"Auswanderung vorläufig nicht möglich. Die Geschichte der Familie Herskovits aus Hannover"*. Göttingen, Wallstein, ISBN 3892445079. English edition: Gutmann, 2013.

Hodge, Deborah, 2012; *"Rescuing the children: The story of the Kindertransport"*. Toronto, Tundra Books, ISBN 9781770492561. [Contains a chapter on the SS *Bodegraven*.]

Italie, Gabriel, 2009; *"Het oorlogsdagboek van dr. G. Italie. Den Haag, Barneveld, Westerbork, Theresienstadt, Den Haag 1940-1945"*. Ed. by Wally M. de Lang. Amsterdam, Contact, ISBN 9789025427917. [The war diary of Gabriel Italie, one of the brothers of Nathan Italie, the director of the Jewish orphanage in Leiden.]

Jong, L. de, 1969-1994; *"Het Koninkrijk der Nederlanden in de Tweede Wereldoorlog"*. http:// www.dbnl.org or http://www.loedejongdigitaal.nl/. [The standard (contemporary) history of the Netherlands during the war. The entire text is available online (with search facility). For more recent interpretations, see Blom et al., 2021.]

Keesing, Miriam, 2013; *"Truus Wijsmuller-Meijer, a forgotten heroine"*. In: *"Celebrating 75 years of Kindertransport"*, pp. 32-33. https://www.dokin.nl/publications/celebrating-75-years-of-kindertransport-truus-wijmuller-a-forgotten-heroine/.

Keesing, M., P. Tammes & A.J. Simpkin, 2019; *"Jewish refugee children in the Netherlands during World War II: Migration, settlement, and survival"*. *Social Science History* 43 (4), 785-811.

Meijer-Wijler, Gerda, 1993; *"A personal history, 1923-1945"*. [Unpublished document (in English), written for her children and grandchildren. Gerda was neighbour to both Emilie van Brussel (before she married Hijme Stoffels) and the family Klein. She played an active role in the Dutch resistance. She emigrated to Israel with other surviving members of her family, building a successful dairy farm in Beth Jitschak (Kopuit, 1974). She also deposited an (English language) report of her activities between September 1944 and May 1945 at NIOD, also available at www.weggum.com.]

Melkman, Jozeph, 1974; *"De briefwisseling tussen Mr. L.E. Visser en Prof. Dr. D. Cohen".* Studia Rosenthaliana 8, 107-130.

Michman, Jozeph, 1987; *"Met voorbedachten rade. Ideologie en uitvoering van de Endlösung der Judenfrage".* Amsterdam, Meulenhoff, ISBN 9029098473. [An analysis of the ideology which gave rise to the Holocaust and how it developed from the moment Hitler declared his intention to remove all Jews from Europe.]

NMG Productions, 2010; *"Bagage van Leiden. Een Joods weeshuis in oorlogstijd".* [A video documentary (50 minutes) about the Jewish orphanage in Leiden. The film can be viewed at https://www.nmgproductions.nl/portfolio?lang=nl.]

Presser, J., 1965; *"Ondergang. De vervolging en verdelging van het Nederlandse Jodendom, 1940-1945".* 's-Gravenhage, Staatsuitgeverij/Martinus Nijhoff. [The entire Dutch text is available online (with search facility) at http://www.dbnl.org. Although written more than half a century ago, the book is still very readable and impressive today.] An English translation was published by E.P. Dutton & Co. in 1969 (ASIN B000LD8D7S), and again in 1988 under the title *"Ashes in the wind: The destruction of Dutch Jewry"* by Wayne State University Press; re-issued in 2010, ISBN 9780285638136.

Stam-van der Staay, Mien, 2003; *"Lotte. 'Ik zing terwijl het binnen in mij huilt'. Lotte Adler, 1925-1943".* Leiden, Museum De Lakenhal, ISBN 9071655172.

Wasserstein, Bernard, 2014; *"The ambiguity of virtue: Gertrude van Tijn and the fate of the Dutch Jews".* Cambridge, MA, Harvard University Press, ISBN 9780674281387. [An earlier version of this book was published in Dutch in 2013: *"Gertrude van Tijn en het lot van de Nederlandse Joden",* Amsterdam, Nieuw Amsterdam, ISBN 9789046814352.]

Zegveld, W.F. van, 1993; *"Joods Wees- en Doorgangshuis Leiden, bewoners 1890-1951".* Originally in: *"De Joden van Leiden".* Unpublished; 4 volumes. [Several copies were made, available (i.a.) at Erfgoed Leiden (ELO) and the Joods Historisch Museum, Amsterdam. The results of his painstaking research have served as a basis for subsequent investigations. Note that his report is an important source of information on children and staff in the Leiden orphanage who are not included in this book because they had left before the move to the new building in 1929, as well as Jewish citizens of the Leiden region who were not connected to the orphanage.]

6   1940 to 1942: Occupation, oppression, persecution

Abstract

Germany invaded the Netherlands on 10th May 1940. The queen and the government ministers escaped to Great Britain. Hitler appointed a *civil* (rather than a military) occupation government dominated by Austrian Nazis. They exerted direct control over the Dutch civil service. The anti-Jewish campaign started early, and was executed with exceptional sense of purpose, vigour, and tenacity. Terror increased and mass deportations of Jews to Buchenwald and Mauthausen took place in early 1941, before the plans to deport all Jews from Western Europe to death camps had taken shape. Jews were systematically identified, registered, separated from the other Dutch, marked by wearing a star, sequestered in their homes, robbed of their possessions, and brought to Camp Westerbork, from where deportations to Auschwitz started on 14th July 1942. By end December 1942 some 38,000 Dutch Jews had been deported and murdered.

Keywords: Persecution of Jews, segregation of schools, February Strike, deportations, Buchenwald, Westerbork, Mauthausen

6.1   10th May 1940: Germany invades the Netherlands

The German army invaded the Netherlands in the early morning of 10th May 1940; it was all over on the 14th when the main defence positions had collapsed and after the air raid and bombardment of Rotterdam.

As opposed to France and Belgium, or Eastern European countries, there was no living memory of war and occupation in the Netherlands in 1940: it had been one and a half centuries since the French occupation (1795-1813), and the Spanish occupation, which gave rise to the independent Dutch Republic, was a full three centuries in the past. Colonial wars such as in Atjeh (Aceh, North Sumatera), 1873-1914, were gruesome but far removed from daily life in Holland. Following neutrality in the First World War, hope had turned into illusionary belief that Holland would not

Focke, Jaap W., *Machseh Lajesoumim: A Jewish Orphanage in the City of Leiden, 1890-1943*.
Taylor & Francis Group, 2021
DOI: 10.5117/9789463726955_CH06

be drawn into a new European war. Country and people were very unprepared for what was to come. The state of the armed forces was affected by years of spending cuts, an unwillingness to find budget for improvements, pacifist beliefs, and endless political debates. Although defence spending increased in the early 1930s, it was too late. Most of Europe was frantically engaged with rearmament, and the Dutch government found itself at the back of the queue. The situation with the navy and its capacity to withstand a Japanese attack on the Dutch East Indies was arguably even more dramatic.[1] This notwithstanding, the poorly equipped army put up a brave resistance, along the *"Grebbelinie"*, but also in the *"Battle for The Hague"*, a German attempt – which largely failed – to capture the three military airports around The Hague (the seat of government) by large-scale air landings (see Herman Stofkooper's exploits, Ch. 9.8, and Truus Wijsmuller's travels, Ch. 9.1).

Responses to the German occupation were varied. Some Dutchmen had sympathy for the invaders or the Nazi ideology, expecting the country to do well as part of the German Reich. Some accepted the new political reality because they thought that German domination was unstoppable and was here to stay for more than a lifetime. It is disconcerting to ponder how accurate their prediction could have been, *if Hitler had not attacked Russia, if Japan had not attacked the USA, if the British had not stood their ground in 1940, if...* Some were shocked but had no clue how to react to the new situation. Others responded more dramatically – 388 people, about half of them Jewish, perceived the evil which had come to the Netherlands to such an extent that they committed suicide in the days following the invasion of 10th May (Ligtenberg, 2017). Still others tried desperately, in most cases too late, to escape overland to France, or over the sea to England. A few exceptional people put up resistance at an early stage of the occupation. But most people did not respond at all, waiting to see how the occupation would develop, and focusing on the survival of themselves and their families.

The Germans had originally planned to install a military government in Holland, as they actually did in Belgium, and France. Hitler had issued instructions that the population should be spared unnecessary violence, and that disruption of the economies should be prevented as much as possible. But just before the formal capitulation, the Dutch queen and the ministers had fled to England.[2] The Germans quickly (Führer's decree of 18th May) filled the gap by putting their own

---

1   The growing threat of Japan to the Netherlands East Indies was perceived from the early 1900's, following Japanese victories against China in 1894-1895 and Russia in 1904-1905. The almost total annihilation of the Russian fleet in 1904 sent a clear message to Western colonial powers. But plans to effectively upgrade the navy were crippled or delayed by parliament. Several warships were still under construction at Dutch wharves in May 1940.

2   The departure of the government shocked many at the time. With hindsight, and by comparing it with what happened in Belgium and France, it seems that it was a wise decision. The army had capitulated, but

civil government in place. Hitler appointed the Austrian Arthur Seyss-Inquart as *Reichskommissar* of the occupied Dutch territories. Four *Generalkommissars*, three of them also Austrians, reported to Seyss-Inquart. Together, they effectively replaced the Dutch government, which put the country under direct Nazi-civil control. The situation in Belgium, which capitulated on 28th May 1940, was much more complex,[3] and developments in France were very different (Chs. 9.7 and 9.8) compared to the fall of the Netherlands.

The departure of the Dutch government had immediate and far-reaching effects. It left the civil service in administrative charge of the country, without day-to-day political guidance from the Dutch ministers, now in London. The most senior Dutch civil servants were the secretaries (or directors) general (SGs or DGs), two of which need to be mentioned: K.J. Frederiks at the Interior Affairs Department (the "Home Office"), and J. van Dam at the Ministry of Education. Before they left for England, the government had instructed the SGs to collaborate with the occupying authority in order to protect the population as best as they could. As a result, the *Generalkommissars* were able to give direct instructions to the SGs. The civil servants in the various government departments, including local government agencies such as the police, were expected to take their cue from the SGs and collaborate with the civil German officials. As a result, direct instructions began to flow from the German to the Dutch authorities at several lower levels. The German police (SiPo/SD) in The Hague simply called the Dutch police station in Leiden if they wanted someone to be arrested.

6.2   1940: The anti-Jewish campaign starts early

From early on, and in fact well into the occupation, the Germans attempted to conciliate the population. Prisoners of war were released; German soldiers were instructed to behave properly and with decorum. Pictures appeared of soldiers strolling the beach and paying for their ice cream, visiting Artis Zoo in Amsterdam. At the same time the Germans made it clear that normal freedoms no longer applied, and repression started long before the conciliation attempts were given up. All newspapers, already in May 1940, had to print a statement of "loyalty" with respect to the German occupation. Criticism was not tolerated. Only a few people

---

not the government, allowing the country to continue the struggle, while maintaining (for the moment) the control over the colonies, including the resource-rich Dutch East Indies (Indonesia).

3   The situation in Belgium was more complex. King Leopold, as commander-in-chief, remained in the country as a prisoner of the Germans, leading to conflicts and making it difficult for the "Free Belgians" to form an effective government in exile in London. It led to a deep constitutional crisis in Belgium after the war.

had the courage (and the foresight about what the Germans had in store) to put up resistance. Truus Wijsmuller did not hesitate for a moment when she heard, in Paris, about the German invasion. She returned to Amsterdam as quickly as possible to rescue as many refugee children as possible from "her own" Kindertransport in 1938 (Ch. 5.2), those who had stayed in Holland, as well as other refugee children, such as Helga and Kurt Gottschalk. Their story will follow in Chapter 9.1.

On 18th May 1940 Bernard IJzerdraat distributed his first anti-German pamphlet, calling for resistance. He was betrayed, arrested on 25th November 1940, and executed by the Germans on 13th March 1941 with fourteen other dissenters and three men who had been part of the February Strike (see below). The trial was widely publicized, as was the execution of the verdict. The message was clear.

The first specific anti-Jewish measure was introduced as early as 1st July 1940, removing Jewish citizens from the air-defence roll. It may have looked rather harmless to many people. The Germans wanted, in the first instance, to drive a wedge between Jewish and non-Jewish Dutchmen, or, in Nazi terminology, between the "Jews" and the "Dutch". Their expectation was that the latter would be willing, as fellow Aryans, to become part of the German Reich just as many Austrians had welcomed the *Anschluss* in 1938.

Many more anti-Jewish measures, far less innocuous, followed in quick succession during the second half of 1940. To name only a few: 6th September: Jews were no longer accepted into government employment; 5th October: All staff in government employment must declare whether they were of Aryan descent or not; 22nd October: Jewish-owned businesses must be registered, a clear step towards expropriation. On 4th November Jewish government staff was suspended (they were dismissed as per 21st February 1941). Some other anti-Jewish decrees issued by the occupation administration in Holland looked like childish harassment, such as the one of 9th January 1941, denying Jews access to cinemas, or 15th September 1941: banning Jews from public parks, zoos, cafés, restaurants, hotels, theatres, and museums. But they were deadly serious, and, with hindsight, the pattern in a great number of measures following each other in quick succession, is unmistakable: identify the Jewish Dutchmen and *isolate them from the rest of the population*, rob them of all their possessions, concentrate them as much as possible in one place, and then remove them from Dutch society altogether. How that was to be done may not have been clear in 1940; the consensus is that the "Final Solution" as the last phase of the Holocaust only gradually developed into genocide during 1941 and 1942. But one can make a cogent case (J. Michman, 1987) that Hitler knew exactly what he wanted long before his own Nazi organization was ready for it (Ch. 7.6).

In Belgium, where religious denomination was not recorded by the Civil Registry (Ch. 8.4), it required two countrywide surveys which "requested" people to declare any Jewish ancestry. If they refused, and if their Jewish identity was not obvious from their family name, appearance or behaviour, there was no easy data source to identify them as Jews (Schram, 2018; Kazerne Dossin Museum). In the Netherlands, however, the Civil Registry had kept record of the religious congregation everybody belonged to, lately based on the 1930 census. During that census, some 112,000 people had responded as belonging to the "Israelite congregation" and were duly recorded as *Israelites* in the Civil Registry, just as Catholics and Protestants were registered (Table 1.1). The Germans were fully aware of that, but the Nazi definition of who was Jewish was based on race, more than on faith, and was defined as anybody being *"of Jewish blood"*. In the German view a Jew was a Jew, irrespective of whether they had chosen to leave the Jewish faith. Some 14% of all Dutch respondents in 1930 had indicated that they did not belong to any religious congregation. Conceivably, this group harboured Jews who had relinquished their religious identity as part of an assimilation process. The Nazis solved this by stepping up two generations and looking for anybody with "Jewish blood" irrespective if it came from only one Jewish grandparent, or two, three or four. A grandparent was Jewish if he or she belonged to the Israelite congregation. This definition ensured that Jews could not escape being classified as such by claiming that they, or their parents, had given up belonging to the congregation. When this was settled, what followed may be considered the most infamous preparatory measure of the Holocaust in the Netherlands: *Decree 6/1941*, issued on 10th January 1941. Every citizen or resident with one or more Jewish grandparents had to go to the authorities and fill in a form, declaring any Jewish grandparent they had.

Only very few people refused to have themselves registered, and many of those, as far as cases have been documented, were registered nevertheless, based on other sources of information available to the Germans, such as the Civil Registry. They had to pay one florin (guilder) for the privilege and carry the proof of their registration (*Bewijs van aanmelding*, Fig. 6.1) with them when out of their house. The declaration was issued by or on behalf of the mayor of the town of residence, but in Amsterdam it was stamped (in blue) by the Jewish star and the signature of A. Asscher, the co-chairman (with D. Cohen) of the Joodse Raad of Amsterdam, which had been established[4] in early February 1941 by German instruction to provide a liaison (rather, a one-way communication channel) between the Nazi authorities and the Jewish community. The card also included a statement about previous location of residence (*"Laatste woonplaats"*) if this had been in the German Reich or the occupied parts of Poland, so that Jewish refugees were included in this registration. Anybody with three or four Jewish grandparents was considered a Jew. If you had "only" two Jewish grandparents, you were classified as a "half-Jew", with one Jewish grandparent: "quarter-Jew", and deportation might be avoided. But to avert deportation, it was not enough to have two non-Jewish grandparents:

---

4   initially for Amsterdam, but soon for the entire country.

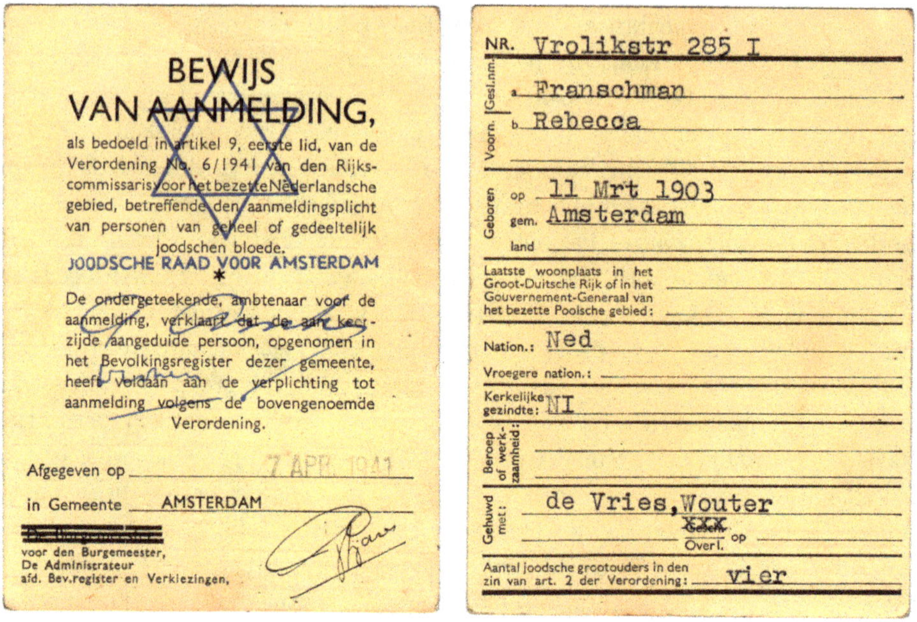
BEWIJS
VAN AANMELDING,
als bedoeld in artikel 9, eerste lid, van de Verordening No. 6/1941 van den Rijkscommissaris voor het bezette Nederlandsche gebied, betreffende den aanmeldingsplicht van personen van geheel of gedeeltelijk joodschen bloede.
JOODSCHE RAAD VOOR AMSTERDAM
De ondergeteekende, ambtenaar voor de aanmelding, verklaart dat de aan keerzijde aangeduide persoon, opgenomen in het Bevolkingsregister dezer gemeente, heeft voldaan aan de verplichting tot aanmelding volgens de bovengenoemde Verordening.
Afgegeven op 7 APR. 1941
in Gemeente AMSTERDAM
~~De Burgemeester,~~
voor den Burgemeester,
De Administrateur
afd. Bev.register en Verkiezingen,

NR. Vrolikstr 285 I
Gesl.nm. a. Franschman
Voorn. b. Rebecca
Geboren op 11 Mrt 1903
gem. Amsterdam
land
Laatste woonplaats in het Groot-Duitsche Rijk of in het Gouvernement-Generaal van het bezette Poolsche gebied:
Nation.: Ned
Vroegere nation.:
Kerkelijke gezindte: NI
Beroep of werkzaamheid:
Gehuwd met: de Vries,Wouter
Gesch. Overl. op
Aantal joodsche grootouders in den zin van art. 2 der Verordening: vier

Figure 6.1: This "proof" that Rebecca Franschman, the mother of Piet de Vries, had "presented herself for registration" was found in the archive of H. and E. Stoffels (see Ch. 7.4). The last entry, "vier", registers her four Jewish grandparents, which made her "fully Jewish" in German eyes. But her husband, Wouter de Vries, was not Jewish. This enabled Hijme Stoffels to save Piet de Vries from deportation two years later, just in time (see Ch. 7.4). Rebecca survived the war. The presence of this card in his archive suggests that Stoffels provided her with false papers (see Ch. 10.3). Private collection

half-Jews such as Hans Kloosterman, Piet de Vries and his sister Marietje, who had incontestably a non-Jewish father and two non-Jewish grandparents, were classified as J2: *"unsafe half-Jew"* by the Civil Registry office (van den Boomgaard, 2019), probably because they were living in a Jewish orphanage, where they were considered to be a member of the Israelite congregation. To be reclassified from J2 to G1 ("safe half-Jew") they needed to submit a *"change request"* to the Civil Registry, to be approved by the German *Entscheidungsstelle* (headed by Hans Calmeyer) or they would be deported with everybody else. It is one of the many shocking facts about the collaboration of the Dutch civil service that they initially classified these youngsters as J2, while their German overlords later accepted their request to be reclassified as G1 without raising the issue that they were firmly embedded in the Jewish community. It seems curious that the Nazis were so finicky about these issues in Holland, compared to the indiscriminate mass murder which took place in Eastern Europe. Without (as yet) finding an answer in the literature, I would surmise that in essence "half-Jew" in Holland implied *"half-Aryan"* in the eyes of the Nazis; and that presented them with a problem.

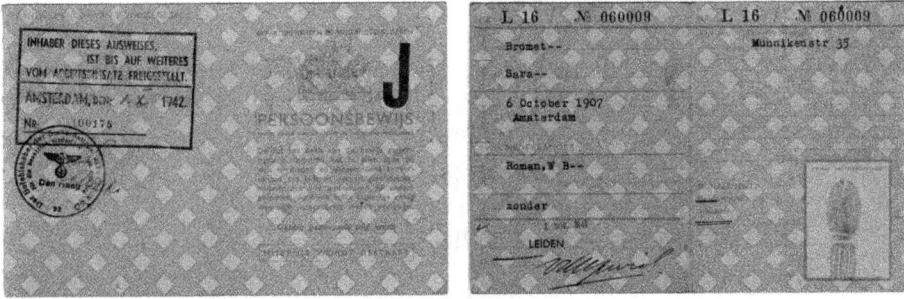

Figure 6.2: The front and back side of the pb of Sara Bromet, with the third page (with the photograph and the second J) torn off. It was found in the private archive of Hijme and Emilie Stoffels (Chs. 6.5 and 10.3). Stoffels provided Sara with a false pb, no. 069051 (van Wijk, 1946). The two stamps in the left corner provided the bearer with temporary exemption from deportation. The significance of these stamps (Sperre) is discussed in Chapter 6.6. Private collection.

Some 160,000 declarations were submitted. Presser (1965, p. 418) lists the official figures, provided by the Dutch Civil Registry office, based on the analysis of these declarations. On 1st October 1941, the Civil Registry reported that there were 117,999 Dutch Jews in the Netherlands, 14,381 German Jews, and 7621 Jews from other countries. Total: 140,001 Jews by the German definition (three or four Jewish grandparents). In addition, 15,000 half-Jews, and 5000 quarter-Jews were registered.

By October 1941 the Germans, using the staff of the Dutch Civil Registry, had effectively updated the 1930 database, which now included those of Jewish ancestry who had not declared themselves as belonging to the Jewish faith in 1930, as well as the c. 22,000 Jewish refugees from the East who were still in the country. Now the Germans knew who was Jewish by their definition, and they knew everybody's address. In that same period (early 1941) a new identity card, the *"persoonsbewijs"*, colloquially called the *pb*, was issued to all citizens from age fourteen. It was instantly connected to the results of the registration: the pbs of Jews were stamped with two big black Js (Fig. 6.2).

The new pb was a personal project of Jacob L. Lentz, the head of the Dutch Civil Registry. It contained a multitude of security features in addition to the special paper with fine multicolour print: a special ink which was not visible under a quartz lamp, a watermark which could only be poorly reproduced, fingerprint, special stamps, and so on. The photograph of the holder could not be removed without destroying a specially printed half-transparent seal with another fingerprint. It was arguably the "best" identity card in occupied Europe. Lentz was very proud of his product, and the Germans were pleased: the pb was more difficult to counterfeit than even the German identity card. The identity cards used in Belgium (see Figs. 8.10 and 8.11, the counterfeit cards for Alexander Lipschits and his father) were "a joke" by comparison. A good counterfeit pb which could survive technical scrutiny was only possible if one could obtain blank originals. And even a technically perfect pb could be exposed as a forgery by comparing the personal data with the data in the Civil Registry. And if the data in the Civil Registry had been "adapted", such as was done by Stoffels and van Wijk, there still was a central record stored in the *Villa Kleykamp* in The Hague, which the police could consult (Ch. 10.3 for details).

A mere twelve to fifteen months into the occupation, they were ready for the next step – segregation: isolation from all other Dutchmen, their removal from all branches of society, from professional and vocational occupation, from government employment, from business ownership. It was a complicated process which was executed by the Nazi administrators in Holland with stunning speed and efficiency. But first, another event would drastically change the attitude of the Nazi authorities in occupied Holland.

6.3   1941: The first razzias, the February Strike, and deportations to Mauthausen

The Dutch Nazi Party (*Nationaal-Socialistische Beweging*, NSB) had gained a one-time high of 7.9% of the popular vote as a populist party in 1935. Just two years later, the NSB fell back to 4.2% of the vote, and in 1939 to 3.9%. The NSB was and remained a marginal party, the more so as people became aware of the growing danger of fascist and Nazi movements elsewhere in Europe. The Dutch government prohibited its employees from being members of the NSB as early as 1933, the Catholic Church banned membership in 1935, and the Protestant *"Gereformeerde Synode"* followed in 1936. Following the German invasion, the NSB saw the opportunity to gain influence or even power. Its leader, Anton Mussert, hoped to be elevated to leader of the Dutch population under German tutelage, but Hitler eventually only gave him the title, without any authority. Seyss-Inquart and his four *Generalkommissars* remained fully in charge. After the war, Mussert was convicted of treason and executed. Notwithstanding Hitler's snub, the NSB gained influence during the occupation because officials who were not loyal enough in the eyes of the Nazis were often replaced by more "reliable" NSB members or sympathizers, such as R.N. de Ruyter van Steveninck, who became mayor of Leiden in April 1941, U.K.L. Hoffmann, who became chief of police in Leiden in June 1942, and Steven van Musscher (Fig. 10.12), who joined the Leiden police force in 1941 to head the *Documentatiedienst*, a special unit to hunt down Jews and other people hiding from the Germans.

In February 1941, members of the WA (*Weerbaarheidsafdeling*, the paramilitary arm of the NSB) and other Dutch Nazis went into the Amsterdam Jewish Quarter to make trouble. The regular police were incapable (or unwilling) to deal with it. There was resistance by Jewish fighting groups armed with sticks and staves, and

ORGANISEERT IN ALLE BEDRIJVEN DE PROTEST-STAKING !!!
VECHT EENSGEZIND TEGEN DEZE TERREUR !!!
EIST DE ONMIDDELLIJKE VRIJLATING VAN DE GEARRESTEERDE JODEN !!!
EIST DE ONTBINDING VAN DE W.A-TERREURGROEPEN !!!
ORGANISEERT IN DE BEDRIJVEN EN IN DE WIJKEN DE ZELFVERDEDIGING !!!
WEEST SOLIDAIR MET HET ZWAAR GETROFFEN JOODSE DEEL VAN HET
                                    WERKENDE VOLK !!!
ONTTREKT DE JOODSE KINDEREN AAN HET NAZI-GEWELD, NEEMT ZE IN
                                    UW GEZINNEN OP !!!!
B E S E F T   D E   E N O R M E   K R A C H T   V A N
        U W   E E N S G E Z I N D E   D A A D   !!!!!
    Deze is vele malen groter dan de Duitse militaire bezetting!
Gij hebt in Uw verzet ongetwijfeld een groot deel van de Duitse
                                    arbeiders-soldaten met U !!!!.

STAAKT!!! STAAKT!!! STAAKT!!!

Legt het geheele Amsterdamse bedrijfsleven één dag plat, de werven
de fabrieken, de ateliers, de kantoren en banken, gemeente-bedrijven
en werkverschaffingen!!

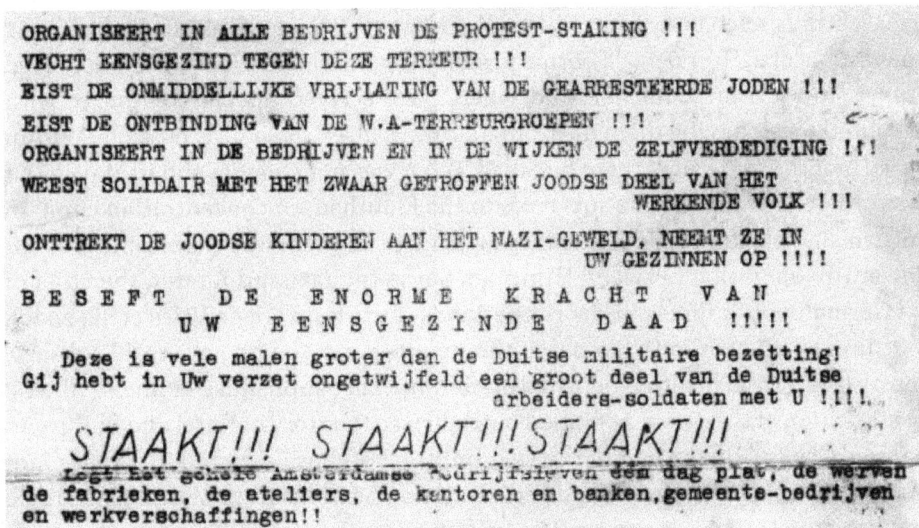

Figure 6.3: The call to strike (Staakt!!), Amsterdam, February 1941.

one NSB man was killed. The actions of the WA were not orchestrated or supported by the Germans, who were keen to maintain order so that they could progress the anti-Jewish campaign without disturbances. They considered sealing off the Jewish Quarter and transforming it into a ghetto, but soon realized that would create more serious unrest, since thousands of non-Jews living there would have to be uprooted and relocated elsewhere in Amsterdam. The first barbed wire fences were erected, but the plan was abandoned after a few days. To suppress any further resistance, razzias were held in Amsterdam on 22nd and 23rd February. Some 400 Jewish men were arrested and taken to the Schoorl concentration camp, near Alkmaar. Among them were Karel van Santen, who had left the Leiden orphanage in 1940 after more than thirteen years, and his brother Philip. They happened to be in Amsterdam that day to visit a friend and were caught by sheer bad luck (Ch. 8.1).

Two days later, on 25th February 1941, a strike broke out in Amsterdam. The initiators, mostly from Communist backgrounds, issued a pamphlet (Fig. 6.3) demanding *"the immediate release of the arrested Jews, [...] the disbanding of the WA terror groups [...] [and that people] show solidarity with the badly hit Jewish part of the population"*. Interestingly it also said that people should *"shield Jewish children from Nazi violence, [and] take them into your own family"*.

By implication it urged Jews to start putting their children into hiding (*"onder-duik"*), a totally unnerving idea at this time (early 1941), when only few Dutch Jews perceived that they would soon be in mortal danger. Initially, the Germans were taken aback. Strikes were unheard of in the Third Reich, and it took them a day to respond, which they did with a vengeance. Seven strike leaders were executed. On

27th February 389 young men from the original group of people arrested during the razzias of 22nd and 23rd February, including Karel and Philip, were deported from Camp Schoorl to Buchenwald, where they received "special treatment" with the intention of having them die from "natural causes" as soon as possible. Within three months some 20 of them had died. But it was not enough, and in May 1941 it was ordered to transfer the survivors to the Mauthausen concentration camp in Austria. It is clear from documentary evidence that there was close contact about the entire operation between Himmler, Seyss-Inquart and Rauter, the chief of all German police forces in the Netherlands (de Vries, 2011; de Vries et al., 2000). Within just a few months, most of the people deported on 22th-23rd February, mostly young and healthy men, had died from exhaustion, mistreatment, illness, or starvation, if they were not killed outright (see the story of Karel and Philip van Santen, Ch. 8.1). By the end of the year only one of those arrested in Amsterdam was still alive. The Germans allowed death notifications from Mauthausen to be published in the Dutch papers. The underground paper *Het Parool* wrote on 11th September 1941:

> *According to official German death notifications (as many as 38 last week), 232 people have died for unknown causes, [...] more than a third of the Amsterdam Jews who were taken from their homes or off the streets and brought to Buchenwald and then to Mauthausen. Despite many rumours we do not know for sure how these young men, not accused of any wrongdoing, were murdered by these bestial Germans.*

It was clear that the deportees were brought to Mauthausen with the premeditated purpose of having them die as quickly as possible. The fear of being sent to Mauthausen played an important role in the *"Great Deception"* when the deportations to the death camps began in July 1942. Contrary to Mauthausen, the true nature of these death camps was kept secret: Auschwitz was supposed to be a labour camp, and nobody had heard about Sobibor until after the war. Many would prefer to take the train to *"labour camps"* in Poland, rather than risk being sent to Mauthausen and what they considered certain death. Even if rumours went around about the death camps, they were difficult to believe for most people. At the same time, the brutality of the German response had a lasting impact on the Dutch population at large. The February Strike as a public protest against German oppression and the persecution of Jews was unique in occupied Europe; but it was also the last.

New decrees followed each other in quick succession. Jews were no longer allowed to give blood (27th February 1941), to possess a radio (15th April), to visit a market (1st May) or swimming pools and beaches (31st May) or enter any public park or sports

Figure 6.4: From left: Louis Fleurima (4), Elchanan Italie (3), Melna Fleurima (4). May 1940. The Fleurima twins had Haitian nationality; they were deported with parents and a younger sister from Westerbork to the Liebenau internment camp for enemy nationals on 9*th* March 1943. They survived the war.

field (15th September). It probably affected the older children from the orphanage more than the younger ones (Fig. 6.4) for whom the building and the vast playground in the garden was most important.

Another round of razzias was held in Amsterdam on 11th June 1941, and some 300 Jewish citizens were deported. On 8th August 1941 Jews were instructed to transfer all money in bank accounts above 1000 florins to a formerly Jewish Bank (Lippmann, Rosenthal & Co., colloquially called Liro) which the Germans had taken over. The great theft had begun. It is only in the last 30 years that complicity in this process by "ordinary" Dutchmen such as civil servants and registry officials, real estate agents, notaries, art dealers, bank officials, tax consultants, and others has reached public discussion and scientific research (e.g. Aalders, 1999; Schütz, 2016).

Camp Schoorl is not well known in the international literature, nor the fact that mass deportation of Dutch Jews started from Schoorl one and a half years before deportations started from Westerbork, Mechelen (Malines, Kazerne Dossin, Belgium) or Drancy (France). On 27th February, 22nd May, and 22nd June, three transports from Schoorl carried 1009 Jews to Buchenwald/Mauthausen. In total, some 2000 Dutch prisoners were deported to Mauthausen during the war, of which more than 1600 were killed (de Vries, 2000, 2011). It has been argued that the context of these early transports was different in that they were of a penal nature, and not part of

Figure 6.5: Henny and Lotte Adler, photographed by Foto Bonte in Leiden, 1st August 1941. From Nathan Italie's personal photo album. Private collection.

the well-planned and centrally organized mass deportations from Westerbork. But the purpose of the transports was the same: to kill the deportees as quickly as possible. The early deportations illustrate the exceptional speed, the sense of purpose and urgency, and the tenacity of the Nazi administration in Holland, much more than the Nazis achieved under the military governments in Belgium and France, or in the area controlled by the anti-Semitic government in Vichy France (Chs. 8.3, 8.4, 9.6 and 9.7).

The orphanage had remained a relatively safe haven in turbulent times, and until the summer of 1941 life in the eyes of the children was not so badly affected. Lotte and Henny Adler were pictured (Fig. 6.5) by a professional photographer[5] on 1st August 1941. They had received Red Cross letters from their mother in New York (Ch. 10.1), who had been trying to obtain immigration certificates for them. Nathan Italie put a print of this photo in his album after writing the date on the back. Presumably the picture was taken to be sent to their mother in New York.

Four weeks later, at the close of the summer holiday of 1941, the next step in the persecution process would drastically change life for the children in the orphanage, as well as for all other Jewish children in the Netherlands.

---

5   Foto Bonte, Korevaarstraat 2a-b, Leiden.

) — ALGEMEEN HANDELSBLAD VAN VRIJDAG 29 AUGUSTUS 1941

Joodsche leerlingen

en -leerkrachten

Worden op scholen gescheiden van niet-Joden.

's-Gravenhage, 29 Augustus.

De Secretaris-Generaal van het Departement van Opvoeding, Wetenschap en Cultuurbescherming brengt het volgende ter algemeene kennis:

Krachtens de opdracht, gegeven door den Rijkscommissaris voor het bezette Nederland-

HONDEN- EN KATTENBROOD

Het Rijksbureau voor de voedselvoorziening in oorlogstijd maakt bekend, dat van 1 tot en met 30 September op bon no. 16 van de voederkaart voor honden wordt beschikbaar gesteld voor honden van: groep 1 10 kg hondenbrood ;groep 2 10 kg hondenbrood; groep 3 8 /kg hondenbrood; groep 4 5 kg hondenbrood; groep 5 4 kg hondenbrood; groep 6 3 kg hondenbrood.

Op bon no. 16 van de voederkaart voor katten wordt voor dezelfde periode 1½ kg kattenbrood beschikbaar gesteld.

Na 30 September zijn de bonnen no. 16 van

Figure 6.6: Announcement in national newspapers of enforced segregation of Jewish and non-Jewish children and teachers. Source: Delpher.nl.

6.4   Schools are closed for Jewish children

On Friday evening, 29th August 1941, a notification appeared in the national papers. In the *Algemeen Handelsblad* it appeared on page 9, next to an article on the rationing of dog and cat food (Fig. 6.6). The article was printed again the next day, more prominently on page 2 of the morning edition of the newspaper.

It announced that the Secretary General of Education, Science and Culture (J. van Dam) had received instruction from *Reichskommissar* Seyss-Inquart, the highest-ranking German authority in the occupied Netherlands, that Jewish children and Jewish teachers would be separated from non-Jewish children and teachers. Schools which could not be classified as a purely Jewish school, were instructed not to allow access to any child "of Jewish blood" as per 1st September. Non-Jewish teachers were no longer allowed to teach Jewish children.

The implementation had been meticulously prepared. Based on the abovementioned directive from Seyss-Inquart, van Dam's department sent letters on 16th August 1941 to all municipal authorities in the Netherlands instructing them to obtain and return to the department a precise inventory, by individual names and by individual schools, of all Jewish children enrolled in schools within their township. On 21st August the city authority in Leiden sent instructions to that effect to all schools in Leiden.

Four days later, headmaster D. Bosma of the *openbare* ULO school at Langebrug provided the information. He listed eight of his pupils, six from the orphanage, and two (of the four) sons of the "sexton" of the synagogue at the Levendaal: Meijer and Tobias Mendelson. Upon receipt on 26th August, the letter was duly logged

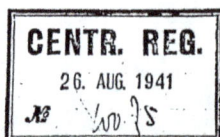

Figure 6.7: Letter by Headmaster Bosma reporting eight Jewish pupils in his school to the authorities, six from the orphanage (Roodenburgerstraat 1a), Meijer and Tobias are sons of the sexton of the Leiden synagogue. Courtesy L.P. Kasteleyn, 2003.

and stamped by the Leiden City Council. Someone at the City Hall ticked off each of the eight children, no doubt against some list with names from other sources. Bosma signed his handwritten letter (Fig. 6.7) with *"Hoogachtend, Uw dw. dnr"*, which stands for "your faithful servant". A similar letter from the head of the ULO Rijnsburgersingel, in which he informs the authorities of one Jewish pupil, Anna Vreeland, enrolled in his school, is even more submissive. It reads:

> *Honourable Gentlemen, In response to your request [...] the undersigned politely takes the liberty to report one Jewish pupil in our school, Anna Vreeland, DOB*

28th December 1929, Janvossensteeg 52. With the highest esteem, he has the honour to be your obedient servant.

Hundreds of such letters were submitted to city councils throughout the country. Although writing in this subservient style may have been normal at the time in a society which was generally much more deferential and respectful to authority than today, the letters are disquieting to say the least. Even without knowing what exactly was going to happen to the children (all nine children named in these two letters were murdered in Sobibor between 26th March and 2nd July 1943), by mid-1941 everybody knew that the Nazi plans were foreboding a very bad future for the Dutch Jews. In addition, the segregation, and the discrimination based on race or religion, however many ordinances the Nazis issued to give it all a pseudo-legal basis, was in flagrant conflict with the constitution and any ethical standard which Dutch society had adhered to for a long time.

Notwithstanding the above, some school boards did realize the immorality at the time. There were about 80 schools in Leiden in 1941: about 40 public (i.e. non-denominational) schools, 20 Protestant schools, and 20 Catholic schools. In contrast to the public schools mentioned above, the Protestant schools did not reply to the letter asking for information. When prompted, and following mutual consultation, they informed the City Council that they would not provide the requested information. The secretary of the Protestant Teacher Training College replied (Fig. 6.8), without salutation and without a polite sign-off, that the governors of the schools had decided that *"they could not, for reasons of principle, comply with the request".*

As far as it is known, the refusal to comply had no consequences. Thanks to the near-perfect Dutch registration systems, updated by the registration exercise of Decree 6/1941, the Germans knew with extraordinary precision who was Jewish in the Netherlands, who their ancestors and their family members were, where they came from, and where they resided. The refusal to comply may seem somewhat gratuitous, since no Jewish children were enrolled in these schools. But that does not make their reply meaningless, not least because the tone of the letters and the refusal to say if any of their students were Jewish carries an unmistakable message of resistance. By summer 1941 expressing anti-German sentiments, even without any active resistance, was dangerous. After the first executions on 13th March 1941 more executions of people who had produced or distributed anti-German pamphlets or papers (*Het Parool, Vrij Nederland* and others) followed later in the year.

The impact of the measure was enormous; it enforced total segregation of all Jewish children in the Netherlands with immediate effect. On that weekend of Saturday, 30th August 1941, Dutch school-going children, including of course those

CHR. KWEEKSCHOOL
TE LEIDEN
—
Secretaris-Penningmeester:
J. VEENENDAAL
Thorbeckestraat 7 · Telefoon 2061
Postgiro t/n Penningm.
Christelijke Kweekschool No. 16077

LEIDEN, 19 September   1941.

CENTR. REG.
19. SEP. 1941
№   IIIIS

162/12.0.

Naar aanleiding van Uw verzoek om een
nominatieve opgave van de Joodsche leerlingen onzer
School, heb ik de eer U mede te deelen, dat ons Bestuur van meening is om principieële redenen zijn medd-
werking niet te kunnen verleenen.

Namens het Bestuur der

Chr. Kweekschool te Leiden,

Secretaris.

Figure 6.8: Letter from a Protestant school in Leiden, refusing to comply with the instruction to report Jewish children "as a matter of principle". Courtesy L.P. Kasteleyn, 2003.

in the Leiden orphanage, were preparing to start a new school year the following Monday, 1st September. Most of the Dutch Jewish children attended ordinary non-Jewish schools, and they were all told two days before the start of the school year that they were no longer allowed to attend classes. At short notice they had to find a Jewish school, but there was not any in Leiden. Frantic efforts followed to find a solution, but it took three months before a Jewish elementary school could be opened on 27th November 1941, on Pieterskerkhof 4, right in the medieval centre of the city (Fig. 6.9). The building, a vacated ULO school of Catholic denomination, still stands in its original condition.

Only two classrooms were required to accommodate them, an "upper" class in front on the right, behind the three gentlemen on the photo, for the combined levels 4, 5 and 6, and a "lower" class right behind it on the backside for levels 1, 2 and 3. The photograph in Figure 6.10 was taken in the lower class and comes from the photo album of Donald de Marcas (1). Level 1 sits in front, level 2 in the middle, level 3 in the back. Rita Klein (2) lived in the Mariënpoelstraat, next door to the family of Emilie van Brussel, who would play an important role in the dark

Figure 6.9: The former Catholic ULO school for boys at Pieterskerkhof 4A served as a temporary Jewish school in 1941-1942.

days to come. The father of Ineke David (3) was professor at the university; Hanna Italie (4), the daughter of Nathan, and Willy Blog (5) were from the orphanage, Eli Bloemkoper (6) lived close to the orphanage; his father was a hazzan in Leiden (Ruth Herskovits lived with the Bloemkoper family until her and Eva's return to Germany in 1941, see Chapter 5.2). With six more in the upper class, the school harboured eight children from the orphanage. Probably also on this photo (L.P. Kasteleyn, personal communication), but not positively identified, are Jacob Bloemkoper, Eli's brother, and at least one son of the sexton of the synagogue, Mendelson.

For the children attending secondary education a solution was found in The Hague. Fanny Günsberg was fourteen and attended the ULO for girls in Leiden. She had not been allowed to go to the "HBS", which would have given her access to an academic education, although she had passed the entry exam (Kasteleyn, 2003). She had to wait until January 1942 before she could attend the Jewish ULO in The Hague on the Waalstraat, near the Hollands Spoor railway station. Her

Figure 6.10: The lower class of the Jewish school at Pieterskerkhof, early 1942. Donald de Marcas (1), Rita Klein (2), Ineke David (3), Hanna Italie (4), Willy Blog (5) and Eli Bloemkoper (6). Photo courtesy Donald de Marcas.

boyfriend Piet ("Daniel") de Vries was sixteen at the time and found himself going to the same school in The Hague. Piet and Fanny enjoyed the fact that they were no longer separated, after attending separate boys' and girls' schools in Leiden. They travelled daily from Leiden to The Hague by the *Blue Tram*, until the summer of 1942, when Piet received his diploma. They stood together on the rear platform since Jews were not allowed to enter the tram itself.

School life for the Jewish children continued as before, or so it was made to appear. Even the traditional school photos were taken, as in every year in Dutch schools (Fig. 6.11). But of course, it was all an illusion.

For the youngest children, of kindergarten age and not yet under compulsory education, the orphanage could probably have made in-house makeshift arrangements for their own resident children. But for the other young Jewish children of Leiden there was no immediate solution. However, the parents asked Lotte Adler to run a kindergarten in one of the rooms of the synagogue complex. This would help the preschoolers and their parents, but also Lotte herself. She had not been allowed to continue her teacher education on 1st September 1941, after her headmaster had reported his five Jewish students to the City Council: Lotte, Inge Salm, Eva Herskovits (also from the orphanage; see Fig. 5.3), Lili Braun, and Meta Labotto. Lotte and Inge had been enrolled since 1937 and 1938, respectively; the

Figure 6.11: Piet de Vries and his girlfriend, Fanny Günsberg, at the same Jewish ULO school in The Hague, spring 1942. Photo courtesy Piet de Vries.

other three were new enrolments in 1941. On 3rd September, the chairman and the secretary of the school's governing board requested an interview with the mayor of Leiden, to obtain an exemption from the segregation measure for their Jewish students. They made the case that there was no Jewish alternative vocational school available anywhere, nor could one be created. Somewhat surprisingly, the mayor, Mr. R.N. de Ruyter van Steveninck, whom the Germans had put in place because he was considered to be "more loyal" than his predecessor, acted on the request, telephoned the Department of Secretary General van Dam, and sent an appeal letter to the department on 15th September with a supporting letter from the school as an attachment. The mayor urged van Dam to make an exception at least for Inge and Lotte, who had all but completed their education. It took three months before the department replied, and of course the appeal was denied. The letters and the hand-scribbled comments, based in part on telephone conversations between the mayor and the department, suggest that even someone like de Ruyter van Steveninck, had not yet, at that stage, perceived that it was all a charade, that the physical segregation of the Jews was all that mattered, and that the whole exercise of providing alternative Jewish schooling had no other purpose than to keep them busy and quiet until they could be deported to Westerbork and the death camps.

In this period, autumn 1941, following the German invasion of the Soviet Union in June, several of these camps, purely for extermination purposes, were in the planning and construction phase. Camp Kulmhof (Chelmno) became operational as an experimental killing factory in early December 1941, while Sobibor (as well as Belzec and Treblinka II) became operational between March and July 1942.[6] It is unnerving and horrifying to observe how it all fitted together, in time and space, step by step, highly coordinated and executed with industrial efficiency. In Holland, another ordinance was issued on 7th November 1941: Jews were no longer

6   https://encyclopedia.ushmm.org.

Figure 6.12: Hijme Stoffels and Emilie Stoffels - van Brussel. From their wartime persoonsbe-wijs. Some of the many security features of the Dutch pb can be seen on Emilie's pb: photo glued within the special paper, Stamp of the Leiden registry, part of on of special stickers (upper right corner), sophisticated microscopic print in complex patterns. Photo's private collection.

allowed to change their residence address without permission. This ensured that the database would remain up to date, and that they could be picked up from home when the time came. Between mid-1942 and 17th March 1943 one after the other of the children in the Jewish classes began to drop out, without notification. Some went into hiding like Donald de Marcas and Ingrid Klein. Most of the others were sent to Westerbork: they were duly written out of the Civil Registry in Leiden and entered in the Civil Registry of Hooghalen, the municipality of Camp Westerbork. Decades later, the Dutch Civil Registry would maintain that Westerbork was their last place of residence before "emigration", a very painful situation for survivors who did not return to Holland after the war, for example, if they required documents from the Civil Registry.

6.5   1942: The arrival of Hijme and Emilie Stoffels-van Brussel

Hijme Stoffels (12th September 1907) was *gereformeerd* (a relatively strict branch of Dutch Protestantism), while Emilie van Brussel (4th August 1918) was *rooms katholiek* (Roman Catholic). They had to postpone getting married from 9th April to 31st July 1942 in order to get permission from their respective church authorities for their inter-faith marriage.[7]

They moved[8] into a townhouse at Cronesteinkade no. 20, on the corner with Roodenburgerstraat 1a, where they became neighbours of the orphanage. From their back garden, they looked directly upon the playground and the rear of the orphanage. Today the view is blocked by two ugly post-war extensions to the building, but in 1942 the mutual view was unimpeded across the large playground of the orphanage. Hijme and Emilie (Fig. 6.12) could not walk the narrow path behind the wire fence in the back (Fig. 6.13) without seeing the children play in their own garden. They quickly made acquaintance with the staff, particularly with Director Italie, and

Figure 6.13: Hanna Italie in the garden of the orphanage, 1938. Behind her is Cronesteinkade no. 20, the future home of the Stoffels.

some of the children, and soon began to perform small services, such as opening mail on Shabbat. By early 1942, following an orthodox lifestyle had become difficult as the Germans increased the harassment of the Jewish community. Mail delivered on Shabbat could be too important to be left unopened.

Stoffels, who held a senior position at the Wijtenburg cigar factory in Leiden (known as *"De Edelachtbare"*), possessed a car long before the war, when the number of private cars was still very low in the Netherlands. He frequently toured Germany in the 1930s, and often visited his nephew E. Jan Stoffels, who had lived in Germany since 1919. Jan was very conscious of the chaos and dreadful poverty in Germany after the defeat of 1918, and the political implications thereof. After working for *De Standaard*, Jan became correspondent in Berlin in 1933 for the Dutch newspaper *De Telegraaf*. He was a good friend of H.J. Noordewier, who was correspondent in Berlin for the *Nieuwe Rotterdamse Courant*. Noordewier frequently sent critical reports back to his editors. Criticism of Germany was generally not appreciated; the Dutch government was very anxious to preserve Holland's neutrality, and Germany used this effectively to suppress critical stories in the Dutch press (Stoop, 1988). Noordewier therefore put his real opinion in secret reports which landed on the desk of only a few senior civil servants in The Hague. These reports have been preserved and published (ibidem). As early as 1933-1935 Noordewier warned about Germany's rearmament, the growing repression of the opposition, the increasing

7   Archive Frits Stoffels, https://sites.google.com/site/stoffelswereldweb/.
8   Hijme left notes indicating that they effectively moved into the house as early as January 1942.

persecution of Jews in Germany, the inevitability of another war, and the plan to defeat Belgium and France in a next war by passing through the Netherlands, a much easier route than going through the mountainous Ardennes, which were heavily fortified by the Belgians.[9]

Hijme, from his own observations and from regularly talking to these two correspondents, had a good idea of what was going on, including the likelihood that Germany would not bypass Holland during a next war. Moreover, he had no illusions about what the Germans would do with respect to the Dutch Jews in case of a military occupation. Even he could not foresee or imagine what exactly was going to happen, but the significance of the German anti-Jewish measures, as described above, was unmistakable to him. Once they had moved to their new house and become neighbours of the orphanage, he started talking to Director Italie, trying to convince him that he should become more proactive and prepare for the worst.

Emilie van Brussel, eleven years younger than Hijme, came from her parental home at Mariënpoelstraat no. 13. It so happened that the family van Brussel had Jewish neighbours on both sides before the war: family Meijer at no. 11, and family Klein at no. 15 (Fig. 7.20). Emilie was well acquainted with the Meijer and Klein children and maintained contact after moving with Hijme to the Cronesteinkade. Just around this time, on 6th March 1942, Jozua Klein, the father, was arrested by the Leiden police. The police archives[10] explicitly report, amongst the other "normal" cases of theft and violence, that Jozua's arrest was made *on behalf [i.e. by instruction] of the German police*. Jozua was put on a transport the next day, and was deported to Mauthausen, where he died on 6th July 1942, four months after his arrest. No doubt the Stoffels heard about Jozua's death, and it only confirmed Hijme's belief that the Dutch Jews were in mortal danger, and that they should not allow themselves to be deported. When the situation became critical on 17th March 1943, Emilie took very assertive action to get Rosi Klein and her children into hiding (Ch. 7.12).

Stoffels escalated his warnings to Nathan Italie that he should take the threats to their lives more seriously. Specifically, he told Nathan to start making his children disappear, and that he, Stoffels and his wife, Emilie, could assist him finding *onderduik* addresses. But these warnings fell mostly upon deaf ears, which upset

---

9   The original German plan for the First World War had included an attack through Holland. But after the death of Von Schlieffen in 1913 the plan was changed, leaving Holland's neutrality intact. The German advance through Belgium in 1914 was significantly delayed by the exceptionally fierce Belgian resistance. Some German analysts had predicted that such a delay would cause Germany to face war on two fronts, which they were likely to lose, as indeed they did. They were not going to make this mistake again in 1940.

10   ELO Dossiers 627 and 571, daily/nightly operations reports, and Dossier 1003 Arrestantenregister.

Hijme at the time, and saddened him after the war,[11] when they found out what had happened to the children and the staff.

6.6   Camp Westerbork and the deportations to Auschwitz

When the number of (illegal) immigrants increased in 1938 and 1939, the Dutch government set up a number of temporary holding camps (such as Camp Reuver, which held the father of Kurt and Helga Gottschalk, Ch. 9.1). But they became difficult to manage and creating a purpose-built larger refugee camp near Apeldoorn was considered. That plan was cancelled following resistance from various sides, including the queen (who lived in Apeldoorn) and the national touring organization ANWB. It was then decided to build a camp near Hooghalen in the province of Drenthe. Refugee Camp Westerbork was opened in October 1939. By the time of the German invasion the camp held some 750 Jewish refugees. The camp was not a prison, but freedom of movement was limited: for each excursion the refugees had to ask permission of the Dutch commandant. There was a plan to evacuate the Jewish refugees in case of a German invasion, but it was doomed from conception, given the location of the camp in the far eastern part of the country. As anybody could have predicted, in the time it would take to move the refugees to the west, the German army would have overtaken them two times over. And that is what happened six months later.

Following the German invasion, the responsibility for the camp was transferred from the Interior Ministry to the Justice Department (now under German control, since the ministers had gone to London), with a new commandant, Jacob Schol, and stricter rules. Although the Germans left him in place during the first two years of occupation, they were clearly interested in the camp: Westerbork was a desolate place, far removed from everything else in the Netherlands, close to the German border and to a major railway line between the cities of Zwolle and Groningen. The decision to use Camp Westerbork as the last holding and collection camp from where the Jews (and Roma and Sinti) of the Netherlands could be efficiently deported to the East was probably taken before the end of 1941 (van Liempt, 2019). In early 1942, the Germans ordered the construction of 24 more barracks to accommodate an additional 5000 to 7000 people. Schol, who was denied additional resources to handle such large numbers, decided to install a form of limited self-government amongst the internees, with departments to handle the provision of food and health, a fire brigade, work, an internal police force (the OD, *Ordedienst*), and the like. Inevitably these departments were run by German

---

11   The Stoffels' own write-up from 1967 and the interview by Kerkvliet and Uitvlugt (1973).

Jews[12] who had been in Westerbork from its early days. When by mid-1942 the first Dutch Jews were arriving in large numbers, they discovered that all senior and influential jobs in the camp, including the most lethal one – registration and preparing the weekly or twice weekly transport list – were in the hands of these *"Alte Insassen"* ("old hands"). They spoke fluent German, knew their master's mindset from before coming to Holland, and therefore knew how best to interact with them. Not surprisingly, many of the *Alte Insassen* managed to survive the war by not being deported.[13] Dutch Jews who understood the system realized that in order to avoid or postpone deportation, they should get a job, if possible an *important* job, within that organization as soon as possible after registration in Westerbork, just as a job with the Joodse Raad of Amsterdam could arrange a – temporary – stay of deportation to Westerbork. Most of those who were put on the first transport following their arrival never had the time to make arrangements for themselves. Obviously, the staff of the orphanage and the older children were not particularly astute in these matters, to say the least, when they arrived in Westerbork on 18th March 1943 (Ch. 7.6).

On 1st July 1942, when they were ready to start the systematic removal of the Jews from the Netherlands, the Germans formally took over the camp and renamed it *Durggangslager* (transit camp). The first two German commandants, Erich Deppner and (from 1st September 1942) Joseph Dischner, were both brutal SS officers, whose personal behaviour created serious unrest amongst the prisoners. On 12th October Albert Gemmeker who was shrewder (and arguably more dangerous) than his two predecessors, became the new commandant of Camp Westerbork. He behaved ostensibly like a gentleman and did everything possible to maintain a "human" regime and to create the illusion that the future of the deportees would possibly be not as bad as feared. He made sure all possible aspects of normal life continued in the camp – healthcare (Abuys & Mulder, 2006), including dental services, workshops, schools, kindergarten, and so on. A small child with an illness which could not be treated in the camp's clinic was sent to a hospital in the city of Groningen. When she had recovered and returned to Westerbork, she was put on the train to Sobibor and killed three days later: *such was the cynicism of the Great Deception.* Jewish festive days were celebrated in the camp, and entertainment was arranged by the prisoners. Gemmeker liked to attend the cabaret staged by the prisoners (better called a "revue") which was of usually high quality given the many professional artists and musicians which passed through the camp.

---

12   The behaviour of some of these officials, such as the head of the OD Arthur Pisk, has been a longstanding controversial issue within the Jewish community.

13   Researchers at Westerbork discovered that the *Alte Insassen* managed to remove their own names from the card system which was used to put together the weekly transport lists.

He also personally attended the loading of the deportation trains and signalled the departure with a wave of the hand. He was also very clever in making sure that no paper trail existed to link him directly with what happened with the deportees after they left Westerbork. These actions, along with a fair degree of luck, allowed him to escape justice after the war (van Liempt, 2019).

On 3rd May 1942, all Jews in the Netherlands from age six were instructed to wear the yellow *jodenster* (Fig. 6.14) on their outer clothing when appearing in public. Like Decree 6/1941 introduced the year before, this was a significant decree. It emphasized the separation

Figure 6.14: The Jewish star, to be visibly worn at all times in public.

which the Germans wanted to create between Jewish and non-Jewish Dutchmen, or, in Nazi terminology, between the "Jews" and the "Dutch". It was part of another flood of anti-Jewish decrees, issued in rapid succession: Jews were not allowed to marry gentiles (25th March 1942), remove any furniture from their homes (26th March), have money in a bank account other than with Liro (12th May). A week later, Jews had to relinquish jewellery, silverware, even teaspoons, to Liro (21st May), they were not allowed to go fishing (29th May), or travel (5th June), or visit non-Jewish vegetable shops or partake in any sports activities (12th June). Organizing the capture of tens of thousands of Jews within a short period and sending them to Westerbork in time to ensure the deportations trains were full and the target number set by Berlin could be met by the commandant in Westerbork was arguably the most complex and sensitive part of the whole operation. It was done with exceptional efficiency.

On 26th June 1942, *SS-Hauptsturmführer* (Captain) Ferdinand aus der Fünten, a prominent executive at the *Zentralstelle* in Amsterdam (Ch. 10.4), informed the Joodse Raad that the deportations to "labour camps" in Germany (which included the annexed Polish territories) were imminent. The Joodse Raad obediently passed on the news through the only Jewish newspaper still allowed, and for good measure the chairmen (Asscher and Cohen) added a stiff warning that all Jews should strictly adhere to the regulations *"in the interest of everybody else".* The *Zentralstelle* had instructed each local (municipal) government to provide updated address lists of all Jews in their municipality; the vast majority obliged without protest. The lists for Leiden and neighbouring villages have been preserved (Kasteleyn, 2003).

The Joodse Raad was instructed to send call-up papers to all men between 16 and 40 to report for transport to Camp Westerbork. When not enough people showed up to meet the target numbers, Jews were picked up from the streets during a razzia in Amsterdam on 14th July, which was easy since they were wearing the yellow star, or from their homes, which was also easy because from 30th June all Jews were placed under curfew, in their own home, between 8 pm and 6 am. With only few exceptions, the Dutch police force faithfully executed the German orders to pick up people from their homes.

From 12th July, trains ran from Amsterdam to Hooghalen, from where they had to walk about 5 km to Camp Westerbork. Within a few days, the camp housed thousands of Jews. The Dutch National Railway Company (*Nederlandse Spoorwegen*, NS) duly sent invoices to the *Zentralstelle*: one-way Amsterdam to Hooghalen, *fl* 4.85 per person.[14] The Nazis were ready to start the actual deportations. On 15th July 1942, the first train left Westerbork for Auschwitz with 1135 persons. Six weeks later, by the end of August, fifteen trains had delivered 12,243 Jews from Holland to Auschwitz, where most deportees were killed upon arrival.

It was all done in an exceedingly clever way, to cause minimal disturbance, with cooperation by the Dutch police and the civil service and using the Joodse Raad to create a smooth process. The illusion that the deportees would go to labour camps was successfully maintained. Camp Westerbork was only lightly guarded, but only few inmates decided to escape. People who were still young and in good health did not give up hope that they would manage, even under difficult circumstances. As long as they had a glimmer of hope, they could not believe rumours that death was awaiting them. Therefore, the fear that not complying could mean being deported to Mauthausen, and certain death, was effectively suppressing notions of resisting the deportation. Nobody knew at the time that the people who boarded the train in Westerbork were effectively already dead (van der Boom, 2012). Nevertheless, some people *"knew"*, or at least felt instinctively, that they were in mortal danger (see the Epilogue).

There is extensive literature on Westerbork, mostly in Dutch. A "professional" account of life in Westerbork is found in the diaries of journalist Philip Mechanicus (1964), while the letters of Etty Hillesum (2002) and the book by Willy Lindwer (1990) have become landmark witness accounts. Paul Siegel (2001) provides a fascinating account of why, like almost all inmates, he was very hesitant to resist, or walk away

---

14   J. Houwink ten Cate, on Dutch television, 27th January 2015, calculated the total charge of the NS at almost 0.5 million guilders, approximately 2.5 million euros in 2015. The NS knew it was transporting Jews for a one-way journey. They apologized in 2005 and decided to make payments to victims or descendants in 2019.

from the camp, and how he finally, after many months in Westerbork, decided to escape after all. Paul (who eventually reached Palestine with Lodi Cohen, Ch. 9.7) was lucky: thanks to being protected (as a member of the Palestine Pioneers) he was given enough time to decide and execute his plan. Most inmates of Westerbork were put on a train too soon to do the same.

Most people could not believe that the Germans would deport the sick or the very young or very old to labour camps in Eastern Europe. Indeed, during the second half of 1942, with deportations to Auschwitz in full swing, the Jewish institutions: orphanages, hospitals, old age homes, mental hospitals, were mostly left alone. The fact that the German or Polish refugee children from the orphanage in Utrecht had already been removed to Westerbork by February 1942 must have been known to the staff in Leiden, but these were refugees, and Westerbork was a refugee camp. Surely the Germans would not treat the Dutch orphans in the same way, they thought, although the dark fate of the refugees had come very close to the orphanage in Leiden in March 1942 (van Zegveld, 1993, p. 168, based on his interviews of Geertje Gebert):

> *Friday evening, 6th March 1942, Shabbat evening. Around 9:30 pm the doorbell rings. The older children in the orphanage are alarmed. Ringing the doorbell [in wartime] on Shabbat did not forebode well. Geertje Gebert, a non-Jewish intern not bound by the Shabbat rules, went to the door with trepidation. It is not a German, but a Dutch policeman. He comes to take away Greta Goldenberg, the cute six-year-old German refugee girl. But she has gone to bed hours ago. And it is Shabbat. The policeman does not care, he is unrelenting. [...] The child must be woken up and is taken away by the policeman into the night.*

The arrest of Greta hit Geertje and the children who were still awake like a bombshell. Only years after the war, Geertje (then Mrs. Bekooy) found out that Greta was murdered in Sobibor on 5th March 1943.

The Germans allowed the Joodse Raad to issue "temporary exemptions" to being deported. If approved, the holder received a stamp in his or her *persoonsbewijs* called a *Sperre*, the German word for "embargo", or "stoppage". The stamp (Fig. 6.2) stated that the *"holder of the identity card is, until further notice, exempted from being sent to a labour camp"*, the German euphemism for deportation. It was issued to people who were doing *"essential work"*. The Joodse Raad submitted more than 32,000 requests for *Sperre* to be allocated, more than half of those to its own employees. The possibility of getting a *Sperre* became a major incentive for people to try and get a job, *any job*, at the Joodse Raad, which quickly became an inflated organization. The Joodse Raad even issued a 35-page booklet,[15] basically an organigram, explaining the huge structure of departments, sections, offices, and providing lists of (only the more senior) officials showing who was who and who was doing what. The booklet was issued on 15th March 1943, when almost half the total Jewish population of the country had already been deported and killed. In Leiden, all the permanent staff members had a *Sperre*, based on their position and function in the orphanage. But the protection of these jobs, and the temporary exemption they provided, was all an illusion, albeit an effective part of the deception. When the Nazis ran out of non-exempted victims to send to Westerbork and on to occupied Poland, they simply cancelled another batch of *Sperre* to make up the shortfall. By that time, it was too late for many to go into hiding. By September 1943, when more than 80,000 Jews had been deported to the East, the Joodse Raad became defunct and its last remaining members, including the two chairmen, were sent to Westerbork.

From 15th July 1942 mass deportations of Jews from the Netherlands took place in a shockingly high tempo. Instructions as to how many people should be deported were sent from the office of Adolf Eichmann at the RSHA[16] in Berlin to the SiPo/SD office of Wilhelm Harster and Willy Zöpf in The Hague, and then passed on to the German commandant at Westerbork.

In the beginning, trains left for Auschwitz twice a week. The efficiency of the logistics, both *before* and *after* Westerbork, was key to the whole operation, which was essentially organized backwards. Trains had to arrive at Auschwitz, and later Sobibor, on specified days or nights. If they arrived too late, or too early, the killing facilities were underutilized on one day, while on the other day too many trains would create chaos. Eichmann's office coordinated the required train schedules for the whole of occupied Europe such that the death camps could be operated without being disturbed or interrupted, like any large-scale cross-border industrial operation. Thus, the trains had to leave Westerbork on exactly specified dates. The train schedule had top priority throughout German-occupied Europe, even over troop and ammunitions transport, and the trains continued to run on time for the entire war period. Only in December 1942 and 1943 were the deportations stalled to give transport priority to soldiers on leave from the front for Christmas.

---

15   "Gids van den Joodschen Raad voor Amsterdam". Westerbork Memorial, G. Abuys, personal communication.

16   The *Reichssicherheitshauptamt* (Reich Main Security Office) was created by Himmler in September 1939 to combine all German police, intelligence and security forces under his own control. Being at the core of the SS state (Kogon, 1974), the RSHA was a huge bureaucratic organization which included Adolf Eichmann's *Referat IV B4*, which coordinated the logistics of the deportations across occupied Europe. See Stiftung Topographie des Terrors, 2018, for a comprehensive and richly documented description of the SS, Gestapo and the RSHA organization. For Wilhelm Zöpf: op. cit., p. 145.

The Nazi organization in Holland had to make sure that there were enough victims ready for transport in Westerbork. Jews were picked up from their homes, or the streets during razzias, and brought to temporary holding pens, such as the Hollandsche Schouwburg, the main *Umschlagplatz* in Amsterdam, which from time to time harboured a few hundred people. From there they were usually brought by tram to the Muiderpoort railway station, and then to Westerbork. If a shortage threatened in Westerbork of Jews who were *"transportfähig"*, that is *"available"* to be put on the list of the next transport to the East, the effort to round up people was increased, or people were put on the transport list who had been protected until that moment.

In the area of The Hague and Leiden, Franz Fischer (Fig. 10.11) was the prominent hands-on executor of this process. In Amsterdam, Aus der Fünten and Lages kept in touch with Gemmeker, and all three were on Eichmann's radar screen (van Liempt, 2019). Each of the major "compartments" of this final stage of the Holocaust: identifying and arresting all Jews in the country, collecting them in a transit camp and smoothly putting them on a train, the railway logistics inside the German Reich and coordinating the transports from so many countries, and finally the smooth running of the death camps, had to be organized efficiently, and they had to be geared to each other. This is the context for the change of destination of the trains from Westerbork, from Auschwitz to Sobibor (Ch. 7.6), in March 1943.

6.7   The staff in 1942

Early in 1942, all residents of the orphanage over a certain age (probably sixteen) had passport photos made. Several copies have survived through various photo albums, and because Mary de Raay preserved her copies in *onderduik* and when moving to Israel. For many, these are the last photographs we have. Nathan and Lies Italie were also photographed (Fig. 6.15). Compared to the photograph taken in his office just three to four years before, Nathan appears to have aged significantly. One can surmise that the stress from the increasing oppression and persecution of Jews, and the uncertainty about the future had taken its toll. It is also clear that during the second half of 1942, with deportations in full swing, the staff began to realize that the orphanage would not be safe after all.

The four women shown in Figure 6.16 were effectively part of the "permanent" staff. They were resident in the building, and they stood out, in more than one aspect. As opposed to many of the temporary staff, they were Jewish; they were responsible for the "parental" guardianship of the children, including physical, spiritual, and cultural-religious aspects. Like Nathan Italie, they were already there before 1929,

Figure 6.15: Nathan Italie and Lies Cohen, 1942.

Figure 6.16: From left to right: Mien Gobes, Rachel Bierschenk, Jet de Leeuw and Floortje Altenberg.

at the Stille Rijn home. They were still there in 1942 when the photographs were taken; and all four stayed with their children until the very end.

Mien Gobes (21st December 1899) had arrived in 1923. She was in charge of the small (school-going) children. She brought the children to school every morning and was a stern disciplinarian. Although the governors, by instructions to the director (or "father", as he was called between 1890 and 1919), had strictly banned corporal punishment, it did not stop Ms. Gobes from using her hands to discipline the children when required, as both Mimi Weiman and Piet de Vries remembered. With some of the older girls she had a more informal, friendly relationship, as seems to be suggested by surviving photographs.

Rachel Bierschenk (1st November 1898) had arrived in 1924. She was chief seam-stress, in charge of the sewing room. She also ran a club for the older girls who

Figure 6.17 : Esther Klein, 1942

Figure 6.18: Jacob Philipson at his desk, c. 1938.

attended secondary school. They could become a member by paying a small weekly subscription: one, two or three cents, depending on age and pocket money. She obviously enjoyed organizing outings with the girls (Fig. 5.12).

Jet de Leeuw (29th December 1888) was under-director and head housekeeper. She had a similar function in Het Apeldoornse Bos, a Jewish psychiatric institution, before she came to Leiden in 1925.

Floortje Altenberg (23rd April 1904) arrived on 7th February 1929 during the last months at Stille Rijn no. 4. She was nanny and seamstress.

Esther Klein (17th August 1909) arrived in Leiden, 14th September 1939. Her photograph (Fig. 6.17) is signed and dated *"1-9-42"*. She lived at Roodenburgerstraat 13, some 40 metres away from the orphanage. She taught Jewish religion and culture, including Hebrew, to the younger children. Since all children attended regular Dutch schools, such teaching had to be done after school hours when the children got home. Hans Kloosterman told us that the secondary school children (from age twelve) were taught by Director Italie himself. Hans considered him a good teacher: half a century later he could still read Hebrew (letter to L.P. Kasteleyn, 19th December 2000). Esther also stayed with the children until the end in March 1943.

Jacob Philipson (24th June 1903) (Fig. 6.18) was the *"administrateur"* of the orphanage, a modest title for a function which is crucial to the administrative "health" of an institution. He was responsible for the proper management of its finances, personnel issues and contracts, legal issues, etc. He lived with his wife, Jet Philipson-Simons, and his five children (Fig. 10.6) at Van der Waalsstraat 34, just 600 metres from the orphanage. He had an office, or at least a desk in the orphanage, on the ground floor of the right (north-western) wing. He was also warned by Stoffels about the growing dangers, and he was more receptive to the idea to

Figure 6.19: Mr. van Ee, the janitor, in front of the main entrance, c. 1938.

prepare for *onderduik*. But he did not abandon the orphanage and waited to the last moment before taking action (Ch. 7.12).

Barend de Vries (20th June 1922) was a salesman, but also worked as physical education teacher in the orphanage. He moved in with the orphanage on 7th December 1942, possibly because he hoped to be safe there, and stayed to the end. Very little is known about him.

Geertje Gebert (Emmen, 7th July 1918), who answered the door when the police came for Greta Goldenberg (above), was a non-Jewish resident *dienstbode* for a salary of 27.50 guilders a month plus board and lodging. She occupied one of the two rooms for *dienstbodes* in the attic of the building (Z in Fig. 3.5), from September 1939 until 1st April 1942, when she was dismissed because non-Jewish staff was no longer allowed to work in Jewish institutions. Her tasks were taken over by Betsy Wolff (who was seventeen at the time) and Corry Frenkel (almost eighteen). Geertje had a collection of photographs from her time in the orphanage, which were passed on via W.F. van Zegveld. One of her photographs is included in this book (Fig. 9.16). Geertje married Dirk Bekooy on 6th May 1942. Jopie Beem, Hans Kloosterman, and a third – unidentified – boy attended their marriage reception, Jopie gave her a wooden serving tray, which he had made as a carpentry "masterpiece" at the technical school. Jopie was fifteen at that time. The tray is on display in the recently established Holocaust Museum in Amsterdam. Hans said that Geertje was concerned about the safety of the boys, showing up in a public place, and that he assured her they had carefully hidden their star when entering the building.

Van Zegveld (1993) lists a total number of 116 non-permanent domestic staff, most of them *"dienstbodes"*, between 1890 and 1943, broken down into 54 Jewish, 42 Protestant, 13 Catholic, and 7 of unknown denomination. More than 35 of these girls and women came from Germany (ibidem). The number of *dienstbodes* at any one time varied from none to eight, but most of the time there were five or six. Some worked in the orphanage for only short periods, others for many years, such as the Protestant Louisa Johanna Helmens (or Helmans, 2nd February 1880), who was there from 1910 to 1918.

When Mr. F. van Ee, the non-Jewish janitor (Fig. 6.19), was dismissed, Piet de Vries took over maintaining the fire of the central heating system. His job as *stoker* (fireman) was duly noted on his Joodse Raad card.

6.8   Late arrivals, late departures

At least seventeen children were placed in the Leiden orphanage *after* the deportations from Westerbork to Auschwitz had begun on 15th July 1942. Presumably, the idea that Jewish institutions like orphanages and hospitals would be safe from deportation will have played a role in many cases.

Etty Heerma van Voss arrived on 28th August 1942. Etty was born on 16th June 1930 in Amsterdam, the daughter of Theodora Noach (Krefeld, Germany, 9th October 1904-Sobibor, 16th April 1943). Her mother legalized her daughter as Etty Noach on 8th July 1931. She was adopted in 1932 by the family Heerma van Voss in Haarlem. They had no children of their own, but on 22nd April 1933 a daughter, Ingeborg, was born (Fig. 6.20). Around this time, Theodora married Samuel Vischschraper (Amsterdam, 30th March 1911-Sobibor, 9th July 1943), but there is no indication that he might have been Etty's biological father. On 24th March 1938 Etty's family name was officially

Figure 6.20: The family Heerma van Voss in Haarlem, c. 1933. From left: Irmi, Inge, Cas, and Etty. Photo courtesy family Heerma van Voss.

Figure 6.21: Etty during her time in Leiden, August 1942 to March 1943.

changed into Heerma van Voss.[17] During the first year of occupation the family must have become aware of the ever-worsening situation of the Dutch Jews. Etty's foster-sister Inge remembers that her mother Irmi took both Etty and Inge to Amsterdam to see Etty's mother:

[I]n Amsterdam, Etty talked to her mother alone, and then Mama talked to her. Mama told me later that she had asked Theodora to say – if asked by the authorities – that Etty's biological father was not Jewish. But I don't know if she was ever asked by anybody, and neither did I ever know who Etty's father really was. (Inge Heerma van Voss to L.P. Kasteleyn, also in Jonkers-Stroink & de Bruin, 2016)

Pauline Jonkers declared (op. cit., p. 77) that Irmi (who was her aunt) had brought a notary statement with her to Amsterdam, to the effect that Etty's biological father had been a (non-Jewish) Norwegian seaman, but Theodora refused to sign it. Obviously, the family was aware that if Etty was registered as "half-Jew", and had been adopted into a non-Jewish family, the risk of being deported would be significantly reduced. Inge: *"Then came the time Etty was denied entry into her school [1st September 1941], and she had to go to a Jewish school. Mama tried to find an onderduik address, but it was difficult, and she was advised to bring her to the Jewish orphanage, where she would be safe."* Etty entered the Leiden orphanage on 28th August 1942 (Fig. 6.21). Half a year later (Ch. 7.11) she was brought to Westerbork with all the other residents.

Benjamin and Louis Bobbe arrived on 7th November 1942. Benjamin was three, Louis was just one year and eight months old. He was the youngest of the orphanage children, at just two years, to be killed in Sobibor. No photograph of the boys has been found, hopefully someday one may come to light. Gusta Wahrhafig entered the orphanage on 12th January 1943, two years old. She must have left again soon, certainly[18] before 17th March. It is not known how and by whom she was taken out. Maurits and Simon Hakker arrived on 15th February 1943, just weeks before the *ontruiming* of the orphanage.

---

17   This required approval by Queen Wilhelmina; apart from notary fees, the government charged the family 250 guilders for legal fees, a small fortune in those days.

18   Based on reports and letters sent to the Stoffels after 17th March 1943.

There were also late departures, such as Louise (Lies) van Straten, fourteen years old at the time, who lived unofficially (de facto as *onderduiker*) in the orphanage, probably from January 1943. She was taken out by her uncle on 16th March 1943, the day before the *ontruiming*. That can hardly be a coincidence. They may have been warned about the impending deportation, possibly by the Stoffels or one of their associates.

Esther (Els) van Santen (Fig. 6.22) most likely made her own decision: she had lived in the orphanage for sixteen years when she left in March 1939, before the war. But she returned in September 1942, when she was 22. She left again on 3rd February 1943 and survived the war in

Figure 6.22: Esther van Santen, 1942

onderduik. She was apparently warned that the orphanage would not be left alone by the Germans by one of the governors who tutored in French[19] and advised her to go into hiding. The early arrest and deportation of her brothers Karel and Philip and their deaths in Mauthausen (Ch. 8.1) may also have influenced her decision, but she was not keen to talk about the war.

Salomon and Bernard Meijers (Fig. 6.23) were brought to the Leiden orphanage probably between August and November 1942. The choice for Leiden, and not The Hague, where they lived, was probably determined by age: Bernard was only two years old in November 1942 and Leiden was the only place willing to accept him (just as in the case of Aron Wolff, Ch. 9.3). They were not officially registered in Leiden, which made them *onderduikers*, but their names appear on an internal accountant report[20] for the orphanage because the money spent on them had to be accounted for.

The parents, Samuel Meijers and Hinde Meijers-Ringer, began to doubt whether they would be safe in Leiden, and – as we now know – rightfully so. Herman Ringer, Hinde's brother, had befriended Giel Lacroix during the mobilization period of the army. Giel lived in Beek in the southern province of Limburg with his wife and daughter, and he correctly perceived the mortal danger for the Dutch Jews. He offered Herman a hiding place at his home in Beek, which was accepted. Later, Herman in turn convinced his sister Hinde and her family to go into hiding, and the Lacroix family provided *onderduik* addresses in Beek and three other villages

---

19 Information provided by Mr. F. Wolters, 2019.
20 A copy is included in the dossier for the brothers Meijers.

Figure 6.23: Salomon and Bernard Meijers, probably c. 1942. Photo courtesy Paula and Albert Ringer.

in Limburg. The *onderduik* history of Herman Ringer and the family Meijers, as well as many others in Limburg, has been documented by van Rens (1994, 2013).

The two boys were taken out of the orphanage on 13th January 1943 and taken to an *onderduik* address in Limburg (van Rens, 2013). But the fact that they were hiding in Limburg was inadvertently revealed to an acquaintance of the family, who then betrayed them. They were arrested and taken to Westerbork on 18th March 1944, where they were put in *Strafbarak* 67, which held people who were caught in *onderduik* or who had been arrested for other violations of the German "legislation". As was usual with such "penal" cases, all four family members were put on the first available transport to Auschwitz on 23rd March 1944, where both boys (seven and four) perished with their mother on or around 26th March 1944. Their father, Samuel M. Meijers, miraculously survived Auschwitz-Birkenau, Monowitz, and Gleiwitz-I, then went via Kosel to Blechhammer, where he was liberated on or around 18th January 1945. He returned to Holland.

By the end of 1942 living conditions for the Dutch Jews – that is, those who had not already been deported to Auschwitz – had become hopelessly difficult. At the beginning of 1943, it would get even worse. In the orphanage, it seems that people were just waiting for what was to come.

References

Aalders, G., 1999; *"Roof. De ontvreemding van joods bezit tijdens de Tweede Wereldoorlog"*. Den Haag, SFU Uitgevers, BSN 9012087473. An English translation was published in 2005: *"Nazi looting: The plunder of Dutch Jewry during the Second World War"*. Bloomsbury, ISBN 9781859737279. [The addition of the word "Nazi" in the translation is misleading, since the more shocking aspect of this book is the complicity of "ordinary" Dutchmen, who were not necessarily "Nazis".]

Abuys, G. & D. Mulder, 2006; *"Genezen verklaard voor … : Een ziekenhuis in kamp Westerbork, 1939-1945"*. Hooghalen Herinneringscentrum, Kamp Westerbork, ISBN 9789023242475.

Boom, B. van der, 2012; *"Wij weten niets van hun lot"*. Amsterdam, Boom, ISBN 9789461054777. [A study of contemporary sources to determine what people knew at the time about the fate of the Jewish deportees.]

Boomgaard, Petra van den, 2019; *"Voor de nazi's geen Jood"*. Hilversum, Verbum, ISBN 9789493028043. [With English summary at the back; *"How more than 2500 Jews were able to escape deportation by evading racial regulations"*; certainly the most comprehensive study to date.]

Hillesum, Etty, 2002; *"Etty: The letters and diaries of Etty Hillesum, 1941-1943"*. Ed. by Klaas A.D. Smelik. Grand Rapids, Wm. B. Eerdmans Publishing Company, ISBN 0802839592. Originally published in Dutch in 1986 by Uitgeverij Balans, Amsterdam.

Jonkers-Stroink, P. & A. de Bruin, 2016; *"Familiekroniek Heerma van Voss. Deel 7b"*. Private publication.

Kasteleyn, L.P., 2003; *"Vervolging en bescherming, joden in Leiden 1933-1945"*. Leiden, Museum de Lakenhal.

Kerkvliet, G. & M. Uitvlugt, 1973; *"Een pot picalilly voor Westerbork. Journalistiek verslag over de vernietiging van het joodse weeshuis in Leiden"*. Den Haag, Q-Producties. Author's collection. [The original stencilled report, containing verbatim quotes from interviews with the Stoffels, Geertje Gebert, and Piet de Vries.] See also Kerkvliet & Uitvlugt, 1974.

Keulen-Woudstra, Alice B. van (ed.), 2000; *"Mauthausen, 1938-1998"*. Utrecht, Van Gruting, ISBN 9075879067/9789075879063.

Kogon, Eugen, 1974; *"Der SS-Staat. Das System der deutschen Konzentrationslager"*. München, Kindler Verlag. [Kogon was a Christian opponent to the Nazi regime who survived 6 years in Buchenwald.]. Dutch edition: Kogon, Eugen, 1976; *"De SS-staat"*. Amsterdam, Amsterdam Boek, no ISBN. English and Dutch translations exist in several editions.

Liempt, A. van, 2019; *"Gemmeker. Commandant van Kamp Westerbork"*. Amsterdam, Balans, ISBN 9789460039782 (hardcover)/9789460039799 (ebook).

Ligtenberg, L., 2017; *"Mij krijgen ze niet levend. De zelfmoorden van mei 1940"*. Amsterdam, Balans, ISBN 9789460038457. [About the sharp increase in suicides immediately upon the German invasion in May 1940.]

Lindwer, Willy, 1990; *"Kamp van hoop en wanhoop. Getuigen van Westerbork, 1939-1945"* [Camp of hope and despair: Witness account from Westerbork]. Amsterdam, Balans, ISBN 9050180981.

Mechanicus, Philip, 1964; *"In dépôt: dagboek uit Westerbork"* [In depot: Diary from Westerbork]. Amsterdam, Polak & van Gennep.

Michman, Jozeph, 1987; *"Met voorbedachten rade. Ideologie en uitvoering van de Endlösung der Judenfrage"*. Amsterdam, Meulenhoff, ISBN 9029098473. [An analysis of the ideology which gave rise to the Holocaust and how it developed from the moment Hitler declared his intention to remove all Jews from Europe.]

Presser, J., 1965; *"Ondergang. De vervolging en verdelging van het Nederlandse Jodendom, 1940-1945"*. 's-Gravenhage, Staatsuitgeverij/Martinus Nijhoff. [The entire Dutch text is available online (with search facility) at http://www.dbnl.org. Although written more than half a century ago, the book is still very readable and impressive today.] An English translation was published by E.P. Dutton & Co. in 1969 (ASIN B000LD8D7S), and again in 1988 under the title *"Ashes in the wind: The destruction of Dutch Jewry"* by Wayne State University Press; re-issued in 2010, ISBN 9780285638136.

Rens, H.A.V. van, 2013; *"Vervolgd in Limburg. Joden en Sinti in Nederlands-Limburg tijdens de Tweede Wereldoorlog"*. Maaslandse Monografieen 76. Hilversum, Verloren, ISBN 9789087043537.

Rens, H.A.V. van, et al., 1994; *"Een voetnoot bij de wereldgeschiedenis. Beek tijdens de Tweede Wereldoorlog"*. Wat Baek os bud #17. Beek, Stichting Herdenking Oorlogsslachtoffers. [For correct dates, see Rens, 2013.]

Schram, Laurence, 2018; *"Dossin. Wachtkamer van Auschwitz"*. Tielt, Lannoo, ISBN 9782390250395. [One of the first comprehensive studies about the transit camp Kazerne Dossin in Mechelen (Belgium), through which 25,484 Jews and 352 Roma and Sinti were deported to Auschwitz, including Alexander Lipschitz and his family. Only 1222 survived the deportations.]

Schütz, Raymund, 2016; *"Kille mist"*. PhD thesis, Free University of Amsterdam. [This study, sponsored by the Dutch Notary Professional Association, brought to light, more than 70 years after the war, the dismal role of Dutch public notaries in registering new ownership of stolen Jewish assets (such as real estate), while hiding the original Jewish ownership.]

Siegel, Paul, 2001; *"Locomotieven trekken wagons, 1933-1945"*. Utrecht, Van Gruting, ISBN 9789075879100. The English translation (Siegel, Paul, 2005; *"Engines pull wagons: A personal story"*. Trans. by Gilda Gordon. Amsterdam, Olive Press, ISBN 9077787011/9789077787014) was not used in preparing this book.

Stiftung Topographie des Terrors (represented by Nachama, Andreas), 2018; *"Topography of terror: Gestapo, SS and Reich Security Main Office on Wilhelm- and Prinz-Albrecht-Straße: A documentation"*. 9th revised edition. Berlin, ISBN 9783941772175.

Stoffels, H. & E. Stoffels-van Brussel, 1967; *"Unpublished"*, 22nd November. [A list of (some of) their activities in support of Jewish citizens of Leiden from February 1942, such as arranging *onderduik* addresses, false papers, etc. The list was written at the request of Elchanan Italie, in support of a proposal by him and the family Philipson-Armon to award the Yad Vashem medal to Stoffels and his wife.

Stoop, P., 1988; *"De geheime rapporten van H.J. Noordewier. Berlijn, 1933-1935"*. Amsterdam, Sijthof, ISBN 9021839954.

Vries, Hans de, 2000; *"Sie starben wie Fliegen im Herbst"*. In: Keulen-Woudstra, 2000, pp. 7-18.

Vries, Hans de, 2011; *"Mauthausen. Een geval apart"*. https://pure.knaw.nl/ws/files/6338408/2011 and search for Vries_MauthausenEenGevalApart.pdf. [In Dutch, summarizing the special significance of Mauthausen in Dutch wartime history.]

Vries, H. de, B. Perz, L. Jacobs, A. Baumgartner & D. Wingeate Pike (eds), 2000; *"Mauthausen, 1938-1998"*. Utracht, Van Gruting, ISBN 9075879067 and 9789075879063.

Zegveld, W.F. van, 1993; *"Joods Wees- en Doorgangshuis Leiden, bewoners 1890-1951"*. Originally in: *"De Joden van Leiden"*. Unpublished; 4 volumes. [Several copies were made, available (i.a.) at Erfgoed Leiden (ELO) and the Joods Historisch Museum, Amsterdam. The results of his painstaking research have served as a basis for subsequent investigations. Note that his report is an important source of information on children and staff in the Leiden orphanage who are not included in this book because they had left before the move to the new building in 1929, as well as Jewish citizens of the Leiden region who were not connected to the orphanage.]

7   1943 to 1944: Liquidation

Abstract

Between the end of January and the end of March 1943 Jewish social institutions were liquidated, including all eight orphanages. On 17th March 1943, 50 children and 9 staff members were arrested in the Leiden orphanage by the Leiden police and sent to Camp Westerbork. Just five days after arrival, all 9 staff members and 25 children were put on a train to Sobibor, where they were killed. The remaining children, together with many others who had left the orphanage before 17th March 1943, were deported to Sobibor, Auschwitz, or other camps in the East. Hans Kloosterman and Piet de Vries did not receive their mixed-blood certificate in time, despite the efforts of their neighbour, Stoffels, but he managed to get them released from Westerbork.

Keywords: Holocaust, Shoah, deportations Belgium, Westerbork, Sobibor, Auschwitz, Bergen-Belsen, Liebenau, Apeldoornse Bos, Barneveld

The facts as presented in this chapter are primarily based on the witness accounts of Hijme and Emilie Stoffels, Betsy Wolff, Piet de Vries, and Hans Kloosterman. Extensive interviews with Stoffels and Betsy Wolff were recorded by Kerkvliet and Uitvlugt (1973) and reported, often verbatim, in their original (stencilled) report of 1973, a copy of which was found in the private archive of the Stoffels.[1] This archive also contains letters and postcards from Westerbork. Interviews with, and letters from, Hans and Piet have been recorded by L.P. Kasteleyn. Additional documentary evidence, such as cards from the *Joodse Raad Cartotheek* and dossiers in the War Archives of the Netherlands Red Cross, has also been included in the study. Although there are small differences between the stories, they are very consistent as to the main facts. No further reference will be made to each of these sources unless relevant.

---

1   Copies are also present in the libraries of the Jewish Museum Amsterdam and the Jewish congregation in Leiden.

Focke, Jaap W., *Machseh Lajesoumim: A Jewish Orphanage in the City of Leiden, 1890-1943*.
Taylor & Francis Group, 2021
DOI: 10.5117/9789463726955_CH07

7.1   The situation in late 1942

During the second half of 1942, some 38,000 Jews were transported from the Netherlands to Auschwitz, including some 20,000 people from the labour camps and their families. This may have contributed to the misguided belief that the deportees were going to labour camps in the East. Many people could still not believe that the Germans were going to deport the sick or the elderly to labour camps, or – for that matter – orphans, and some parents decided, even as late as November 1942, to lodge their children in one of these Jewish institutions, where they thought they would be better protected, as mentioned in Chapter 6.8. Other people, adults, took refuge in these institutions themselves, by assuming a staff position. Such positions were available because from January 1942 non-Jewish staff were no longer allowed to work in Jewish institutions. Staff vacancies in Jewish institutions also increased because Jewish patients had to be removed from non-Jewish institutions. The number of patients in Het Apeldoornse Bos, a Jewish psychiatric institution, grew from c. 750 in 1939 to more than 1000 in January 1943. Thus, within a year, the Nazis had managed to effectively separate the Jewish from the non-Jewish people in Holland. At the same time, they were systematically being dispossessed, robbed of all their possessions and assets, before being deported to Eastern Europe.

During this period (the second half of 1942) the Jewish social institutions were not included in the deportations, but they were stripped of their independence, as well as their finances, when the Germans forced them all to merge into a single unit under the Joodse Raad of Amsterdam, the *Joodse Vereniging voor Verpleging en Verzorging* (Jewish Association for Nursing and Care), colloquially called the J4V. The official letters of the orphanage were duly adapted by typing the name of the J4V above the letter head.

Of the eight Jewish orphanages (Table 1.1), the one in Utrecht had taken in more refugee children from Germany and the East than the others. By early 1938 there were eight, then eleven refugee children in Utrecht (Crone, 2005). After *Kristallnacht* the numbers increased, and in November 1938 the summer holiday villa which the orphanage had in nearby Den Dolder was used to house 56 refugee children for whom there was no place in Utrecht itself. In October 1939, the building in Den Dolder was requisitioned by the Dutch army and had to be relinquished. The children were dispersed, while some 28 refugees remained in Utrecht.

As early as 12th February 1942, a full year before the destruction of the other Jewish institutions, 23 refugee children from Utrecht were deported to Camp Westerbork (ibid.), which at that time was officially still a "central refugee camp" with a Dutch commandant. On 15th October 1942 the orphanage in Utrecht was shut down altogether, by order of the *Zentralstelle*, and approximately 30 children who were still there and the resident staff were transferred to temporary buildings in Amsterdam. The director, B.S. Themans, who, like Nathan Italie in Leiden, had lived in the orphanage with his wife and two small children, considered to let the children go into hiding. But when it transpired that no more than ten *onderduik* places could be found[2], he preferred to keep them all together and move to Amsterdam as ordered.

The closure of the orphanage in Utrecht, in the context of all the other anti-Jewish measures, probably had an impact on the staff in Leiden, but they managed to keep their anxiety hidden from the children. For the younger children the relatively undisturbed way of life continued as much as possible. Even the older children, such as Betsy Wolff, Hans Kloosterman and Piet de Vries, were relatively unconcerned. This may have been partly appearance, because all three were willing to allow Stoffels, with the approval of Director Italie, to start a "mixed blood" procedure on their behalf at the Civil Registry to prevent their deportation (Chs. 7.7 and 9.2).

Children who were approaching the age of eighteen or those who had finished school and had found a job were supposed to leave the orphanage and move on. But from 7th November 1941 Jews were not allowed to change residence without a special permit. Such was the case with Sally Montezinos, who had a job, and who would become eighteen on 6th May 1942.

7.2 Sally Montezinos becomes "an old hand" in the orphanage

Sally (Fig. 7.1, in 1942) was ten years old in 1934 when an assembly photograph (Fig. 5.4) was taken. He completed elementary education in 1935 or 1936, and the ULO in 1940 when he was sixteen years old. After the ULO, he needed a job, preferably with further education. The management of the orphanage considered vocational and apprentice training as appropriate further development for most of the children. Only very rarely (e.g. Lodi Cohen, Ch. 9.6) did they support a pupil to attend a higher level secondary school (HBS or grammar school), which prepared for further higher technical or academic education. Accordingly, they found him a job, probably in autumn 1940, in the shop of Mr. Brussé, who was making horse saddles and other leather products, at Middelweg 21 in Leiden. Mr. Brussé's son,

---

2 Although finding *onderduik* addresses required having (very) reliable contacts and effective outside help, such as provided by Stoffels, to secure funds, ration stamps and food, this is a surprisingly low number. Help was also available in Utrecht and there were (student) resistance groups in Amsterdam as well as in Utrecht at that time, engaged with finding hiding addresses for children. Possibly Themans was not aware of that at the time.

Figure 7.1: Sally Montezinos, 1942, when he was eighteen.

Figure 7.2: Mr. L. Brussé Jr. (left) in front of his sail-making shop at Middelweg 21, where Sally worked for Mr. Brussé's father, 2007. Private collection.

Loek, was eleven at the time, and still worked in the same shop, making sails on order when I met him in 2007 (Fig. 7.2). He remembers[3] Sally very well. His father accepted Sally as an apprentice and assistant because he liked him at first sight. Sally *"was always a merry person to have around, always laughing"*. Indeed, Sally is laughing on all the photographs which survived. Sometimes he stayed for dinner, which was, of course, not kosher and, strictly speaking, not allowed. One evening in early December 1941[4] when the family celebrated the Dutch children's festival of *Sinterklaas* Sally acted as *Zwarte Piet* (Black Peter) with a black mask and a red carpet around his shoulders.

Sally did not want to go into hiding. He had arrived in the orphanage, then still in the ramshackle building on the Nieuwe Rijn, in December 1926 as a two-and-a-half-year-old toddler (Ch. 2.3), and he witnessed the move to the new building in 1929. It was his home; they were effectively his family. He was never interested in moving to the Sephardic orphanage in Amsterdam when he was old enough to be admitted, or to the orphanage in The Hague where his other siblings lived.

German horse-riding officers liked Brussé's craftsmanship and often came to the workshop (Fig. 7.2) to place or inspect orders. They noticed Sally, wearing the yellow star, working there. Some of them warned him: *"Disappear, go into hiding, now that you still can do it."* But Sally did not want to consider it. *"If we have to go, I'll go as well,"* he said to the Brussé family.

3   Interview note, 21st September 2007; Mr. Brussé's two sisters were interviewed in 2008.
4   Possibly 194., Mr. Brussé Jr. was not certain.

7.3   January 1943: Jewish institutions are not safe at all

On the last day of the year 1942 the Germans raided the Jewish *Ramaer* psychiatric hospital in The Hague, arresting Jews who were impersonating patients. They were not really in *onderduik* because they were not hiding their presence in the clinic, or the fact that they were Jewish: they hoped that *as patients* they would be safe from deportation.[5] But the idea that the Germans would leave the institutions alone was nothing more than wishful thinking.

Three weeks later, during the night of Thursday/Friday, 21st/22nd January 1943, all the patients (possibly[6] more than 1000) of Het Apeldoornse Bos, a Jewish psychiatric institution, were taken from their beds, thrown into trucks, some unclothed and bound to a mattress, others in straitjackets, and delivered to the Apeldoorn railway station, together with some 50 staff who had decided not to go into hiding. Early in the morning of Friday, 22nd January, the train left Apeldoorn and brought them straight to Auschwitz, where everybody on board was killed upon arrival. Apparently, Eichmann himself had arranged this special train for the occasion. It was arguably one of the most brutal and gruesome liquidations of a Jewish institution in Holland during the war (de Jong, 1969-1994, vol. 6, pp. 319-326). Aus der Fünten, one of the prominent Jew hunters in the German administration, had come down to Apeldoorn in person. So had Gemmeker, the commandant of Camp Westerbork, who claimed he had no idea about the fate of the deportees (Ch. 10.4).

Among the staff who remained with their patients was Marietje de Vries, Piet's sister. After leaving the girls' orphanage in Amsterdam, she moved to Het Apeldoornse Bos as an apprentice nurse on 11th November 1941 (Fig. 7.3). She wrote letters to Piet in Leiden, and the last two of her letters have been preserved.[7] In her letter of 3rd January 1943, she writes: *"What is the situation with your star? Did you hear anything? They are working hard on my [star]. Were you told, like I was, to send the birth certificates of father's parents?"* Like Piet, she was waiting for a decision after submitting a "change request" to the *Entscheidungsstelle*, which supervised the Dutch Civil Registry in these matters. Although both had two non-Jewish grandparents via their father (Wouter de Vries), they had been classified by the Civil Registry who handled the "VO 41/6" registration exercise for the Germans as J2: *"unsafe half-Jewish"* (van den Boomgaard, 2019. See also story on Betsy Wolff, Ch. 9.2). To escape deportation, they had to be reclassified as G1, essentially *"half-Aryan"*.

---

5   Research by C. Glaudemans, 2019. The clinic was liquidated on 18th/19th February 1943.
6   A list of patients who were there by end 1942 has only recently come to light; Trouw 21st January 2013, see also the Joods Monument. But there is no reliable list (yet) of names for those deported on 22nd January 1943.
7   Courtesy M. de Vries, Piet's daughter, personal communication, 2014.

Figure 7.3: Marietje de Vries, Piet's sister. Nurse in Het Apeldoornse Bos, the Jewish psychiatric institution, 1942. Courtesy Marianne de Vries.

Stoffels was pushing the change request on behalf of Piet, as described in the next chapter. Marie's wording *"they are working hard"* suggests that she also had someone working on it on her behalf. The fact that Stoffels only narrowly succeeded in getting the G1 approval for Piet (he was already in Westerbork) demonstrates how important it was that someone was following up on the procedures, chasing the authorities, and banging on doors. The tragedy is that the G1 approval did arrive for Marietje in March 1943, two months after she was killed in Auschwitz. In some cases (ibidem) deportation could have been prevented if the registry had passed on a positive decision by the German authorities more promptly. This is probably not the case for Marietje, because the decision for Piet, being chased by Stoffels, also arrived only in March.

Marietje was on a night shift Wednesday/Thursday, 20th/21st January, when she wrote her last letter to Piet:

It is now midnight. We have night watch, however, under abnormal circumstances. You may have heard already what is going to happen to us, and if not, you will surely understand. So, we have not been safe here either, [...] but we will keep up our hopes that it will someday change again for the better. You may hear from us now and then from Westerbork. Don't be too concerned. We are young and capable of enduring [this], and until now we have been lucky. So, we have a sound basis [for survival] and when this is all over, we will start a new life again. [...] Give my regards to Mr. & Mrs. [Italie] and the staff. [...] I send you my greetings and kisses, and wish you all the best, your sister, Marietje. Please write to Mother as often as you can, because I cannot do it anymore, and try to comfort her. Bye.

The day she wrote the letter (Wednesday, 20th), members of the OD (*Ordedienst*, the Jewish auxiliary police in Westerbork) had arrived to "assist" with moving the patients. Their arrival made it clear to all the staff that deportation was imminent. They had arrived too early by mistake; the Germans arrived only the next day (Thursday, 21st) and the deportation started that evening. She takes it for granted that Piet (and thus everybody else in the orphanage old enough to be aware) realized she was talking about deportation, and confirms that she, like so many others, had originally assumed that the mental institute would be safe. She thinks they will first be brought to Westerbork and talks about a better future after the war. If she had heard rumours about death camps in the East,

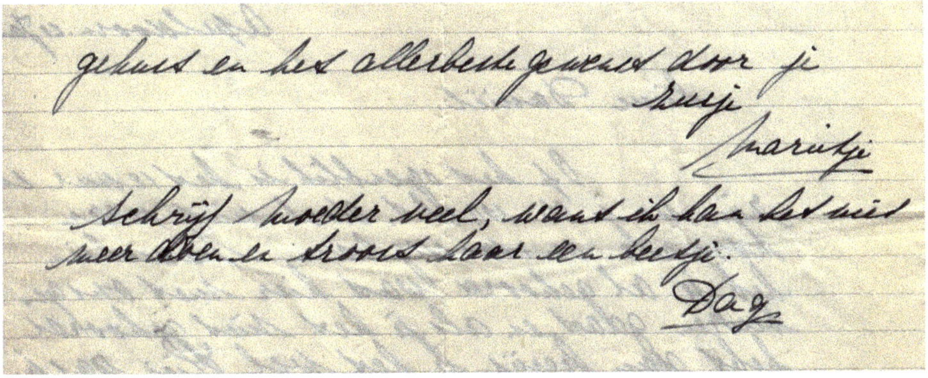

gekust en het allerbeste gewenst door je
Zusje
Marietje

Schrijf moeder veel, want ik kan het niet
meer doen en troost haar een beetje.
Dag

Figure 7.4: Closing sentences of Marietje's last letter to her brother Piet de Vries, 20th/21st January 1943. Courtesy Marianne de Vries, 2015.

she would not have believed it. At the same time, the closing sentences (Fig. 7.4) of her letter have a terrible aura of finality. *"Dag"* is about the shortest possible way to say *goodbye* in Dutch. Nowhere in the letters does she even mention the possibility to leave her patients and go into hiding, and she went along with them to Auschwitz. Piet had the photograph of Marietje (Fig. 7.3) in his living room in Hilversum after the war. Both letters have been included in Piet's dossier, courtesy of his daughter.

Het Apeldoornse Bos was not the only Jewish institution which was liquidated in the first weeks of 1943: in rapid succession Jewish hospitals and old-age homes, were *leeggehaald, "forcefully emptied"*, the people brought to Westerbork, where most of them were put on the first planned deportation train. Two weeks after the liquidation of Het Apeldoornse Bos, the Nazis began to deal with the orphanages:

- 10th February: All four Jewish orphanages in Amsterdam were liquidated and the children brought to Westerbork to await deportation. Probably some 220 children (including the children who were brought to Amsterdam when the Germans closed the orphanage in Utrecht in October 1942) were taken away that day.
- 25th February: Nathan Italie must have realized that the days for his orphanage were numbered. The evening of 25th February Nathan and Lies went to The Hague to say goodbye to Nathan's brother Gabriel, who expected to be evicted from The Hague and be sent to Barneveld (see below) any day, based on a "visit" by the German police who were interested in his house and his furniture (Italie, 2009).
- 26th February: The Jewish orphanage in Rotterdam was *ontruimd*, the euphemism for "liquidated". Children and staff were brought to Westerbork, together with the people taken out of the Jewish Hospital and Old Age Home

in Rotterdam. In total some 260 children, sick and old people, and staff. Most of them were deported on the first planned train to Sobibor on 2nd March.

– 1st March: The remaining 236 patients of the *Joodsche Invalide*, the Jewish Hospital in Amsterdam, were violently[8] taken out of their famous[9] institution and deported.

– 5th March: In the evening and during the night, the Leiden police arrested 25 Jews and handed them over to the SiPo in The Hague, Franz Fischer's office, from where the order for the arrests had come as recorded in the Leiden police archives (Kasteleyn, 2003). The SiPo itself arrested eight others in the Elizabeth Hospital in Leiden. Among those lifted from their bed that night was Donald de Marcas (Fig. 6.10). The following morning, Donald and his parents were delivered by truck to the Hollands Spoor railway station in The Hague, to board a train to Westerbork. Donald's father managed to get a temporary reprieve from Fischer himself. They decided to go into hiding, Stoffels arranged new identities for them ("van den Heuvel" and "Heskes") and new pbs (van Wijk, 1946).

– 6th March: The Jewish orphanage in The Hague was liquidated, also in a brutal and violent manner.[10] Van Creveld (2004) lists 44 children and seven staff taken to Westerbork. In total 51 people, of which 42 were killed a few days later. Of the other nine, only two girls survived the war.

Any remaining illusion that the Germans would not deport orphans, the old, sick or mentally ill to "labour camps" in the East, indeed the very idea that such "labour camps" even existed, should have been shattered upon the liquidation of Het Apeldoornse Bos and the other institutions, hospitals and orphanages. The news of the liquidations became known quickly in the other institutions, such as the orphanage in Leiden. Although Jews were not allowed to use the telephone from June to July 1942, there were other means of communication, via non-Jewish friends such as Stoffels, and by letters, such as those sent by Marietje de Vries. Everybody in Holland, Jewish or not Jewish, realized or should have realized that nothing good was awaiting them, and that their survival was far from certain, even if nobody knew what exactly the Germans had in store for them.

No preparations were made to let children go into hiding. On the contrary, rucksacks had been made from the banded red/white cloth of the exterior awnings for each of the children to carry the most essential items for when the day

8   De Jong quotes a witness who saw an elderly patient being thrown down the stairs.
9   Crown Princess Juliana visited the *Joodsche Invalide* in 1938. See also Hannah van den Ende, May 2021; *"De Joodsche Invalide"*. Boom, Amsterdam. ISBN 9789024418848
10   CABR Dossier Vas, National Archives, The Hague.

of deportation would arrive, such as warm clothing and an extra pair of shoes. Only the two blankets from each bed were to be added at the last moment. Each rucksack carried a number (Piet de Vries' number was 41). Clearly, the staff, but also most of the older children, were resigned to the fact that the time of their own deportation could not be far off.

After the war, Hijme and Emilie Stoffels told Kerkvliet and Uitvlugt (1973) about their many attempts in the weeks before 16th and 17th March to convince Nathan Italie to organize *onderduik* for as many of his children as possible. Stoffels recalled (ibid., p. 22): *"I told him: Take action, send children into hiding. But Italie said, 'I cannot do that. The children have been entrusted to me; I cannot let them go. If our fate is to be taken away, I accept that.'"* Then he said: *"They may unlawfully take us out of our home and deport us, but surely they are not going to kill us."* Stoffels was not so sure of that, although even he, with his good connections, including German officers, whom he provided with bottles of genever (Dutch gin) and cigars from the Wijtenburg factory, did not know the reality of what happened to the people deported to occupied Poland.

Kerkvliet and Uitvlugt also interviewed L. Levisson (Fig. 2.7), who himself survived the war in hiding, and who had known Nathan for more than fifteen years. They asked him specifically why the governors of the orphanage had not been more active in organizing *onderduik* for the children. Levisson replied: *"Suggesting onderduik was out of the question. All my attempts foundered on the mentality of not only the director [Italie], but also some of my fellow governors. They lacked the mental attitude to resist the plans to deport them."* Moreover, the official role of the governors had been annulled by the Germans in 1942. He also added that those colleagues who did agree with him (to resist deportation) were already in hiding themselves in March 1943 and were no longer able to exert influence.

It is difficult to know what Nathan's mindset was at the time. The quote from Stoffels (above) suggests that Nathan did not want to release responsibility for the children but given his willingness to leave them and go to Barneveld (see below), this may not be convincing. It seems more likely that his resistance to the idea of *onderduik* was based on his aversion to do *anything illegal*, an attitude which was common in the pre-war Dutch Jewish and non-Jewish Christian bourgeoisie.[11] That may also explain why Nathan *did* consent to the Stoffels' proposal to try and arrange G1 status ("safe half-Jewish") for four of his children, although they all had Jewish mothers. Being classified G1 was one of the few ways to escape deportation

---

11 When in early 1942 Jews were ordered to hand over their bicycles, Hans Kloosterman (letter to L.P. Kasteleyn) decided to put his bicycle in hiding with Salomon Ritmeester who worked at the horticulture farm across the "Vliet". But the absence of the bicycle was noticed by Ms. Gobes, and when Hans told her where he had hidden it, he was forced to collect the bike and bring it to the Leiden police station.

"legally", i.e. with permission of the Nazi authority. The different pre-war attitude towards "authority" is one of the many factors to consider before judging wartime behaviour today.

Stoffels started the G1 requests after the summer of 1942, in November at the latest, for Piet de Vries and Hans Kloosterman because they demonstrably had non-Jewish fathers, and for Bram Degen and Betsy Wolff because it was not known who their fathers were, and non-Jewish fathers could therefore be concocted for them.

Bram Degen was sixteen when he left the orphanage on 13th July 1942. So Stoffels, who had moved into his new house around the corner of the orphanage in January 1942 (months before his postponed marriage), knew him. Bram joined Ralph Litten's Hachsharah farm (for Palestine Pioneers) in Gouda, better known as *Catharinahoeve*. His G1 certificate was issued in time for him to remove his star and leave Catharinahoeve before the inhabitants were told to report to the Vught concentration camp. The correspondence between Litten and Stoffels shows that Bram's rescue was a close call (Ch. 9.6).

Betsy Wolff had arrived in January 1932. She was eighteen when Stoffels, drafting the letters for Italie to sign, started a descendance investigation on her behalf. The whole "investigation" was a hoax, and served only to create a non-Jewish father, and fabricate the required documentary evidence. Betsy's G1 certificate (Fig. 9.6) arrived in Leiden on 9th March 1943, after the Civil Registry (and the *Entscheidungsstelle*) had accepted D.J. Dommerholt as her father. From then on, she was to be called Betsy Dommerholt. When she was still regarded as Jewish, she was not allowed to leave the orphanage; now that she was classified as G1, she had to leave the orphanage forthwith, entirely in line with the strict separation which the Nazis enforced between Jewish and non-Jewish Dutchmen. Stoffels offered her accommodation and employment, and the next day, 10th March, she officially moved in with Hijme and Emilie. A few days later the orphanage was liquidated: she had moved just in time. Her story is detailed in Chapter 9.2 and the relevant documents are included in her dossier.

For Hans Kloosterman and Piet de Vries, no G1 decision had been received, and both boys were arrested and taken to Westerbork with all the others (Table 7.1) on 17th March. Their story will unfold below.

7.4   17th March 1943: The orphanage is liquidated

Stoffels knew on Tuesday, 16th March, that the following day a major razzia would be held in the town, ordered by the German police and to be executed with full deployment of the (Dutch) police force in Leiden. He had also been told by one of his German contacts in The Hague about the special train being ordered for the following day. He went over to the orphanage and tried again to convince Nathan Italie to send his children into hiding, telling him (again) that he and Emilie could help in finding *onderduik* addresses even at this very short notice.

That same evening of Tuesday, 16th March, Hijme and Emilie organized a group of trustworthy acquaintances to warn all the remaining Jews in Leiden to seek hiding places immediately. One of the first to be warned was Jacob Philipson's family. Stoffels, having contacts with staff as well as (the older) children in the orphanage, had been advising Jacob long before March 1943. Jacob and his wife were sure to heed the warnings (see Ch. 7.13). The resident staff was also informed about the imminent threat and may have considered going into hiding themselves. But none of them did.

Gerda Meijer was a close contact of Emilie (Stoffels) van Brussel from the time when both lived in the Mariënpoelstraat, and she was already active in the resistance at this time, March 1943 – although she concentrates on later years in her own report (Meijer-Weyler, 1993). Gerda was also involved in passing on the warning to other Jewish families. Her family had moved to the Thorbeckestraat close to the orphanage. She probably did not need to convince her own family members (see the story of Eva Herskovits, Ch. 5.2) but she did visit her "other" erstwhile Jewish neighbours on the Mariënpoelstraat: Rosi Klein and her three children Rita, Ingrid and Ben. Their detailed report (Klein-Roskin, 1995) provides further insight in the events of March 1943 and thereafter, and the role played by Stoffels (Ch. 10.3).

On Wednesday, 17th March, Stoffels went to Italie around 15:30 for a last-ditch attempt to convince him. *"Open the doors; let the children go."* But again Nathan refused: *"I will keep us all together as long as possible, come what may."* Later, around 17:30, Hijme and Emilie went together to see Nathan, now to say goodbye. He took Betsy, who had been living in the orphanage for eleven years, and who had only moved to the Stoffels' house six days earlier, with him. Hijme reported (Kerkvliet & Uitvlugt 1973, p. 26): *"While we were talking, the building was suddenly surrounded by ten to twelve policemen, led by van Musscher, Biesheuvel, and de Groot. Van Musscher was in charge"* (Fig. 10.12). They immediately ordered Stoffels to leave the building. He was shocked by being confronted by the reality of the eviction, despite his accurate foreknowledge of what was going to happen. When he got home, he suddenly realized that he had left Betsy in the building. He ran back, a mere 50 metres around the corner, where Biesheuvel, who was in charge outside, initially refused to let him in. Once inside, he succeeded in convincing van Musscher to let Betsy go. Other witnesses, including the son of the janitor of the Leiden police station (Kasteleyn, 2003) counted at least 20 policemen, including members of the German police.

Sally Montezinos who had ignored earlier advice from German officers (Ch. 7.2) to go into hiding, had worked that day as usual in the leather shop of Mr. Brussé. When he got home at the end of the day the orphanage was surrounded by the Dutch police. According to Stoffels (Kerkvliet & Uitvlugt, 1973), one policeman stopped him and whispered: *"Go away. You will all be arrested,"* but Sally just repeated what he had told Brussé: *"If we have to go, we'll all go together."* Hans Kloosterman remembered that Salomon Ritmeester, who came home from work on the horticulture farm around the same time as Sally, was also warned by one of the policemen not to enter the building and disappear as fast as he could. But like Sally, Salomon, who had turned fifteen the day before, ignored it.

The smaller children were delivered to the Leiden railway station later that evening in a bus provided by Eltax (Kerkvliet & Uitvlugt, 1973); the older children were marched to the station on foot. Emilie Stoffels happened to see them around 22:30, walking through the Breestraat under police escort that evening. She came back from bringing a Jewish boy to Valkenburg (Ben Klein?, Ch. 7.12; she did not mention a name to Kerkvliet and Uitvlugt). She realized with sadness that she could not do anything for the orphanage children anymore.

Piet de Vries realized much later that he could have hidden himself easily (with his girlfriend, Fanny Günsberg) in the many nooks and crannies in the building. He knew the cellar well since he had taken over the job as *stoker* (fireman) from Mr. van Ee. But none of the children was mentally prepared to take such a momentous, consequential, decision.

Upon arrival at the station, they were told to enter one of wagons of the old (passenger) train, which had been positioned at the far end of the platform. The wagons had separate compartments. Piet remembered that, once in the train, reality hit them hard. Guidance by the staff had collapsed, children were crying, every feeling of comfort and security which the big building had provided during almost three years of occupation had evaporated. They knew that they would be sent on from Westerbork to "labour camps" in Eastern Europe. Everybody mixed and moved between the compartments as they wished. Some tried to keep up their spirits, talking about how to survive in the camps. Lotte Adler managed to send a postcard to her friend from the Haanstra *kweekschool*, Jopie Vos (Mrs. Schröder), probably while still on the train, telling Jopie that they were doing their best to be strong, but that, while singing songs (no doubt for the smaller children), she was weeping inside. The card was lost after the war, but the photo album which Lotte gave to Jopie for safekeeping was preserved and is now in the Camp Westerbork museum. Lotte's photos could be dated and almost everybody on them identified, which helped to reconstruct life in the orphanage.

The train left Leiden around midnight. The whole operation, at the orphanage, as well as the arrest of the other Jews in Leiden who had not gone into hiding, was carried out by the Leiden police force, while the German police remained in the background, although they were also seen in the Roodenburgerstraat (Kasteleyn, 2003). As shown (ibidem) by notes in the Leiden police archives, Franz Fisher (Ch. 10.10) was present in Leiden that day. Only very few Dutch policemen objected to taking part in the razzia, notably J.P. Rozemeijer, and Chief Inspector van de Wal, who was locked up in the police station when he insisted on taking a day off on 17th March. His wife, who was told by a colleague of her husband that he had been locked up, called Stoffels to warn him that the razzia was imminent. Van der Wal survived. Stoffels arranged a false pb for his son (Hugo) later in the war, to keep him out of *Arbeitseinsatz* in Germany. Rozemeijer was arrested later for another act of defiance, and was deported to Buchenwald, where he died on 12th March 1945, aged 46. Stoffels was very critical of the Leiden police force; his personal archive contains lists of a few dozen policemen whom he wanted prosecuted by the special tribunals after the war, in some cases for offences which today look rather trivial.

Piet de Vries remembered the *ontruiming* as calm and orderly. But Stoffels told Kerkvliet and Uitvlugt that it was chaotic, with some children crying and screaming, and throwing stuff around. Geertje Gebert (Mrs. Bekooy) told van Zegveld (1993, p. 169) that she cycled past the now empty orphanage on 18th March and spoke to Betsy (Wolff) Dommerholt. Betsy also said that children threw tins of syrup down the stairs in anger. The memory of Hijme and Betsy appears to be confirmed by Leo van der Meide, a young underground co-worker of Stoffels; they went back into the building the next morning and found the place in a chaotic state.[12]

Hans Kloosterman and Mieke Dagloonder (Figs. 7.5 and 7.7) were inseparable in the early years since they arrived in 1929 as two-year-old toddlers (Ch. 4.2). At the beginning of the occupation they were about thirteen years old, and they had begun to grow apart. But in the train which brought them to Westerbork in the small hours of the night 17th/18th March, they cuddled up.

In the weeks before the razzia, Stoffels had offered Nathan to try and get him (and his family) added to the *"List van Dam"*, so that he would end up in Barneveld rather than Westerbork. Nathan's brother Gabriel was on this list. He had indeed been interned in Barneveld since 27th February 1943 (de Lang, 2009). *Barneveld* was considered "special treatment".[13] Van Dam was Secretary General of the Education Ministry. With his colleague Frederiks of the Interior Ministry, they put together a list of Jewish Dutchmen whom they tried to safeguard from

---

12   Letter, Leo van der Meide to Emilie Stoffels, 22nd March 1993 (in Dossier Stoffels).
13   Not much later, the Barneveld Jews were sent to Westerbork after all, but many of them continued to be treated as special cases. Gabriel and his wife survived the war in Theresienstadt.

Figure 7.5: Hans Kloosterman.
Private collection.

deportation because of prominence and valuable contributions to Dutch society before the war. It says a lot about Hijme and his perception of the Nazis that he knew about things like the "Barneveld route" and the G1 procedure. One may speculate that Hijme, who was both assertive and astute, made the offer in conjunction with the pressure he put on Nathan to let children go, hoping to neutralize Nathan's view that he could not abandon his wards. But Nathan had not told Hijme to go ahead. However, he posted a card to Stoffels when the train halted at the Zwolle railway station just an hour away from its destination, Westerbork. *"Dear friends, can you please do everything in your power to expedite the Barneveld papers."* Stoffels was shocked that Italie seemed ready to leave his orphanage children, after refusing to let them go into hiding. He was still angry (in 1967) that Nathan made this reversal too late for him to get more children into hiding, but he assumed that Nathan had lost his self-assurance in the train and decided there and then to seek the special "Barneveld" treatment after all. But when Gabriel's war diary was published (de Lang, 2009), it transpired that Nathan had already written to his brother the week before 17th March, asking him if he could try to get Nathan and his family added to the Barneveld list as well. He did not ask Hijme Stoffels to arrange this for him, nor did he inform him.

Etty Heerma van Voss, one of the "late arrivals" in Leiden (Ch. 6.8), sent a postcard (Fig. 7.6), dated 18th March, which was pre-addressed and pre-stamped by her foster parents, and which she wrote on the train to Westerbork: *"Thursday, 18th March. We are gone. Wednesday night at 9 they came to take us away. I am now in the train, getting close to Westenborg. Goodbye everybody, lots of kisses, Etty."* The tone is raw, more so than can be captured in translation; the words are abrupt *"weg"* (gone), *"weggehaald"* (taken out, removed, as if concerning pieces of furniture).

The train of 17th/18th March brought the last large group of Jews from Leiden to Westerbork: 59 from the orphanage, and probably 41 who had not gone into hiding and who had been picked up by the Leiden police mostly from their own homes. Some 50 people had already been deported in earlier months. At least 51 had gone into *onderduik*, warned by Stoffels, Gerda Meijer, Beb Bedak and others[14].

---

14   More people, not original residents, were in hiding in Leiden; see www.herdenkingleiden.nl for results of ongoing research.

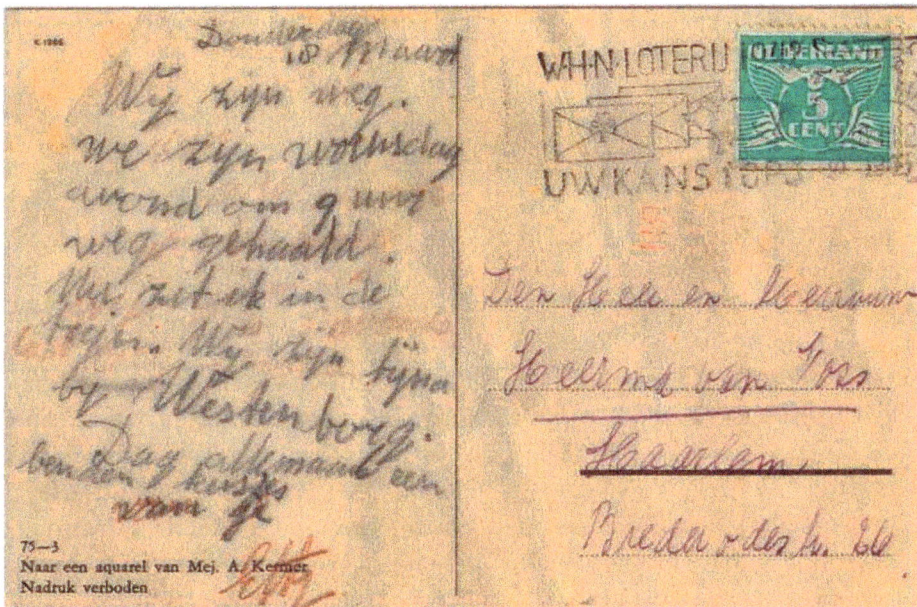

Figure 7.6: The postcard Etty wrote on the train to Westerbork, 18th March 1943.

These were actively hunted down by the above-mentioned Dutch policemen, Biesheuvel and de Groot, who (just as Steven van Musscher) had been placed in the *Documentatiedienst*, a unit of the Leiden police force created specifically to make arrests on behalf of the German police. From the approximately 500 Jewish residents in Leiden and neighbouring townships (reviewed by Kasteleyn, 2003, p. 38), 271 were deported and murdered. Similar police units had been created in other cities. The shocking role of the Dutch Jew hunters is described by van Liempt (2005).

Table 7.1 lists the 59 people who were forcefully removed from the orphanage on the night of 17th/18th March 1943. They were all registered by the Joodse Raad as having arrived and registered in Westerbork on 18th or 19th March. It is not impossible, but unlikely, that there were more people in the orphanage on or just before 17th March. Not everybody who was taken in by the orphanage in 1942 and 1943 was officially registered (for example, Salomon and Bernard Meijers, Ch. 6.8). The police had a list of 198 Jewish citizens of Leiden, of which 74 were supposed to be in the orphanage (Kasteleyn, 2003). Some of these, such as Gusta Wahrhaftig, left the orphanage before 17th March. In Westerbork, some of the older children maintained a careful weekly accounting of the names of those put on transports and those who remained in the camp. They reported this "live" in letters to Stoffels. The dates also match with the registration dates that were recorded by the Joodse

Raad. The list of 59 persons is therefore probably as accurate as possible. Yet, some uncertainty always remains.

7.5   Westerbork, a camp of "hope and despair"

Upon arrival in Camp Westerbork in the early morning of Thursday, 18th March, the group was registered.[15] Nathan sent a second postcard to Stoffels to inform him that they were lodged in Barrack 66. There was no breakfast for them, so they used the emergency rations which the staff had put in each of the rucksacks. Nathan tried to recreate order by having the tables laid with cutlery, also from the rucksacks. When Nathan asked who had brought their prayer book, it turned out that only Hans Kloosterman, probably the "least Jewish" of them all, had done so. Three days after arrival in Westerbork, Sunday, 21st March, they celebrated Purim, the feast of the Book of Esther, commemorating how the plans of Haman, the vizier to the Persian king, to have all Jews in the empire killed, were foiled. During the yearly memorial in March by students from the Erasmus College in Zoetermeer (Ch. 10.5) the story of Esther[16] is told, with sinister relevance.

No doubt that on that Sunday the staff and the senior children had begun to understand that the entire life in Westerbork was focused on the upcoming transport, expected to leave Westerbork on Tuesday morning, and the question of who would be on the transport list. Camp Commandant Gemmeker, of course, had the power to add people to (or remove them from) the list, and he did so if someone annoyed him for some trivial reason (van Liempt, 2019). But otherwise, the preparation of the transport list was in the hands of the relevant department (*Dienstbereich*) within the Jewish organization, and their boss *Oberdienstleiter* Kurt Schlesinger. They used a card index for that purpose and special lists of those who were exempted. To keep the system active, the cards of those deported were removed or destroyed. Schlesinger's organization[17] in Westerbork included the *Antragstelle*, which was headed by Hans Ottenstein, also a Jewish refugee from Germany. It was an important office for anybody who could make a reasonable claim to special status, to be exempted from deportation (temporarily, at least). Examples relevant to the story of this book are the Palestine connection of Mindel Färber (Ch. 9.3) and the mother of Aron Wolff (aka Ronnie de Paauw, Ch. 9.3), the Haitian nationality of Melna and Louis Fleurima, or the ongoing "Calmeyer" descendancy investigation

15   Some of the Joodse Raad cards used in this study give 19th March as registration date.
16   Courtesy Mrs. Malka Polak, who has provided the introduction for many years. Purim is almost always in mid-March in the Jewish calendar.
17   The complex workings of the Westerbork Jewish organization and the relation with the departments of the Joodse Raad in Amsterdam and The Hague are described by Schütz (2011).

for Etty Heerma van Voss, Hans Kloosterman and Piet de Vries. All the above were initially protected against being selected for deportation. Nevertheless, the pressure of meeting the weekly target number could cause any of these people to suddenly appear on the next transport list. Hans[18] and Piet found their names on the list more than once. They were only taken off again thanks to the assertive actions of Stoffels (see below). It caused them great anxiety, not in the least for Piet, who was aware that his sister Marietje, who had been in an identical situation as he was now, had been deported on 22nd January and nothing had been heard from her since.

It is probably impossible to fully appreciate the impact which the weekly announcements must have had, even after reading the surviving witness accounts (e.g. Etty Hillesum, 2002; Philip Mechanicus, 1964). During the days and the night before each deportation, tensions rose to a terrible peak, until, usually on Monday evening, the names on the list were revealed. Each barrack supervisor read out the people on the list who were in his or her barrack. A terrible moment of breaking tension: condemned to depart to an uncertain but fearful future next morning, or relief: another seven days to stay in the camp. Willy Lindwer (1990) chose an apt title for his account of Westerbork: *"Camp of hope and despair"*. Once the list was revealed, frantic efforts were made by some to get a last-minute reprieve, for example, by asking the doctor to declare them unfit for deportation (Cohen, 1979). But even if one found a sympathetic ear, such requests posed a terrible dilemma: if granted it implied that somebody else would have to take his or her place because the target number of people to be on the train was sacrosanct.

Except the special cases mentioned above, the group from the orphanage in Leiden had no protection, no connections, and no strings to pull in Westerbork, and whoever was responsible to make up the target number for the upcoming transport of 23rd March decided to put 34 of the 59 new arrivals on the list. When the names were read out in Barrack 66, just four days after arrival in Westerbork, the news must have hit them terribly. Included were all nine staff members: Director Italie, his wife, Lies, and their two children, Hanna (seven) and Elchanan (six); the female staff Gobes, Bierschenk, de Leeuw, Klein, and Altenberg; Alice Blitz, as well as Barend de Vries. Also Izak Ensel (four), Salomon Rotstein (five) (Fig. 7.8), the four children van Kam: Arthur (five), Herman (eight), Hijman (ten) and Mary (twelve), Willy Blog (nine), Lotte Adler, who had just turned eighteen, and her sister Henny (twelve), whom she looked after as she had promised her mother Clara in back in Frankfurt; Herman Rozeveld (twelve); Ralph Protter (twelve); Fanny Günsberg (sixteen; Piet's girlfriend) (see Fig. 6.11), and her brother Lothar (fourteen) (see Fig. 7.8); Mieke Dagloonder (fifteen), the early days' girlfriend of Hans; Jopie Beem (sixteen); Chaim Kirschenbaum (sixteen); Max van Stratum (sixteen), Bertha Goudsmit (eighteen),

18   Letter #5 to L.P. Kasteleyn.

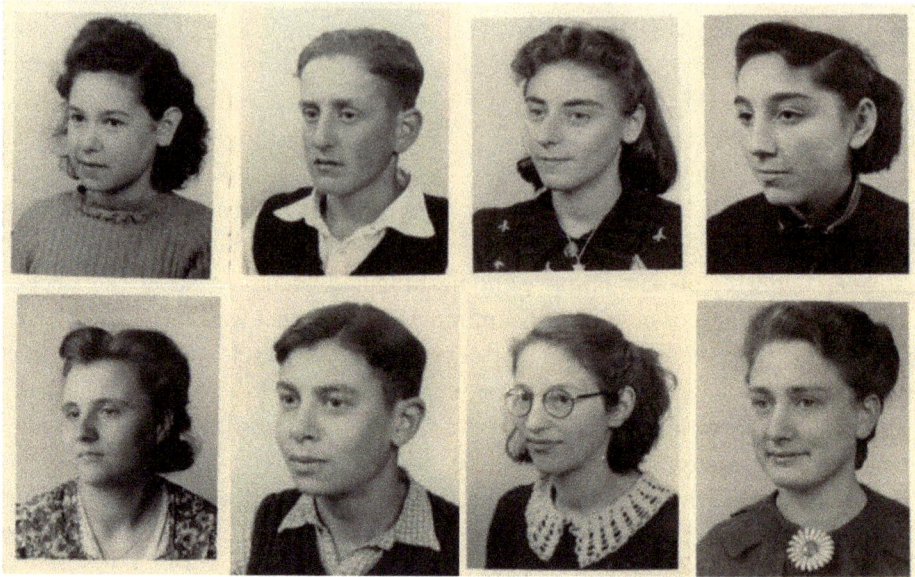

Figure 7.7: Passport photographs taken in 1942; courtesy Mary Vromen-de Raay, Israel. Names from top-left to lower-right:

Lotte Adler	Joop Beem	Jet Bobbe	Mieke Dagloonder
Corrie Frenkel	Chaim Kirschenbaum	Reina Segal	Alice Blitz

Jetje Bobbe (eighteen); Reina Segal (eighteen), Margarita (eighteen) and Marianna Velleman (sixteen), and Corry Frenkel (eighteen).

The next morning the selected people were walked to the train, standing ready in the middle of the camp, by members of the OD, and "guided" into one of the cattle wagons. All other camp inhabitants were under curfew to prevent emotional outbursts. By then, each deportee had been reduced to utter destitution; everything had been taken away from them: money, papers, basic rights. When the doors of the wagons were shut, they had effectively even lost their identity: although possibly the list of deportees was given to the German guards who travelled with the train, there is no evidence that anything was ever done with it, and nobody in Sobibor had any interest in the identity of the arrivals. The administrative staff in Westerbork made a secret copy of each list, and all the copies have survived the war, allowing us to know who was deported and on which date (Schelvis, 2001).

The passport photos that were taken in 1942 were the last. For the seven staff members, see Figures 6.16 to 6.18. For eight others, including Alice Blitz, see Figure 7.7. No photograph was found of Barend de Vries, the P.E. teacher. Jopie Beem and Chaim Kirschenbaum, who had just turned 16, were included in the photo

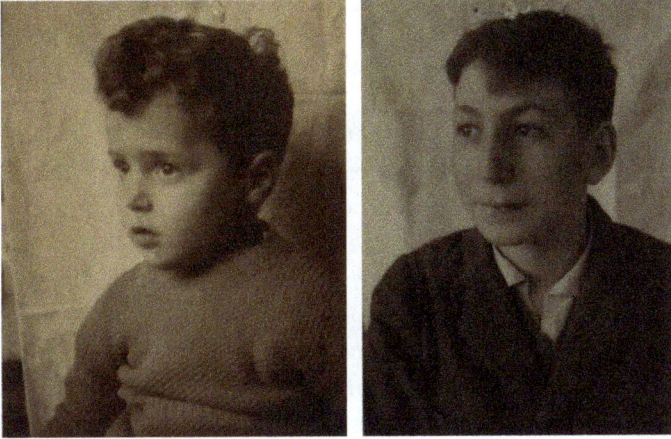

Figure 7.8: Left: Salomon Rotstein; right: Lothar Günsberg. Joods Monument.

session. Chaim and Lothar Günsberg were friends. They shared a Polish refugee background and may even have spoken some Yiddish. For the younger children who were being deported on 23rd March, no contemporaneous photos exist. The photos of Salomon Rotstein and Lothar Günsberg (Fig. 7.8) were taken earlier by or for the Dutch alien police (courtesy the Joods Monument).

The train left Westerbork on 23rd March with 1250 deportees on board, who had no clue where they were going. The destination was Sobibor, an obscure place in occupied Poland. Auschwitz, supposedly a labour camp, was known as the destination for almost all deportation trains from Westerbork in 1942 and early 1943. But nobody had ever heard of Sobibor. Even today, this death camp is not very well known internationally. It was constructed to murder large numbers of Jews in Poland and other occupied territories in Eastern Europe, while Auschwitz remained the preferred death factory for Jews from Holland, Belgium and France and occupied Southern and South-eastern Europe. What caused the Germans to divert the deportations from Holland to Sobibor for a period of five months?

7.6 Sobibor and the "Final Solution"

During 1940 and into 1941 the Nazi leadership had begun to realize that previous ideas about relocating the Jews from the annexed parts of Poland further to the East and relocating the Western European Jews in the same area, was not workable: the numbers were simply too large. The invasion of Poland in 1939 had brought more than 2.5 million Jews under German control. The local

German administrators of the occupied territories in the East were putting up resistance to the idea that *"even more Jews would be unloaded on them"* from Western Europe.

The invasion of the Soviet Union in June 1941 brought even more millions of Jews within German control, but by that time the Nazi thinking had already shifted from relocation ("emigration") to downright liquidation. It is estimated that the four *Einsatzgruppen* which followed[19] the German army into Soviet-controlled Eastern Poland, the Baltic states, Belarus, Ukraine, and the western part of Russia, killed at least some 1.1 million Jews (and other people in undesired categories, such as Roma, Poles and Soviet prisoners). But it was soon realized that even for these dedicated killing squads, the numbers were too high. Moreover, the daily killing of so many men, women, and children, mostly by shooting, took its toll even on the toughest members of these squads. A more efficient and "anonymous" method was needed to prevent the perpetrators from being in direct contact with each individual victim they killed. Experiments with gassing took place early in 1941 even before the invasion of the Soviet Union, originating from the pre-existing T4 euthanasia programme in Germany and Austria. The brother of Els and Karel van Santen, Philip, was killed in August 1941 in such a T4 facility in Austria (Schloss Hartheim, Ch. 8.1). These and other gassing experiments, mainly with carbon monoxide, led to the building of dedicated facilities, such as Chelmno (Kulmhof), which began its killing operation on 8th December 1941. Auschwitz I, started in May 1940 as a prison and labour camp mainly for Polish and Russian prisoners, installed a gas chamber in 1941 and experimented with Zyklon B (a cyanide-based insecticide). Auschwitz II (Birkenau) was much bigger. Construction started in late 1941, and the camp became operational in 1942 specifically to handle large numbers of Jewish deportees. The senior Nazis who participated in Heydrich's Wannsee Conference (20th January 1942) were duly impressed with the staggering numbers of Jews to be destroyed in each of the occupied countries and territories, and the enormous logistical challenges associated with the plans to remove them from the face of the earth. Even a much bigger Auschwitz could never handle the numbers involved. New death camps were therefore built as part of *Aktion Reinhard* to handle the vast numbers of Eastern European Jews, and with only one purpose: to kill and destroy as many humans as possible, as efficiently as possible. Belzec became operational in March, Sobibor in May, and Treblinka II in July 1942.

---

19   In view of the scale of the operation, and the numbers involved, local auxiliary forces were added to the Einsatzgruppen who did much of the killing under German supervision.

The rapid and systematic step-by-step evolution of the Holocaust into a "final solution", the coherence of the components and the way it all fitted together, suggest the presence of a strong central planning. Jozeph Michman (1987) argued that Hitler, who was in a hurry to realize his ambitions, but who also was a good tactician and patient enough to wait for the right moment, knew exactly what he wanted long before the war, but that he had to wait for his own Nazi organization to come on board with the idea of genocide. He also realized he had to wait until the German army was ready for all-out war in the East before he could execute his plans for the Jews. This could explain the apparent paradox between making a pact with Stalin in August 1939 and invading the Soviet Union in 1941: he needed the time. However, the current historical consensus is that the plans for mass murder at an industrial scale developed gradually, "organically", as Germany expanded eastward between 1939 and 1942, with a marked acceleration from June 1941 during the invasion of the Soviet Union. In the absence of unambiguous documents, it is not clear what Hitler's role was during this period, and when and by whom certain decisions were taken. Both points of view may have merits. The T4 euthanasia programme already used gas to kill victims as early as 1940, and used it to kill Jewish deportees from Mauthausen in 1941, including Philip van Santen, the brother of Karel (Ch. 8.1).

Following the early deportations out of Camp Schoorl to Mauthausen in 1941 (Ch. 6.3), it took one and a half years before the plans to deport all the Jews of Western Europe had taken shape. By mid-1942 Westerbork had been taken over by the Germans, and the preparations to identify all Jews in the Netherlands, sequester them in their homes, strip them of all possessions and collect them in Westerbork ready for deportation, had been completed. Preparations to "process" the deportees at Auschwitz were also ready by mid-1942. Systematic deportations from Westerbork to Auschwitz began on Wednesday, 15th July 1942, more or less at the same time as deportations from Drancy (France) and Kazerne Dossin in Mechelen (Belgium). Eichmann's office at the RSHA in Berlin (for a description of the central SS bureaucracy, see Stiftung Topographie des Terrors, 2018) coordinated the railway transports with frightening efficiency. Trains had to depart Westerbork on schedule because *they had to arrive at the camps on schedule*; if not, chaos would be the result. In each occupied country, a regular "supply" of Jews to the transit camps should ensure that each train could be loaded with some 1000 to 2000 people. Although Westerbork was periodically overloaded, the execution of the deportations was near perfect, far more so than in Belgium (see the story of Alexander Lipschits, Ch. 8.4). This fact did not escape the attention of Eichmann.

Between 15th July 1942 and 23rd February 1943, 50 trains left Westerbork, to deliver 44,000 Dutch Jews to Auschwitz. As train loads of deportees arrived there from all over Europe and more gas chambers were built, the "capacity" to murder people increased to unimaginable figures. The most serious problem was not how to kill so many people, but how to dispose of the bodies. When the well-known German oven company Topf of Erfurt installed their new highly efficient ovens at Auschwitz, the killing and destruction capacity rose to some 20,000 *per day*.[20] It was not enough. When deportations from the Greek city of Thessaloniki (Salonika), which boasted one of the oldest, largest and most famous Jewish communities in the Mediterranean,[21] started in March 1943 (Mazower, 2005), deportations to Auschwitz from other countries, notably France, had to be suspended. But the transports from Westerbork were not halted. It seems that Eichmann was so impressed with the progress and efficiency of the deportations from the Netherlands that it was decided not to interrupt the deportations, and to divert the transports to Sobibor instead. The first train to Sobibor left Westerbork on Tuesday, 2nd March 1943, with 1105 deportees: the last one left on Tuesday, 20th July, with 2209 people. The journey usually took three days. As a rule, all deportees on board the train were killed upon arrival. There was no labour camp in Sobibor; the camp's only purpose was to kill as many people as efficiently as possible. Only in a few cases some 40 young and healthy people were picked from a newly arrived transport to work in one of the sub-camps supporting the main camp. Thus, Sally Montezinos (see below) was probably selected to work in the sub-camp Dorohucza, digging up peat for combustion.

In total, nineteen trains carried 34,314 people from Westerbork to Sobibor, of which 34,296 did not survive. In other words, the survival rate for Sobibor was practically zero. For each train, the transport list as put together in Westerbork has been preserved. One of the eighteen Dutch survivors was Jules Schelvis, who published a description of his ordeal (2007a), as well as an analysis of the workings of the camp (2007b). He also published the transport lists (2001) of the nineteen trains from Westerbork to Sobibor. This accuracy, and the fact that we know the names, is unique: it is estimated that between 170,000 and 250,000 Jews were murdered in Sobibor between April 1942 and October 1943, mostly from Poland and other occupied regions in the East. But in the absence of documentation,

---

20 Topf specialists visited Auschwitz to investigate what the SS required in terms of oven type and capacity. The invoices show that Topf was fully aware that the ovens were used for cremating thousands of bodies of killed people per day. Their ovens used advanced technology, using the combustible components of the human body effectively to reduce fuel consumption. In 2011, Topf & Sons established a Place of Remembrance at the former company grounds in Erfurt (Germany), to acknowledge their role in the Holocaust. See www.topfundsoehne.de/ts/.

21 According to German records, some 45,000 Jews were deported from Thessaloniki to Auschwitz between March and August 1943.

nobody knows for sure how many were killed in Sobibor, nor do we know their names (see Epilogue).

No words can describe the horror of the three-day trip in the cattle cars[22] and the arrival in Sobibor, but try we must: a bucket as a toilet for some 60 to 70 people, no privacy whatsoever, no room to sit or lie down, no food and little water; upon arrival, the humiliation which the staff must have felt walking naked to the gas chambers with the 25 children of the transport of 23rd March, the shock when people started to suspect what was going on, the terrible asphyxiation caused by the exhaust fumes of a captured Russian tank. It could take more than 20 minutes before the screaming stopped (Schelvis, 2007a, 2007b).

Following the revolt on 14th October 1943, the Germans liquidated the camp by killing the remaining prisoners and demolishing the structures, covering it with soil, planting trees and disguising it as a farm. The satellite camps were liquidated on 8th November.[23] Several documentaries exist about the revolt in Sobibor, including one by Claude Lanzmann (2001). A joint Polish, Israeli and Dutch team of archaeologists[24] started excavations at the site in 2006. They uncovered the foundations of eight gas chambers (Schute, 2020), the train platform, and traces of the postholes that marked the path of what the Nazis cynically called the *Himmelfahrtstrasse* (Ascencion Road or the "Road to Heaven", the path along which the prisoners were marched to the gas chambers), and several small rings and other small pieces of jewellery. Surely, for us in the Netherlands, the most moving finds to date are the metal identification tags of three Dutch children.[25]

7.7   The miraculous release of Hans Kloosterman and Piet de Vries

Hijme and Emilie Stoffels had successfully arranged a G1 (mixed blood) certificate for Betsy Wolff (Ch. 7.4, details in Ch. 9.1), as well as for Bram Degen (Ch. 9.5). But the G1 status had not yet been approved for Piet de Vries and Hans Kloosterman. Their case was, in principle, more straightforward, because both boys indisputably had non-Jewish fathers, and there was no need to fabricate non-Jewish grandparents. The registry had classified them as J2 ("unsafe half-Jewish") as they had done with Marietje de Vries. It would appear (van den Boomgaard,

22   Visitors may enter such a cattle in the USHMM in Washington, but even if one would get inside with 60 or 70 people it is difficult to imagine the horror.

23   Witness accounts recorded by the Red Cross, second edition February 1947; in NIOD library (EVDO02_NIOD05_7880.pdf.

24   W. Mazurek, Y. Haimi and I. Schute.

25   Deddie Zak, Lea Judith de la Penha, Annie Kapper; see the Joods Monument or the site of Stichting Sobibor.

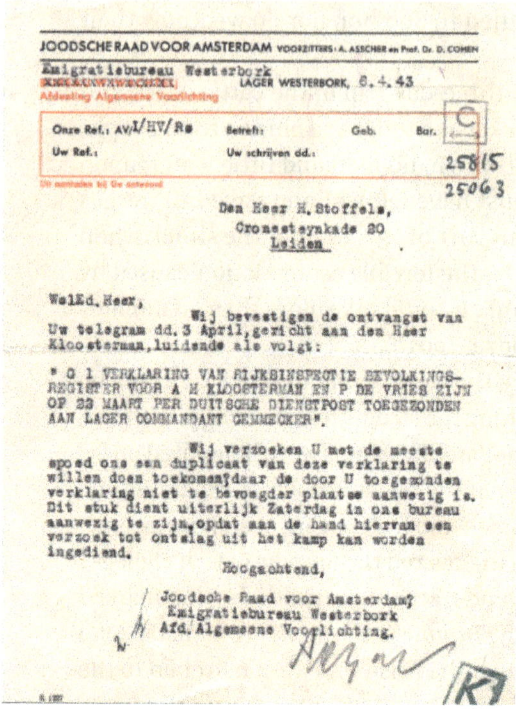

JOODSCHE RAAD VOOR AMSTERDAM VOORZITTERS: A. ASSCHER en Prof. Dr. D. COHEN

Emigratiebureau Westerbork
LAGER WESTERBORK, 6.4.43
Afdeeling Algemeene Voorlichting

Onze Ref.: AV/I/HV/Rs Betreft: Geb. Bar.
Uw Ref.: Uw schrijven dd.:

25815
25063

Den Heer H. Stoffels,
Cronesteynkade 20
Leiden

WelEd. Heer,

Wij bevestigen de ontvangst van Uw telegram dd. 3 April, gericht aan den Heer Kloosterman, luidende als volgt:

" G 1 VERKLARING VAN RIJKSINSPECTIE BEVOLKINGSREGISTER VOOR A H KLOOSTERMAN EN P DE VRIES ZIJN OP 23 MAART PER DUITSCHE DIENSTPOST TOEGEZONDEN AAN LAGER COMMANDANT GEMMECKER".

Wij verzoeken U met de meeste spoed ons een duplicaat van deze verklaring te willen doen toekomen, daar de door U toegezonden verklaring niet te bevoegder plaatse aanwezig is. Dit stuk dient uiterlijk Zaterdag in ons bureau aanwezig te zijn, opdat aan de hand hiervan een verzoek tot ontslag uit het kamp kan worden ingediend.

Hoogachtend,

Joodsche Raad voor Amsterdam,
Emigratiebureau Westerbork
Afd. Algemeene Voorlichting.

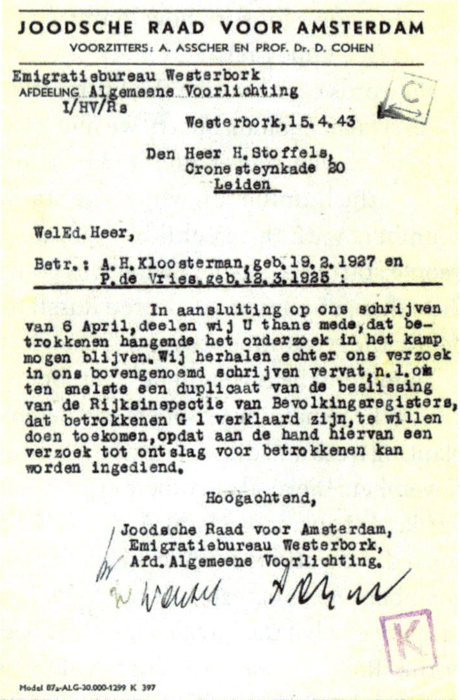

JOODSCHE RAAD VOOR AMSTERDAM
VOORZITTERS: A. ASSCHER EN PROF. Dr. D. COHEN

Emigratiebureau Westerbork
AFDEELING Algemeene Voorlichting
I/HV/Rs

Westerbork, 15.4.43

Den Heer H. Stoffels,
Cronesteynkade 20
Leiden

WelEd. Heer,

Betr.: A.H. Kloosterman, geb. 19.2.1927 en P. de Vries, geb. 12.3.1925 :

In aansluiting op ons schrijven van 6 April, deelen wij U thans mede, dat betrokkenen hangende het onderzoek in het kamp mogen blijven. Wij herhalen echter ons verzoek in ons bovengenoemd schrijven vervat, n.l. om ten snelste een duplicaat van de beslissing van de Rijksinspectie van Bevolkingsregisters, dat betrokkenen G 1 verklaard zijn, te willen doen toekomen, opdat aan de hand hiervan een verzoek tot ontslag voor betrokkenen kan worden ingediend.

Hoogachtend,

Joodsche Raad voor Amsterdam,
Emigratiebureau Westerbork,
Afd. Algemeene Voorlichting.

Model 87a-ALG-30.000-1299 K 397

To H. Stoffels; Westerbork, 6th April 1943.
We confirm receipt of your telegram of 3rd April to Mr. Kloosterman to the effect that "G1 certificates issued by the Civil Registry Office for A.H. Kloosterman and P. de Vries were despatched by German Military mail service to Lager Commandant Gemmecker." We request that you send us a duplicate of the certificates with utmost urgency, since the original have not arrived at their destination. They must arrive in our office [this] coming Saturday [10th April] at the very latest, for an application to be released from the camp to be submitted.

To H Stoffels; Westerbork, 15th April 1943.
Further to our message of 6th April, we can now inform you that the above-mentioned boys may stay in the camp, pending the outcome of the investigation. However, we reiterate our urgent request to send us a duplicate of the statements containing the approval by the Civil Registry Office of their G1 status, in order for an application to be released from the camp can be submitted.

Figure 7.9: Two of the many documents underpinning this chapter (see text). For the other documents, see the dossiers of Hans and Piet. Translation below. Both documents are in a private collection.

2019) that the German *Entscheidungsstelle*, headed by Hans Calmeyer, who had to approve the requests for a change in status, was more lenient than the Dutch Civil Registry, and the G1 status for both Hans and Piet was approved on 18th March and despatched to the orphanage in Leiden by registered mail. But the orphanage had just the previous night been liquidated, there was no one to sign for receipt, and the certificates were returned[26] undelivered to the Civil Registry, where they probably arrived on 22nd March 1943.[27] Stoffels realized that the two boys were at serious risk when they were taken to Westerbork on 17th March without proof that the G1 decision had come through. He used one of his German contacts[28] to find out that the approval had been given on the 18th and arranged for the certificates to be sent by official German military mail service, on 23rd March, directly to Commandant Gemmeker in Westerbork. Stoffels assumed that this ensured timely delivery, but the documents never arrived at their destination (or Gemmeker dismissed them).

On that same day, 23rd March, 34 of the orphanage group were sent to the East, and during the following six days the two boys experienced the growing tension as the moment to announce the names for the transport of 30th March approached. With no news about their G1 status, they realized they were increasingly at risk. But their names were not called for the transport of 30th March. The documents in Stoffels' archive show that there were discussions within the Westerbork bureaucracy (probably involving the *Antragstelle*) about their status. On 2nd April Hans sent a telegram to Stoffels: they had been told that they would not remain "*zurückgestellt*" (i.e. temporarily exempted from deportation to German-occupied Poland), for much longer. Stoffels was surprised and replied to Hans the following day (3rd April) to inform him and Piet that both G1 statements had been despatched already on 22nd (23rd) March. Hans took this telegram to the officials of the Joodse Raad, who then told Stoffels (letter, 6th April, Fig. 7.9) that the statements had not arrived, and asking Stoffels to arrange duplicates *"with utmost urgency"*, and that the G1 statements *"must be in our office [this] coming Saturday [10th April] at the very latest"*.

That was a very serious and dangerous threat. It gave Stoffels just three days to fix it. He probably managed to communicate with the Joodse Raad officials directly or via a (German) contact, because on 15th April they sent another letter to Stoffels (Fig. 7.9) to tell him that the threat of imminent deportation had been softened:

> *Further to our message of 6th April, we can now inform you that the above-mentioned boys may stay in the camp, pending the outcome of the investigation. However, we reiterate our urgent request to send us a duplicate of the statements containing the approval by the Civil Registry Office of their G1 status, in order for an application to be released from the camp can be submitted.*

26 Letter, Stoffels, 22nd April 1943.
27 Date stamp on the G1 certificate for Hans.
28 An unidentified *Obersturmführer* (Kerkvliet & Uitvlugt, 1973).

This gave Stoffels time to get hold of duplicates and send them to Westerbork. On 18th April Hans writes to Stoffels that they had been earmarked for deportation twice but taken off the list again. Piet sends two postcards and Hans one, to thank Stoffels for sending them food parcels. On 22nd April Stoffels sends the newly acquired duplicate G1 certificates to the "Emigratiebureau Westerbork" by registered mail, under covering letter. He adds: *"I trust that you will now submit a request to release the [two boys] without delay."* On 28th April, the Joodse Raad confirms to Stoffels that they have received the certificates, and that the boys can now submit an official request (to Commandant Gemmeker) to be released.

On 16th May Piet sends another postcard to thank him, also on behalf of Didia Klein, for yet another parcel. But he regrets:

> *that the parcel did not contain a new pair of shoes for me, since the only pair I have is falling apart. No further efforts to secure our release can be made, since the matter is now in the hands of the commandant. Photographs for our new persoonsbewijs have been made, and we hope to be released on the coming Friday. The day after, we plan to show up in Leiden. We will send a telegram from Assen. A [new] camp regulation prohibits receiving parcels from non-Jewish friends, or from anybody not resident in Amsterdam.*
> *We hope to see you soon. Please give our regards to Bets and van Ee [...] Daniel. Barrack 64.*

(Curiously he signs again as Daniel, and not Piet as he had done after 17th March.) It took another ten days of waiting. On 26th May he sends the promised telegram from Assen: *"On the way home. Arriving tomorrow. De Vries."*

Hijme and Emilie Stoffels must have spent an enormous amount of time to get from the German and Dutch (Civil Registry) bureaucracy what they needed to get the two boys out of Westerbork. It is sobering to realize how easily it could have gone wrong for both boys, as it did for Piet's sister Marietje, who had also submitted a "G1" change request. While going through the records and realizing the efforts they made on behalf of so many other people, my admiration for Hijme and Emilie increased accordingly (Ch. 10.3).

Notice the bureaucratic nature of the letters (Fig. 7.9), with reference indicators, no less than five initials indicating checks and approvals, and two stamps, and underneath the official letterhead of the Joodse Raad, the euphemism *"Emigratiebureau Westerbork"*.

7.8   March to June 1943: Letters from Westerbork

Including Piet and Hans, 25 children and young adults (from the original group of 59) remained in Westerbork after 23rd March. For the first time ever since they entered the orphanage (for Sally Montezinos: sixteen years) they found themselves on their own: the formerly ever present guidance and direction of the staff had disappeared overnight (although there was someone in charge of the children who remained in Barrack 66). It is a testimony to how well Stoffels had been able, in just about one year, to build a relationship, not only with Nathan Italie, but also with quite a few of the (older) children, that so many of them started using their once-a-fortnight writing privilege to send a postcard or a letter to Stoffels.[29] It can be somewhat disconcerting to read how easily, as a matter of course, they expected Stoffels to send them regular packages with articles ranging from foodstuffs to a new pair of shoes. But by March-April 1943 there was no one else they could write to for help. They frequently sent postcards back to Stoffels to thank him. Indeed, within two or three days from 17th March, Hijme and Emilie began to send parcels to Westerbork, containing food and all sorts of articles to make their life easier. Sally Montezinos, always the cultured one, wrote a letter on 23rd March (Fig. 7.10) to thank him for the parcels, informing Stoffels that many of the group had been sent to the East that very morning. He ends the letter expressing hope that he will meet Stoffels again soon. *"Sending you regards on behalf of all children, and once again our gratitude for the more than outstanding way you care for us by sending us parcels. [...] [I] hope to meet again in the near future."* Harry sent a postcard (Ch. 7.11) on the same day (23rd March), thanking them for the food package which had reached them the day before.

Piet de Vries also wrote to Stoffels, his undated letter was most likely written on 24th or 25th March. He takes the trouble of listing the 25 children who remained in Westerbork after 23rd March. Together with the Joodse Raad cards, the other letters from Westerbork, and the municipal Civil Registry, it allows the reconstruction with some certainty of the list of the 59 persons who were taken from the orphanage to Westerbork on 17th/18th March (Table 7.1). Piet tells Stoffels that the staff took most of the supplies with them on the train so that *"there is hardly enough left [for the others] to take to Poland"*. He adds a rather long shopping list: they are particularly short of bed sheets, towels, toilet paper, soap, cooking pans, as well as bread, butter, vinegar, lemons, apples, piccalilli, salt, matches. Ms. Bierschenk had told them that they would have enough sheets and towels because the Leiden laundry service van der Loo had promised to send them many items which were left with him the week before.

---

29   Some of the letters were given to NIOD by Emilie in 1988, the others were found in her archive.

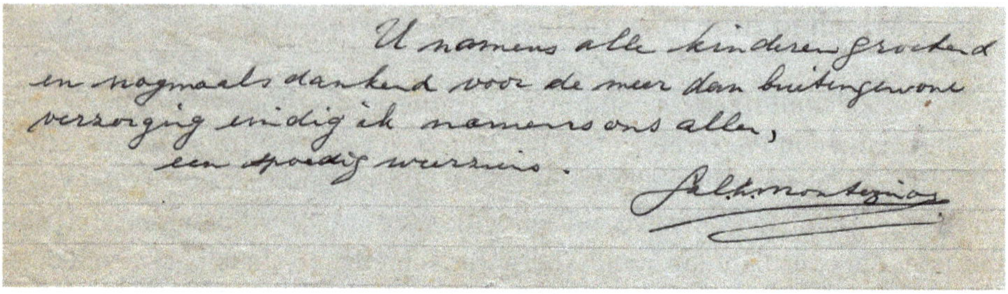
U namens alle kinderen groetend
en nogmaals dankend voor de meer dan buitengewone
verzorging en dig ik namens ons allen,
een spoedig weerzien.

Figure 7.10: Letter (closing sentence) from Sally Montezinos in Westerbork to Stoffels, 23rd March 1943, the day the first large group from the orphanage was put on the train to Sobibor. From the private archive of Emilie Stoffels. Original Private collection.

Jet Mogendorff wrote to Stoffels on 6th April to thank him for more food parcels, asking him to send them more kitchen utensils and candles, and to urge van der Loo again to send them the laundry. There is no indication that the laundry ever arrived in Westerbork. If it did, it may have been sequestered by others as the orphanage group had become small and dispersed in Westerbork after the deportation of the first group on 23rd March.

For 20 days, the remaining 25 children from the group of 17th March were left alone. No one was called for the transports of 30th March or 6th April, which together took 3275 men, women and children to Sobibor. As a result, they had a chance to "settle", and, for the older ones, to be given something useful to do. A day after arrival, Sally was given a job as "Essenholer [*food distributor*] *in the* Krankenhaus [*hospital*], *which gives me extra rations of porridge and 200 grams of bread."* He continues:

> *Didia has a deep tan as a result of working 'on the heathland' surrounding the camp, Frieda Lichtenbaum is* ordonnans [*orderly, attendant*] *of her own barrack, so is Harry Spier to Barrack 66, and Hans Kloosterman to the* 'Voorzorg' [*another unit within the self-administration of the camp*]. *Piet is doing earth work, Cecilia assists with looking after the boys above twelve years, and Jet* [*Mogendorff*] *with the children ten to twelve.*

Then, unexpectedly, Etty Heerma van Voss, and she alone from the remaining orphanage group, was selected for the transport of 13th April. Her sudden deportation must have shocked the others, who were rudely reminded that they were also likely to be called, unexpectedly, any Monday evening before the weekly transport. Indeed, Sally wrote to Stoffels a few days later that he was surprised to be still there. The background of Etty's lone selection for transport is described in Chapter 7.11.

Various remarks in the letters suggest that the optimism which had characterized so many of them during the preceding two years and ten months of occupation was rapidly eroding. Jet Mogendorff writes to Stoffels on 19th April 1943, after first thanking him for receiving yet more packages with food items, and telling him how it had improved their meals, that the four oldest boys: Daniel (Piet) de Vries (who had just turned eighteen), Hans Kloosterman (sixteen), Harry Spier (seventeen) and Sally Montezinos (eighteen), had been transferred to Barrack 64, because of the mixed sleeping arrangement which in Westerbork was not the norm. It was not considered appropriate or acceptable to whomever was in charge. She goes on to complain that the children who remain in Barrack 66 have now been split into age groups, meaning that they still had their meals in the same barrack, but at different tables depending on age. One wonders what possessed the (Jewish) administrators[30] in the camp to forbid the children from Leiden, who spent all or most of their life together, to remain in the same barrack, and even to forbid those who stayed in Barrack 66 to have their meals at the same table. She reports their joy of being allowed a shower once a week; they all suffered from the windy, dusty (and if it rained: muddy) conditions at Westerbork. More ominously, Jet adds that they have heard that the G1 papers for Hans and Piet have gone missing, so that *"we are not so confident anymore that they will be allowed to go back [to Leiden]"*.

Nothing, so it seems, could dampen the optimism of Sally Montezinos and Harry Spier. Sally, almost a month after deportation to Westerbork, is still *"fairly content, given the circumstances"* (or so he claims in his letter to Stoffels of 19th April). He is happy with his extra rations, but they lack something to drink. The water in that part of Drenthe is heavy with iron compounds, making it unsuitable for drinking or for making coffee or tea. He plays soccer on Sunday. The fact that they had to move to a different barrack which upset Jet (above), does not seem to bother him. But Sally was from all accounts a reserved, reticent person, and he probably had a fair idea of how precarious their situation was, without wanting to bother Stoffels with his personal fears.

Harry (Fig. 7.11) was a quite different character, unpretentious and uncomplicated, who took life as it came, often in high spirits.[31] He probably had no need to hide his fears from Stoffels: he simply did not have any, or so it seems. He sent four postcards to Stoffels, the first one, like the letter from Sally, on Tuesday, 23rd March, just after the train of that day had taken 34 of them away to the East. *"Dear All, I arrived here in good health and good spirits. They put me in a barrack for orphans, which is very nice. The food is also quite OK. [...] Yesterday we received the food parcels, also the fish pie. [...] Regards to Betsy and your wife."* All his four postcards are in the

---

30   Jet Mogendorff mentions (letter, 6th April) that a Mrs. Prins was in charge of all the "orphans" in Westerbork, but whether she played a role in all this is not known.

31   Although the Joodse Raad noted on his card "not very strong (*"flink"*) for his age.

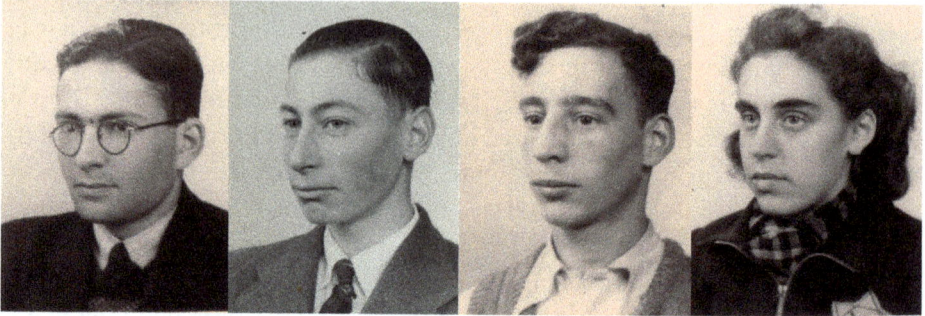

Figure 7.11: They all used their once-a-fortnight privilege to write to Stoffels. Passport photos, Leiden, autumn 1942.

Names from left: Sally Montezinos, Harry Spier, Piet de Vries and Jet Mogendorff

same spirit. Everything is *"fine"* the food is *"OK"*, and many thanks for sending so many parcels.

On 10th April Salomon Ritmeester sent a postcard to thank Stoffels for "parcels"; on 6th May Hans Kloosterman does the same. Hijme and Emilie must have sent dozens of parcels between 18th March and May 1943, when the inmates of Westerbork were no longer allowed to receive parcels from non-Jewish friends outside the camp, and any Jewish friend they may have had, had disappeared from life in Holland.

On Tuesday morning, 27th April, the ninth train from Westerbork to Sobibor took away Jet, Cecilia and Roza Mogendorff, and Sally Montezinos (Fig. 7.11).

Although in Sobibor there was no "selection" as there was in Auschwitz-Birkenau, the SS and their Ukrainian assistants occasionally required labourers in or around the camp. It is known that from this transport (which probably arrived on 30th April) several tens of people were selected for work (Schelvis, 2001). They were often forced to send a postcard to family or friends back home, typically saying things like: *"I am in good health. I have to work hard, but the food is OK,"* and so on. From seven people from this transport of 27th April such a card was received (as registered by the Joodse Raad before the card was forwarded). One such card, from the Sobibor sub-camp Dorohucza, was from S. Montezinos, addressed to A. van Nood in Amsterdam.[32] It was assumed after (and possibly already during) the war that the card came from Sally. The card itself did not survive, and it seems strange, given all the letters from Westerbork, that Sally would not write to Stoffels. There is no information about this Mr. van Nood, nor anything which would connect

32   Abraham van Nood, Eerste Oosterparkstraat 28, Amsterdam; list of 8th November 1943. Information about him would be very welcome.

him to Sally or the orphanage in Leiden. On the other hand, in spite of the many members of the families Montezinos (and Montesinos) who were deported to Sobibor, and with the initial S, only Sally was the right age to be selected, so indeed it may have been him.

The exact date of Sally's death is unknown, but it is extremely unlikely that he survived the liquidation of Sobibor on 14th October 1943 and all its sub-camps on 8th November. Sally's official date of death (4th November 1943) established after the war for legal reasons, is probably as good as any. Many official dates of death of Jews who were selected for work before being killed, particularly in Auschwitz (Croes & Tammes, 2004; Schütz, 2011), but also in Mauthausen (Ch. 8.1), are incorrect. In many cases the information available in local registries (such as *Sterbebücher*) was not used after the war, and even if it was used, the date and cause of death were often falsified, particularly when larger numbers of prisoners were killed on the same day. The list at the end of this book therefore maintains the official dates, and readers investigating a particular person should be aware of this.

7.9   The transport of 4th May 1943

On Tuesday, 4th May, a train left for Sobibor with 1187 people on board. None of them survived. The youngest of the remaining "Leiden" children were on this transport: Benjamin (four) and Louis (two) Bobbe, and Regine (René) Klausner, who was just one and a half years old when someone brought her to the Leiden orphanage on 30th April 1942. All three children went to their death without their parents and without their guardians from Leiden, who had already been deported (on 23rd March). The mother of René, Marie Schmarag, was gassed on 7th September 1942; her father Isaak was doing forced labour in Auschwitz-Fürstengrube, a coal mine for IG Farben; he died on 31st January 1943. The father of Benjamin and Louis had been deported on 16th October 1942; he perished in Buchenwald on 1st March 1945. Their mother, Eva Fuld, was deported to Sobibor on 8th June, a month *after* Benjamin and Louis. She was listed as *Häftling*, which suggests that she may have been caught while in hiding. If so, it raises the question why she did not arrange *onderduik* for the children, or maybe she did try, without success. It may also be surmised that she thought they were relatively safe in the orphanage, because being caught in *onderduik* meant certain death.

Also on this train were Philip (twelve) and Harry (two) Poons, but they were possibly reunited in Westerbork with their mother, Roosje Poons-Swaan. All five above-mentioned children were originally from The Hague. Philip and Harry had been in hiding in the orphanage, probably from early 1943. Thanks to their erstwhile

Figure 7.12: Philip Poons, The Hague, c. 1932. Courtesy Mrs. Henny Schippers.

neighbour in The Hague who came forward in 2017, there is one photograph of Philip (Fig. 7.12), but none of Harry, Benjamin, Louis or René.

Frieda Lichtenbaum (Fig. 7.13) was born in Ginneken, the Netherlands, but her mother, Jospa Lichtenbaum, was a refugee from Poland, who lived in Antwerp, Belgium. Jospa was a nurse, and she was stateless, which probably means that both Poland and Germany refused to give her a passport, before the war. Jospa was deported from *Kazerne Dossin* (Mechelen, Belgium; Ch. 8.4) to Auschwitz on 11th August 1942. Frieda was registered by the Dutch alien police on 10th October 1932, but the photo (Fig. 7.13) must have been taken much later. Frieda arrived in the orphanage in Leiden on 18th August 1932 and had lived there for more than ten years. She appears on many photographs, such as Figure 4.7 (1932) and Figure 5.10 (1939). She wrote (26th February 1940) in a verse album of a classmate (probably the last year in elementary school, at age twelve): *"Vergeet mij niet, in vreugde en verdriet"* ("Forget me not, in joy or sorrow"). Frieda uses some empty space on Henriette's letter of 19th April to thank the Stoffels for all their efforts on their behalf, and to wish them a happy Easter (25th-26th April 1943).

Harrie Spier had sent his fourth postcard to Hijme Stoffels on 3rd May with his habitual comments:

Dear Sir, Madam and Betsy. How are things in Leiden? Here everything is 'healthy'. [...] Today we had barley soup with meat. It tasted quite good. [...] The Mogendorfs and Sally Montezinos have departed [on 27th April], but Leo Auerhaan is still here, Betsy, he sends his regards. [...] Mr. and Mrs. [Stoffels], best regards.

Figure 7.13: Frieda Lichtenbaum, c. 1939. Photo: Alien police.

Figure 7.14: Postcard of 3rd May 1943 from Harry Spier to Mr. and Mrs. Stoffels and Betsy Wolff. Back side in dossier.

He scribbles a postscript to Betsy Wolff (Fig. 7.14, next to his signature) *"Bets, can you please send us a jar with piccalilli? Thanks."* It provided the title of Kerkvliet and Uitvlugt's report (1973).

Four days after writing this postcard, Harry, the once indomitable optimist, was no longer alive. He would have been eighteen a month later.

7.10   The transports of 18th and 25th May and 1st June 1943

On the 18th May, the next train to Sobibor took away Maurits Hakker (fourteen) and his brother Simon (ten), Rika Alvares Vega (ten) and her siblings Isaac (almost nine) Henrietta (four), and Willem (three), and Salomon Ritmeester (fifteen). Salomon was transported to Sobibor without his brother, Barend, or his father, Hartog, who were deported two weeks later. His mother had died in 1932 when he was three. He had stayed in Barrack 66, while Barend was in Barrack 58. Their father had been *wehrmachtgesperrt* (exempted from deportation) because as a metal worker he was valuable to the German army, but in the end the plans to eradicate everything Jewish always took precedence over economic or military considerations.

Several children who had left the orphanage shortly before 17th March were also deported on 18th May: Simon Korper (four), Enny Hamerslag (seven) and her siblings

Judith (five) and David (three), the youngest of this group. Many had spent overlapping periods in the orphanage, and they must have known each other. There is no way of knowing if they were put in the same or a different cattle wagon. Ies Cohen was the oldest, at 23, of the in total twelve children who had lived in the Leiden orphanage who were sent to Sobibor on this day. He had lived there for more than eight years, from 1932 to 1938. His brother Lodi Cohen survived the war (Ch. 9.7).

Isaac Slap (seven), who had lived in the orphanage for three months in 1939, follows them a week later, on the 25th, with his father, Joseph.

On 1st June, the weekly train to Sobibor took away Salomon's brother, Barend Ritmeester (thirteen), and their father, as well as Benno Redisch (four), who had left the Leiden orphanage in July 1942, and Harry de Vries and Jupie Pront, who had left the orphanage in 1932 and 1935. Benno sits on the bench with Aron Wolff and other children (Fig. 9.16) in July 1941, the last surviving last photo of him, taken on behalf of Geertje Gebert (Mrs. Bekooy). Barend (Fig. 4.7) lived in the Leiden orphanage from September 1932 to March 1939. He needed special care; in 1939 he was transferred to the Rudelsheim Clinic in Hilversum.

To the best of current knowledge, 59 people were forcefully taken out of the orphanage on 17th March 1943 and delivered to Camp Westerbork the following morning (Table 7.1). By the end of May, two had been released by the Germans; 54 had been deported to Sobibor, and by early June not a single one of those was still alive, with the possible exception of Sally Montezinos who may, at best, have survived until the liquidation of the Sobibor sub-camps on 8th November 1943. The last of the nineteen trains to Sobibor left Westerbork on Tuesday, 20th July 1943, after which transports went to Auschwitz again. At that time 3 of the original 59 were still in Westerbork: Didia, Bram and Mindel. Didia Klein, who became eighteen in May 1943, had married Heinz Cahn in Westerbork. They were both deported to Auschwitz on 21st September 1943. Didia survived Auschwitz, but at unimaginable personal cost (Ch. 9.5). Bram de Beer (five) had a brother, Hartog, who was two years older. Their mother was Betje Meents, who died in 1939. Hartog was taken in by his grandparents from father's side, Bram was lodged in the orphanage in Leiden in July 1942. Their father, Joseph de Beer, married again, with Elizabeth Turfreijer, and they had a son, Simon, who was born in Camp Westerbork on 24th August 1943. Simon therefore was Bram's half-brother. Elizabeth had three daughters from before her marriage with Joseph de Beer; they were Bram's stepsisters. One of these stepsisters died in 1941 in infancy; all the other family member perished in the Holocaust. Bram was in Westerbork when his father, Joseph, arrived in Westerbork with his new wife, Elizabeth, and he was there when Simon was born. There is a letter from Bram's father to Stoffels in his private archive (freely translated):

Westerbork, 7th May [1943]

Dear family,
You probably do not know me, but you are acquainted with my son, whom I have found
again here. He has not yet lost his timidity and is still the quietest boy in the camp. I
also received your package, for which I thank you very much. I was unable to thank
you properly in my previous letter, so I take the opportunity of this postcard to do so.
Sir, I regret I don't know what else to write to you, therefore I end this message, again
with many thanks on behalf of my son.
J. de Beer, Barrack 65, Westerbork

By the time this postcard arrived in Leiden (it was written on 7th May but stamped at the Assen post office only on 19th May), Stoffels had sent yet another package to Bram. Joseph and Bram sent another card to acknowledge receipt of this parcel on 14th May. This card was postmarked 15th May and it arrived in Leiden first. All family members de Beer and Turfreyer were deported to Auschwitz on 16th November 1943 and killed on 19th November, except Bram's father Joseph who perished on or around 31st March 1944, 28 years old.

Mindel Färber was the very last one of the 59 to be deported (Table 7.1), on 11th January 1944, to Bergen-Belsen, which at that time was a holding camp for Jews in "special categories" who were not to be killed outright. Mindel was in such a category because her mother was in Palestine, and Mindel was eligible for a (British) Palestine entry visa. Her story follows in Chapter 9.3. See also Chapter 9.4 about Aron Wolff.

Paula Jacobsohn, mentioned above, was deported one week after Mindel. Six more erstwhile inhabitants of the orphanage were deported in 1944, all to Auschwitz: Hijman Cohen (deported on 25th January), Leo Auerhaan (3rd March), Salomon and Bernard Meijers (23rd March), Hetty de Jong (19th May) and Ihno ten Brink (4th September). Hetty was killed with her husband and her son, Edward Frankenhuis, who was born in Westerbork on 24th February 1944.

7.11 Etty and Harry in Westerbork and the efforts of the Joodse Raad

Why was Etty Heerma van Voss not included in the first group for the transport of 23rd March, and why was she then selected and deported all on her own three weeks later? The Joodse Raad left four "work cards", which are shown and translated in Figure 7.15.

Etty had arrived in Leiden late, when deportations from Westerbork were already in full swing, after an attempt by her foster parents to arrange a G1 status (Fig. 6.20) had failed. Nevertheless, the Joodse Raad (probably in Amsterdam or The Hague) made significant efforts (Fig. 7.15) to find out if she could qualify for

Heerma - van Voss, Etty   Leiden   25343
            16-6-31   Roodenburgerstr.

19 MAART 1943 >H 1553/B : heeft 2 Joodsche grootouders.
                      S.v.p. onderzoeken
22 MAART 1943 < ⊕ verzorg gele kaartje + neg. verkl. N.I.G.
23 MAART 1943 : CV aan Mr. H Burgersdijk, Leiden: verzorg gele kaartje
                   + neg. verkl. N.I.G.
24 MRT. 1943 < op 18/3: verzoeken met spoed gele kaartje en negat.
             verkl. N.I. Leiden. Zonder deze bewijsstukken request onmogelijk.
             Verzoeke J.R. Den Haag hiervan in kennis te stellen. - 24/3
24 MAART 1943 : CV → JR Haag: Antwoord op request doorgegeven

25 III 43 JR Haag → CT → Bev. Reg. A'dam
           Geboortebewijs verzorgen.
26 MAART 1943 >B/Theeboom: Mr. Burgersdijk deelt mede,
            dat gele kaart niet te verzorgen, omdat
            in gesloten weeshuis, verder dat Bet. geen
            lid van Joodsche gemeente. Wil zaken bij
            M. B. neg. verkl. aanvragen.
26 MAART 1943 : CV → JR Haag, Onderhoud met Mr. Meulenaar
            bevestigd (zie voorafgaande notitie). Verzorgt
            afschrift gele kaart + neg. verkl.
31 MAART 1943 >Theeboom /C. neg. verkl. N.

Heerma - van Voss, Etty   I   25342
            16-6-31

31 MRT. 1943 < op 26/3: voor bet. is verzoek ingediend.
           Verzoeken de noodige stukken met spoed te bezorgen. - 31/3.
3 APR. 1943 > Boas /A: uittr. uit geb. reg. A'dam. Erkend door
           Theodora Noach, naam 1938 veranderd in Heerma van Voss.
           Mr. Veth is van meening dat niet zonder meer 2 joodsche
           grootouders kunnen worden aangehouden aangezien pleeg-
           ouders 4 grootouders hebben opgegeven. Waar is haar
           moeder? Nagaan wie verwekker is
5 APR. 1943 < 31/3 verzoeken nieuwe negatiefsverklaring van N.I.Leiden,
           dat bet. op ?/?/9-5-40 niet lid der I gemeente of niet lid is
           geweest. Toegezonden verklaring onvoldoende. - 5/4

8 APR. 1943 JR Haag: adres pleegouders: S. Heerma van Voss,
            Brederodeln. 26 Haarlem.
8 APR. 1943 CV aan bovengenoemde : hilt
10 APR. 1943 >C/Theeboom: Neg. verkl. Ned. I. gem. Leiden
10 APR. 1943 ⊕> Neg. verkl. N. per koerier
15 APR. 1943 < op 10/4 Verzoek afgewezen. - 17/4 -
3 MEI 1943 < op : bijgaand stukken retour hiere stappen
           geen doel. - 29/4

19 Maart 1943: >H1553/13: heeft 2Joodse grootouders. svp ouder zoeken.

19th March: Has 2 Jewish grandparents, pls find parent;

22 Maart 1943: < x verzorg geel kaartje + neg. verkl. N.I.G.

22nd March: "Yellow card and negative statement NIG"

23 Maart 1943: CV aan Mr. H. Burgersdijk, Leiden, verzorg geel kaartje + neg.verkl.

23rd March: "CV to Mr Burgersdijk, Leiden : arrange yellow card + neg. decl NIG";

24 Maart 1943: < op 18/3: verwachten met spoed geel kaartje en negat. verkl NIG Leiden. Zonder deze bewijsstukken request [tot goedk.G1] onmogelijk. Verzoeke J[oodse] R[aad] Den Haag hiervan in kennis te stellen- 22/3

24th March: "Urgently require yellow card and neg. statement ", without these documents request [to approve G1] cannot be made. Please inform JR The Hague";

24 Maart 1943: CV>JR Haag: Antwoord op request doorgegeven

24th March: CV>JR Hague: Response to request passed on".

25.III/43: JR.Haag L> CV>Bev.Reg. A'dam Geboorte-bewijs verzorgen

25th March: JR Hague L-7 CV L-7, Civil Registry Amsterdam

26 Maart 1943: >/Theeboom: Mr Burgersdijk deelt mede, dat gele kaart niet te verzorgen, omdat in gesloten weeshuis, verder dat betr. geen lid van Joodsche Gemeente. x>J [?] zullen bij Mr.B. neg. verkl. aanvragen

26th March: B/Theeboom: Mr Burgersdijk informs yellow card cannot be arranged because orphanage is closed, but negative declaration NIG possible. We will ask him to arrange that decl.

26 Maart 1943: CV>JR Haag. Onderhoud met dhr. Meuleman bevestigd (zie voorafgaande notitie) Verzorgt afschrift gele kaart + neg. verkl.

26th March: JR Hague, interview with mr Meuleman Confirmed, he will arrange duplicate yellow card and neg. decl.

31 Maart 1943: >Theeboom/C: neg. verkl.N.

31st March: >Theeboom/C: neg. decl. N

31 Mrt. 1943: <op 26/3: voor betr. is verzoek ingediend. Verzoeken de nodige stukken met spoed te verzorgen. -30/3

31st March: On 26/3 request has been submitted; please arrange the required documents with utmost urgency 30/3

3 Apr. 1943: >Boas/A: uittr. uit geb. reg. A'dam. Erkend door Theodora Noach, naam 1938 veranderd in Heerma van Voss. Mr. Veth is van meening dat niet zonder meer 2 joodsche grootouders kunnen worden aangenomen aangezien pleegouders 4 J. grootouders hebben aangegevn. Waar is haar moeder? Nagaan wie verwekker is.

3rd April: >Boas/A excerpt birth certificate A'dam. Recognised as her child by Theodora Noach, name changed 1938 Heerma van Voss. Mr Veth is of opin-ion we cannot assume [only] 2 Jewish grandparents just like that, because foster parents have registered 4 Jewish grandparents. Where is her mother? Check who is her biological father.

5 Apr. 1943: <31/3 verzoeken nieuwe negatiefver-klaring van NIG Leiden, dat betr. op of na 9-5-1940 niet tot de J. Gemeente of nooit lid is geweest. Toegezonden verklaring onvoldoende. -3/4

5th April: We requested on 31st March new neg. decl from NIG Leiden to effect that this person (ie Etty) was not a member of the NIG on or after 9-5-40, or for that matter, ever. The declaration we received is insufficient.

6 & 8 Apr. 1943: JR Haag: adres pleegouders en naam bovengenoemde ?niet

6th April: JR Hague provided address foster parents Haarlem. Name of above: (unreadable)

8th April: JR Hague: address foster parents

10 Apr. 1943: >Theeboom: Neg.Verkl. NIG

10th April: C/Theeboom: neg. decl. N. by courier

10 Apr. 1943: x Neg.verkl. per koerier

10th April: Neg. decl despatched by courier

15 Apr. 1943: < op 10/4 verzoek afgewezen

15th April: on 10/4: request denied -14/4

3 Mei 1943: bijgaand stukken retour. Verdere stappen geen doel. - 29/4

3rd May: Returning documents. Further actions serve no purpose - 29/4 -

Figure 7.15: Four "work cards" of the Joodse Raad for Etty Heerma van Voss, recording the efforts of the JR officials to determine whether Etty was "full- or half-Jewish". Translation on the right. Not all scribbles are clear as to their meaning. Courtesy of the Red Cross War Archives, The Hague, 2017.

Frantic efforts to obtain confirmation and documents from the NIG (the Jewish Congregation) in Leiden were of course fruitless: all Jews who had not been arrested and deported in Leiden were in hiding, and no official could be reached. Yet somehow a "Negative declaration" was obtained and sent to Westerbork by courier on 10th April. to support the request to classify Etty as "half Jewish". The request was denied on the same day, and Etty was put on the list for the upcoming transport 3 days later. The last entry of 3rd May reads: *"Further actions serve no purpose"*: Indeed, Etty was put on the train to Sobibor on 13th April, where she was killed on 16th April 1943.

G1 status. Two Joodse Raad officials stand out, both using a fountain pen and dark-grey ink. Their annotations occur on many of the cards which were reviewed for this study.

The very first entry (19th March, the day after she arrived in Westerbork) observes that she has two Jewish grandparents (implying that she might have two non-Jewish grandparents). Assuming that the information was shared with the *Emigratiebureau* and/or the *Antragstelle* in Westerbork, this was likely the reason why Etty was not put on the transport of 23rd March. But on 3rd April the Joodse Raad official notes that the [foster] parents were unable to attest that the other two grandparents were not Jewish, since Etty's biological mother declined to support such a claim (Ch. 6.8). For the same reason they could not make a credible claim that her adoptive father was also her biological father.

Irmi (Etty's foster-mother, Fig. 6.20) wrote her a letter (Kasteleyn, 2003, p. 43) on 12th April. It was postmarked for receipt in Assen (the city nearby Westerbork) on 15th April and sent back to Haarlem when it transpired that Etty was not in Westerbork anymore. The efforts by the Joodse Raad continued for another two weeks until they concluded (last entry 3rd May) that further action served no purpose (Fig. 7.15). No doubt someone in Westerbork had informed him that Etty had been deported on 13th April. As far as we can tell, she made the journey to Sobibor alone; there were no other children from the orphanage group, the people she had lived with for the preceding seven months, on this transport. She was eleven years old. I can only hope that someone in Etty's cattle car cared for her.

Theodora Noach, Etty's biological mother, was imprisoned in Camp Vught according to the Joodse Raad card (the red V at the top, Fig. 7.16) on 24th February 1943, and deported to Auschwitz on 8th June via Westerbork with her husband and their two children. All four were killed on or around 11th June.

Harry Spier had entered the orphanage, not yet three years old, in May 1928, before the inauguration of the new building. Little is known about him, or his family, except that his mother was Froukje Spier, born in Haarlem on 29th January 1883. Froukje married a certain Wellink, who may or may not have survived the war. The Joods Monument comments as follows:

> *We have been unable to determine whether one or more members of this family survived the war. While their names do not appear on the lists of survivors, we have not been able to trace them in In Memoriam, either. They are therefore labelled as 'surviving' and their names are not listed.*

When Harry arrived in Westerbork, Joodse Raad officials, probably in Amsterdam because they refer to the Joodse Raad office in The Hague, embarked on an investigation into the possibility of declaring Harry G1, just as they tried to do

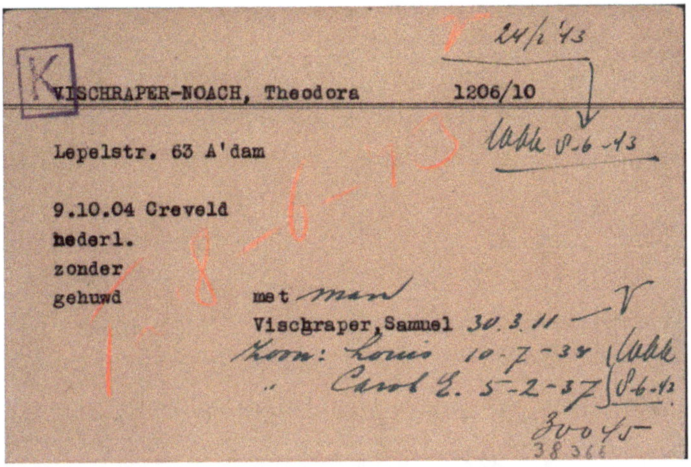
K
VISCHRAPER-NOACH, Theodora 1206/10
Lepelstr. 63 A'dam
9.10.04 Creveld
nederl.
zonder
gehuwd
met man
Vischraper, Samuel 30.3.11
Zoon: Louis 10-7-38
" Carol E. 5-2-37

Figure 7.16: The Joodse Raad card for Etty's biological mother, Theodora Vischschraper. The V at the top stands for Camp Vught. Courtesy Red Cross Netherlands, 2017.

for Etty (Fig. 7.17). In fact, comparing both sets of cards shows how busy the unknown *"official with the fountain pen"* has been in trying to keep Etty and Harry, and who knows how many others, out of the claws of the Nazis, *the official way*, that is: strictly within the pseudo-legal boundaries as determined by the Germans and faithfully executed by the Dutch civil service, in this case the *Rijksinspectie der Bevolkingsregisters*. The efforts included getting documentary evidence that Harry was never a member of the Israelite congregation in Leiden. On 24th March: *"We continue to ask as a matter of urgency for the yellow card*[33] *and negative statement by the Jewish congregation Leiden."* But the last members of that congregation had been arrested and deported in the preceding weeks, or they had gone into hiding; there was nobody left who could comply. Three more cards detail the many efforts, until on 3rd May the Joodse Raad bureau in The Hague is requested to take up Harry's case with the Civil Registry. But, just as with Etty (above), on 7th May the "fountain pen" records that further action is futile: indeed, the news must have reached him[34] that Harry had been deported on 4th May.

The cards of Etty and Harry, and some of the documents for Piet and Hans, are of an utterly unreal, almost phantasmagorical nature. The cards seem to reflect a busy, effective organization, with so many officials working hard, no doubt in good

33 I have not been able to determine its meaning.

34 I feel, possibly mistakenly, that the handwriting suggests a male official. Note that there were at least two officials using a fountain pen.

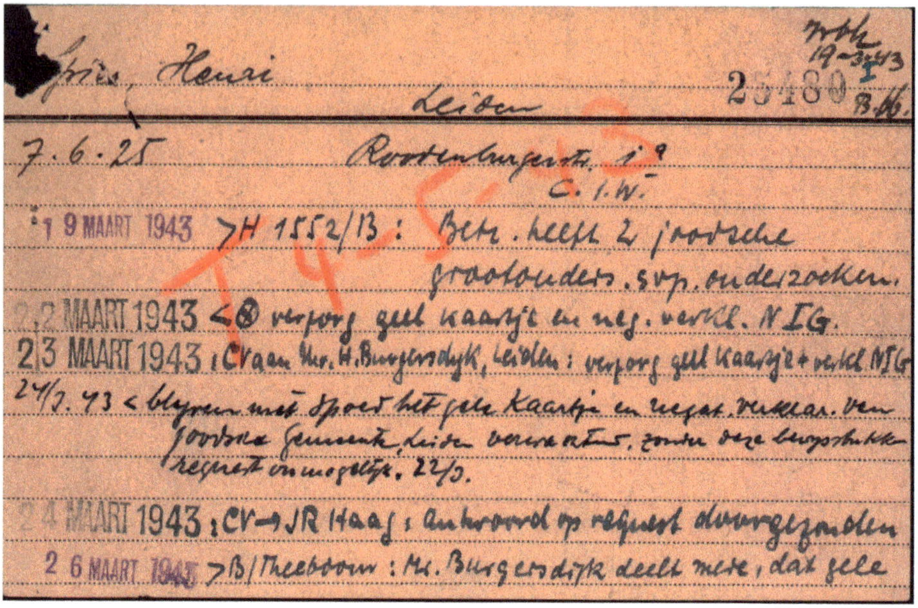
Spier, Henri
Leiden
25480
7.6.25
Roodenburgerstr. 1a
19 MAART 1943 >H 1552/13: Betr. heeft 2 joodsche grootouders. svp. onderzoeken.
22 MAART 1943 < verzorg geel kaartje en neg. verkl. N.I.G.
23 MAART 1943: CV aan Mr. H. Burgersdijk, Leiden: verzorg geel kaartje + verkl. NIG
24/3.43 < blijven met spoed het gele kaartje en negat. verklar. van Joodsche Gemeente Leiden verwachten, zonder deze bewijsstukken request onmogelijk. 22/3.
24 MAART 1943: CV→JR Haag: antwoord op request doorgezonden
26 MAART 1943 >B/Theeboom: Mr. Burgersdijk deelt mede, dat gele

Figure 7.17: One of four work cards of the Joodse Raad for Harry Spier (see text).

faith, to save a pitiful few people from deportation (see the Joodse Raad organigram of March 1943). But month after month during 1943, the whole structure was fading away, dissolving as the *Sperre* were cancelled, one after another, or batch by batch, and the number of vacant positions in the Joodse Raad organization increased until no one was left to answer the phone. Then Asscher and Cohen were also sent to Westerbork (September 1943), and the Germans could proudly declare a village, or city, or country *"Judenfrei"*.

7.12 Jacob Philipson and Jozua Klein and their families

Jacob Philipson (Fig. 7.18) was a member of the permanent staff, but he lived independently with his wife and five children at Van der Waalsstraat 34, a mere 650 metres away from the orphanage. He was its *"administrateur"*, a modest-sounding title for a function which probably included the bookkeeping, the financial and personnel management, and so on; tasks essential to safeguard the short- and long-term financial and organizational health of such an institution.

Jacob refused to go into hiding (testimony of H. Stoffels, 22nd November 1967) and stayed in function until Stoffels told him on 16th March 1943 that the orphanage would be liquidated the following day, and that on the same day a razzia was planned to arrest all Jews still living in Leiden. The Stoffels had prearranged *onderduik* for Jet Philipson-Simons and her five children, and maintained contact with Jet and the foster parents of (at least some of) the children all through the remaining years of the war. Jacob joined his parents-in-law at their hiding address, Oude Rijn 48. But they were found and arrested by Biesheuvel and de Groot, the infamous Jew hunters of the Leiden police force (Fig. 10.12), on 23rd June. Jacob and his wife's parents were deported from Westerbork and murdered in Sobibor on 23rd July 1943. He was 40 years old.

Figure 7.18: Jacob Philipson, 1942.

Jet and the children were delivered by different people to different addresses. When Hijme and Emilie Stoffels were asked by Elchanan Italie (in November 1969) to put together a list of people who they warned about the impending razzia of 17th March 1943, and assisted in finding *onderduik* addresses, they put the family Philipson on top of their shortlist of four families. Sara was brought to the house of Piet "Sik" van Egmond in the village of Rijnsburg. She is included in the family photo (Fig. 7.19). Contrary to the story in de Beer (2015, p. 69), Sara is the only *onderduiker* on the photo; everybody else belongs to Piet's family. Sara narrowly escaped arrest by de Groot and Biesheuvel: Bertha Colijn (no. 4 on the photograph) hurried her away during the raid (Ch. 10.4).

The other children (see Fig. 10.3) were delivered to various addresses by helpers (including Kit and Henna Winkel). They all survived the war. It has always been assumed that Sara was betrayed while in Rijnsburg, but no evidence has (yet[35]) been found. Rijnsburg, which harboured a surprisingly large number of (Jewish) *onderduikers* (ibidem), was a tight-knit community, and even the local NSB member never dared to betray anybody. It is quite possible that Biesheuvel and de Groot were attracted to Piet's house by the resistance activities of Johannes Post and his comrades (see Hovingh, 1995).

The year before, on 6th March 1942, Jozua Klein, a neighbour of Emilie Stoffels on the Mariënpoelstraat (Fig. 7.20), had been arrested by the Leiden police (Ch. 6.5). Jozua was put on a transport the next day, and was deported to Mauthausen, where he died on 6th July 1942, four months after his arrest. No doubt, the Stoffels heard about Jozua's death, and it only confirmed Hijme's belief that the Dutch Jews

---

35 More research of the police records is required, which has become easier now that the wartime police archives have been declassified.

Figure 7.19: Piet van Egmond (1), his wife, Jannetje de Mooi (3), Sara Philipson (2) and Bertha Colijn (4), 1943 (see text; de Beer et al., 2015, and Chapter 10.2). Photo courtesy Historische Vereniging Rijnsburg.

were in mortal danger and that they should not allow themselves to be deported. After Jozua's arrest, Rosi Klein-Mendel had continued to live at Mariënpoelstraat 15, next to the parents of Emilie (Stoffels-)van Brussel. Rosi was warned to leave her house on 16th/17th March 1943, but when Gerda (who had been the other neighbour in the Mariënpoelstraat) and Emilie checked on that fateful Wednesday afternoon, they found out Rosi was still there with the three children. It prompted Emilie to take assertive action. From the Klein family's reports (1995; freely translated by the author):

> Early morning on the 17th March, Gerda Meijer (who was involved with resistance activities) knocked on our door and told my mother to leave the house and go into hiding [...] because the trains are standing ready at the railway station, and they will come to take all of you away. My mother refused to move: 'I lost my husband. I will not give up my children, and I have a doctor's attestation to the effect that we have diphtheria.' But Gerda replied, you [may] all have doctor's attestations, and yet they will come and take you all away. She was in a hurry to go, since she had lived for a year just two houses down the street from the Klein family, and

she was afraid someone would recognize her. She told us that Emilie [Stoffels] would drop by around 11:00. The first thing Emilie asked when she arrived was: Has Gerda been here to talk to you? Yes, she was here. Emilie talked to my mother to convince her to flee until she gave in. [...] Emilie and a woman who lived in our house put Ingrid and Ben on the back of their bicycle and brought them to Oegstgeest. At 17.30 my mother and I walked through the park (Leidse Hout) to a safe house. An hour later the police van to take us away stopped in front of our house! [...] In the evening [of 17th March] Emilie and my mother brought Ingrid and Ben by bicycle to Valkenburg.[36] Next day Emilie returned to pick up Ben [to bring him] to an address in Sassenheim.[37] He was just two and a half years old and lived there for the remainder of the war. (Klein-Roskin et al., 1995)

Figure 7.20: Jozua Klein and family at Marienpoel-straat 15, 1941. They were neighbours of Emilie van Brussel before she moved in with Hijme Stoffels in 1942. From left: Ingrid, mother Rosi, Benjamin, Rita.

The Stoffels took care of Ingrid, who had a difficult time. They moved her a few times, but she was unhappy, until Emilie found an elderly couple in the small farming village of Nieuwe Wetering, where she felt safe. She stayed there until the end of the war. Rita was brought to a hiding place in Rijnsburg, just as Sarah Philipson. She was given the name *Rita Roelofs* and was supposed to be a homeless refugee from the bombardment of Rotterdam in May 1940 (just like Aron Wolff, Ch. 9.4). Rita's *onderduik* parents were Jan and Grietje van Egmond-Star. She attended school with the children of Jan and Grietje (Fig. 7.21). On occasion, when a razzia was expected, they brought Rita by bicycle to Sassenheim to stay with the family Ciggaar, who was sheltering her brother Ben. Like so many other Jewish children in *onderduik*, both Sarah and Rita appear on "family" photographs taken during their sojourn in hiding (see de Beer et al., 2015).

36   Like Rijnsburg, Valkenburg is a small village west of Leiden.
37   In the flower bulb region, north-west of Leiden. Nieuwe Wetering is north-east of Leiden. All these villages are within bicycle distance from Leiden.

Figure 7.21: Rita Klein, aka Rita Roelofs (right), with the two children of her onderduik parents, Jan and Grietje van Egmond.

It is difficult to imagine how Emilie and Hijme managed to take care of the children under the stressful conditions, a razzia going on, German police present in the city, and all by bicycle. They made use of their extensive social networks, covering both Protestant (Hijme) and Catholic (Emilie) communities. They could rely on a number of safe houses and addresses where people were prepared to accept "guests" at very short notice. They never bragged about it after the war and were obviously not concerned that their role in arranging *onderduik* was not always acknowledged.[38]

Table 7.1   Jewish Orphanage in Leiden; Arrested on 17th March 1943 and brought to Westerbork (listed by deportation date from Westerbork)

	Place of birth	Date of birth	Deported on:	Date of death	Place of death	Age
Adler, Lotte	Frankfurt a/M	8-2-1925	23-3-1943	26-3-1943	Sobibor	18.1
Adler, Henny Henriette	Frankfurt a/M	23-7-1930	23-3-1943	26-3-1943	Sobibor	12.7
Beem, Jozef David	Rotterdam	4-7-1926	23-3-1943	26-3-1943	Sobibor	16.7
Blog, Wilhelmina (Willy)	Apeldoorn	1-1-1934	23-3-1943	26-3-1943	Sobibor	9.2
Bobbe, Jetje (Jetty)	The Hague	25-4-1924	23-3-1943	26-3-1943	Sobibor	18.9
Dagloonder, Mietje (Mieke)	Amsterdam	29-11-1927	23-3-1943	26-3-1943	Sobibor	15.3
Ensel, Izak	Rotterdam	20-8-1938	23-3-1943	26-3-1943	Sobibor	4.6
Frenkel, Cornelia (Corry)	Rotterdam	25-4-1924	23-3-1943	26-3-1943	Sobibor	18.9
Goudsmit, Bertha	The Hague	14-8-1924	23-3-1943	26-3-1943	Sobibor	18.6
Günsberg, Fanny Susanne	Gelsenkirchen	15-1-1927	23-3-1943	26-3-1943	Sobibor	16.2
Günsberg, Lothar	Gelsenkirchen	22-4-1928	23-3-1943	26-3-1943	Sobibor	14.9
Italie, Hanna Sara	Leiden	11-5-1935	23-3-1943	26-3-1943	Sobibor	7.9
Italie, Elchanan Tsewie Italie	Leiden	8-2-1937	23-3-1943	26-3-1943	Sobibor	6.1
Kam, Marianne (Mary) van	Rotterdam	16-1-1931	23-3-1943	26-3-1943	Sobibor	12.2
Kam, Hijman van	Rotterdam	15-3-1933	23-3-1943	26-3-1943	Sobibor	10.0
Kam, Herman van	Rijswijk	18-1-1935	23-3-1943	26-3-1943	Sobibor	8.2
Kam, Arthur van	Rijswijk	23-8-1937	23-3-1943	26-3-1943	Sobibor	5.6
Kirchenbaum, Chaim (Charles)	Belfort	2-9-1926	23-3-1943	26-3-1943	Sobibor	16.6
Protter, Ralph Heinz	Köln	10-5-1930	23-3-1943	26-3-1943	Sobibor	12.9
Rotstein, Salomon	Amsterdam	20-7-1937	23-3-1943	26-3-1943	Sobibor	5.7

38   Post-war attention naturally focused on the host families which provided the shelter, more than on those who arranged the contact.

	Place of birth	Date of birth	Deported on:	Date of death	Place of death	Age
Rozeveld, Herman Bert	Leiden	25-12-1930	23-3-1943	26-3-1943	Sobibor	12.3
Segal, Reina	Amsterdam	5-1-1925	23-3-1943	26-3-1943	Sobibor	18.2
Stratum, Mozes (Max) van	Groningen	3-3-1927	23-3-1943	26-3-1943	Sobibor	16.1
Velleman, Margarita Henriette	Rotterdam	4-3-1925	23-3-1943	26-3-1943	Sobibor	18.1
Velleman, Marianna Rosa	Rotterdam	6-9-1926	23-3-1943	26-3-1943	Sobibor	16.6
Altenberg, Floortje (staff)	Amsterdam	23-3-1904	23-3-1943	26-3-1943	Sobibor	39.0
Bierschenk, Rachel (staff)	Amsterdam	1-11-1894	23-3-1943	26-3-1943	Sobibor	48.4
Gobes, Mietje (Mien) (staff)	Amsterdam	21-12-1899	23-3-1943	26-3-1943	Sobibor	43.3
Italie, Nathan (staff)	Leeuwarden	10-4-1890	23-3-1943	26-3-1943	Sobibor	53.0
Italie-Cohen, Lies (staff)	Leiden	2-3-1902	23-3-1943	26-3-1943	Sobibor	41.1
Klein, Esther (staff)	Oldenzaal	17-8-1909	23-3-1943	26-3-1943	Sobibor	33.6
Leeuw, Jet de (staff)	Barneveld	29-12-1888	23-3-1943	26-3-1943	Sobibor	54.2
Vries, Barend de (staff)	Leiden	20-6-1922	23-3-1943	26-3-1943	Sobibor	20.8
Blitz, Alice (staff)	Leiden	18-7-1923	23-3-1943	26-3-1943	Sobibor	19.7
Heerma van Voss, Etty	Amsterdam	16-6-1931	13-4-1943	16-4-1943	Sobibor	11.8
Mogendorf, Henriette (Jetty)	Amsterdam	23-11-1925	27-4-1943	30-4-1943	Sobibor	17.4
Mogendorf, Cecilia	Amsterdam	5-11-1926	27-4-1943	30-4-1943	Sobibor	16.5
Mogendorf, Roza	Amsterdam	1-12-1932	27-4-1943	30-4-1943	Sobibor	10.4
Montezinos, Salomon Levie (Sally)	The Hague	6-5-1924	27-4-1943	4-11-1943	Dorohucza	19.5
Bobbe, Benjamin	Rotterdam	11-2-1939	4-5-1943	7-5-1943	Sobibor	4.2
Bobbe, Louis	The Hague	7-3-1941	4-5-1943	7-5-1943	Sobibor	2.2
Klausner, Regine (René)	The Hague	22-7-1940	4-5-1943	7-5-1943	Sobibor	2.8
Lichtenbaum, Frieda Ita	Ginneken	17-10-1927	4-5-1943	7-5-1943	Sobibor	15.6
Poons, Philip	The Hague	6-12-1930	4-5-1943	7-5-1943	Sobibor	12.4
Poons, Harry	The Hague	13-7-1940	4-5-1943	7-5-1943	Sobibor	2.8
Slier, Henriette (Henny)	Rotterdam	26-12-1930	4-5-1943	7-5-1943	Sobibor	12.4
Spier, Henry (Harry)	The Hague	7-6-1925	4-5-1943	7-5-1943	Sobibor	17.9
Hakker, Maurits	The Hague	29-3-1929	18-5-1943	21-5-1943	Sobibor	14.1
Hakker, Simon	The Hague	24-2-1933	18-5-1943	21-5-1943	Sobibor	10.2
Ritmeester, Salomon	Amsterdam	16-3-1928	18-5-1943	21-5-1943	Sobibor	15.2
Vega, Rika Alvares	Amsterdam	17-9-1932	18-5-1943	21-5-1943	Sobibor	10.7
Vega, Isaac Alvares	Amsterdam	19-6-1934	18-5-1943	21-5-1943	Sobibor	8.9
Vega, Henriette	Amsterdam	1-9-1938	18-5-1943	21-5-1943	Sobibor	4.7
Vega, Willem Alvares	Amsterdam	5-8-1939	18-5-1943	21-5-1943	Sobibor	3.8
Klein, Didia	Paris	12-5-1925	21-9-1943		Survived	
Beer, Abraham (Bram) de	Amsterdam	10-8-1939	16-11-1943	19-11-1943	Auschwitz	4.3
Färber, Mindel	Düsseldorf	5-4-1939	11-1-1944		Survived	
Kloosterman, Anthonius H. (Hans)	Amsterdam	19-2-1927		Not dep'd	Survived	
Vries, Piet (Daniël) de	Amsterdam	12-3-1925		Not dep'd	Survived	

References

Beer, W. de, et al., 2015; *"Een veilig nest voor vervolgden. Verhalen over Joodse onderduikers in Rijnsburg"*. Genootschap Oud Rijnsburg. [A collection of stories about the many Jewish *onderduikers* (including Sara Philipson and Rita Klein) who found shelter in this small strictly reformed Christian village in the Leiden area. The stories are included as they were told, without being checked against other sources or documents.]

Boomgaard, Petra van den, 2019; *"Voor de nazi's geen Jood"*. Hilversum, Verbum, ISBN 9789493028043. [With English summary at the back; *"How more than 2500 Jews were able to escape deportation by evading racial regulations"*; certainly the most comprehensive study to date.]

Cohen, E.A., 1979; *"De negentien treinen naar Sobibor"*. Amsterdam, Elsevier, ISBN 9010025136.

Creveld, I.B. van, 2001; *"Het wezen van wezen. Joodse wezen in Den Haag 1850-1943. Een monument"*. De Nieuwe Haagsche, ISBN 9077032096. [Describes the history of the Jewish orphanage in The Hague and its liquidation in 1943.]

Creveld, I.B. van, 2004; *"Hulp aan wezen in oorlogstijd"*. De Nieuwe Haagsche, ISBN 9077032711. [Reports on new information about the orphanage in The Hague based on the orphanage's archives, upon their recovery and return from Russia.]

Croes, M. & P. Tammes, 2004; *"Gif laten wij niet voortbestaan. Een onderzoek naar de over-levingskansen van joden in de Nederlandse Gemeenten"*. Rijksuniversiteit Groningen. [Dutch text; for an (abbreviated) English summary, see Croes, 2006.]

Croes, M., 2006; *"The Holocaust in the Netherlands and the rate of Jewish survival"*. Holocaust and Genocide Studies 20 (3), 474-499.

Crone, F., 2005; *"Voorbijgaand verblijf. Joodse weeskinderen in oorlogstijd"*. Amsterdam, De Prom, ISBN 9068011162. [Focused on refugees from Germany and the Jewish orphanage in Utrecht.]

Hillesum, Etty, 2002; *"Etty: The letters and diaries of Etty Hillesum, 1941-1943"*. Ed. by Klaas A.D. Smelik. Grand Rapids, Wm. B. Eerdmans Publishing Company, ISBN 0802839592. Originally published in Dutch in 1986 by Uitgeverij Balans, Amsterdam.

Hovingh, G.C., 1995; *"Johannes Post. Exponent van het verzet. Een biografie"*. Kampen, Kok, ISBN 9024264626. 2nd ed., 1999.

Italie, Gabriel, 2009; *"Het oorlogsdagboek van dr. G. Italie. Den Haag, Barneveld, Westerbork, Theresienstadt, Den Haag 1940-1945"*. Ed. by Wally M. de Lang. Amsterdam, Contact, ISBN 9789025427917. [The war diary of Gabriel Italie, one of the brothers of Nathan Italie, the director of the Jewish orphanage in Leiden.]

Jong, L. de, 1969-1994; *"Het Koninkrijk der Nederlanden in de Tweede Wereldoorlog"*. http://www.dbnl.org or http://www.loedejongdigitaal.nl/. [The standard (contemporary) history of the Netherlands during the war. The entire text is available online (with search facility). For more recent interpretations, see Blom et al., 2021.]

Kasteleyn, L.P., 2003; *"Vervolging en bescherming, joden in Leiden 1933-1945"*. Leiden, Museum de Lakenhal.

Kerkvliet, G. & M. Uitvlugt, 1973; *"Een pot picalilly voor Westerbork. Journalistiek verslag over de vernietiging van het joodse weeshuis in Leiden"*. Den Haag, Q-Producties. Author's collection. [The original stencilled report, containing verbatim quotes from interviews with the Stoffels, Geertje Gebert, and Piet de Vries.] See also Kerkvliet & Uitvlugt, 1974.

Klein-Roskin, Ingrid, 1995; *"Observations on the end of an era"*. Private report. Author's collection. [Contains the wartime memories and history of Ingrid, Rita and Benjamin Klein.]

Lang, Wally de, 2021; *"De razzia's van 22 en 23 februari 1941 in Amsterdam. Het lot van 389 Joodse mannen"*. Amsterdam, Uitgeverij Atlas Contact, ISBN 9789045042749. [This first comprehensive account of the razzias which preceded the February Strike, and the fate of the deportees to Buchenwald and Mauthausen was published just before the present book went to press.]

Lanzmann, Claude (dir.), 2001; *"Sobibor: 14th October 1943, 16:00"*. [A 95-minute documentary containing a detailed witness account by Yehuda Lerner of the revolt in Sobibor, which caused the Germans to close down the camp and its subsidiary camps and kill all the remaining prisoners.]

Liempt, A. van, 2005; *"Hitler's bounty hunters: The betrayal of the Jews"*. New York, Berg, ISBN 1845202031/9781845202033.

Liempt, A. van, 2019; *"Gemmeker. Commandant van Kamp Westerbork"*. Amsterdam, Balans, ISBN 9789460039782 (hardcover)/9789460039799 (ebook).

Lindwer, Willy, 1990; *"Kamp van hoop en wanhoop. Getuigen van Westerbork, 1939-1945"* [Camp of hope and despair: Witness account from Westerbork]. Amsterdam, Balans, ISBN 9050180981.

Mazower, Mark, 2005; *"Salonica – City of ghosts: Christians, Muslims and Jews, 1450-1950"*. London, Harper Collins, ISBN 9780007120222.

Mechanicus, Philip, 1964; *"In dépôt: dagboek uit Westerbork"* [In depot: Diary from Westerbork]. Amsterdam, Polak & van Gennep.

Meijer-Wijler, Gerda, 1993; *"A personal history, 1923-1945"*. [Unpublished document (in English), written for her children and grandchildren. Gerda was neighbour to both Emilie van Brussel (before she married Hijme Stoffels) and the family Klein. She played an active role in the Dutch resistance. She emigrated to Israel with other surviving members of her family, building a successful dairy farm in Beth Jitschak (Kopuit, 1974). She also deposited an (English language) report of her activities between September 1944 and May 1945 at NIOD, also available at www.weggum.com.]

Michman, Jozeph, 1987; *"Met voorbedachten rade. Ideologie en uitvoering van de Endlösung der Judenfrage"*. Amsterdam, Meulenhoff, ISBN 9029098473. [An analysis of the ideology which gave rise to the Holocaust and how it developed from the moment Hitler declared his intention to remove all Jews from Europe.]

Schelvis, Jules, 2001; *"Vernietigingskamp Sobibor. De transportlijsten"*. Amsterdam, De Bataafse Leeuw, ISBN 9067075167. [A most important document, it published the deportation lists made, and secretly copied, in Camp Westerbork. It contains the names and date of birth of 34,313 people deported in 19 train transports from Westerbork to Sobibor, a journey which took 3 days. Only 18 people (including Schelvis) survived.]

Schelvis, Jules, 2007a; *"Binnen de poorten. Een verslag van twee jaar Duitse vernietigings- en concentratiekampen"*. Amsterdam, De Bataafse Leeuw, ISBN 978906707626. [Schelvis is one of the 18 survivors of the 34,314 people deported from Westerbork to Sobibor. This is his own account of his deportation and survival.]

Schelvis, Jules, 2007b; *"Sobibor: A history a Nazi death camp"*. Oxford, Berg, in association with USHM, ISBN 978184520418. Republished in 2014 by Bloomsbury, ISBN 1472589068.

Schute, Ivar, 2020; *"In de schaduw van de nachtvlinder"*. Amsterdam, Prometheus, ISBN 9789044642438. [A recent publication by a member of the Sobibor archaeology team.]

Schütz, Raymund, 2011; *"Vermoedelijk op transport. De Joodsche Raad Cartotheek als informatiesysteem binnen sterk veranderende kaders: repressie, opsporing en herinnering. Een archiefwetenschappelijk onderzoek naar de herkomst, het gebruik en het beheer van een bijzondere historische bron"*. MA thesis, Free University of Amsterdam. [An indispensable report when interpreting the index cards kept by the Joodse Raad of Amsterdam on all people who were to be deported from the Netherlands. The cards were kept by the Red Cross (War Documentation) in The Hague until February 2018; now in the Holocaust Museum, Amsterdam. Also ITS Arolsen. Dutch text available at https://www.joodsebibliotheek.nl.]

Wijk, Cor van, 1946; *"Mijn werk in de Nederlandse Verzetsorganisatie 'Strijdend Nederland'"*. Typescript, Regionaal Archief Leiden (now Erfgoed Leiden & Omgeving). [An account of his wartime activities, including the provision of (at least) 420 blank but genuine pbs to the Leiden underground movement. No less than 124 of these were used by Stoffels.]

Zegveld, W.F. van, 1993; *"Joods Wees- en Doorgangshuis Leiden, bewoners 1890-1951"*. Originally in: *"De Joden van Leiden"*. Unpublished; 4 volumes. [Several copies were made, available (i.a.) at Erfgoed Leiden (ELO) and the Joods Historisch Museum, Amsterdam. The results of his painstaking research have served as a basis for subsequent investigations. Note that his report is an important source of information on children and staff in the Leiden orphanage who are not included in this book because they had left before the move to the new building in 1929, as well as Jewish citizens of the Leiden region who were not connected to the orphanage.]

8 So many more

Abstract

Most of the children who had left the orphanage before 17th March 1943 were deported. Karel van Santen was caught with his brother Philip in the razzias in Amsterdam in February 1941. They were deported to Buchenwald, Mauthausen, and Schloss Hartheim. The life of Barend Bora Kool illustrates the social circumstances which brought many children into orphanage care: large extended families, poverty, death of a parent, poverty, multiple marriages. One boy was caught by the Germans while living in hiding in Belgium, another in France. The family of Sally Montezinos illustrates how terribly effective the Holocaust was in the Netherlands. The entire family of 20 people, living in various places in the country, was caught and murdered. Even the memory of their existence as a family was almost lost.

Keywords: Razzias, Amsterdam, February Strike, Camp Schoorl, deportation, Buchenwald, Mauthausen, Schloss Hartheim, T4, Kazerne Dossin, Pithiviers

The previous chapter focused on the 59 people who were removed from the orphanage on 17th March 1943. Some of the 62 children who left the orphanage before 17th March 1943, and who did not survive the war, also found a place in Chapter 7, but so many more could not be included. The stories which follow are dedicated to their memory.

Chapter 8.1 is about Karel van Santen, who was, to the best of my knowledge, the first of the (erstwhile, since 1929) inhabitants of the Leiden orphanage to perish in the Holocaust. He and his brother Philip were deported in February 1941, first to Buchenwald, then to Mauthausen, just nine months into the German occupation of the Netherlands.

Little is known about Barend Bora Kool (Ch. 8.2), but his extended family illustrates the social circumstances which brought many children to the orphanage in the first place, although most of them still had one or even two living parents.

Jacques Witteboon was deported from France (Ch. 8.3), where conditions for Jews were complicated by the division between occupied France and the area controlled by the Vichy government (see also Chs. 9.7 and 9.8).

Focke, Jaap W., *Machseh Lajesoumim: A Jewish Orphanage in the City of Leiden, 1890-1943*.
Taylor & Francis Group, 2021
DOI: 10.5117/9789463726955_CH08

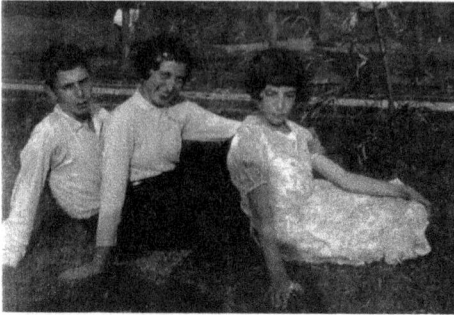

Figure 8.1: Karel, Jenny and Esje (Els) van Santen, c. 1927, when all three were resident in the orphanage.

Figure 8.2: Els and Karel, c. 1938.

Alexander Lipschits was caught in Brussels and deported from Mechelen (Ch. 8.4). Compared to the Netherlands, circumstances in Belgium were different: it was under authority of the German army, the king had stayed behind, and there was initially no central registration telling the Germans who was Jewish.

Chapter 8.5 is about the family of Sally Montezinos, who is one of those who "carry the story" throughout this book. Most of the children in the orphanage, including Sally, came from families which were not in a strong social position. They generally had no protection against the fanatic and tenacious nature of the persecution of Jews. It did not matter where they were, distributed over the country, in all sorts of homes and institutions. Their children, parents, siblings, grandparents, nephews, and cousins were all caught, deported, murdered. It is disconcerting to observe how close the Nazis came to eradicating even the memory that they ever existed.

8.1   Karel van Santen

Three of the children van Santen from The Hague lived in the Leiden orphanage: Jenny (1914) for almost eight years, Karel (1918), ten years or more, and Esther ("Els", 1920) for more than sixteen years. From December 1926, when Karel was the last to arrive, to April 1932, when Jenny was the first to leave, they were all three living in the orphanage in Leiden (Figs. 8.1 and 8.2). Karel was drafted for military service in 1937; he had become eighteen on 16th September the year before; at that time boys were initially drafted for half a year, so he probably did not actually live in the orphanage for the whole of 1937. He was called up again when Holland mobilized in August 1939, together with Herman Stofkooper (Ch. 9.7). Even if he was not resident, he certainly appeared frequently in the orphanage where practically everybody knew him. He was only officially written out of the Leiden registry on 2nd July 1940 when he was 21.

Figure 8.3.: Dutch Jews from the very fi rst mass deportation from Holland, on the day of their arrival in KL Buchenwald: 28th February 1941. The N on their jacket stands for Niederlände. Karel and Philip van Santen were both part of this group. Photo courtesy Gedenkstätte Buchenwald and many other sources.

Karel and his brother Philip[1] happened to visit a friend in Amsterdam[2] on 22nd February 1941, when the Germans took revenge for the street fighting in Amsterdam's Jewish Quarter the week before. Both boys were caught during the two-day razzia; in total some[3] 400 men were arrested on 22nd and 23rd February and brought to Camp Schoorl. On 27th February 1941, arguably in response to the February Strike (Ch. 6.3), a train took 389[4] of them from Alkmaar (the nearest railway station) to Weimar in Germany, from where they were force-marched to Buchenwald, the same camp where Lotte Adler's father had been killed in 1938. It was the first mass transport of Jews from the Netherlands, just nine months after the invasion, and one and a half years before systematic mass deportations to Auschwitz started from Westerbork. The context of these early (February 1941) deportations from Holland is often said to be different from the later (July 1942) deportations from Westerbork, Mechelen (Belgium) and Drancy (France). In early 1941 the plans for genocide on

1   His full name was Philip Karel. He was born in Amsterdam on 6th November 1915. He never lived in the orphanage.
2   Testimony of Esther van Santen, as recorded by her son.
3   The list of arrested people had to be reconstructed by the Red Cross based on incomplete data.
4   The group also changed slightly as men who were arrested in other places were added to the transports, while others from the original group were not included in the transport to Buchenwald. Thus, comparing the number of people in each group as transported from Amsterdam to Schoorl, Buchenwald and, eventually, Mauthausen, is not always exact.

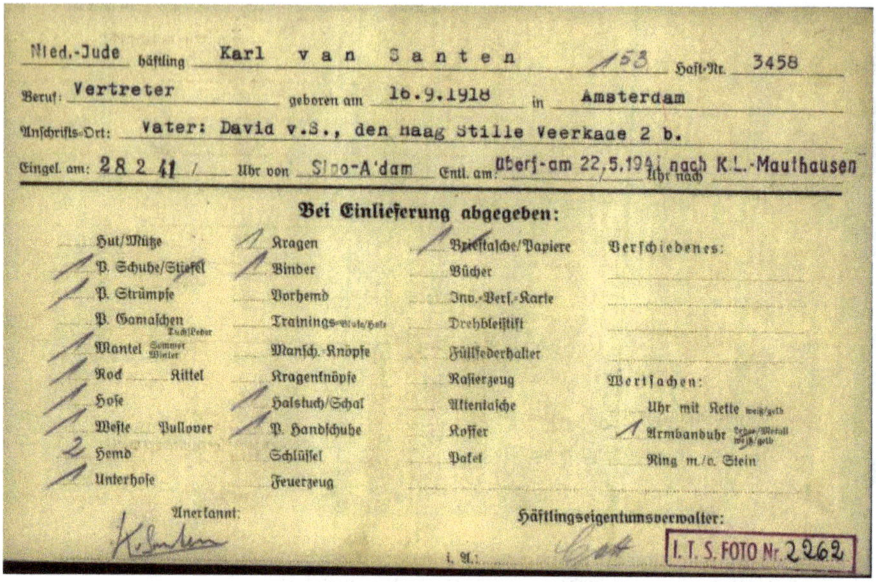

Figure 8.4: The meticulous administration of this stage of the Holocaust, before it developed into the "Final Solution", is astounding. Above: Karel's Buchenwald registration card, duly recording the date of his arrest, arrival in Buchenwald, and his transfer to Mauthausen, as well as itemizing each piece of clothing taken from him, including his wristwatch. Below: another Buchenwald registration card, with *Häftling* (prisoner) number, Sipo Amsterdam having made the arrest (not The Hague as could be suggested by the typing), arrival date in Buchenwald (28th February 1941) and further deportation to Mauthausen on 22nd May 1941. Both documents courtesy ITS Arolsen.

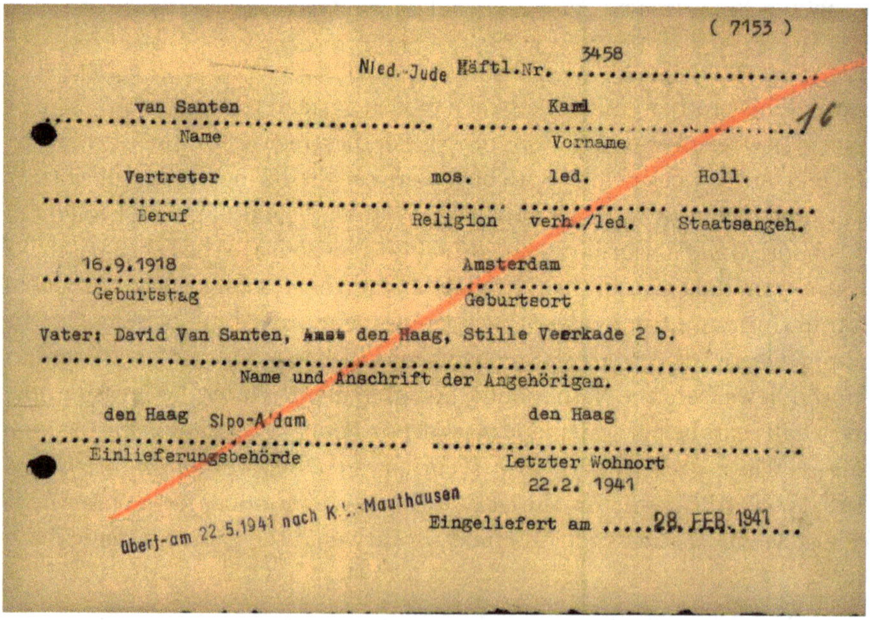

a massive scale had not yet crystallized. But the purpose of the deportations was the same: the deportees, randomly picked from the streets of Amsterdam and other cities, only because they were Jews, were meant to die as soon as possible. If anything, the deportations of February 1941 and the deliberately arranged murder of all deportees illustrate how fanatical, deadly and efficient the persecution of Jews was in the Netherlands.

The deportations took place in a very orderly and efficient manner. Upon arrival in Buchenwald the men were registered and even photographed (Fig. 8.3) and given striped clothing with the appropriate star symbol and a big N for *Niederlande* attached. Figure 8.4 shows two of Karel's Buchenwald registration cards, duly signed by himself and the *"Häftlings-eigentumverwalter"*, the camp's custodian of confiscated property.

In Buchenwald the men were put to work building more barracks, or, if they were unlucky, in the quarry. The new Dutch arrivals were treated more harshly than the "regular" inmates. Their condition quickly started to deteriorate due to lack of food, hard labour, cold weather, inadequate clothing and footwear, standing on roll call for up to seven hours and other forms of direct maltreatment. Within a month the first deaths occurred; three months after arrival more than 30 had died. But in the eyes of the Nazis it was not enough, and it took too long. On 22nd May, 341 of the remaining men were transferred to the Mauthausen concentration camp near Linz in Austria, where conditions were even worse. The order for the transfer came from the SS in Berlin, probably from Himmler himself; he had been kept in the loop by Rauter and Seyss-Inquart from the start of the unrest in Amsterdam (H. de Vries, 2000, 2011). The entire deportation process was meticulously recorded, as shown by the selected documents in this chapter. Figure 8.5 shows part of the transfer list from Buchenwald to Mauthausen. This bureaucracy did not last as the number of victims increased. Jews who were not immediately killed in Auschwitz a year later were still registered (and tattooed) when they arrived, and registered again when they died, but not those who went directly to the gas chambers. When deportations to Sobibor started in 1943, nobody bothered anymore with such bureaucratic niceties. There was no need: the process of robbing them from their possessions and their identity had already been completed before they left Westerbork.

KL Mauthausen was operated from 8th August 1938, five months after the *Anschluss* of Austria. With Gusen, a major sub-camp just 2 km east of Mauthausen, it was classified *Lagerstufe-III*, the hardest possible regime of all camps (until December 1941, when the death camps in occupied Poland became operational). Reading the detailed description of the bestiality of the SS guards in Buchenwald by Eugen Kogon (1974) and others, it is hard to believe that conditions in Mauthausen were even worse. Karel and Philip arrived in Mauthausen-Gusen around midnight

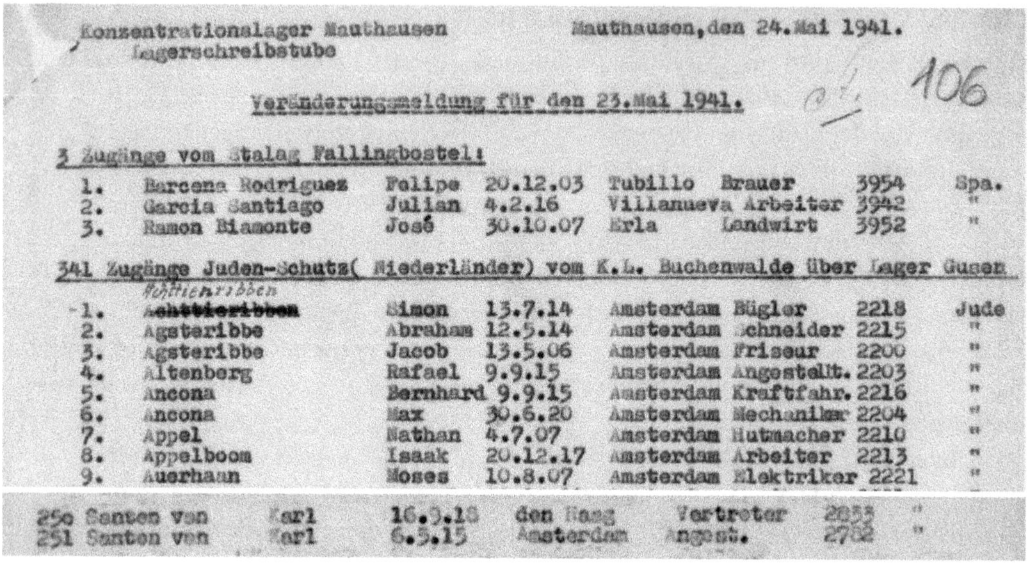

Konzentrationslager Mauthausen — Mauthausen, den 24. Mai 1941.
Lagerschreibstube — 106

Veränderungsmeldung für den 23. Mai 1941.

3 Zugänge vom Stalag Fallingbostel:

1.	Barcena Rodriguez	Felipe	20.12.03	Tubillo	Brauer	3954	Spa.
2.	Garcia Santiago	Julian	4.2.16	Villanueva	Arbeiter	3942	"
3.	Ramon Biamonte	José	30.10.07	Erla	Landwirt	3952	"

341 Zugänge Juden-Schutz(Niederländer) vom K.L. Buchenwalde über Lager Gusen

1.	~~Achttienribben~~ [Achttienribben]	Simon	13.7.14	Amsterdam	Bügler	2218	Jude
2.	Agsteribbe	Abraham	12.5.14	Amsterdam	Schneider	2215	"
3.	Agsteribbe	Jacob	13.5.06	Amsterdam	Friseur	2200	"
4.	Altenberg	Rafael	9.9.15	Amsterdam	Angestellt.	2203	"
5.	Ancona	Bernhard	9.9.15	Amsterdam	Kraftfahr.	2216	"
6.	Ancona	Max	30.6.20	Amsterdam	Mechaniker	2204	"
7.	Appel	Nathan	4.7.07	Amsterdam	Hutmacher	2210	"
8.	Appelboom	Isaak	20.12.17	Amsterdam	Arbeiter	2213	"
9.	Auerhaan	Moses	10.8.07	Amsterdam	Elektriker	2221	"
250	Santen van	Karl	16.5.18	den Haag	Vertreter	2853	"
251	Santen van	Karl	6.5.15	Amsterdam	Angest.	2702	"

Figure 8.5: The arrival in Mauthausen of 341 Dutch Jews from Buchenwald on 23rd May 1941 as recorded on the following day. The top part of page 1, and below the entries for Karel (no. 250) and Philip (no. 251) on page 6. Philip's full name was Philip Karel; the official listed him also as Karl. Courtesy Gedenkstätte Mauthausen, list AMM/Y/50.

on 22nd/23rd May 1941. Some 50 men were killed that same morning, the others were put to work in the quarry. Mauthausen had the quarry with the infamous staircase, where the prisoners were forced to carry heavy rocks up the 148 steps; Gusen had a quarry as well. The death rate increased dramatically: some were shot "while trying to escape", some were sprayed with ice-cold water to make them sick, some killed themselves. Within four months following their transfer from Buchenwald, most of these men were no longer alive. Their death was duly reported to their next of kin in Holland, and obituaries appeared in the newspapers, and the name Mauthausen as the place of death was not kept secret. This instilled fear in the community: *Do not resist, do as you are told, or you will be sent to Mauthausen and to certain death.*

According to the entry in the Mauthausen *Totenbuch,* Karel died on 10th September 1941, at 13.30. Cause of death: "Phlegmone li. K'sch., Allg. Sepsis" (i.e. 'phlegmons on the left patella, general sepsis'). But his death, if he was not killed outright, was due to the conditions in the camp which induced the prisoners to die "from natural causes". Both the cause of death, and the date, may be concocted, such as was the case for his brother Philip (see below), and many others, often to hide the fact that a large group had been killed on the same day (Jacobs, 2000). To the best of our knowledge, Karel was the first one from the erstwhile orphanage children (those who lived there from 1929; list at the back of this book) to be murdered after deportation. Of the 341 Jews from this transport who were delivered to Mauthausen not even one survived the unbelievable conditions in this camp.[5]

Philip's death a week before Karel, ostensibly in Mauthausen on 2nd September 1941, was recorded in the Netherlands (Red Cross War Archives, The Hague), probably based on an official death notification sent from Mauthausen. But contrary to Karel, the death of Philip was not recorded in the *Totenbücher* and both the date and place of death as officially recorded in Holland were false. Documents preserved in the Archives of Mauthausen show that Philip was deported on 11th August 1941 from Mauthausen to the *"Lager Sanatorium – Dachau".* This was the code name for Schloss Hartheim, a "T4" euthanasia facility some 40 km east of Mauthausen. He was part of a group of 70 Jewish prisoners, 65 of them Dutch, transported to Schloss Hartheim on 11th August 1941, and duly recorded on a transport list (Fig. 8.6). There were no holding facilities at the castle, and according to the staff of the Mauthausen Memorial all were killed in the gas chamber of Schloss Hartheim the same day.

Following rare public protest[6] in Germany, Hitler ordered the halting of the T4 programme on 24th August 1941, but the facilities remained in use. Between May 1940 and 1945 some 30,000 people[7] were killed at Schloss Hartheim in a gas chamber, people with disabilities or mental illnesses, but also increasingly prisoners from Mauthausen, Gusen, and Dachau.

The connection between the T4 programme and the development of the "industrial" killing facilities like Kulmhof (Chelmno), Belzec, Sobibor and Treblinka is well known (e.g. Kogon, 1983). In fact, Christian Wirth, one of worst perpetrators of *Aktion Reinhard*, was "technical director" of the killings in Schloss Hartheim before he became active in occupied Poland. Franz Stangl, later commandant of Sobibor and Treblinka, also worked in Schloss Hartheim. Step by step the persecution of Jews developed toward genocide during 1941.

Two more trains left Alkmaar (the train station "serving" Camp Schoorl), on 22nd May and 22nd June 1941, bringing the total of deportees to Mauthausen to 1009. Two smaller transports to Mauthausen took place from Enschede and Arnhem in September and October. Fear for Mauthausen was one of the factors which made many Jews in Holland very reluctant to go into hiding, even if they had the opportunity.

5   Two men survived the deportation to Buchenwald, but they were not sent on to Mauthausen (de Vries, 2000, 2011).
6   By people who began to realize that their hospitalized family members, and disabled patients in general, were dying in large numbers.
7   Of which some 23,000 have been recorded in the Hartheim Memorial Book; see also www.schloss-hartheim.at/.

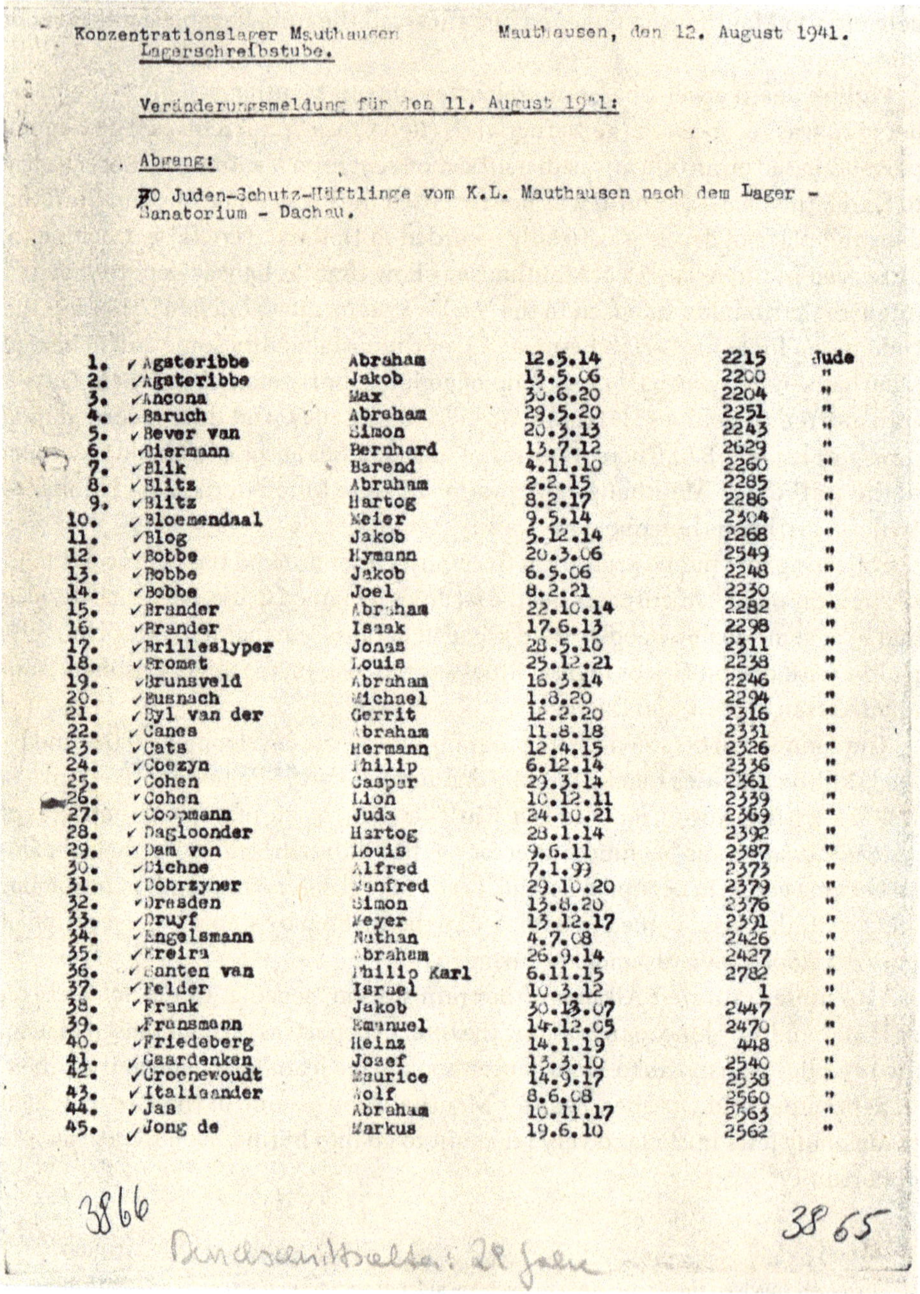

Konzentrationslager Mauthausen   Mauthausen, den 12. August 1941.
Lagerschreibstube.

Veränderungsmeldung für den 11. August 1941:

Abgang:

70 Juden-Schutz-Häftlinge vom K.L. Mauthausen nach dem Lager -
Sanatorium - Dachau.

1.	Agsteribbe	Abraham	12.5.14	2215	Jude
2.	Agsteribbe	Jakob	13.5.06	2200	"
3.	Ancona	Max	30.6.20	2204	"
4.	Baruch	Abraham	29.5.20	2251	"
5.	Bever van	Simon	20.3.13	2243	"
6.	Biermann	Bernhard	13.7.12	2629	"
7.	Blik	Barend	4.11.10	2260	"
8.	Blitz	Abraham	2.2.15	2285	"
9.	Blitz	Hartog	8.2.17	2286	"
10.	Bloemendaal	Meier	9.5.14	2504	"
11.	Blog	Jakob	5.12.14	2268	"
12.	Bobbe	Hymann	20.3.06	2549	"
13.	Bobbe	Jakob	6.5.06	2248	"
14.	Bobbe	Joel	8.2.21	2230	"
15.	Brander	Abraham	22.10.14	2282	"
16.	Brander	Isaak	17.6.13	2298	"
17.	Brilleslyper	Jonas	28.5.10	2311	"
18.	Bromet	Louis	25.12.21	2238	"
19.	Brunsveld	Abraham	16.3.14	2246	"
20.	Busnach	Michael	1.8.20	2294	"
21.	Byl van der	Gerrit	12.2.20	2316	"
22.	Canes	Abraham	11.8.18	2331	"
23.	Cats	Hermann	12.4.15	2326	"
24.	Coezyn	Philip	6.12.14	2336	"
25.	Cohen	Casper	23.3.14	2361	"
26.	Cohen	Lion	10.12.11	2339	"
27.	Coopmann	Juda	24.10.21	2369	"
28.	Dagloonder	Hartog	28.1.14	2392	"
29.	Dam von	Louis	9.6.11	2387	"
30.	Dichne	Alfred	7.1.99	2373	"
31.	Dobrzyner	Manfred	29.10.20	2379	"
32.	Dresden	Simon	13.8.20	2376	"
33.	Druyf	Meyer	13.12.17	2591	"
34.	Engelsmann	Nathan	4.7.08	2426	"
35.	Freira	Abraham	26.9.14	2427	"
36.	Ganten van	Philip Karl	6.11.15	2782	"
37.	Felder	Israel	10.3.12	1	"
38.	Frank	Jakob	30.13.07	2447	"
39.	Fransmann	Emanuel	14.12.05	2470	"
40.	Friedeberg	Heinz	14.1.19	448	"
41.	Gaardenken	Josef	13.3.10	2540	"
42.	Groenewoudt	Maurice	14.9.17	2538	"
43.	Italiander	Wolf	8.6.08	2560	"
44.	Jas	Abraham	10.11.17	2563	"
45.	Jong de	Markus	19.6.10	2562	"

3866   38 65

Durchschnittsalter: 28 Jahre

Figure 8.6: *"Veränderungsmeldung"* (mutation list), dated 12th August 1941, recording the transport of 70 Jews from Mauthausen to Schloss Hartheim, where they were all gassed upon arrival. Philip is listed as no. 37. No. 37 is Israel Felder, with Mauthausen no. 1. He was the first prisoner to arrive in August 1938. Courtesy Gedenkstätte Mauthausen AMM B 15 06-11.8.41.

Esther (Els) van Santen had left the orphanage in 1939, but she returned on 25th September 1942. She will have heard about the death of her two brothers in September or October, since death notifications were sent back to Holland. It may have been a reason for her to return to the orphanage, thinking she would be safe there. But after receiving a warning, she left the orphanage again on 3rd February, six weeks before its liquidation. She survived the war in *onderduik*. Els was never keen to talk about her wartime experiences. She died in The Hague on 3rd March 2016. Her sister Jenny (Jansje) survived deportation and emigrated to the USA with her husband. She died in New York on 9th September 1962. The father, David van Santen (Amsterdam, 23rd March 1889), also perished in Mauthausen (7th October 1943), two years after his sons.

Just two weeks before this book went to press, a comprehensive account about the razzias in Amsterdam, and the fate of the 389 victims was published (de Lang, 2021), just in time to include the reference, but without time to incorporate any new research results in the narrative above.

8.2   Barend Bora Kool

Barend Bora was born on 24th August 1927 in Amsterdam. He was brought to the orphanage in Leiden when he was two and a half years old. No stories about him have survived, and he could not be identified on any of the photographs from that period. But his family details, as far as they could be uncovered,[8] are illustrative for the social circumstances which brought so many children into childcare, despite not being true orphans. Including all the names below is necessary to paint the overall picture.

His mother was Sientje Grootkerk (24th May 1886), and his father was Barend Kool (23rd November 1894). His father had two children from a previous marriage[9] with Leentje Grootkerk (no direct relation of Sientje): Eva (12th January 1918) and Mozes (21st March 1944). Sientje also had children, nine in fact, from a previous marriage (in 1907) to Meijer van West, who had died in 1922 at age 41. So Barend Bora had a whole suite of half-brothers and half-sisters. One of them, Adriana van West, also lived in the orphanage in Leiden (from 17th June 1926 to 27th November 1929; she left before the arrival of Barend Bora). The father, Barend Kool, died on 16th December 1927, four months after his marriage, 33 years old. Barend Bora was born just under eight months later, so he never knew his father, and he was brought to the orphanage in

---

8   See https://www.schenk.nl/.

9   The marriage was on 10th January 1917; the divorce was on either 25th February or 25th May 1927 (Schenk Genealogie).

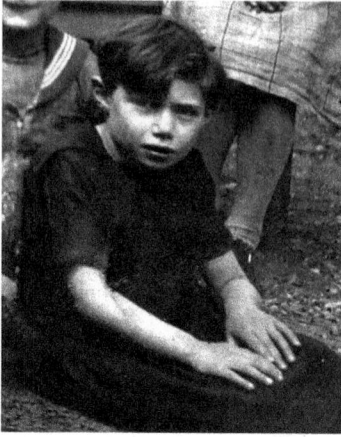

Figure 8.7: Adriana van West, Barend B. Kool's half-sister, at the Langebrug school in Leiden, 1927/1928.

Leiden on 16th January 1931. Circumstances as a widow in an age without comprehensive social welfare will have been difficult for Sientje, but on 25th May 1932, she married for a third time, to Arend van de Kar, a rag merchant. Just five days later, she collected Barend Bora from the orphanage in Leiden, to live with his mother and new stepfather in Rotterdam. The municipal family register (courtesy Roy Schenk, personal communication, October 2018) shows that his other half-siblings, Adriana, Roosje and Schoontje van West, from Sientje's first marriage, also joined their mother and new stepfather. But Barend Bora was obviously not doing well, since he was taken in by *Achisomov*, the children's ward of the Jewish mental institution Het Apeldoornse Bos (Ch. 1), on 20th January 1936. He would stay there until the fatal night of 21st/22nd January 1943 when all the patients, close to 1000, were lifted from their beds and taken directly from Apeldoorn to Auschwitz (Ch. 7.3).

From all the above-mentioned family members, only Adriana and Rebecca van West survived the war. Barend Bora was fourteen when he was murdered. There is no photograph of him, but his half-sister Adriana van West appears on a photograph at the Langebrug school in Leiden (Fig. 8.7).

8.3   Jacques Witteboon is deported from France

Jacques Maurice Witteboon (Fig. 8.8) was born in Amsterdam 26th April 1918, from a second marriage of his father, Salomon (Amsterdam, 6th January 1875). His mother, Marianne Sarphati (Amsterdam, 23rd December 1878), had a daughter from a previous marriage. Jacques spent almost nine years in the Leiden orphanage, from 1927 to 1936. He appears on the group photograph from 1932 (Fig. 4.14, no. 21). In 1940-1941 he worked as a salesman, living with his mother in Amsterdam.

There is no information available about how Jacques got to be in France in 1942. Was he trying to escape via Spain or Switzerland? Records show that he was deported to Kosel/Auschwitz from Pithiviers. The Pithiviers Camp was one of the first such camps in occupied France. It initially held Jews with non-French nationalities, arrested by the French police on instructions from the Germans or the collaborative French government in Vichy. Children were separated from their parents, who were often deported without them.

Six transports left Pithiviers between 25th June and 21st September 1942, carrying 6079 people to Auschwitz or Kosel; 4027 were selected for work (2652 men and 1375 women) of which 162 (4% of those selected, 2.7% of the total number of deportees) survived (156 men and 6 women). Jacques Witteboon was part of the second transport (17th July 1942), and did not return. Some sources (see the Joods Monument references) suggest that he was killed on 19th July, i.e. upon arrival, but as far as is known, everybody on this transport was selected for work upon arrival. Indeed, the Netherlands Red Cross reported that he was part of the group going through Kosel. His death is reported as 2nd September 1942 in the Auschwitz *Sterbebücher* (as recorded in his Red Cross dossier).

The Pithiviers Camp is not as well known as the camp at Drancy, which served as the main holding and transfer camp for Jews in France. Between June 1942 and July 1944 some 67,400 Jews were deported in 64 transports from Drancy to the extermination camps in the East. Only 1542 (2.3%) were still alive in 1945.

Figure 8.8: "Jack (Jacques) Witteboon with Dikky and Semmy" in front of the annex, 1936. (Comment attached to original photo as donated to the Joods Historisch Museum. Dikky is Herman Rozeveld, Semmie is Willem van Weddingen.) Photo F1635-1, courtesy Jewish Historical Museum Amsterdam.

8.4   Alexander Lipschits is caught in Belgium[10]

Alexander was born in Bergen op Zoom, Netherlands, on 24th August 1926; he entered the orphanage on 15th May 1930 when he was three years old and left again on 13th October when he was four.

His father was Mozes ("Max") Lipschits (Maastricht, 23rd July 1901), and his mother was Marianne Walvis (Rotterdam, 4th October 1899). His parents were registered by the Belgian alien police in 1924 but must have returned to the Netherlands, since Alexander was born there, and the family was later registered in Breda

10   This chapter was made possible by the exceptional assistance given to the author by the staff of the State Archives of Belgium in Brussels (ARA) and Kazerne Dossin (Mechelen/Malines): Mrs. Alexandra Matagne, Mr. Felix Strubbe and Mrs. Laurence Schram. I also thank Mr. Ron Bosten who provided the photographs.

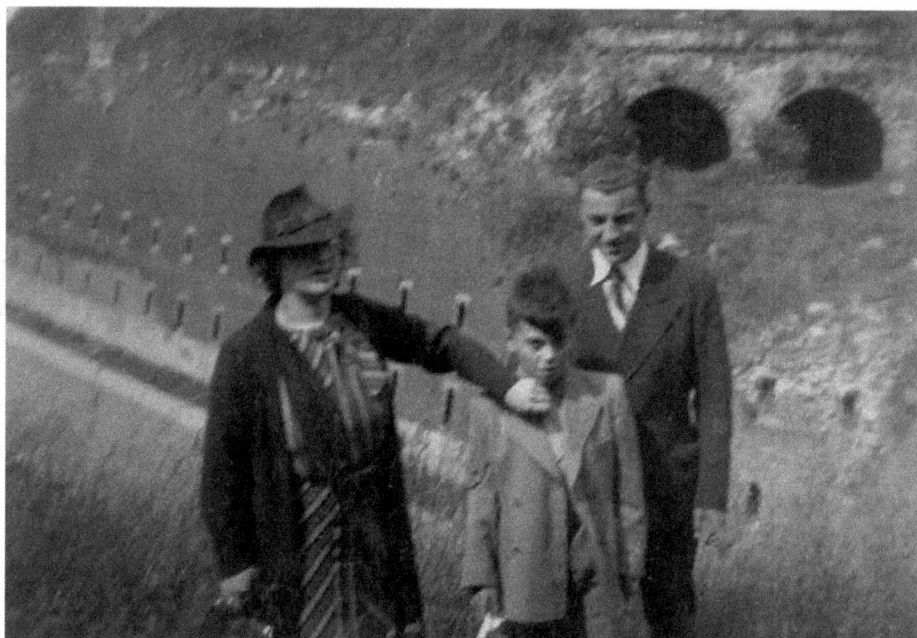

Figure 8.9: Alexander Lipschits with his mother, Marianne Walvis, and his uncle, Levie (Louis) Walvis, c. 1937. Note in the background two entrances to the Maastricht cave system. Photo courtesy R. Bosten, grandson of Louis Walvis.

and Maastricht. Other members of the Lipschits family also had close ties with Maastricht as well as with Antwerp.

The circumstances which brought Alexander to the orphanage are not known. The choice for Leiden was most likely determined by his young age. He was reunited with his parents later that year. When war broke out, the family lived in Maastricht, close to the St Pietersberg, a prominent hill penetrated by countless tunnels and caves as a result of mining the Cretaceous limestone (Fig. 8.9). In the spring of 1942, even before deportations from Westerbork had started, they were preparing to go into hiding in Belgium. The family of Uncle Louis Walvis (Fig. 8.9), who survived the war, thinks that they escaped to Belgium through the above-mentioned cave and tunnel system, together with Abraham Levie, who had lived in their house in Maastricht, and who, it seems, provided the hiding address in Brussels.

They managed to obtain fake Belgian identity cards (Figs. 8.10 and 8.11), ostensibly issued by the municipal authorities in Wetteren, a small community near Ghent in Belgian Flanders. The ID card for Max ("Hendrik Willems") is dated 5th May 1942, for his wife, Marianne ("Maria van Dam"), 5th July, and for Alexander ("Jan Willems") and their friend Abraham Levie ("Johan Wouters"), 8th July 1942.

From November 1941 (re-enforced on 5th June 1942), Jews in the Netherlands were no longer allowed to move to another address without a special permit. The move of the Lipschits family was therefore "illegal" and they were duly recorded as fugitives, together with Abraham Levie (*Algemeen Politieblad*, no. 37, 17th September 1942, 1044, notice 1931).

After living in hiding for some ten months, the family was arrested. Relatives of the family think that Abraham Levie was arrested first, when he could not resist the temptation to go out on the streets of Brussels, but the sequence of events, and the remarkable number of documents which have been preserved, may not support this assumption. On 25th May 1943, the Lipschits family was brought to Kazerne Dossin in Mechelen (Malines), which served as the main holding and transit place (Fig. 8.12) for Jews being deported from Belgium. Abraham Levie was brought to Kazerne Dossin much later, on 6th April 1944. He was deported to Auschwitz with Transport XXV on 19th May 1944.

Figure 8.10: Alexander Lipschits in 1942, from his counterfeit identity card in the name of Jan Willems. The fake ID of his father is shown in full in Figure 8.11 because it shows remarks added by the SD after their arrest. Photo courtesy Archief Oorlogsslachtoffers (AOS), Brussels.

The Lipschits family was arrested on 24th May 1943, or maybe the day before. The German police added the date to their comments on the fake ID card of Mozes, after their arrest (Fig. 8.11).

Unlike Camp Westerbork, which was situated in the middle of nowhere, close to the border with Germany, and out of sight of most people in Holland, Kazerne Dossin is situated in the medieval city of Mechelen, on the banks of the Dijle River. Prisoners were delivered by truck (Fig. 8.12), and a convenient spur line connected the barracks to the national railway network of Belgium. It fitted the German plans to *"solve their so-called Jewish problem"* (Schram, 2018). Between August 1942 and August 1944, 25,274 Jews were deported to Auschwitz, with only 1218 survivors (4.8%). The transports (ibidem) also deported 354 *Zigeuner* (*"Gypsies"*: 33 survivors, 9.3%) and 218 "special cases" (144 survivors, 66%).

The names of the deportees were recorded on 28 administrative transport lists, numbered I to XXVI, with list XXII split into A and B, and one list numbered Z2 (Z for *Zigeuner*), corresponding to 22 actual train transports. The Lipschits family was entered on the list of Transport XXI as numbers 336, 337 and 338 (Fig. 8.13). The date in the upper-left corner, 25th May 1943 does *not* refer to the departure

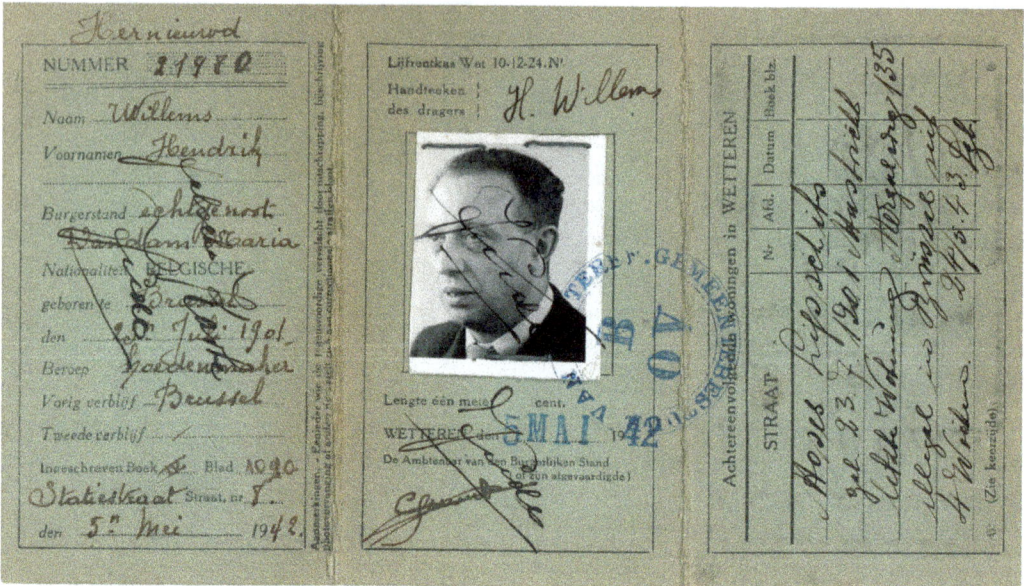

Figure 8.11: The counterfeit Belgian ID card of Mozes Lipschits, Alexander's father, including remarks added by the German police after their arrest. On the left-hand part of the card, obliquely across the original text, he wrote *"falsche Karte"* (counterfeit document), and below that *"Jude"* (Jew). Across the middle part again *"Jude"* across the photograph and again below it. On the right-hand part of card, intended to keep track of address changes, he added Max's real name, date and place of birth, and his last address in Maastricht: Mergelweg 135, and the remark *"illegal in Brüssel seit 4 Wochen"* ("illegally in Brussels for four weeks"), and the date, 24th May 1943. Finally, unreadable, are his initials? Photo courtesy Archief Oorlogsslachtoffers (AOS), Brussels.

of this transport; it is the date on which the people on this page were registered in Kazerne Dossin. Transport XXI left on 31st July 1943, the seventeenth train from Dossin. It carried 1552 Jews to Auschwitz, of which 21 survived. Alexander and his parents were probably killed upon arrival in Auschwitz on or around 2nd August 1943. The Lipschits family was locked up in Kazerne Dossin for more than two months before their transport left on 31st July. Most people who entered Dossin in 1943 had to wait there one to three months before being deported. The previous year, during the month of September 1942, four trains left Dossin, carrying 6790 Jews to Auschwitz. During October three trains took away 4842 people. But then the deportations slowed down with "only" one train in January, April, July and September, an astounding difference with the deportations out of Westerbork.

By early 1943, the *Sicherheitsdienst* (SD) had difficulties in meeting its target number of Belgian Jews caught and ready to be deported. And that target was not as "ambitious" as it was in Holland to begin with. Many more Jews in Belgium survived the war (60%) than did in the Netherlands (25%). This has led commentators to wonder if the level of anti-Semitism and active local collaboration with the Germans has been significantly higher in Holland as compared to Belgium or France. But

Figure 8.12: Arrested Jews waiting in the courtyard of Kazerne Dossin in Mechelen, Belgium, 1942. JMVD Fonds Kummer.

there seems to be no evidence for any such claims. Anti-Semitic riots in Antwerp and Brussels in 1939 and early 1940 had no significant equivalent in the Netherlands, and Kazerne Dossin has dedicated much effort in highlighting the collaborative role of city mayors, civil servants, police, etc., which seems to have been as common there as it was in the Netherlands.

In Holland, until the arrival of refugees in 1933, the vast majority of Jews had Dutch citizenship. They were duly recorded by the Civil Registry as belonging to the Jewish faith just like Catholics and Protestants (Ch. 1), and it was very easy for the Germans to complete their inventory of who was Jewish and where they lived. Because they had already been registered before the war, not complying with Decree 6/1941 would have made little difference.

In Belgium however, more than 95% of the Jews were aliens, with German or Polish nationalities, or without nationality papers at all. Moreover, registering people's faith was unconstitutional in Belgium, and the Germans needed two

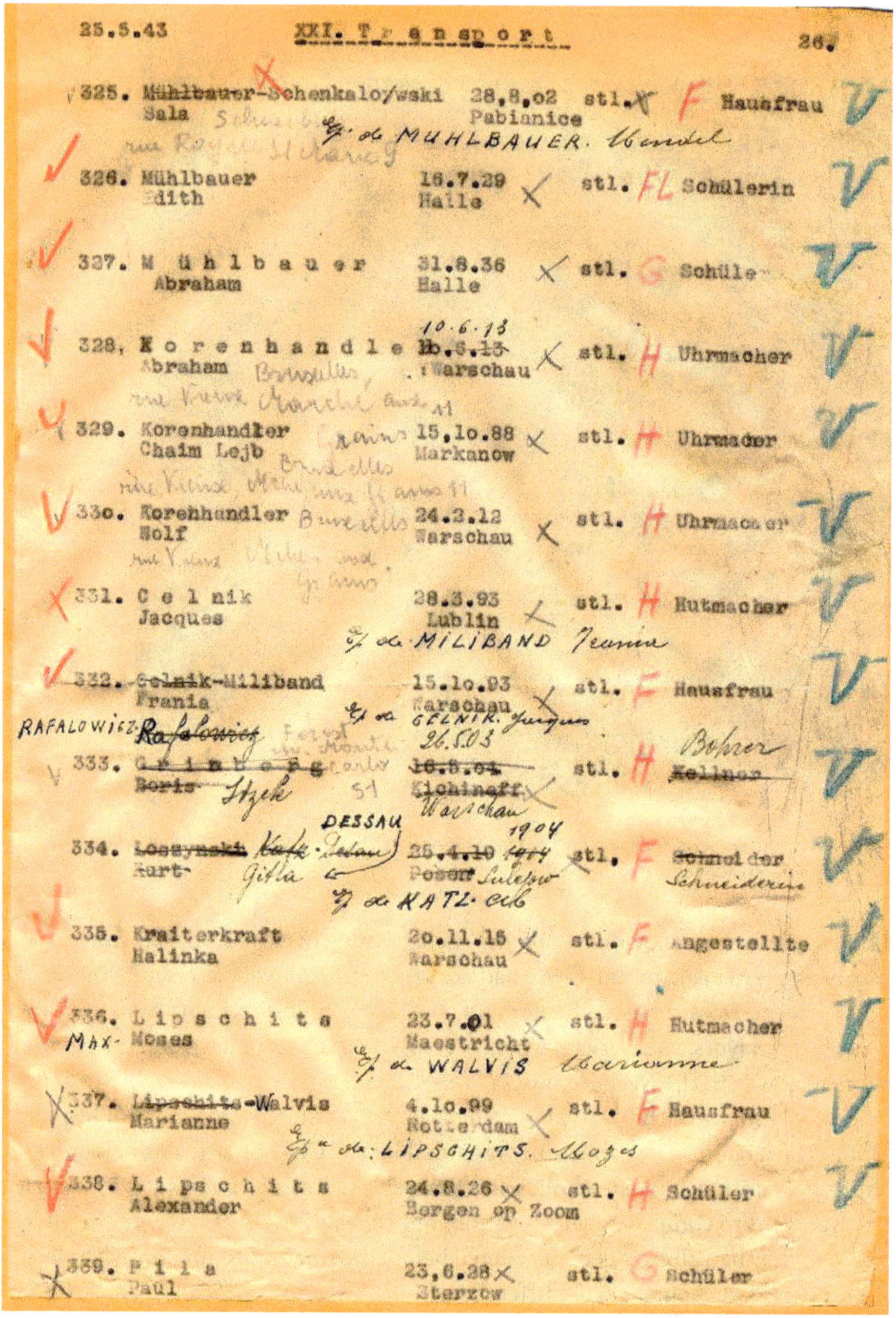

25.5.43 XXI. Transport 26.

325. Mühlbauer-Schenkalowski 28.8.02 stl. F Hausfrau
Sala Pabianice
Ep. de MUHLBAUER. Mendel

326. Mühlbauer 18.7.29 stl. FL Schülerin
Edith Halle

327. Mühlbauer 31.8.36 stl. G Schüle
Abraham Halle

328. Korenhandle 10.6.13 stl. H Uhrmacher
Abraham Warschau

329. Korenhandler 15.10.88 stl. H Uhrmacher
Chaim Lejb Markanow

330. Korenhandler 24.2.12 stl. H Uhrmacher
Wolf Warschau

331. Celnik 28.3.93 stl. H Hutmacher
Jacques Lublin
Ep. de MILIBAND Jeanine

332. Celnik-Miliband 15.10.93 stl. F Hausfrau
Frania Warschau
Ep. de CELNIK. Jacques

RAFALOWICZ Rafalowicz 26.5.03
333. Grinberg 16.8.04 stl. H Kellner Bohrer
Boris Itzek Kichineff Warschau

DESSAU 1904
334. Loszynski Kafe. Dessau 25.4.10 stl. F Schneider Schneiderin
Kurt Gitla Posen Sulejow
Ep. de KATZ. Ch.

335. Kraiterkraft 20.11.15 stl. F Angestellte
Halinka Warschau

336. Lipschits 23.7.01 stl. H Hutmacher
MAX- Moses Maestricht
Ep. de WALVIS Marianne

337. Lipschits-Walvis 4.10.99 stl. F Hausfrau
Marianne Rotterdam
Ep. de: LIPSCHITS. Mozes

338. Lipschits 24.8.26 stl. H Schüler
Alexander Bergen op Zoom

339. Pila 23.6.28 stl. G Schüler
Paul Sterzow

Figure 8.13: The page of the list for Transport XXI showing Alexander Lipschits and his parents (see text). Note that the date in the upper-left corner indicates the arrival date in Dossin, not the date of the transport, which left on 31st July 1943. Courtesy Kazerne Dossin and AOS, Brussels.

public exercises instructing Jews to register themselves as Jews (Schram, 2018). There were some 90,000 Jews living in Belgium in 1940, and some 45,000 of them did not comply with the order to register themselves, a significant difference with the situation in the Netherlands. The fact that about the same number *did* comply may be equally significant.

The level of suspicion in Belgium, having been the victim of a previous brutal German occupation just 25 years earlier, was much higher than in Holland, and resistance developed earlier. Some people managed to escape from the Belgian train transports, and one transport was even stopped by three young men from Ukkel to let the deportees escape (Schram, 2018). Belgium was administered by the Wehrmacht, whereas in Holland the German civil administration, run by four fanatic Austrian Nazis, had a free hand from May 1940.

This book is not the place to discuss the significant differences in survival rates between the Netherlands (27%), Belgium (47%), and France (75%), but the above-mentioned factors suggest that one must be careful before drawing conclusions from the bare numbers. For a comprehensive treatment of the Holocaust in the three countries, the reader is referred to Griffioen and Zeller (2010).

8.5   So many more – the family of Sally Montezinos

All 168 children on the list at the end of this book had family: one or even two parents, siblings, uncles, and so on. Many, like Barend Bora Kool (Ch. 8.2) or Barend and Salomon Ritmeester, had extended families. Inevitably, during the investigations it was discovered what happened to these family members.

Table 8.1 lists the family of Sally Montezinos, who, as told in Chapter 7.2 and 7.4, preferred to stay with his orphanage friends rather than join his "real" family, as it was in 1941. Sally's father had died before the war. His mother, Louise Hagenaar, had nine children, six children-in-law, and four grandchildren. The table *only* includes Sally and his direct family, in total 20 people, without his uncles, aunts or cousins.

They lived in The Hague, Leiden, Amsterdam, Apeldoorn, and other places. It did not make a difference where they were: they were all caught up in the persecution and deported with nine different transports between August 1942 and July 1943. Not one of them survived.

Such was the effectiveness of the Holocaust in the Netherlands.

Surely, there were photographs of these family members, albums for the grandchildren, or stacked in boxes. Despite the long-standing efforts of the Westerbork Memorial Museum, the Joods Monument, and individual authors

Table 8.1   The family of Sally's mother: Louise Montezinos-Hagenaar, her children and grand-children

	Mother:		
	Louise Hagenaar	b 11-01-1887	d 23-04-1943 Sobibor
	Children:		
1.	Branca	b 01-10-1909	d 09-07-1943 Sobibor
	– C. Hakker	b 21-01-1912	d 09-07-1943 Sobibor
	– Lea	b 19-12-1935	d 09-07-1943 Sobibor
2.	Jacob	b 27-03-1911	d 13-03-1943 Sobibor
	– J. Elburg	b 04-05-1910	d 13-03-1943 Sobibor
	– Louise Jeanne	b 06-11-1937	d 13-03-1943 Sobibor
3.	Grietje	b 21-09-1912	d 30-09-1942 Auschwitz
	D. Agsteribbe	b 31-01-1911	d 09-10-1942 Auschwitz
4.	Anna	b 05-01-1914	d 13-03-1943 Sobibor
5.	Bilha	b 11-04-1916	d 11-12-1942 Auschwitz
	– Sal. Levij	b 26-05-1916	d 28-02-1943 Auschwitz
	– Alida	b 06-02-1941	d 11-12-1942 Auschwitz
6.	Eva	b 30-08-1917	d 26-08-1942 Auschwitz
	– L.Tokkie	b 06-09-1913	d 30-09-1942 Auschwitz
	– Bettie	b 01-04-1939	d 26-08-1942 Auschwitz
7.	Abraham	b 23-08-1919	d 31-01-1943 Auschwitz
	– L. Cohen	b 20-01-1916	d 01-10-1942 Auschwitz
8.	Josephina	b 17-05-1922	d 13-03-1943 Sobibor
9.	Sally	b 06-05-1924	d 04-11-1943 Dorohucza*

* Official date. Both date and place of Sally's death are uncertain. He will most likely not have survived the liquidation on 8th November 1943 of Dorohucza and the other satellite camps of Sobibor.

to "add a face" to the names of the victims, not a single photograph has (yet) come to light for any of Sally's nineteen family members. Sally is the only one of the entire family of whom photographs exist, all taken during his sixteen-year stay in the orphanage. On 6th September 2011,[11] a notice appeared on the Joods Monument that several members of the family were entitled to payments out of a life insurance, and asking relatives, however remote, to come forward. But there is no one left to make a claim. When this book went to press, the notice was still there.

By December 2020, the Joods Monument showed only two of the nineteen family members on the page "family of Louise Montezinos-Hagenaar"[12] with the comment

11   Possibly the notice has already been posted in earlier years.
12   https://www.joodsmonument.nl/nl/page/144387/louise-montezinos-hagenaar. To be precise: The other family members are individually included on the Joods Monument, but the memory that they belonged to one family was not yet recognized.

"(as yet) no other family members are known". It is in no way criticism about the Joods Monument. On the contrary: it shows how frighteningly close the Nazis came to not only eradicate entire families, but even destroy the evidence, the memory, that they ever existed.

It seems to be a miracle that there were any survivors at all. Maybe it is. The survivors who contributed so much to the stories in this book are mentioned in the previous chapters. The following chapter presents nine survivor stories in more detail.

References

Griffioen, P. & R. Zeller, 2011; *"Jodenvervolging in Nederland, Frankrijk en België, 1940-1945. Overeenkomsten, verschillen, oorzaken"*. Amsterdam, Boom, ISBN 0789085068112. [Comparison of Jewish victimization rates in the Netherlands, Belgium and France.] An English summary of the dissertation which preceded (2008) the book is available from the University of Amsterdam at https://pure.uva.nl/ws/files/4255606/58120_12. pdf. See also P. Griffioen & R. Zeller, 2006; *"Anti-Jewish policy and organization of the deportations in France and the Netherlands, 1940-1944: A comparative study"*, Holocaust and Genocide Studies 20 (3), 437-473, and a similar comparative study with respect to Belgium: P. Griffioen & R. Zeller, 1998; *"The persecution of the Jews: Comparing Belgium and the Netherlands"*, Netherlands J. Social Sciences 34 (2), 126-164.

Jacobs, Luise, 2000; *"De verborgen massamoorden in Schloss Hartheim"*. In: Keulen-Woudstra, 2000, pp. 31-42. [Relevant to understand the false death details of Philip van Santen (Ch. 8.1) recorded in Holland.]

Jong, L. de, 1969-1994; *"Het Koninkrijk der Nederlanden in de Tweede Wereldoorlog"*. http://www.dbnl.org or http://www.loedejongdigitaal.nl/. [The standard (contemporary) history of the Netherlands during the war. The entire text is available online (with search facility). For more recent interpretations, see Blom et al., 2021.]

Kogon, Eugen, 1974; *"Der SS-Staat. Das System der deutschen Konzentrationslager"*. München, Kindler Verlag. [Kogon was a Christian opponent to the Nazi regime who survived 6 years in Buchenwald.]. Dutch edition: Kogon, Eugen, 1976; *"De SS-staat"*. Amsterdam, Amsterdam Boek, no ISBN. English and Dutch translations exist in several editions.

Kogon, Eugen, 1983; *"Nationalsozialistische Massentötungen durch Giftgas. Eine Documentation"*. Frankfurt a/M, S. Fischer Verlag, ISBN 3100404025.

Lang, Wally de, 2021; *"De razzia's van 22 en 23 februari 1941 in Amsterdam. Het lot van 389 Joodse mannen"*. Amsterdam, Uitgeverij Atlas Contact, ISBN 9789045042749. [This first comprehensive account of the razzias which preceded the February Strike, and the fate of the deportees to Buchenwald and Mauthausen was published just before the present book went to press.]

Schram, Laurence, 2018; *"Dossin. Wachtkamer van Auschwitz"*. Tielt, Lannoo, ISBN 9782390250395. [One of the first comprehensive studies about the transit camp Kazerne Dossin in Mechelen (Belgium), through which 25,484 Jews and 352 Roma and Sinti were deported to Auschwitz, including Alexander Lipschitz and his family. Only 1222 survived the deportations.]

Vries, Hans de, 2000; *"Sie starben wie Fliegen im Herbst"*. In: Keulen-Woudstra, A.B. van, 2000, *"Mauthausen, 1938-1998"*. Utrecht, Van Gruting, ISBN 9075879067, pp. 7-18.

Vries, Hans de, 2011; *"Mauthausen. Een geval apart"*. https://pure.knaw.nl/ws/files/6338408/2011 and search for Vries_MauthausenEenGevalApart.pdf. [In Dutch, summarizing the special significance of Mauthausen in Dutch wartime history.]

9   1943 to 1946: Survivors

Abstract

Nine stories, each very different from the other, show how some (erstwhile) residents in the orphanage survived by plan, personal courage, outside assistance,
sheer coincidence, or fortuitous events. Kurt and Helga Gottschalk were lucky
in being transferred, just before the German invasion, to the Burgerweeshuis in
Amsterdam, where Truus Wijsmuller picked them up; Betsy Wolff and Bram Degen
were saved by a neighbour, Stoffels, who arranged mixed-blood certificates for
them based on concocted Aryan fathers. Mindel Färber had the good fortune to
have parents in Palestine and being much too young to become an enemy soldier,
so the Germans let her join the *Austausch* train from Bergen-Belsen to Haifa. The
mother of Aron Wolff had the courage to send him into hiding, where he was safe
during the war. Didia Klein married a musician with a *Sperre* in Westerbork, and
survived gruesome medical experiments in Auschwitz, paying an unimaginable
price for her survival. Lodi Cohen was infused with resistive ideas by the young
Palestine Pioneers he looked after. He joined the Westerweel Group, arranged
hiding and escape routes for the young refugees, and escaped himself over the
Pyrenees. Herman Stofkooper tried to reach Spain but ended up in Switzerland;
he was exceptionally lucky, safely crossing four borders and hostile Vichy France.
Elchanan Italie was provided by Hijme Stoffels with a false identity and a genuine
working position in a forest camp near Berlin in Germany.

Keywords: Mixed-blood certificate, G1, Antragstelle, Calmeyer, Albersheim list,
Palestine certificate, Bergen-Belsen, *Austausch* train, Transport 222, Palestine
Pioneers, Hachsharah, Paviljoen Loosdrechtse Rade, Catharina Hoeve Gouda, Aliyah
Bet, Joop Westerweel, Vichy France, *onderduik*, SS *Bodegraven*, Truus Wijsmuller

Our parents never talked about their wartime
experiences, and we never asked.[1]

---

[1]   André Boers about the hazardous escape of his parents to Spain in 1942 (Huisman, 2018; see Chs. 9.7
and 9.8 about escape lines to Spain and Switzerland).

Focke, Jaap W., *Machseh Lajesoumim: A Jewish Orphanage in the City of Leiden, 1890-1943*.
Taylor & Francis Group, 2021
DOI: 10.5117/9789463726955_CH09

Without the willingness of survivors to talk about the past, and the cooperation and permission of their relatives to use their reports and documents, it would not have been possible to write this book. After the war (Ch. 10) many had a difficult time. It took a long time before it was recognized how deeply they were affected by their experiences and the loss of so many or all their loved ones. Many were unable to talk about the war. Some were only able to talk about the war decades later, not to their children, but to their grandchildren. They were troubled by the question of why they had survived and so many others had not. Countless are the unanswered questions: *What if…?*

The nine stories in this chapter are all different from each other. Survival is commonly the result of a combination of many circumstances: being (even if by chance) one of Truus Wijsmuller's children, and being in the right place at the right time; the tireless efforts of Hijme Stoffels; the willingness of a civil servant in an obscure farming village to sign an obviously false parentage declaration; sheer luck; having family in Palestine; being selected by a perverted "doctor" for gruesome experiments; the willingness to resist; being affected by the more realistic view within the Hachsharah movement about the intentions of the Nazis; the willingness to provide *onderduik* shelter for Jewish children even if you have a baby of your own; personal courage to walk into a barbershop in Breda asking how to illegally get across the Belgian border, and travel south without any pre-planned support, and so on. The stories below stand on their own, but together they provide insight in the conditions and circumstances which determined the individual's fate during the German occupation.

9.1   Helga and Kurt Gottschalk escape on the SS *Bodegraven*

Helga (18th November 1932) and Kurt (15th July 1937) Gottschalk were refugees (Table 5.1). They were born in Geilenkirchen, Germany, just a few kilometres from the border with Dutch Limburg. Their parents Friedrich and Regina also hailed from Geilenkirchen. Friedrich was in Holland on business before November 1938. Calling Regina at home in Geilenkirchen she told him that the SS had come by to look for him, and that he should stay in Holland, which he did. Although he had travel documents, he was interned in Camp Reuver near Roermond in the province of Limburg. This suggests that he had no residence status, and that his continued presence in Holland was in fact illegal. By March 1938, the Dutch government had virtually closed the border, and illegal immigrants were liable to be sent back to Germany if they were caught (Ch. 5). But in the wake of Kristallnacht (Ch. 5.6) it was grudgingly recognized that Germany had become too dangerous for Jewish refugees to be sent back there and many were allowed to stay. To retain control over the increasing numbers of refugees the government created four facilities to hold the adult males while women and children could stay with relatives or friends. Camp Reuver (van Rens, 2013, and references therein) was one of those facilities, under responsibility of the Justice Department. They were in fact places of detention[2] guarded by the *Marechaussee* (military police). After some six months the status of the refugees could be legalized, then they could transfer to Camp Westerbork where their families could join them.

Helga, Kurt and their mother had stayed behind in Geilenkirchen, but after Kristallnacht they were evicted from their home by the SS. They fled first to Aachen, then to Holland. Crossing the Dutch border illegally at night, by car and with a friend (Kurt Gottschalk, personal communication, 2020), they went to Valkenburg (Dutch Limburg), where Regina's brother lived, and then to Amsterdam, where she found no place to stay with the children. Following quarantine in Rotterdam from 30th March 1939 (Kasteleyn, unpublished) Helga and Kurt were taken in by the Jewish orphanage in Leiden on 20th April 1939.

On 10th July they were transferred from Leiden to the *Burgerweeshuis* in Amsterdam,[3] one of the oldest (founded in 1580) non-denominational orphanages in the country. As the number of refugee children increased, the *Burgerweeshuis* was designated as a dedicated home for refugee children in March 1939 (Keesing, 2013). Most of the children, but not all, were unaccompanied by parents and many had arrived by Kindertransport. Truus Wijsmuller, who had been involved with children war victims and refugee work for 20 years and who had talked to Eichmann in person in Vienna in 1938 to arrange her own Kindertransport (Ch. 5.2), inevitably became involved with the *Burgerweeshuis*. She became a member of the governing board, which extended her special link with these children (Fig. 9.1). Post-war testimonies suggest that many of the children who had arrived without parents had similar feelings for *"Tante Truus"*.

Helga and Kurt had not arrived by Kindertransport, nor was their escape from Germany facilitated by Truus, but their transfer to Amsterdam made them effectively part of her group. With hindsight it was a very fortuitous transfer since Truus continued her pre-war efforts to assist Jewish refugees even when Holland was invaded on 10th May 1940. The narrative below follows Truus' own original report (Wijsmuller-Meijer, 1961) which is well worth reading in some detail and therefore part of it is included here (it seems no English translation is available).

On 6th May Truus had gone to Emmerich just over the Dutch border in Germany to collect an 84-year-old blind woman and bring her to Holland. She had a talent in exuding authority (which she did not have) and making an impression on German

---

2   They were cared for, very well it seems (Michman et al., 1999) by the Dominican sisters of the Heilige Hart Convent in Reuver, and a Support Committee in Venlo (van Rens, 2013, p. 58).

3   Now home to the Amsterdam Museum.

Figure 9.1: Truus Wijsmuller (the woman standing third from left, looking at the children) and "her" children of the Burgerweeshuis, Amsterdam, probably early 1940. The picture includes refugee children from previous Kindertransports but also refugee children who came to Holland by other means, such as Helga Gottschalk (the girl in the third row from the front, standing, fifth from the right, in a dark jumper (1)). Kurt is missing; he was in the hospital. Photo NIOD, Amsterdam. More identifications are welcome. Picture licensed under Creative Commons 4.0 International.

officials (including Eichmann). She was cordially received by the local Gestapo chief in Emmerich, who proudly showed off his status and his own authority. He also told her about the armoured forces standing ready in his area, and that he expected the invasion of Holland to take place on the coming Thursday. He then allowed her to take the old woman to Holland. Back in The Hague she reported her recent observations to government officials, and the warning about the coming invasion. But there had been such alarms before, and her story was dismissed.

Wednesday, 8th May, she travelled to Paris to bring a Jewish girl on the way to safety in Spain. The girl was taken over by another helper halfway to Spain and Truus returned to the Hotel Terminus in Paris on Thursday evening (for a map, see Fig. 9.36). She was woken up early Friday morning, 10th May, by air raid sirens and the news that the Germans had invaded Belgium and Holland, on the way to France. *"I stayed in bed but finished a bottle of wine to suppress my feeling of utter despondency"* (ibid., p. 147). She must have realized that all efforts to rescue Jewish children from Nazi Germany, in as far as they had remained in Holland, would be totally undone by the German invasion, and decided to return to Holland immediately. The Dutch

consulate in Paris, closing for the Whitsun
weekend and hardly yet conscious of the
invasion of Holland, told her to come back
in three days. She went to the Belgian
consulate to get a transit visa, and noticed
Belgian volunteers, seeking transport
back home to defend their country against
the Germans. When a group of volunteers
left Paris that evening for Belgium, she
managed to obtain French permission
to join them on the train. It took Truus
three days to reach Holland through utter

Figure 9.2: The KNSM ship Bodegraven, c. 1939-1941. Wiki
public domain.

chaos, experiencing German air raids in several places, changing trains, and talking
herself past officials who tried to stop her. At that time, allied forces, not yet aware
that the German army would speed through Belgium much faster than in 1914,
were moving north towards Holland, which was presently no longer a neutral
country. At the same time, in Belgium, large numbers of people were fleeing from
the advancing Germans, first east towards Brussels, then south, remembering the
First World War. She reached Brussels and found transport to Antwerp.

The second leg of her journey, from Antwerp into Holland, across the major
rivers via Numansdorp and Maassluis to The Hague and Leiden, was even more
adventurous. The Germans had dropped large numbers of airborne troops around
The Hague and Leiden on the first days of the invasion and the "Battle for The
Hague" had been raging for three days already (see map, Fig. 9.35) when Truus
tried to travel right through the area. In Leiden, she was arrested on suspicion of
being an airborne German spy impersonating a woman. But whenever she got into
difficulty, there always was somebody around who knew her personally, or so it
seems. When the military in Leiden discovered their mistake, they provided Truus
with a car (Monday, 13th May), a driver and an officer to bring her to Amsterdam.
The car brought her to her husband, then to the *Burgerweeshuis* and to Gertrude
van Tijn of the CJV (Committee for Jewish Refugees) (see Ch. 5; Wasserstein, 2014)
with whom Truus had worked in close cooperation before the war. Gertrude was
formally responsible for the *Burgerweeshuis* as a refugee home. After being arrested
for a second time by the Dutch (military) police and released again after a few hours,
she was contacted by the garrison commandant of Amsterdam with a message from
England requesting her to try and get the refugee children from the *Burgerweeshuis*
on board a ship in IJmuiden.[4] Back at the CJV she asked Gertrude van Tijn to agree,

4   Remember (Ch. 5.6) that Truus had been working for the British refugee committee in 1938-1939,
organizing Kindertransports when the UK special visas became available.

and at about 13:30 (Tuesday, 14th May) she brought five buses to the orphanage to collect the children who were present, including Helga Gottschalk, then seven years old. Her brother Kurt, then two and three-quarters years old, was not there: he had been hospitalized. Going back again to the office of the CJV, which was no longer staffed, she picked up some 40 desperate Jews who did not know where to go and then drove to the hospital where Kurt was being treated to pick him up as well.

Driving to IJmuiden they were stopped at roadblocks and at the harbour. The travel permit from the Amsterdam garrison commander proved worthless once the buses were outside his area of control. At the harbour, several thousands of people were seeking transport to England, but Dutch government officials tried to prevent people getting to the ships[5] and Truus was stopped as well. But, as always, there were friends around to help: an official of the KNSM (a major Dutch shipping agency), and an officer of the Dutch navy. Truus managed to get her 74 children and the other people she had brought safely on board the KNSM ship *Bodegraven* (Fig. 9.2). Truus was an exceptionally imposing and authoritative women, and she used her umbrella to amplify the effect. She also had a very effective network and she knew how to use it. Yet her exploits during the invasion represent an uncanny achievement. That day, Rotterdam was bombed by the Luftwaffe, and the main defence line in the centre of the country (the *Grebbelinie*) had collapsed. Queen and government had fled to England. Nobody knew what was going to happen.

Some accounts suggest that Truus knew about the *Bodegraven* before leaving Amsterdam, although she does not confirm that in her memoir. Others[6] suggest that she did not have any prearranged commitments when driving to the harbour of IJmuiden. Hans Levy[7] (Hodge, 2012, p. 34) remembers that she *"went from ship to ship to persuade the captains to take us on board. The captain of the* Bodegraven *agreed but explained there was very little food. Once aboard the ship [she] bade us farewell. We begged her to come with us. By then, we looked upon her as a mother."* Truus was aware of the children's feelings: *"I told the captain, who also wanted me to stay on board, that I could not. I knew the children were scared and I left my coat and bag on board to reassure them and suggest that I would join them."* She went back to Amsterdam to fetch more people but realized her window of opportunity was closing. That afternoon (14th May) the Dutch army capitulated, there were plans to sink the *Bodegraven* to block the entrance to the harbour[8] and the captain

---

5   Truus in 1961: *"Madness! They should have allowed them all to get on board even if by hanging off the railing by their fingernails; anything was better than falling into the hands of the Germans"* (op. cit., p 157).
6   As always, there are small inconsistencies between various witness accounts and reports.
7   Hans and his brother Oscar were in Manchester together with Helga and Kurt.
8   Or to destroy the large sea locks giving access to Amsterdam; there were British military personal in IJmuiden.

realized this was his last chance to escape. "*The* Bodegraven *left IJmuiden harbour at 10 to 8 [pm]; I waved it goodbye, that was the end"* (ibid., p. 158). While moving into open sea, the ship was strafed by German war planes, and the children down in the hold heard the bullets hit the ship. The *Bodegraven* was launched for the KNSM at the van der Giessen shipyard in 1929 and had (in theory) room for 59 crew and 48 passengers. It left IJmuiden with 74 refugee children and some 190 other people trying to escape from the Germans (Keesing, 2013). It was not prepared for carrying so many passengers, there were no bunks and there was not enough food. It was cold and there were no blankets.

When approaching the British coast, they were not allowed to dock to land the children. Most of them had German nationality. They may have been regarded as refugees in 1938, but in May 1940 they were "enemy aliens". The

Figure 9.3: Kurt and Helga, Lymm Children's Home, UK, c. 1941. Photo courtesy Kurt Gottschalk.

ship bypassed the southern English harbours[9] and steamed into the Irish Sea, apparently to try and land the refugees in Belfast. But it received permission to dock in Liverpool on 19th May after a very rough trip. The children under the age of sixteen, including Helga and Kurt, were allowed to land in Liverpool, but the older ones were interned on the Isle of Man.

Helga and Kurt went to the Lymm Children's Home, somewhere between Liverpool and Manchester (Figs. 9.3 and 9.4). Towards the end of the war, they were transferred to an orphanage in Manchester (Fig. 9.5). It seems others such as Hans Levy and his brother were in a similar home in the town of Wigan, also in the general area between Liverpool and Manchester, until they were also moved to the orphanage in Manchester.

While Helga and Kurt had been transferred to the *Burgerweeshuis*, their father, Friedrich, was released from Camp Reuver and was transferred to Westerbork on 22nd April 1940, three weeks before the German invasion. Regina joined him there on 8th July. At that time Westerbork was still a refugee camp under Dutch administration (and German oversight). The camp was not closed, although the refugees had to

---

9   Except for a short stop at Falmouth to allow the burial of Mr. Jacques Goudstikker, a Dutch art dealer who fell to his death in the ship's hold during the night of 15th/16th May.

Figure 9.4: Lymm Children's Home, probably 1941-1942. No. 11 in school uniform: Helga; no. 19: Matron Bluman. Photo courtesy Mirjam Spziro (no. 8). More identifications are welcome.

get permission from the commandant to travel. Practically all internal affairs were administered by the (mostly German) refugees themselves. By the time (the end of 1941) the Germans started preparations to take over and enlarge the capacity of the camp, this self-government had grown into an extensive organization, running reception, administration, work, medical, sports and education activities, a kitchen, even internal police (Ch. 6.6). Friedrich and Regina were able to secure a position within the administration of the camp before mass deportations of Dutch Jews started from Westerbork in July 1942. They both worked in the camp kitchen. They were effectively *Alte Insassen*, which possibly explains why they both managed to stay for four years in the camp without being deported to Auschwitz or Sobibor. They were still in Westerbork in September 1944, when France and Belgium had been liberated, and the total removal and destruction of Jews from the Netherlands was just about complete. On Sunday, 3rd September, the very last train left Westerbork to Auschwitz with 1019 persons, including the family of Anne Frank. Next day, Monday, 4th September, the last train to Theresienstadt left Westerbork with some 2085 persons on board, including Friedrich and Regina.[10] Their "protection" had

10   Only one more train would leave Westerbork for Bergen-Belsen. It departed on 13th September 1944, with 279 people on board, including young children whose parents were unknown.

run out. Theresienstadt was in part a "showcase" ghetto, maintained to suggest that the deported Jews were allowed to create new, self-contained communities in the East. To maintain that fiction the Theresienstadt camp was cleaned up and beautified in 1944 in anticipation of an inspection visit by an International Red Cross representative, who was successfully hoodwin- ked (Lanzmann, 1997). But in fact, large numbers of prisoners died in Theresienstadt, while others were deported to Auschwitz when the German commandant considered that overcrowding would damage the image of the camp. Friedrich

Figure 9.5: Helga and Kurt in the orphanage in Manchester, 1946. Photo courtesy Kurt Gottschalk.

was deported three weeks after arrival, on 29th September, and killed in Auschwitz Birkenau on or around 1st October 1944. Regina had to work in the mica (*"Glimmer"*) factory, where her fingers became infected. She was liberated in Theresienstadt by the Soviet army on 8th May 1945. She had difficulties in getting back to Holland through the chaos and devastation. Helga and Kurt remained in the orphanage in Manchester (Fig. 9.5), and returned to Holland only in December 1947. Kurt remembers his mother waiting for them on the quayside. It was a difficult time, large parts of the country were in ruins, the economy was stagnant since the Germans had removed anything of value to Germany following Operation Market Garden (September 1944), food and all other essential supplies were lacking, and the distribution system had to be continued into the 1950s. Most people were focused on getting back on their feet again and had little interest in the fate of returning war victims. Being reunited after seven and a half years of separation may also have been more difficult than they were prepared for (see other stories in Ch. 10). Kurt was two and a half years old when he saw his mother for the last time, and ten when he saw her again. Helga at fifteen had probably become a young adult by the time she saw her mother again.

It may have taken a long time before Regina had confirmation of Friedrich's death. She married again in 1951 and settled in Dutch Limburg, the region she knew well. She was concerned that history might repeat itself in the future, and she wanted the children to go to the USA as she may have had in mind in 1939 already.[11] Indeed, Helga left for the USA in 1953, and settled in Arizona. Kurt followed her in January 1958; he lives in California. Helga and several other *"Bodegraven* children"

---

11   Kurt could not confirm this, but Hans Kloosterman remembered Helga and Kurt, and a plan to move to the USA. He can only have heard about such plan in the orphanage, before the war.

such as Mirjam Szpiro provided many details about their escape on 14th May in the documentary *"De kinderen van Truus"* (Sturhoofd & van Tijn, 2020).[12]

In addition to the actions of Truus Wijsmuller, and their timely transfer from Leiden to Amsterdam, the escape of Helga and Kurt to the UK was also made possible because they had not yet joined their parents in Westerbork on 10th May. Anni Schlesinger and Bermann David (Ch. 5.2) were not so fortunate: they moved from the *Burgerweeshuis* to Westerbork on 15th April and 6th May 1940, respectively, and therefore could not be picked up by Truus.

Kurt made significant contributions to this chapter and was keenly interested in the book coming out. Sadly, he passed away in early February 2021.

9.2   Betsy Wolff and her fictitious father

Early March 1943 Hijme and Emilie Stoffels managed to get Betsy out of the orphanage just six days before all the children and the staff were arrested by the Leiden police, and brought to Westerbork (Ch. 7.4). Betsy (Fig. 9.6) was a descendant of Gompert Schlosser (c. 1819-1898), who moved from Ahaus, just across the border in Germany, to the small Dutch village of Den Ham near Ommen in the province of Overijssel, a distance of barely 55 kilometres. Gompert had a daughter, Betje Schlosser (Den Ham, 24th April 1875-15th February 1921), who married Jacob Wolff (Boxmeer, 21st June 1861-Sobibor, 16th April 1943). They lived in Den Ham. Betje and Jacob had a daughter: Leea Johanna Wolff (Den Ham, 24th July 1903-Den Ham, 28th December 1928), who gave birth to "our" Betsy in Den Ham on 13th July 1924. Leea was not married; she legally recognized Betsy as her child on 1st August 1924, as recorded (Fig. 9.7) by D.J. Maneschijn, in charge of the Civil Registry in the small township of Den Ham. So, Betsy carried the family name of her maternal grandfather: Wolff. Her grandmother (Betje Schlosser) died in 1921, aged 45. When her mother, Leea, died in 1928, aged 21, Betsy was just four years old. She was taken care of by other family members, until she was taken in by her grandfather Jacob Wolff around 1928. But Jacob was in poor health and could not continue to care for Betsy, who was taken in by the orphanage in Leiden on 11th January 1932. The story, only very briefly summarized above, is very illustrative for

Figure 9.6: Betsy in Leiden, c. 1942.

12   An English version is expected to be available on Netflix in June 2021.

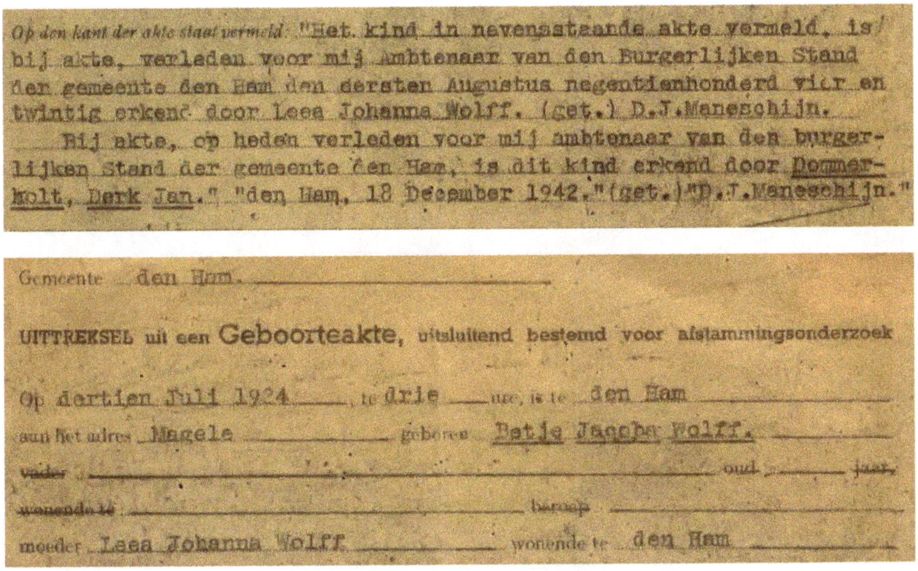

Figure 9.7: The all-important birth certificate issued by the municipality of Den Ham on 21st December 1942, which made Betsy's rescue possible. The text contains two official statements: the legal recognition of parenthood by Leea Wolff dated 13th August 1924 and signed by D.J. Maneschijn, and below that the legal recognition by Derk Jan Dommerholt that he is Betsy's biological father, dated 18th December 1942 and signed by the same D.J. Maneschijn as chief of the local Civil Registry (see text). All documents from the Stoffels' private archive. Private collection.

the social circumstances which led to children being lodged in orphanages (of any denomination) in pre-war Holland, even if they still had one of both parents.

Betsy was one of the four children saved by the Stoffels by arranging a G1 ("half-Jew"; see van den Boomgaard, 2019) certificate: Betsy Wolff, Bram Degen, Hans Kloosterman and Piet de Vries. All four of them officially had two Jewish grandparents. For Hans and Piet, the other two grandparents were officially registered as non-Jewish, but they were classified as Jewish nevertheless (J2, "unsafe half-Jewish") probably because they were firmly embedded in the Jewish environment and assumed to be members of the Dutch Jewish congregation). For their story, see Chapter 7.7. For Bram (see Ch. 9.6) and Betsy the paternal grandparents were not known.

Having two Jewish grandparents (Jacob Wolff and Betje Schlosser), Betsy needed her father and both other grandparents to be non-Jewish to be spared deportation to the East. But nobody knew who Betsy's natural father was, not even Betsy, since she was only four years old when her mother died.

Stoffels had to create an imaginary non-Jewish father for Betsy before he could submit a request to change Betsy's status from J2 to G1. There is an all-but-complete paper trail in the Stoffels archive boxes, containing the many letters he drafted for Nathan Italie to sign. Some of these documents are included in this

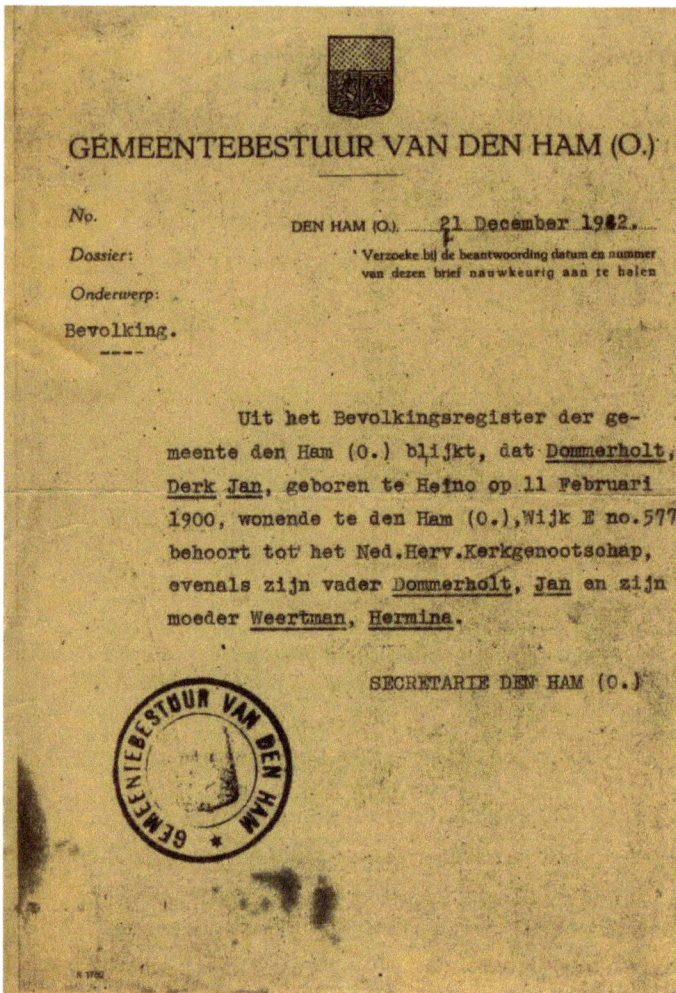

Figure 9.8: Certificate showing that Derk Jan, as well as both his parents, were members of the Dutch Reformed Church. Documents from the archive of Emilie and Hijme Stoffels. Private collection.

book (Figs. 9.8 and 9.9), the others can be found in the dossier[13] of Betsy Wolff. They provide insight about what was required before a change request could be submitted to the authorities with a chance of success. The original classification was made by the (Dutch) Civil Registry. Requests for a reclassification (to a more favourable category, like G1) had to be approved by the *Entscheidungsstelle*

13   These dossiers are held by the author until a home can be found for them.

headed by Hans G. Calmeyer on behalf of *Generalkomissar für Verwaltung und Justiz* F. Wimmer.

Betsy was eighteen years old in 1942 and attended the *Huishoudschool* in Leiden (a vocational institute, training girls in domestic duties, housekeeping, cooking, and being a good wife to a future husband). One of the teachers was a Mr. Dommerholt, who came from the same village (Den Ham) as did Betsy, her mother and grandmother. He arranged, or suggested to Stoffels to contact Derk Jan Dommerholt (Heino, 11th February 1900-Den Ham, 30th April 1949). Derk Jan was married to Janna Wilhelmina de Graaf, but the marriage had taken place on 2nd September 1932, long *after* the birth of Betsy, while his first wife had died *before* Betsy was born. Derk Jan agreed to pretend that he was Betsy's biological father. Betsy told her daughters that he was paid 350 florins for his cooperation, and that she had to agree that she would not use the false declaration of parentage to claim on any future Dommerholt inheritance. If indeed Dommerholt was paid for his cooperation, the funds would likely also have come from or via Stoffels, since Italie certainly did not have funds available for such purpose.

In December 1942 Stoffels and his wife started getting the paperwork together necessary to submit a G1 petition to the Civil Registry, by drafting letters for Nathan Italie to sign. Stoffels orchestrated the entire procedure, as shown by the fact that he kept carbon copies of the originals in his private archive, together with the replies which Italie received and passed on to Stoffels.

On 18th December 1942 he managed to get Derk Jan Dommerholt to recognize Betsy as his biological daughter at the town hall of Den Ham, and on 21st December he obtained an official birth certificate for Betsy stating that Leea Wolff and Derk Jan Dommerholt were her biological parents. The certificate was signed by the same D.J. Maneschijn (Fig. 9.7), who had witnessed and recorded Leea's recognition of Betsy as her child in 1924. Stoffels also obtained a certificate from the registry in Den Ham that Derk Jan and both his parents were members of the Dutch Reformed Church (Fig. 9.8).

By the end of 1942, Stoffels had obtained the most essential documents to claim that Betsy had two non-Jewish grandparents. Since Stoffels was well aware that the deportations were already in an advanced stage, we assume that the request to classify Betsy as G1 was made soon after 21st December 1942. But it may not have been enough for the *Rijksinspectie*, because six weeks later Stoffels had Italie send a letter to Derk Jan Dommerholt asking for more information about Betsy's grandparents. He obliges and returns the letter (Fig. 9.9) with the requested data added by hand, but he makes a curious mistake: he provides the details for Rika Camphuisen. Rika had been his father's wife since 8th November 1907, but she was not his mother, and therefore also not Betsy's "supposed" grandmother. His mother was Hermina Weertman, but she had

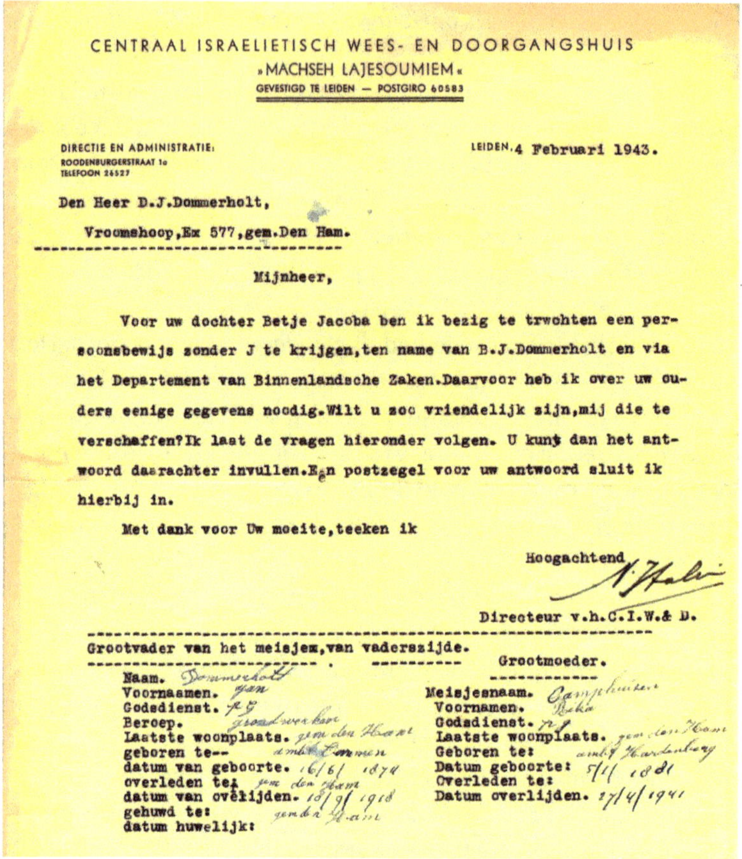

Figure 9.9: Letter of 4*th* February 1943, written by Stoffels, signed by Italie: "Sir, I am trying to obtain a *persoonsbewijs* [the national ID card] without a J [the bold black stamp on the pb indicating the holder was Jewish] for your daughter Betje Jacoba, [...] via the Department of the Interior. For that I require some data about your parents. See questions below. Would you be so kind to provide this data and return the letter to me? A postal stamp is included." Dommerholt duly returned the letter to Nathan (Stoffels) after filling in the requested details. However, he mistakenly provided the details of Rika Camphuizen. The mistake could have had fatal consequences (see text). Private collection.

died (6th September 1906) when Derk Jan was still very young. Making such a strange mistake only makes sense, I think, from the perspective that the whole exercise was a scam. One wonders if anybody on the *Rijksinspectie* staff ever noticed the mistake. Possibly Stoffels himself was not aware of the mistake, since he was involved in many other attempts to frustrate the Germans. On 12th February 1943 another letter was despatched to Den Ham, asking for details about Betsy's Jewish family (Schlosser).

This is also a strange letter, seemingly written in a hurry, and – almost as if by afterthought – asking about the parents of Jan Dommerholt, without mentioning that it should concern the *first* wife of Dommerholt's father. Den Ham duly replies on 24th February with the data on Betje Schlosser but cannot provide data on Dommerholt. Cost of the reply: 50 cents. Then Stoffels asks the municipality of Boxmeer on 26th February (this is three weeks before the orphanage is liquidated) for information on Jacob Wolff, Betsy's Jewish grandfather. Boxmeer replies (free of charge) by returning the original letter (signed by Italie) with the data filled in. Obviously Italie passed on all these originals to the Stoffels, who kept them in their archive. Noteworthy, the local Civil Registry does not follow the German, racial, definition of being Jewish, but the Dutch religious definition. Although grandfather Wolff obviously came from a Jewish family, he was not registered as belonging to the "Israelite faith", so his religion is given as "unknown". It made no difference to the Germans.

On 10th March 1943 the all-important approval of her G1 status was sent by registered mail by the *Rijksinspectie*. A duplicate was sent to Emilie Stoffels (Fig. 9.10), which suggests that she handled much of the work described above. The original was signed by or on behalf of Jacob Lentz,[14] the chief of the Dutch *Rijksinspectie voor de Bevolkingsregisters*, on behalf of Generalkommissar Wimmer, but in fact approved by Calmeyer's *Entscheidungsstelle*.

The degree of collaboration of the Civil Registry in confirming people as being Jews in the context of the German plans is shocking. Yet there were also (Dutch) officials at the registry as well as (German and Dutch) officials at the *Entscheidungsstelle* who were prepared to let dubious claims pass unchallenged, if the proper procedure had been followed and supporting documents presented (van den Boomgaard, 2019). Calmeyer is also credited with approving G1 decisions which could easily have been rejected, as long as the request contained a proper paper trail, including supporting documents (ibidem). The fact that Dommerholt's recognition of Betsy as his biological daughter was made as late as December 1942, together with the fact that he apparently never cared about Betsy during her eleven years in an orphanage, could have been reason enough for a serious challenge. The same applies to the G1 claim for Bram Degen (Ch. 9.6), which was also approved on rather flimsy grounds. Some people regard Calmeyer as a hero because he approved many such flimsy claims. Others point out that he rejected many others, but it is doubtful that he could have done more without jeopardizing his position (See review by van den Boomgaard, 2019). Yet he was part of the Nazi organization in

---

14 He was the godfather of the Dutch *persoonsbewijs*, or pb. See Chapter 6.

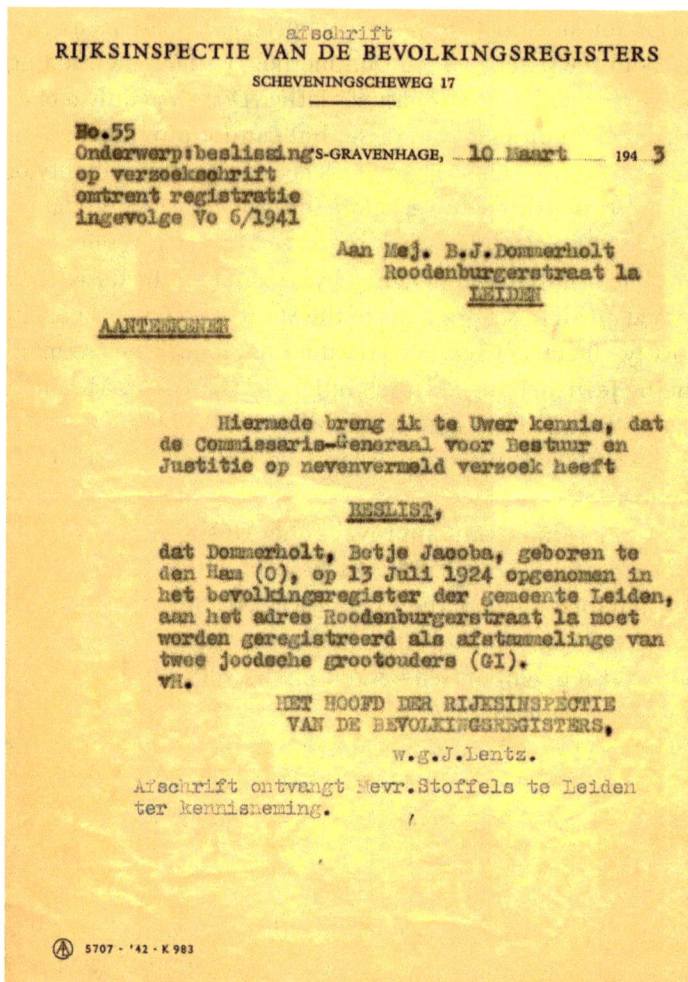

afschrift

RIJKSINSPECTIE VAN DE BEVOLKINGSREGISTERS

SCHEVENINGSCHEWEG 17

No.55
Onderwerp:beslissings-GRAVENHAGE, __10 Maart__ 194 3
op verzoekschrift
omtrent registratie
ingevolge Vo 6/1941

                         Aan Mej. B.J.Dommerholt
                              Roodenburgerstraat 1a
                                   LEIDEN

AANTEKENEN

            Hiermede breng ik te Uwer kennis, dat
         de Commissaris-Generaal voor Bestuur en
         Justitie op nevenvermeld verzoek heeft

                    BESLIST,

         dat Dommerholt, Betje Jacoba, geboren te
         den Haag (O), op 13 Juli 1924 opgenomen in
         het bevolkingsregister der gemeente Leiden,
         aan het adres Roodenburgerstraat 1a moet
         worden geregistreerd als afstammelinge van
         twee joodsche grootouders (GI).
         VH.
                  HET HOOFD DER RIJKSINSPECTIE
                  VAN DE BEVOLKINGSREGISTERS,

                         w.g.J.Lentz.

         Afschrift ontvangt Mevr.Stoffels te Leiden
         ter kennisneming.

(A) 5707 - '42 - K 983

Figure 9.10: The official approval of Betsy's G1 status, dated 10th March 1943, i.e. one week before the orphanage was liquidated.

Holland and as such co-responsible for its actions. The controversy continues to this day.[15]

The next day, based on the G1 certificate, the municipality of Leiden issued a *verhuisvergunning* (relocation permit) (Fig. 9.11). Jews were not allowed (as of 7th

---

15   He was awarded the Yad Vashem medal, but a proposal to name a Holocaust museum in Osnabrück after him (May 2020) met with fierce protest from Holland. He approved some 2500 requests and rejected some 1500 others. From c. September 1943 it became more difficult for him to approve flimsy claims, as (Dutch) co-workers with Nazi sympathies began to complain about it (op. cit.).

November 1941) to change residence, one of the German measures to ensure all of them could be easily picked up later. One of the conditions of getting G1 status (not mentioned on this document, but it is written on the G1 certificate for Hans Kloosterman) was that the person involved should be *"removed immediately from the Jewish milieu"*. The address she is moving to, Cronesteinkade 20, is the house of Hijme and Emilie Stoffels. They took her in until she found a new home in Hilversum.

The paper trail of the story illustrates several aspects of the Holocaust in the Netherlands, such as the German tendency to make even premeditated murder part of a "legal" process, in sharp contrast with the Holocaust in Eastern Europe. All steps were underpinned by laws or decrees promulgated by the Nazi civil government, and duly noted by the Dutch civil service, the police, and other government or private institutions, who were left in a subordinate position to the German authorities when the government left for London. It is a strange but illuminating fact that what is known in other countries as the "Resistance", is often called *"de Illegaliteit"* in the Netherlands. Respect for authority was ingrained in pre-war Dutch society, particularly with the bourgeoisie, including of course the Jewish bourgeoisie, which was better developed and integrated in Holland than in other countries (Ch. 1). One may wonder why Nathan Italie consistently refused to allow Stoffels to arrange *onderduik* for any of his children, while not having a problem with letting go the four G1 children, although each had a Jewish mother. But Nathan was also inclined to submit to official regulations: The G-1 escape route was *legal*, and *onderduik* was not. Jews who moved to a new address without permission listed in the police bulletins as wanted criminals, probably an unthinkable idea in Nathan's mind.

The paper trail also illustrates the amount of work and the time which was required to achieve this result for only one person. The records show that it is highly unlikely that Betsy, or Bram, Piet and Hans, would have obtained the G1 certificate in time to save them without the tireless efforts of the Stoffels.

As always, many questions remain. Was the birth certificate issued in December 1942 genuine, or was the document a falsification altogether? If genuine, then who was this D.J. Maneschijn? It was only in 2019 that I had opportunity to go to the village of Den Ham (now part of Vriezenveen) to verify that indeed a Mr. D.J. Maneschijn was in charge of the Civil Registry of Den Ham, in 1924 (when Leea recognized Betsy as her biological daughter) as well as in 1942, when he recorded the parental recognition by Derk Jan Dommerholt. Was he aware of the role he was playing in saving Betsy from deportation? It came to light[16] that Maneschijn was

16   With the help of a notary in Den Ham, Mr. A. Endendijk, who interviewed his youngest son in January 2019.

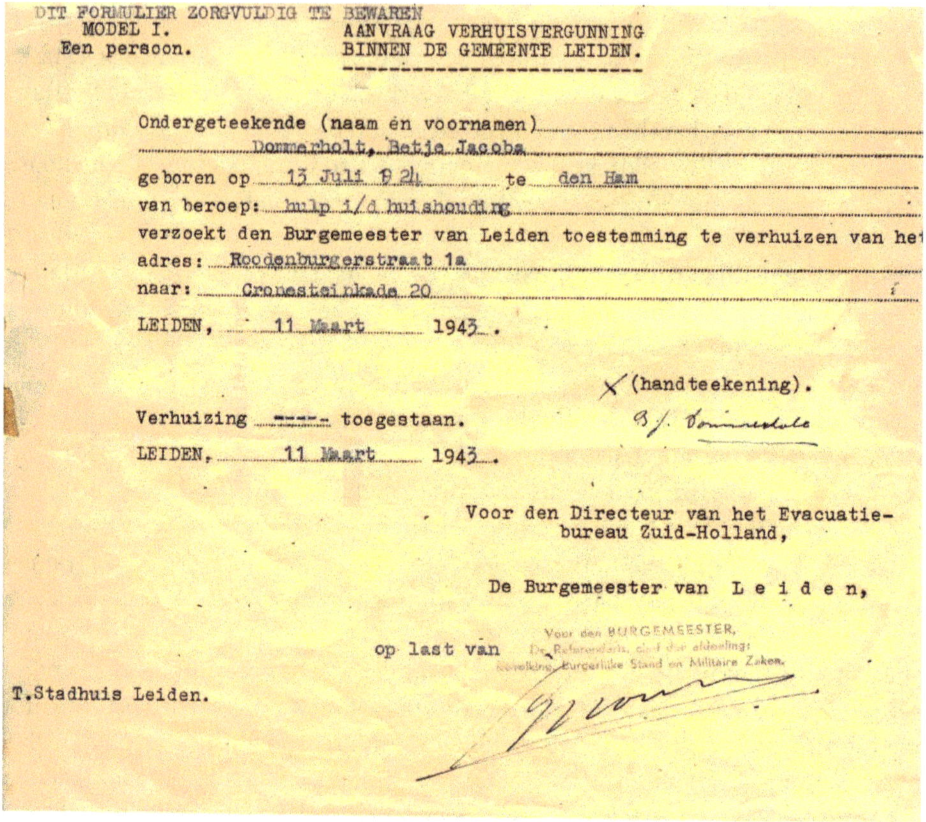

DIT FORMULIER ZORGVULDIG TE BEWAREN
MODEL I.
Een persoon.

AANVRAAG VERHUISVERGUNNING
BINNEN DE GEMEENTE LEIDEN.

Ondergeteekende (naam en voornamen) Dommerholt, Betje Jacoba

geboren op 13 Juli 1924 te den Ham

van beroep: hulp i/d huishouding

verzoekt den Burgemeester van Leiden toestemming te verhuizen van het

adres: Roodenburgerstraat 1a

naar: Cronesteinkade 20

LEIDEN, 11 Maart 1943.

(handteekening).

Verhuizing ---- toegestaan.

LEIDEN, 11 Maart 1943.

Voor den Directeur van het Evacuatie-
bureau Zuid-Holland,

De Burgemeester van Leiden,

op last van

Voor den BURGEMEESTER,

T.Stadhuis Leiden.

Figure 9.11: The authorization to leave the orphanage, and move in with Stoffels, dated 11th March 1943 (see text). Private collection.

arrested in 1944 after someone in the area was caught with false identity papers, and the trail led back to him. Maneschijn, who evidently did not provide the police with names of other people for whom he had arranged false documents, was interned in Camp Erika.[17] This relatively small concentration camp near Ommen served as a prison for people caught for illegal activities such as black market trading or acts of resistance like hiding Jews. Clearly, Maneschijn was aware that he took part in a clandestine effort to keep a Jewish girl out of Nazi grip. As far as we know, he never asked for, nor was he given any recognition of his acts. According to his son, he was criticized after the war by his superiors in the civil service for his actions, in as far as they were "illegal", or because he overstepped the boundaries of his authority. Apparently, he not only assisted people to resist the occupation authorities, but

17 He is included in a list of prisoners for March 1945 (Archive NIOD Amsterdam).

also provided municipal financial support to people who were in need without having the authority to do so.

Soon after liberation, Betsy married Laurentius van der Kroft; her wedding photo was included in the Stoffels' photo album. She was reputed to be always cheerful, but she did not have an easy life. She joined her husband to live in Germany and had five children who survived pregnancy and infancy. Betsy became ill and died in November 1988.

9.3   Mindel Färber escapes from Bergen-Belsen by *Austausch* train

Mindel was born in Düsseldorf, Germany, on 5th April 1939. Her family came from Oświęcim, in Poland, better known by its German name: Auschwitz. This region, around Krakau, had a large Jewish population[18]; but many Jews migrated to Germany after the First World War,[19] often without having a well-defined nationality, coping with shifting borders and virulent anti-Semitism. After Hitler's takeover in 1933, Germany wanted to eject these stateless Jews, who had nowhere to go without proper passports and visa.[20] Mindel's parents Bernard Färber (Oświęcim, 20th May 1901) and Cirl Fradel Hoffnung (Potgorze, 14th October 1909) came to Holland as illegal immigrants in May 1939, and did not register with the alien police, obviously out of fear of being sent back to Germany. Later, Mindel was registered by the Dutch alien police as "stateless". The parents left Holland on the *Aliyah Bet* ship[21] the *Dora*, a 50-year-old Greek coal freighter. The *Dora* left Amsterdam on 19th July 1939 under great stealth and secrecy first to Vlissingen (Flushing) with 20 Dutch and 300 German, Polish or stateless refugees, including many young *chalutzim* from *Werkdorp Wieringermeer* and Deventer. She picked up another 160 Jews in Antwerp, and managed to deliver all 480 refugees to the beach at Shefayim (some 20 km north of Tel Aviv) on 12th August 1939. Gertrud van Tijn played a crucial role in organizing the illegal enterprise. David Cohen (her boss) was kept in the dark since he opposed

---

18   Immortalized, in the nick of time, by photographer Roman Vishniac in *"A vanished world"* (1983).

19   There were severe pogroms in Eastern Europe: 1881, 1903-1906, and 1917-1921.

20   In October 1938 the Germans pushed some 18,000 Polish Jews across the Polish border, where they were not admitted. This led to the murder in Paris of a German diplomat, and the German revenge during Kristallnacht.

21   Mossad leAliyah Bet: the organization for illegal immigration to Erets Jisrael, past the British blockade, c. 1934-1948. Headed in 1939 by Shaul Avigur, later part of Ben Gurion's government. He witnessed the landing of the *Dora* from Golda Meir's apartment. See Daniel Abraham's website, http://danielabraham.net/tree/related/dora/.

all such illegal activities, but the Dutch government cooperated, being happy to see refugees move on to other countries. Such were the paradoxes of politics at the time.

In view of the risks and uncertainties of these illegal enterprises (the *Dora*'s ostensible destination was Thailand), small children were not allowed on board. Mindel, just three months old, was lodged with the family of Abraham Leizer Färber in The Hague.[22] It seems self-evident that the parents, like so many others, did not foresee the German invasion of Holland in May 1940 when they left their child behind in the care of family. Mindel could not stay at the family however; she was taken in by the *Huize ten Vijver* refugee home in The Hague. From that moment (if not before) she became a ward of the Dutch Ministry of the Interior[23] like the other refugee children from Germany[24] (Ch. 5). When on 3rd June 1940 Huize ten Vijver was closed by the Germans because it was too close to the coast, a young woman from ten Vijver, Ilse Braun,[25] took Mindel with her. When Ilse Braun had to leave her house in September 1940, Mindel returned to her uncle, Abraham Färber. But Abraham and his wife, Beile, who had three children of their own, moved to Het Apeldoornse Bos, a Jewish psychiatric institution, in 1941 or 1942. From there they were deported to Auschwitz on 22nd January 1943,[26] together with all the other patients. Obviously, Mindel could not stay in The Hague, and being just one year and nine months old, she was taken in by the orphanage in Leiden on 8th January 1941, where she stayed until the orphanage was liquidated on 17th March 1943. From the surviving stories it is clear she was a character, but she had an angelic appearance (Fig. 9.12), and she seems to have been easily accepted by the much older children and the staff in the orphanage.

She was also frail and required frequent medical attention. In a letter of 28th January 1942 to the *Gnouzeir Dalliem* Jewish society, the treasurer of the board of governors asked for (another) financial donation, explaining that the orphanage had to bear the cost of regularly bringing Mindel and a supervising nanny by tram to the children's clinic in the Leiden University Hospital. The society, according to handwritten note on the side, obliged with a donation of ten guilders. During the night of 17th/18th March 1943, Mindel was arrested by

22   The family included Abraham's wife, Beile Ringer (1905), and their children Leo (1934), Richard (1935) and Jeanne (1937). They lived at Hofwijckstraat 29.

23   However, the documents in the dossier were retrieved from the Justice Ministry Archives 2.09.45/490, courtesy Miriam Keesing.

24   See Dokin.nl for a description and a group photo of refugee children. Most of them had arrived without parents by Kindertransport. See Chapter 5.2.

25   Charlotte de Bourbonlaan 33. See documents on Dokin.nl, courtesy Miriam Keesing.

26   Of their children, Leo died in Den Haag on 31st August 1942. Richard and Jeanne were deported from Westerbork and killed in Sobibor on 13th March 1943.

the Leiden police and put on the train to Westerbork with all the other residents of the orphanage (Ch. 7).

In Westerbork she was registered (on 19th March) (Fig. 9.13) as in possession of an Albersheim letter, in which the Joodse Raad declared that the holder was *"in the process"* of obtaining a "Palestine certificate" and should therefore be regarded as a potential candidate for a "prisoner exchange" between Germany and the UK, by Swiss mediation. Mindel was therefore temporarily exempted from further deportation, pending decisions on further prisoner exchanges. She stayed in Westerbork while one after the other of the Leiden orphanage children was taken away to Sobibor or Auschwitz (Ch. 7). When Abraham de Beer, four years old, had left on the train to Auschwitz on 16th November 1943, Mindel was the only one

Figure 9.12: Mindel Färber in Leiden, 1942.

of the group of 17th March 1943 who was still in Westerbork.

Clara Asscher-Pinkhof, wife of a rabbi, child carer, schoolteacher, and writer, is better known in the USA as Clara Pinkhof, the author of *"Star children"*, a hair-raising tale of the Holocaust through the eyes of children. She had a daughter, Roza, in Palestine, and Clara was therefore also on the Albersheim list. Clara had involved herself in the orphanage in Westerbork, and got to know Mindel, who was indeed not a character to be overlooked. Clara described (Asscher-Pinkhof, 1966) the encounter, as well as the train journey which brought Mindel and herself to Palestine, in her autobiography *"Dancer without legs"*[27]:

She looked like a translucent feather, when I first met Mindeltje[28] in Westerbork.
Having suffered from repeated pneumonia, she looked like a two-and-a-half-year-old

27 *"Danseres zonder benen"* is an impressive document which has unfortunately not been published in English. This and following fragments have been freely translated by the author as relevant for the story of Mindel.

28 In her book, she is called Mindel Fuld, presumably for reasons of privacy. Clara Asscher Pinkhof confirmed to Emilie Stoffels (fide van Zegveld, 1993, p. 169) that Mindel Fuld was indeed Mindel Färber. The child which is shown with Clara in Westerbork on the USHMM website, however, is not Mindel Färber.

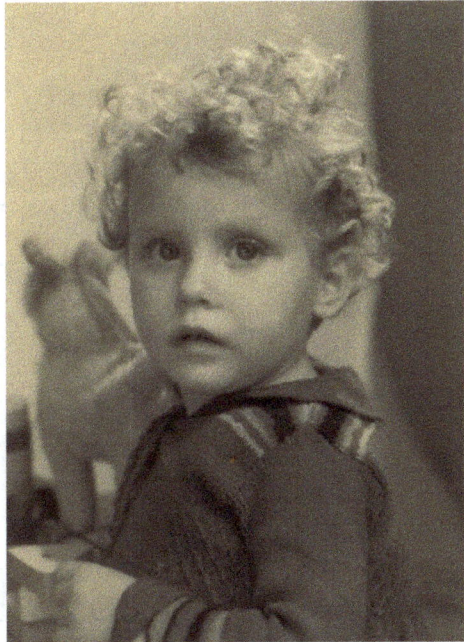

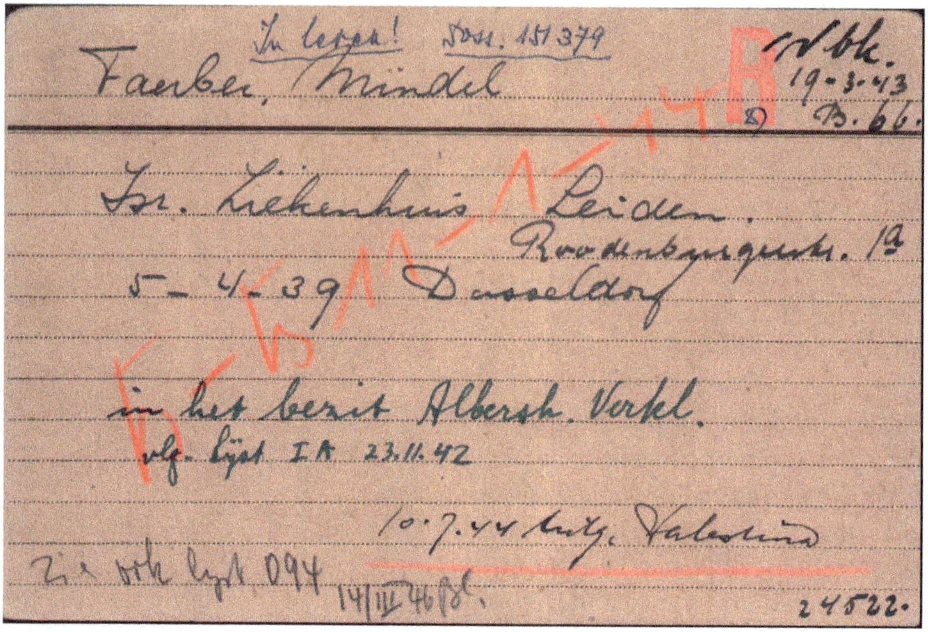

In leven! Doss. 151379

Faerber, Mindel

Wbk. 19-3-43 B. 66.

Isr. Ziekenhuis Leiden.

5-4-39 Dusseldorf

in het bezit Albersh. Verkl.

vlg. lijst I.A. 23.11.42

10.7.44 Uitg. Palestina

24522.

Figure 9.13: The Joodse Raad card for Mindel stating her status as having an Albersheim letter, her registration in Westerbork on 19*th* March 1943 (she arrived on 18*th* March) and post-war additions about her deportation (to Bergen-Belsen) on 11*th* January 1944 and her arrival in Palestine on 10*th* July 1944. At the top, *"in leven!"* i.e. "she is alive!" Courtesy Red Cross War Archives, The Hague, 2016.

> *toddler, but she was in fact four, and she was precocious, talking like a six-year-old. She had blond hair, with dancing silky curls, and fiercely blue eyes. The adults around her whispered: her parents are in Palestine, they left their baby behind in Holland, without papers, when she was just one year old.* [...] *Just around this time, I received my Palestine certificate, and a preposterous idea got hold of me. Here was a toddler whose parents were in Palestine, while I had a certificate; maybe I was predestined to return this child to her parents in Palestine.*

Clara writes that someone from outside the Westerbork camp tried to have Mindel escape, and that she prevented that in order to take her to Palestine.[29] Also, that she managed, with serious difficulty, having been refused in the first instance, to have Mindel attached to her own certificate, and that in the following weeks a relationship grew between them. There is no clue as to who could have tried to get Mindel to escape from Westerbork, and I was unable to corroborate the story. But when on 11th January 1944 a train left Westerbork with 1037 persons on board for

29 Although she could not have known at that time, still in Westerbork, if that was a realistic notion.

the Bergen-Belsen concentration camp, in northern Germany not far from Hanover, both Mindel and Clara were on that train.

As opposed to Auschwitz-Birkenau or Sobibor, Bergen-Belsen was not designed to kill the prisoners outright upon arrival.[30] Several thousand prisoners were held in sub-camps,[31] in special categories (e.g. on the basis of having non-European passports or being candidates for possible exchange with German nationals in allied hands). They had certain privileges while waiting for an exchange, at least until mid-1944. More than a thousand people were on the Palestine list. In fact, apart from small-scale exchanges in 1941/1942, only one such exchange took place, carrying 222 Bergen-Belsen prisoners to freedom on a railway journey via Vienna and Istanbul in early July 1944. Clara writes (1966) how she and Mindel were listed for this – one and only – Palestine exchange, but that she herself was taken off the list at the second selection. She found another woman to take Mindel under her wing and was sent back to the main camp. Clara remarks, seemingly with a little chagrin, that Mindel had no trouble attaching herself to an entirely new "foster mother", and this is not the only qualifying remark about Mindel she makes in her book. A month later (probably May 1944), everybody who had been initially selected for the exchange was sent back to the main camp. Suddenly, at the end of June 1944, the original 250 people, including Mindel and Clara's mother, but now without Clara herself, were called up again. Then, at the very last moment, to her complete surprise, Clara was added to the group again, together with some others, including an entire family, to replace people who had dropped out for various reasons. Going through the gate to the small holding camp for the second time in a matter of weeks they passed Clara's brother[32]: *"Again we looked into each other's eyes and exchanged a wordless farewell. Once in the holding camp, Mother and I saw only his back because he was there on guard duty. Never again would we see his sweet, boy-like face."*

On Friday, 30th June 1944, the group boarded a train at Celle Station, some 25 km south of Bergen-Belsen. Clara is struck by the observation that from that moment the prisoners are suddenly and unexpectedly treated as human beings again. The

---

30 Nevertheless, some 70,000 people died in Bergen-Belsen from exhaustion, lack of food, untreated disease, mostly in the last six months before liberation in May 1945, when the camp was transformed into a "regular" concentration camp and tens of thousands of prisoners were brought in from camps which were on the brink of liberation by the Russian army. Anne Frank and her sister Margot died in Bergen-Belsen in that period.

31 See US Holocaust Memorial Museum, n.d., *"Bergen-Belsen in depth: The camp complex"*, in *Holocaust encyclopedia*, https://encyclopedia.ushmm.org/content/en/article/bergen-belsen-in-depth-the-camp-complex.

32 This (I assume) was Joseph (Amsterdam, 26th April 1906-Bergen-Belsen, 7th January 1945).

train out of Vienna, where another 61 prisoners from France[33] came on board, turns out to have a dining car. A Red Cross representative in Turkey arranges for her to dine with her mother; a young Turkish soldier tucks her in with a blanket, on the way to Istanbul.

Six days out of Bergen-Belsen the train reached Istanbul (Fig. 9.14), where people from the Jewish Agency looked after them. Changing trains twice, after crossing into Asia, they reached Haifa ten days after leaving Bergen-Belsen. Mindel had not come back to Clara during the journey; she stayed with her newly acquired "foster mother". But in Haifa Clara took her to the British administration office of the Atlit camp (Fig. 9.15) where the certificates were checked, when suddenly she heard a sharp woman's voice call out, *"Where is Mindel?"* Clara could return Mindel to her mother, fulfilling the *"preposterous idea"* conceived when they met for the first time in Westerbork. A few days later a camp official allowed Mindel's parents to take her home. I wonder if they fully realized at that time what a miracle Mindel's escape had been. Another few days later, Clara was taken by car to her daughter in Jerusalem. Stepping out of the Atlit camp into freedom, she burst uncontrollably into tears. Two weeks later Mindel and her mother paid Clara a visit in Jerusalem: *"At last the questions which had bothered me for more than a year were answered: How did Mindeltje get separated from her parents? How did the parents reach Palestine, leaving their baby daughter in exile?"*

The mother answered (Asscher-Pinkhof, 1966):

> [T]hey had been in Germany still, when she was pregnant of Mindel. The mother, being born in Poland, was due for deportation but her pregnancy gave her a reprieve. Once Mindel was born, she fled to Holland, where she could board an illegal immigration ship to Palestine in July 1939. Babies and toddlers were strictly not allowed on board the ship, because the journey could take a long time, they could easily become ill, and they could betray the illegal immigrants if they were unable to keep silent. Mindel was lodged with family in The Hague with a view to get Mindel over to Palestine legally as soon as possible. This became impossible after the German invasion of May 1940. There were some Red Cross letters, but after a while no replies were received any more from Holland. The parents assumed that Abraham and his family, including Mindel, had either gone into hiding, or that they had been captured. They had not been aware that Mindel had gone to

---

33   From Vittel (50) and from Laufen (eleven). Small differences exist in numbers as reported. The total number of people reaching Haifa on 10th July 1944 as quoted by sources varies between 281 and 283. A passenger list is available at https://www.ushmm.org/online/hsv/person_advance_search.php?SourceId=20664.

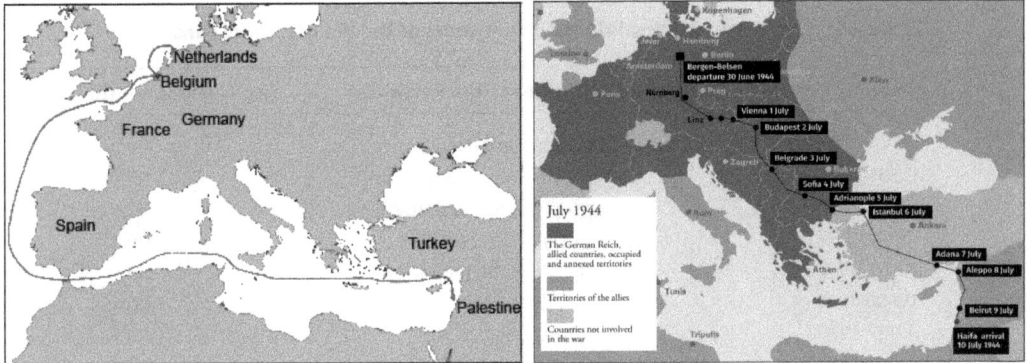

Figure 9.14: Left: The route of the Aliyah Bet ship *Dora*, which brought Mindel's parents to Palestine in August 1939. Courtesy Daniel Abraham. Right: The route of the *Austausch* train from Bergen-Belsen, which brought Mindel to Palestine in July 1944. The mother of Aron Wolff was also on this train (see Ch. 10). Courtesy of Groeschlerhaus, Jever.

Leiden, Westerbork and Bergen-Belsen until the news of the Exchange transport reached them.

The fact that Mindel was considered "a character" is not surprising if we try to imagine the impact which the many moves, summarized in Table 9.1, must have had on Mindel. Each of them represented an enormous upheaval in her life; from being separated from her parents as a baby to travelling across Europe to a mother she had not seen in five years. Relatively speaking, the two years and two months in Leiden may have been the most stable period in the first five years of her life.

Figure 9.15: The British detention camp Atlit, south of Haifa, Palestine. Free Image Coll. Project. If you visit the Atlit Museum, I recommend to take the guided tour which includes an Aliyah Bet display inside the ship which is on the terrain.

Table 9.1   The many upheavals in the 5 first years of the life of Mindel Färber

Date	(Parents were refugees from Poland)	Age (years/month)
05-04-1939	Born Düsseldorf (Germany)	
Ca 01-05-1939	Illegal immigration to Holland	1m
Ca 01-06-1939	Lodged with Abr. L. Färber	2m
19-07-1939	Parents left for Palestine	3m
Ca 01-09-1939	Children's Home ten Vijver	5m
03-06-1940	To Ilse Braun	1y 2m
12-09-1940	Back to Abr. L. Färber	1y 6m
08-01-1941	Orphanage Leiden	1y 9m
17-03-1943	Deported to Westerbork	3y 9m
11-01-1944	Deported to Bergen Belsen	4y 9m
10-07-1944	Escape to Palestine	5y 3m

Clara, like so many others, had to adapt to freedom, and to Palestine as it was at the time. She took a few months in isolation from the outside world, and then sat down to write *"Star children"*, one of her most successful books. She probably received news about her family, who had survived and who had not. She died in Haifa on 25th November 1984. About Mindel, there is no further information except that she moved to Canada at some stage.

9.4   Aron Wolff (Ronnie de Paauw) becomes "Ronald Witteveen"

It so happened that the mother of Aron Wolff, Serlina de Paauw, was on the same *Austausch* train which brought Mindel and Clara from Bergen-Belsen to Palestine in early July 1944 (previous chapter). But Aron was not with her, and like the mother of Mindel who arrived by ship in 1939 (see map, Fig. 9.14), Serlina arrived in Palestine without her child.

Statements and quotes in this narrative are based on an interview with Aron[34] (now Roni Maor) by the author on 6th September 2017; the voluminous reports by Johan van Straten (1992); post-war letters by Serlina de Paauw to Johan and Dien van Straten; post-war letters by Fré de Paauw to her family in Palestine, in as far as published (Melkman-de Paauw, 2002), including comments by her husband, Jozeph Melkman (Michman), and her son, Dan Michman. Relevant parts of van Straten's report have been copied into Aron's dossier, including the post-war letters from Serlina (courtesy Mr. Bert van Straten). The stories of these families are

---

34   I thank Menachem Philipson-Armon for arranging the contact in 2017.

interconnected and illuminating for the wartime problems and post-war issues of *onderduik* children in Holland.

Serlina was a daughter of Aron de Paauw, a rabbi in Amsterdam and governor of the *Beurs voor Diamanthandel*. Serlina (1902) had a sister, Sara (Saar, 1904), and two half-sisters from her father's second marriage: Jeanette (Nettie, 1909), and Frederika (Fré, 1913).[35] Fré was married to Jozeph Melkman,[36] who is "Uncle Jo" in the narrative below.

Nettie had emigrated to Palestine in 1935. Their father was upset: *"Why in the world would you go to such a place of sand and desert?"* She will not have realized at the time that her move to Palestine would be of life-saving significance, for herself as well as for many of the above-mentioned family members. Saar and *"oma"* Hanna (mother of Fré and stepmother of Saar and Serlina) were also on the Austausch train, joining Nettie in Palestine in July 1944.

Aron was born on 27th July 1938 in Amsterdam. His father was Dr. Mozes (Max) Wolff, who was chairman of the Jewish Community Council in Haarlem; he had six children from a previous marriage. Max and Serlina were divorced. Aron was living in Amsterdam with his mother when war reached Holland in 1940.

Serlina had a secretarial job. In September 1941, when Jewish children were segregated from all other children (Ch. 6.4), she became a teacher at Jewish Primary School no. 10 at Jekerstraat 86 in Amsterdam. She needed the income, and when conditions became difficult, she brought Ronnie to the Jewish orphanage in Leiden on 13th September 1940 on the advice of Uncle Jo. It may seem strange, with four Jewish orphanages in Amsterdam, to send Aron to Leiden, but like Mindel Färber he was too young (just two years in September 1940) and the orphanage in Leiden was probably the only one which would accept him. He was registered in Leiden as Aron Wolff, but quickly became known as "Ronnie de Paauw". He was included in one of the photographs taken by or for Geertje Gebert on the bench behind the building (Fig. 9.16, second from right). Almost a year later he appears (Fig. 9.17) with the group of small children in the care of Mary de Raay (later Mrs. Vromen). From here on he can be called Aron or Ronnie (or Roni, as he is called today).

In the autumn of 1942, when the deportations from Westerbork to Auschwitz were in full swing, Uncle Jo told Serlina: *"I don't really know what is happening to all those people sent east, but it is surely no good and we never hear of them anymore. You should take Aron out of the orphanage; it is not a safe place."*

That is what she did. Mary de Raay remembered that Aron's mother came to collect him in Leiden on or around 12th November 1942 to take him home to

---

35   These are only the family members who are important in Aron's story. More details on the families de Paauw, Wolff and Melkman are included in the dossier of Aron Wolff.

36   Later Prof. Jozeph Michman, co-author of *"Pinkas"* and director general of Yad Vashem from 1957.

Figure 9.16: Geertje Gebert sitting on the bench behind the orphanage in Leiden with five of the children in her care and Aron Wolff on her lap. On the far right: Debora Sanders. On the left is an unidentified girl, Benno Redisch, and (probably) Salomon Rotstein. The windows are taped, to prevent dangerous shattering of glass in case of a bombardment. Probably July 1941.

Amsterdam. That same November 1942, Jo and Fré decided to send their one-year-old son Awraham to *onderduik* in Blaricum, where he was registered as a *vondeling*, an abandoned child,[37] and given the name "Kees". But Serlina was not yet ready to follow their example: *"If we have to go, we'll go together,"* she said, according to Aron. But one day in January 1943, around 11 o'clock at night, a policeman knocked on the door. Serlina was initially relaxed; as a teacher she had a *Sperre*: the infamous *"temporary reprieve from deportation"*. The *Sperre* also applied to Aron.[38] But the policeman said he had come specifically for Aron. They were arresting Jews who had recently changed their residence address. He brought them to the *Hollandse Schouwburg*, the main *"Umschlagplatz"* of Amsterdam from where people were brought by tram and train to Westerbork. At the *Hollandse Schouwburg* Serlina noticed other Jews who had recently moved address without permission. She concluded that the arrest of Aron was part of a planned, concerted effort. She

---

37 Three months later the Germans put an end to this loophole, declaring all foundlings Jewish by default.

38 As confirmed by another card from the Joodse Raad Cartotheek, included in Aron's dossier.

Figure 9.17: May 1942. The children of nanny Mary de Raay, including Aron Wolff, not yet four years old, and Mindel Färber, then three years old. Three children are wearing the star.

back row from left:
Willy Blog
Louis or Melna Fleurima
Mary de Raay
Melna or Louis Fleurima
Rika Alvares Vega
unidentified

middle row from left:
Henriette Alvares Vega
Willem Alvares Vega
Izak Ensel (?)
Salomon Rotstein
Hanna Italie
unidentified
unidentified
Aron Wolff (Ronnie de Paauw)
Benno Redisch

front row from left:
Mindel Färber
Elchanan Italie
unidentified

argued that she would join Aron, and she would be missed as a teacher the next day. They were both released and sent home. The Germans were relatively relaxed about letting people go in that stage of the deportations, knowing they would have little problem to arrest and deport them later. Such decisions were occasionally taken in a whimsical manner, depending on the mood of the German official in charge. Ferdinand aus der Fünten, the chief Jew hunter of Amsterdam (Fig. 10.11), was often personally present at the *Hollandse Schouwburg*. Serlina writes (letter to van Straten, 2nd October 1945) that another attempt to arrest Aron was made in mid-March. A month later colleagues from her school were arrested during the major razzia in Amsterdam of 20th-21st May 1943. This time, her colleagues were *not* released although they had a *Sperre* just as Serlina had. She realized she had no choice but to get Ronnie away into hiding as soon as possible. Fré came by to collect Ronnie on 1st June 1943 and pass him on to an unknown helper, who brought him to a hiding address which was also unknown to them. A few days later Serlina was preparing a suitcase with clothes for Ronnie, to be sent to his hiding address. He had left the orphanage in Leiden with only one set of extra clothes and she was still working on getting a new set of clothing ready for him. But that evening the police came by to arrest the neighbour in whose apartment Serlina and Aron were living. She had two small children who were in hiding. But they had been found, and now they had come to arrest the mother as well. During the arrest, Serlina was interrogated to find out where Ronnie was, and she told them on impulse that he was with his father. But Ronnie's small bed was still there for all to see, and Serlina fled from the apartment without delay, leaving the suitcase with clothes behind. Serlina mentions that the Amsterdam Civil Registry was helpful by not mentioning Ronnie on her change-of-residence form. That would appear to be a rare case where the Dutch civil authorities did not loyally follow German instructions. It may have helped to keep Ronnie off the radar screen from June 1943. He is also not mentioned on his mother's Joodse Raad card.

Ronnie's escape from arrest was a close call indeed. Two weeks later, on 20th June, Serlina was arrested during the next major razzia in Amsterdam and brought to Westerbork. At that time, most of the children she had been teaching had been deported already and Serlina's work at the Jewish school no longer served as a reason for the Germans to postpone her deportation. Both Fré and Serlina had been kept in the dark about Ronnie's destination, which was the home of Johan (Wim[39]) and Dien van Straten in Huizen (in the province of North Holland).[40] From that moment he was called "Ronnie Witteveen". The couple already had a baby of their own, Johnny (17th January 1943) (Fig. 9.18), and another Jewish girl of about Ronnie's age: Marjon (Jonnie) Polak, who was given the *onderduik* name "Marietje Smidt". Marietje and Ronnie became "permanent" guests with the van Stratens, but at times, quite frequently, they sheltered other Jewish children and adults in their home as well, such as Leo Vis, who became "Theo Mulder", and his twin brother, Arthur Vis, who became "Jan Mulder". Theo was also present in May 1944 when the photo of Figure 9.18 was taken. *"No one turned these children in to the authorities, even though they attended school and were obvious strangers. In addition to hiding Jewish children, Johan also helped many Jews in hiding by bringing*

---

39 In all wartime-related documents, as well as the Yad Vashem website, he is called Johan. However, his full name was Jan Willem, and he was always called Wim.

40 Van Straten recorded that a Mr. Denekamp (or Deenekamp) delivered Ronnie to him. There may have been other in-between helpers involved. There was confusion; van Straten was told to expect "Flipje", but received Ronnie instead, because he was considered an emergency case.

Figure 9.18: The family van Straten with four *onderduikers* in their back garden, on Whit Sunday, 27ᵗʰ May 1944. Back row from left: "Cobie" (Serlien Prins), Mr. Johan van Straten, "Theo" (Leo Vis), Mrs. Dien van Straten. Front row from left: "Ronnie" (Aron Wolff), "Marietje" (Jonnie Polak), and Johnnie van Straten. All four *onderduikers* survived the war. Photo from van Straten report. Courtesy Mr. Bert van Straten.

them food [ration] cards" (Michman & Flim, 2004, p. 718). Later, they were joined by a young woman who also helped to run the extended household: "Coby", whose real name was Lien (Serlien) Prins. Coby also became a "permanent resident". She is also present in Figure 9.18.

Johan arranged forged statements by the child foster care department of the *Nederlandse Volksdienst* (a Nazi organization) that they were sending to van Straten the children Marietje and Ronnie who *"came from a war-ravaged area [i.e. Rotterdam], and had become homeless in May 1940"*. He also managed to obtain official ration cards (*Distributie Stamkaart*) for each of them under these aliases.[41] The children did not require a pb (ID card), but without a ration card (and coupons) they could not be clothed or fed. On 19ᵗʰ July 1943 Johan was involved in the heist at a *Distributie Kantoor* (the local government office in charge of rationing of food, textiles, and other essential goods), getting away with blank ration cards and hundreds of coupons. The fake legal documents allowed both Marietje and Ronnie to attend school and play outside the house, which was important because

---

41 Maria Geertruida Smidt (*Stamkaart* no. 065547) and Ronald Witteveen (no. 065602).

locking up young children for extended periods in some dark hiding place would have been unsustainable. But the risks were there. Johan recalled:

> One day around dinner time we could not find Ronnie and Marietje. They had played in the street with other children who lived around us. We were not afraid they would be betrayed because we had onderduikers before [...] and we believed we had good papers. [...] We could not find them. One of the kids around suggested they could be at the house of Alex Wunnink, obliquely across the street [he was director of Carré Theatre in Amsterdam and he had a Jewish wife]. We did not want to knock on their door, but one of the kids in the street [...] went to ask. It turned out that they were with Pluyster, together with Wunnink's kid.

Johan suggests that he was not too worried. Yet on the same page he reports that Jewish *onderduikers* within the group of Mr. Denekamp (the one who delivered Ronnie) in Utrecht had been arrested: *"It must have been a case of denunciation because the Germans knew exactly which houses to visit. Most foster parents in Denekamps group had forged Volksdienst declarations such as we had for Ronnie and Marietje, but in case of betrayal they were of no use."*

Not long afterwards Dien and Johan are upset and angry when the father of Marietje unexpectedly visits them in Huizen. Like Serlina and Fré he was not supposed to know where Marietje was in hiding. He refuses to tell them how he found out that Marietje was in Huizen and does not honour Dien's urgent request not to make himself known to his daughter because that would unnecessarily complicate her *onderduik*. He said that he did not know their name or address, but simply walked around Huizen until he spotted Marietje playing with Ronnie and other children in the street.

While having two, four or even five Jewish children at home themselves, Johan and Dien were also supporting Jewish *onderduikers* at other addresses, such as Zwaluweweg 2 in nearby Blaricum, where six people were in hiding in June 1943. The *onderduikers* needed money and most of all ration cards and coupons, and Johan had reliable contacts to supply this. He delivered the goods himself most of the time.

During a visit to these *onderduikers* on Friday, 9th July 1943, Johan had a hunch that something was wrong:

> It was dark that evening of Friday, 9th July. Shabbat had begun, and my call to leave immediately did not make them move. 'Why? There is no danger. We know that now, don't we?' [There had been a previous raid on the house, which had not revealed the hidden door.] They decided to stay put, and I had nothing more to warn them than a hunch.

But the hunch must have been based on something: on the next day, Saturday, 10th July 1943, Johan went to Amsterdam to collect *fl* 300 – from Geert van Oorschot (of Querido Publishing House). Coming back, he took the tram from Hilversum to Blaricum and Huizen:

The tram consisted of two parts, I sat in front, on a long bench with my back to the window and the street. The tram stopped at the regular Blaricum station, opposite the Post Office, but I was sitting with my back to the platform. A member of the Marechaussee [the Dutch military police force] entered the tram and told all passengers in the front to move to the back compartment. I rose from the bench, and turned, [...] and saw our six onderduikers and Leenie, under guard. I was shocked and thought about my failed attempt the evening before to make them leave their shelter. [...] I got out of the tram [in Huizen] and walked along the Naarderstraat to my home when the tram[42] *passed me. I saw them all, sitting on the bench looking away from me, but one, I think it was Bram, turned his head and saw me. I gave him a sign of hopelessness and resignation. [...] [being practical, we] wanted to retrieve the ration coupons; Dien collected them that same afternoon and came back with the story what happened from Neelie's sister: A few days earlier a couple from Amsterdam had approached Neelie. They wanted to hire a room again for a holiday, but Neelie told them they were full. But before returning to Amsterdam they went upstairs to talk to one of the elderly women they knew from the previous year. The woman, without thinking, told them they were full because they harboured six Jewish onderduikers in the house. The couple returned to Amsterdam and they probably betrayed them. [...] Years later, in 1984, I found the names of the [Blaricum] onderduikers, killed in Sobibor on 23rd July 1943. [...] The people who were caught knew our address and we expected them to be interrogated before going to Westerbork, so we decided to go into hiding ourselves [in July 1943]. [...] We borrowed the carrycot again from our neighbours and took the train to Deventer. [...] When we arrived on the platform [in Hilversum], the train had started to move already, a long series of single-door carriages drawn by a steam engine. We ran obliquely across the platform, carrying Johnnie in the carrycot between us, and holding Marietje and Ronnie with our other hand. The train accelerated very slowly, and someone opened the door of the carriage from the inside. We pushed the carrycot inside, I picked up Ronnie and then Marietje and shoved them inside, Dien jumped in, then I did. 'That was a close call,' one of the passengers who helped us to get inside said. But given the poor and infrequent train service of the time, they agreed it was worth the risk. Then one of*

---

42   The tram line continued in the direction of Amsterdam. I assume the prisoners were brought to the SD offices in Amsterdam. I have not been able to find the names of the arrested people, so more information would be welcome.

the ladies remarked how peculiar it was that the baby was so blond, while Ronnie
and Marietje were so dark-haired. We replied that they were also blond as a baby,
but their hair darkened as they grew older.

Johan had arranged a month of sick leave.[43] In Deventer, the family (including Ronnie
and Marietje) stayed with his in-laws lived, lying low. Having had no news about
the German (or the Dutch) police looking for him, they returned to Huizen on 14th
August 1943. Serlien Prins (Coby) joined at around this time, and Johan and Dien
resumed their work to create false papers, ration cards, and to ensure a constant
supply of ration coupons for several groups on *onderduikers*, in Huizen, Blaricum,
Utrecht and even for someone hiding in the East of the country.

While Ronnie was hiding in Huizen, his mother, Serlina de Paauw, was transported to Westerbork; she was registered there on the day of the razzia, 20th June 1943
(Fig. 9.19), as were her sister, Fré, and her husband, Jo Melkman. They were not
immediately sent through to the East as were most others. The Joodse Raad had
noted (Figs. 9.19 and 9.20) that both Serlina and Aron (and the other family members) qualified for a Palestine certificate, thanks to her sister Nettie having been
a Palestine resident since 1935. Like Mindel (previous chapter) they were kept in
Westerbork waiting for a future transport to Bergen-Belsen together with other
"special cases".

On 11th January 1944 Serlina was deported from Westerbork to Bergen-Belsen,
together with her sister, Sara, and her stepmother, Hanna, as well as Jo and Fré
Melkman and a small boy, Nicky Hakker, whom they took along; an amazing
story in its own right.[44] Aron is not mentioned on Serlina's own Joodse Raad card,
although she is mentioned on his card. She probably kept silent about him even
when she was put on the train for Bergen-Belsen, hoping that he would be safe
in *onderduik*.

In Bergen-Belsen Serlina was put to work in the *Shuh Kommando*. Every week
train loads with thousands of shoes, adult as well as kids' shoes, arrived in Bergen-
Belsen. The shoes came from all over Germany and had to be taken apart to recycle
the material, particularly the leather. Serlina told Aron after the war that shoes
also arrived from Auschwitz, and that their task was to look for any gold or other

---

43 His boss was aware of his illegal activities.
44 Fré and Jo "adopted" two-year-old Nicky on the train to Westerbork, by suggesting to his mother that
he would possibly have a better chance of survival if they registered Nicky as their own son, Awraham,
who was in *onderduik*, and possibly benefit from his Palestine status. Nicky stayed with them all through
the war and returned to Holland with Jo and Fré in 1945. Awraham ("Kees"), just three days older than
Nicky, also survived (see Melkman-de Paauw, 2002). If Clara Asscher (previous chapter) found her idea
about Mindel "preposterous", Nicky's survival is even more miraculous.

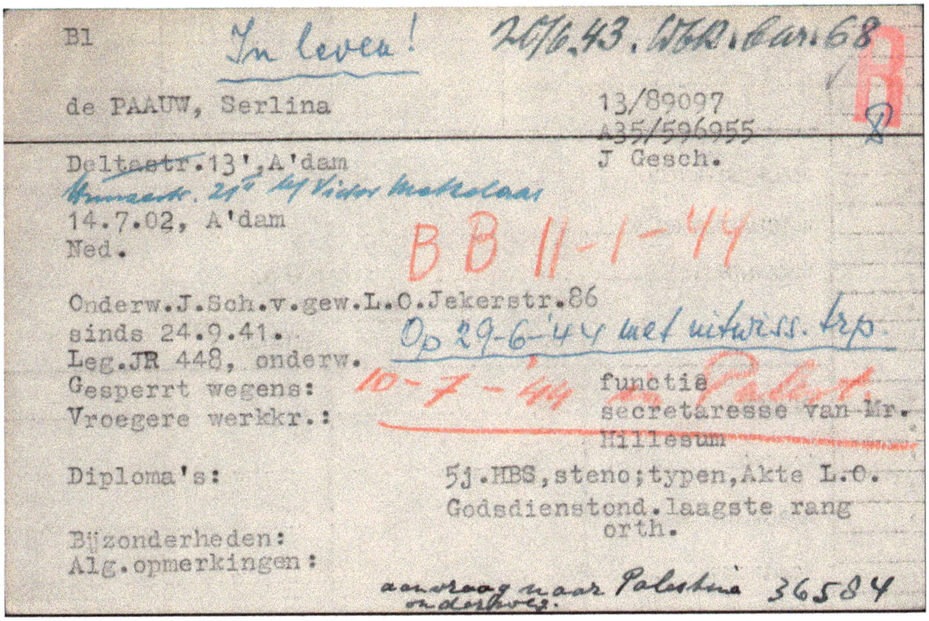
B1 In leven!

de PAAUW, Serlina 13/89097 ~~A35/596955~~

~~Deltastr.~~13',A'dam J Gesch.

14.7.02, A'dam

Ned.

BB 11-1-44

Onderw.J.Sch.v.gew.L.O.Jekerstr.86

sinds 24.9.41.

Op 29-6-'44 met uitwiss. trp.

Leg.JR 448, onderw.

Gesperrt wegens: 10-7-44 n. Palest.

Vroegere werkkr.: functie secretaresse van Mr. Hillesum

Diploma's: 5j.HBS,steno;typen,Akte L.O. Godsdienstond.laagste rang orth.

Bijzonderheden:

Alg.opmerkingen:

aanvraag naar Palestina 36584

Figure 9.19: The Joodse Raad cards for Serlina de Paauw. In blue at the top is a post-war addition: *"In leven!"* ("She is alive!"), just as is found on Mindel's card (Figure 9.13). The red notations of her deportation to Bergen-Belsen on 11th January 1944, and her arrival in Palestine on 10th July 1944 are also post-war. Both cards courtesy Netherlands Red Cross War Archives, 2017.

valuables hidden in them.[45] She could not believe at the time that the owners had all been killed, even when other inmates told her so. *"Impossible"*, she told Aron after the war. *"Surely they have been given other shoes by the Germans, more suitable to the conditions in the labour camps."* It was beyond her capacity to believe that the owners had been killed upon arrival in Auschwitz.

At the end of June 1944 Serlina, Sara and Hanna de Paauw were selected for the *Austausch* train, but Fré and Jozeph were not (Melkman-de Paauw, 2002). The Germans did not want to send able bodied men to Palestine, where they could become enemy soldiers. So out of a thousand or so candidates in Bergen-Belsen, they choose more women than men, the elderly, the very young and the weak. Serlina weighed only 39 kilos in Bergen-Belsen. Upon arrival in Palestine she spent a year in hospital. Later in 1944 and early 1945 the situation in Bergen-Belsen became desperately bad, when thousands of prisoners arrived from camps in the East. The

45 Although several survivors other than Serlina declared that they knew the shoes came from Auschwitz, and had to be inspected for hidden valuables, there is no documentary evidence for this. However, experts at the *Bergen-Belsen Gedenkstätte* consider it quite possible, or even likely, that Auschwitz was one of the sources of the shoes (courtesy Dr. Thomas Rahe, Dr. Jens Binner, stiftung-ng.de).

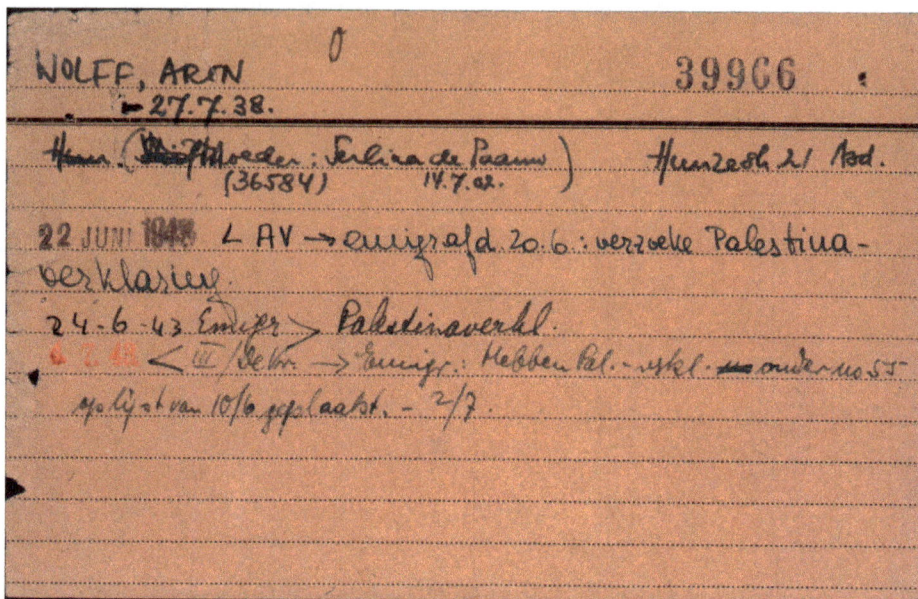

Figure 9.20: From 22nd June the Joodse Raad in Amsterdam was working to get Aron on the Palestine list, which was confirmed on 4th July. Serlina had arrived in Westerbork two days before. Aron was already in hiding at that time.

Russian army was making impressive advances and was about to overrun the camps. It is in this period that Anne Frank and her sister arrived in Bergen-Belsen. Jo, Fré and Nicky survived this period. They boarded one of the trains leaving Bergen-Belsen (at the Celle train station) on 10th April 1945, seemingly with Theresienstadt as its destination. When they reached the halfway point, near Tröbitz in eastern Germany, Soviet troops were getting close, so the two SS guards left the train and the prisoners were free to leave as well.

Jo, Fré and Nicky stayed in Tröbitz for two months without any contact with Holland and could only get home thanks to French efforts to repatriate their own nationals, and the Americans organizing effective hospital transports through the war zones.

Around the time of the *Austausch* train (July 1944), the many activities of Johan and Dien van Straten were – at last I would think – attracting the attention of the German police, and they decided to go again into hiding themselves, but not before arranging new hiding addresses for their *onderduikers*. No doubt he had contacts through his activities in the resistance, but nevertheless it is a remarkable achievement that he managed to find new homes for the children, and that they remained safe until the war was over. Aron was brought to Apeldoorn. Whereas the van Straten family was firmly secular, the family in Apeldoorn[46] was strictly Christian, and Aron, then six years old, suddenly found himself obliged to follow Protestant (*Gereformeerde*) prayer rituals at dinner. He could still perform them 73 years later. But as far as we can tell no attempt to convert him was made, and the routine may have helped to keep him safe.

The van Stratens were not caught. Upon liberation in May 1945, knowing where each of them was lodged, they collected the children, and brought them back to Huizen, where they were quickly collected by family members.[47] But there was no news about Aron's mother, and he continued to live with them again from May 1945. When they began to realize how many parents of *onderduik* children had not survived the war, they wondered if they should consider adopting Ronnie. It took four months before contact with his mother was established. According to his aunt Fré (letter, 16th August 1945)[48]:

> We could not find Ronnie for many weeks; he had to be relocated several times as his regular foster parents had to go into hiding themselves. But we found him! He lives in Huizen with a family van Straten, [...] where he is quite OK. The family cares for him very well. The children of Cis Vis [Theo and Jan Mulder, see above] were also in hiding there. Ronnie has grown a lot, but his face still looks as we remember him. [...] Kees [her own son, Awraham, in hiding in Blaricum] and Ronnie live close together and we can on occasion visit them both on the same day. [...] Mrs. van Straten asked us about the address of Serlien so that she can write to her about Ronnie. [...] They needed to get him new clothes twice since he arrived with very few belongings. [...] He looks fine, [and] even has new shoes. Shoes are almost impossible to get; if we had not brought pilfered shoes from Germany, we would be going about barefoot. [...] The van Stratens are not asking for money, but we told Max [Wolff] that in our opinion he should compensate them for their expenses.

On 30th September 1945 Serlina wrote her first letter to the van Stratens:

> Dear family van Straten. At last, yesterday, I received your address. I do not know how long Ronnie has been living with you, but since he calls you Daddy and Mummy it must have been a long time. I wish I could get on a plane and come over, not just to see Ronnie again, but also to shake your hand and thank you all for everything you have done and risked on his behalf. It is not possible to do this properly in a

---

46 After the war, Serlina tried to contact a family Bakker at Welgelegenweg 33; I have not been able to confirm if this is where they lodged Ronnie from July 1944 to April/May 1945
47 Marietje (Jonnie Polak) was collected by her father, but he brought her back later to stay with the van Stratens again when Marietje's mother was expecting another child.
48 Melkman-de Paauw (2002, p. 43). Freely translated by the author.

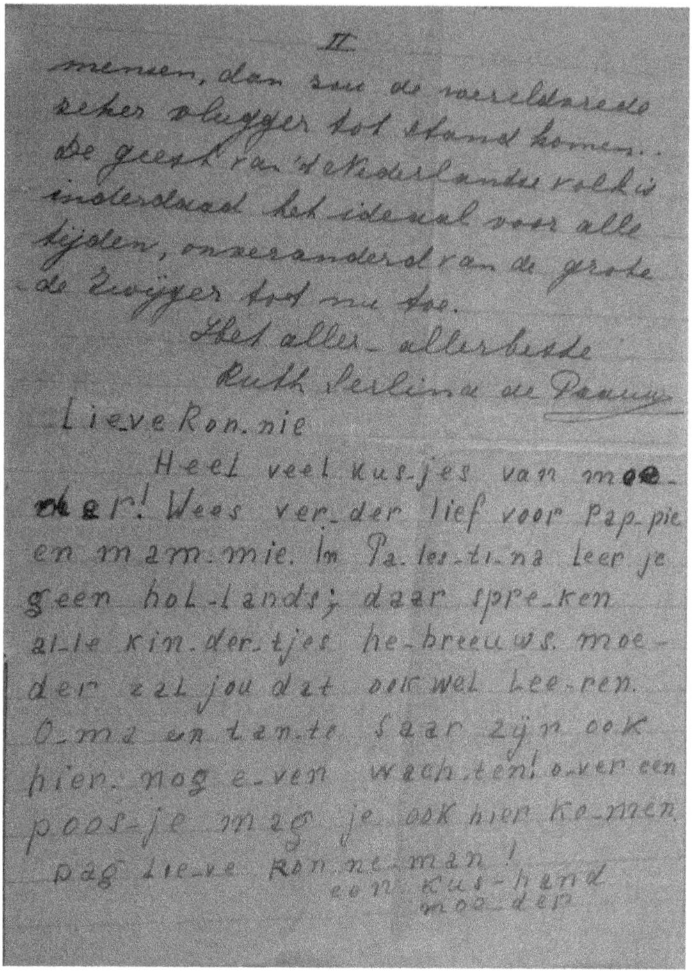

II
mensen, dan zou de wereldvrede
zeker vlugger tot stand komen..
De geest van 't Nederlandse volk is
inderdaad het ideaal voor alle
tijden, onveranderd van de grote
de Zwijger tot nu toe.
Het aller-allerbeste
Ruth Serlina de Paauw
Lieve Ron-nie
Heel veel kus-jes van moe-
der! Wees ver-der lief voor Pap-pie
en mam-mie. In Pa-les-ti-na leer je
geen hol-lands; daar spre-ken
al-le kin-der-tjes he-breeuws. moe-
der zal jou dat ook wel lee-ren.
O-ma en tan-te Saar zijn ook
hier. nog e-ven wach-ten! o-ver een
poos-je mag je ook hier ko-men.
Dag lie-ve Ron-nie-man!
een kus-hand
moe-der

Figure 9.21: The last part of Serlina's letter of 30th September 1945. Not knowing how well Ronnie could read, she separated the letters from each other, and each word into its syllables.

letter. Please when he comes home to me let him bring a photograph of your family so that I can visit you, with him, in thought. I hope he has not been too much trouble for you. He could be rather stubborn, but also affectionate and helpful. [...] *How was his health during these years? Both my sister Melkman and Ronnie's brother Elchanan*[49] *told me he looked very well, and that you had pampered him.*
Ruth Serlina de Paauw

49 Second child (1923) of Max Wolff from his first marriage.

She adds a text for Ronnie in easy-to-read handwriting (Fig. 9.21), sending kisses and telling him that she will help him to learn Hebrew. The letters confirm the initial conjecture that neither Fré nor Serlina knew where they had brought Ronnie when they let him go for *onderduik* in June 1943.

One day after sending her letter, a letter from van Straten arrived in Palestine, and Serlina replies on 2nd October 1945, expressing her gratitude and admiration, and explaining why he had arrived with only so few clothes.

> *Ronnie went to the Jewish orphanage in Leiden in July*[50] *1940. I took him out in November 1942 because the orphanages were in danger, while I had a certificate that I was* 'unentbehrlich für den Unterricht an jüdischen Kindern' [*indispensable for providing schooling for Jewish children*]. *I thought that would give Ronnie a better chance of avoiding deportation,* [...] *although moving him to Amsterdam was also a serious risk because all changes of residence were recorded.* [...] *Indeed, in January 1943 the police came by to arrest Ronnie.*

She continues, describing how she was shaken by her landlady being arrested and decided to let Ronnie go into hiding immediately:

> *My sister Melkman collected Ronnie on 1st June '43.* [...] *I was arrested on 20th June, so Ronnie escaped deportation in the nick of time, or he would have gone through the camps.* [...] *I cannot think about it, except being thankful to our Creator who spared us and directed us towards you. May He bless and protect you as He protected us.* [...] *Immediately upon the liberation of Holland I wrote to the family de Jong in Eindhoven about Ronnie, and I also asked many other acquaintances to try and find out where he was.* [...] *Please tell Ronnie (I presume he may not yet be reading, if he did not attend school)*[51] *that I am cooking meals for no fewer than 130 boys here in Palestine. We live here on a high hill, often without water in a very small village (Kfar Haroeh), some 65 families without postal service. That is why letters must be sent to POB 50 in Chedera.* [...] *Please tell Ronnie that the drawing he made for me* [...] *stands on my cabinet.* [...] *P.S.: I would be very happy if you can send me a photograph of your family with Ronnie.*

A ceremonial portrait was made by Tadema Wielandt Photography in Bussum on 12th January 1946 (Fig. 9.22). Fré's letters describe the situation in Holland for the benefit of her relatives in Palestine. The lack of almost everything, no public transport to speak of, lack of housing, the difficult search for and retrieval of

---

50   Ronnie was registered in Leiden on 13th September.
51   In fact, Ronnie did attend school, in Huizen.

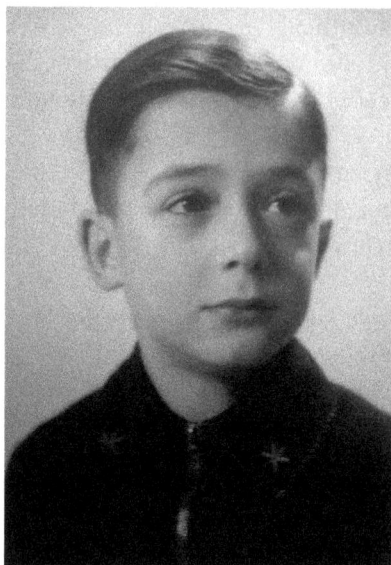

Figure 9.22: Aron Wolff, 12th January 1946, seven and a half years old. From Van Straten's report, courtesy Bert van Straten.

property given to others for safekeeping, and worst of all, the search for relatives and friends, often in vain. Some families (Ch. 8.4) had been wiped out without a single survivor. The few who did survive looked at each other differently than before the war. Attitudes and beliefs changed. Some survivors abandoned their Jewish identity altogether; others were keen to collect any surviving family members before trying to make a restart. Many began to realize that they could not simply start all over again in Holland, or in any other country for that matter, without a philosophy about what would be needed to rebuild an identity, a family, a community (see D. Michman's introduction to Fré's letters in Melkman-de Paauw, 2002). Difficult decisions had to be taken before a restart could be considered.

Fré and Jo Melkman were also confronted with the dilemmas when they claimed custodianship for Bram and Tsipora, two (of the three) children of Jo's sister, Leni. Jo's family had been decimated, and the wish to bring the remnants together was strong. But Tsipora had been living with foster parents who were not prepared to release her. Jo (in Melkman-de Paauw, 2002, pp. 139-140) recalled:

> The childless couple who had hid Tsipora had become much attached to her, and her father [Jo's brother-in-law] had promised them she could stay with them in case he and his wife did not survive the war. [...] When Fré and I submitted a claim to custody for Bram and Tsipora, her foster parents did the same for Tsipora. [...] They were bitterly disappointed when the OPK [Commission for Wartime Foster Children] decided in our favour and they had to say farewell to Tsipora.

At the same time, Jo and Fré had brought Nicky back from Bergen-Belsen, and their premonition that his mother would possibly not survive had proven correct: Jo:

> We had assumed that Nicky, to whom we felt strong attachment, would grow up as part of our family, but had not yet submitted a custody claim. When she entrusted him to us in Westerbork, Nicky's mother had made us promise that we would not abandon him in case he survived but she did not. But then to our surprise Nicky was

claimed by an uncle and aunt who had survived Auschwitz, with a view to reunite the remnants of their family. This caused us a terrible dilemma: should we go ahead with our intention to claim custody or not? [...] After extended deliberations Fré and I came to the conclusion that if the OPK would give us custody of Bram and Tsipora on the basis of reuniting family members, they would be unlikely to refuse to do the same for Nicky's uncle and aunt, who asked for custody on the same grounds. It would be unacceptably cruel to them, after surviving Auschwitz. With great sorrow we decided to let Nicky go.

Nicky, now five years old, fiercely resisted the transfer. To make matters worse, the transfer did not work out (ibidem).[52]

The question of what to do with the orphaned children, particularly if there were contesting claims for custody, belongs to the most painful issues that arose in the post-war years. We should not pass judgement from our distant armchair, not having lived through it at the time. There were no analytical solutions to these dilemmas: giving preference to one argument or one party only implied injustice to another.

In Ronnie's case, once it transpired that his mother had survived, it was considered self-evident that he would return to her. But the immigration procedures were slow due to the political situation in Palestine, and the British desire to limit the number of (Jewish) immigrants as much as possible. The expectation was that it could take a long time for Ronnie's immigration certificate to be issued by the British Mandate Authority. The political situation in Palestine was worsening and becoming repressive as the British began to realize that their position in Palestine was hopeless.[53]

Jozeph adds to Fré in a letter of 17th October 1945:

Fré already discussed Ronnie in this letter. Please tell Serlien [...] that given our own situation (even Kees has not come back to us yet), it seems best that Ronnie stays with the family van Straten, expecting that it will not take too long before he gets his certificate; his foster parents have already prepared him to go to Palestine.

But then Fré had to tell them (letter, 9th November 1945, op. cit., p. 77) that Serlina had asked them to arrange for Ronnie to be transferred to a Youth Aliyah home in Dieren, in preparation for going to Palestine, *before* his certificate would arrive. Serlina had not discussed it in her letters to Johan and Dien, to whom it came as a shock. Fré (9th December 1945) wrote: *"Ronnie was happy to see us. He asked how long he would have to wait before taking the boat to Palestine. He always looks neat*

---

52 To (begin to) understand the traumas caused by these dilemmas, see the 2009 interview with Nikky (in Dutch) at http://getuigenverhalen.nl/interview/nabestaanden-interview-13-nathan-hakker.

53 For a thrilling review of the Mandate period, from the British perspective, see Sykes (1965).

and well-cared for, and evidently he feels at home with van Straten." In a letter dated 26th December, Fré wrote:

> *We talked again in Huizen about Ronnie going to Dieren, which was not well received. They think Ronnie will adapt to the new country quickly enough and have no sympathy for the idea to move him to yet another place now. They feel hurt, the more so because we left Ronnie with them in the first instance. They said: "It would have been better if you had taken Ronnie away upon liberation." As you see, the fact that Max has still not arranged any financial compensation has not affected their wish to keep Ronnie as long as possible. Ronnie himself reacted likewise: "Why should I move again? Always to yet another home, I don't understand it."*

Ronnie's reaction is not surprising, given the many upheavals in his life since 1940: divorce, orphanage, staying with his mother, collected by Aunt Fré, brought to total strangers in Huizen by another total stranger, hiding in Deventer, back to Huizen, hiding in Apeldoorn, back to Huizen.

Fré (20th January 1946) wrote: *"Ronnie is still in Huizen. The children's Aliyah home will move from Dieren to Santpoort in February. We do not want to relocate Ronnie before that time. The van Stratens still object, but they acquiesced."* This is the last reference to Ronnie in Fré's letters (as published). On 9th March 1946 van Straten received a letter from the OPK about his imminent transfer (to Santpoort). About one week later (given the postal delivery times), a long letter from Serlina arrived (dated 4th March 1946), explaining her reasons for taking Ronnie away from them: 1) He needed a minimum understanding of Hebrew before he could attend elementary school; 2) it may yet take many months before his certificate is ready; 3) he would then be eight years old and still have to attend preschool first to prepare him for elementary school.

Van Straten had written her two letters (27th December 1945 and 21st January 1946) expressing his feelings. He did not keep a copy of his own letters but concluded (in 1992) from reading her response, *"I must have written a less than friendly letter"*. Serlina wrote:

> *My reasons are purely practical. If Ronnie were only four, you could have kept him until his departure to Palestine. [...] The family he is going to now lives in Santpoort, not so far away from you. It has therefore grieved me very much to read your reproaches to me. [...] I am not angry; on the contrary, I am touched by your unambiguous attachment to my child. I can understand your feelings of bitterness.*

She includes a long exposé about her religious feelings, and the role played by her father, whose name Ronnie had inherited, not realizing that van Straten would be entirely unimpressed by any such arguments. Fré had actually warned her, and tried to explain the negative reaction, observing that van Straten probably had leftish, secular and anti-nationalistic convictions (op. cit., p. 121), and that he would have little sympathy for religious or Zionist ideals. From his own report, her assessment was correct on all three accounts. Johan abhorred all nationalistic ideas: attending a post-war event to celebrate the liberation from the Germans, the Dutch national anthem was played; Johan and Dien did stand up like everybody else, not to make a public scene, but they did not partake in the singing.

Serlina did not change her decision to move Ronnie. But nothing came of it: around 15th April, much sooner than expected, Serlina sent a postcard: *"Today I received Ronnie's certificate from the British government. [...] It looks like your wish that he will leave for Palestine directly from your home will be fulfilled."* In June 1946

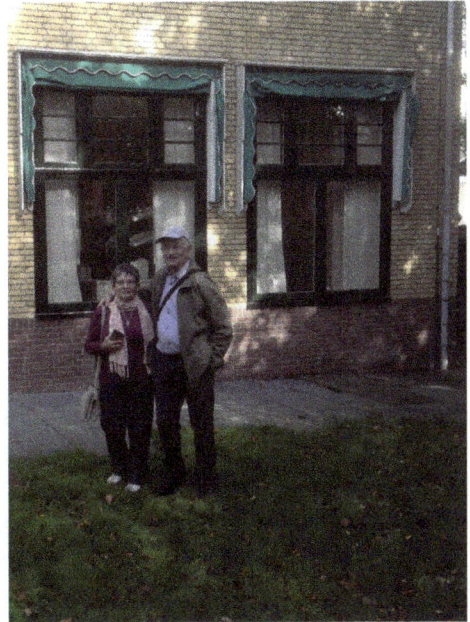

Figure 9.23: Rivka and Roni Maor in the back garden of the former orphanage in September 2017, the same spot where the picture with Geertje Gebert was taken Figure 9.16. Photo by the author.

Ronnie departed for Palestine, by boat from Marseilles. In subsequent letters Serlina describes her emotion at being reunited again after three years and how well-cared for Ronnie looked (10th July 1946), her frustration about not seeing him often enough (because Ronnie lived in a children's home in Jerusalem), and her plan to move closer to him (10th March 1947). That is the last of her letters in the van Straten archive.

Serlina had wished for them to bring Ronnie to the boat, but, apparently, they said goodbye to each other in Huizen. Not much is said about his departure in van Straten's report. Later, he could not remember how Ronnie left them or with whom. It is difficult to escape the impression that the discussions about Dieren and Santpoort cast a shadow over Ronnie's last few months in Huizen. But it did not stop the families from maintaining contact. The problems, issues, dilemmas, possibly frictions which are described above, occurred – in various shapes – in many other reports about wartime resistance activities and how they were closed out after the war, not only with respect to *onderduik* children. The war brought people with different backgrounds and beliefs closely together, people who would be unlikely to have socialized in peace times. Inevitably, once the war was over some of the differences surfaced.

Johan and Dien visited Israel several times and were nominated by Serlina for the Yad Vashem award (Ch. 10.3).

I met Ronnie and his wife, Rivka, in September 2017 in the hills west of Jerusalem to hear his remarkable story and to tell him about this book as it was in preparation. Ronnie visited the van Stratens several times after the war, but he had never gone back to the old orphanage until we had met in September 2017. He and Rivka came to Leiden a few weeks later. Figure 9.23 was taken in the garden at the back of the building, the same spot where the photograph of Ronnie with Geertje Gebert was made (Fig. 9.16) 75 years earlier.

9.5   Didia Klein survives Auschwitz I

Didia was born in Paris on 12th May 1925. It was not known who her father was. She had an affinity with the world of arts, probably from an early age. Piet de Vries told us that she had suffered abuse before coming to the orphanage, with scars from cigarette burns on her body. She was a sociable girl, who appears on many photographs with other children, and she was a good friend of Betsy Wolff and of Corrie Frenkel, her classmate at the ULO for girls on the Breestraat. She became salesperson (and thus independent) at the well-known dress shop of Gerzon, also on the Breestraat. Like Sally Montezinos, she was not allowed to leave the orphanage anymore in 1942-1943.

The same (?) Joodse Raad official "with the fountain pen" who did his best for Etty Heerma van Voss and Harry Spier (Ch. 7.11) also started a descendancy investigation for Didia (Figs. 9.24 and 9.25). On 19th March 1943 (the day after their arrival in Westerbork) he notes, *"two Jewish grandparents. Please investigate."* Probably he assumed simply from the fact that the father was unknown, that she could have two non-Jewish grandparents, and considered that enough justification to investigate. As far as we can tell, nothing came of it. It is not clear why Stoffels, who was engaged with assisting so many people in that period, did not involve himself in her case. It is possible that Didia herself was not aware of what the official was doing. She wrote to Stoffels from Westerbork on 2nd May 1943, reporting: *"The Mogendorff girls have gone. They were very courageous and took care of many things until the very end."* She

Figure 9.24: Didia Klein, 1942.

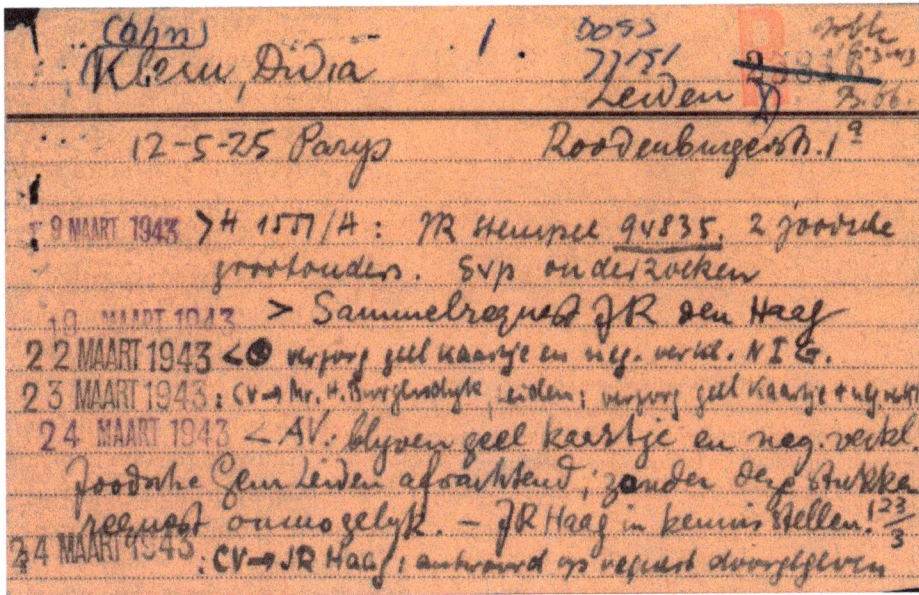

Figure 9.25: One (out of six) index card showing the efforts by the Joodse Raad to get Didia reclassified as G1. Archives Red Cross, The Hague.

includes a long list of items and asking him to arrange it. Clothing for herself, but also items for others.

> As you can see, there are many things we desperately need here in Westerbork. Could you send the parcels to the boys in Barrack 64 to prevent them getting lost because we are being moved from one barrack to another. I entirely forgot to mention that Sally Montezinos has also left. [...] Nothing else to report. Regards from those of us who are still here.

She was almost eighteen when she entered Westerbork, where she met Heinz Cahn, who was working in the camp as a musician. They married on 10th May 1943. It was most likely an opportunistic marriage: Cahn had a Westerbork *Sperre*. Once married, the *Sperre* applied also to Didia. But of course, the *Sperre* were no more than an illusion, and both were deported on 21st September 1943. Nevertheless, the *Sperre* may have saved Didia in a cynical manner: it probably delayed her deportation, so that she was not sent to immediate death in Sobibor, but to Auschwitz, where she was selected for the gruesome medical experiments in Block X. After the war, she told the authorities that it was Johannes Goebel who experimented on her. Goebel, a chemistry PhD, was looking for ways to chemically sterilize Jewish women en masse. Figure 9.26 shows Block X on the left. The entrance to the courtyard between

Figure 9.26: Block 10 in Auschwitz, where prisoners were subjected to horrific medical "experiments". At the far end of the courtyard between block 10 and 11 (behind the gated entrance) was the death wall, where executions took place. The windows of block 10 were boarded up on this side to block the view. Inset: Goebel after his arrest.

X and XI is blocked by a gate; at the end of the courtyard was the "death wall" where executions took place. Some 200 to 400 prisoners were kept on the second floor of Block X. The windows on that floor were boarded up to prevent the women seeing what happened at the death wall.

Didia was moved from Auschwitz to Ravensbrück probably in mid-January 1945, and from there to other camps in the Leipzig area. On 1st April 1945 she was moved to Buchenwald/Taucha, where she was liberated on or about 26th April.

After liberation Didia did not want to talk about the war or her experiences in Auschwitz. Upon return in Holland, she wrote a letter (to a Miss Burgerhout, 19th July 1945):

> You will not remember me, but I was tutored by Mrs. Blitz of the Zoeterwoudse Singel. [...] I spent two and a half years in a concentration camp [...] and could tell you a lot about what the basterds did there. [...] What is the situation with the other people from Leiden? Did anybody else come back? I have no hope for the family Blitz; they were probably put to the gas straightaway.

She was lodged in Eerde to recover, asks for the Stoffels' address, and the status of properties given to friends for safekeeping. Didia was probably badly traumatized. She did not wish to be confronted with the past and spent years in the artists' colony of Bergen, in North Holland, becoming a close friend of the poet Adriaan Roland Holst.[54] She and Cahn had separated immediately after the war, and at some stage (before May 1953) Didia married Kees de Boer. She died in Bergen on 6th May 2001.

---

54 Didia moved into his house when Roland Holst vacated it c. 1966 and lived there until her death in 2001.

9.6   Bram Degen invents his own father

Bram (Fig. 9.27) was born in Leiden on 27th October 1926. His mother, Theresia Degen,[55] was not married. Bram was taken in as a baby by foster parents,[56] who had him baptized on 8th May 1927. They gave him up just a few years later. Bram arrived in the Leiden orphanage on 6th June 1930, three years old, and stayed there for twelve years.

By decision of the Amsterdam magistrate of 24th November 1930 the guardianship over Bram was given to the Misgab Lajeled (Refuge for a Child) Society in Amsterdam. We see Bram, one of the more easily recognizable children in all the photographs, in Figure 4.10 as a six-year-old boy, and in Figure 5.18 when he was twelve. Like the other children he attended the Langebrug primary school, where, according to a classmate, *"he was the clown of the class"*. From c. 1938 he probably attended the ULO School.

Figure 9.27: Bram Degen, probably before moving to Gouda.

He left the orphanage on 13th July 1942 and joined the *Joodse Tuinbouwschool* in Gouda, one of a number of Hachsharah schools (Table 9.2), where fourteen- to seventeen-year-old students were being trained to be Palestine Pioneers, in preparation of moving to Palestine as soon as an entry permit could be obtained from the British or an illegal entry arranged. For many centuries Jews in Europe had been banned from landownership or farming; the idea of buying land in Palestine, *any land, even desert or marshland*, and cultivate it had a special significance from the earliest days of Zionism. The school in Gouda – also known by the name of its farmhouse, Catharinahoeve[57] – concentrated on horticulture. It was led by Manfred Litten and his wife, Sjosjana (Jansje) Serlui (Figs. 9.28 and 9.29). Manfred was born in Posen, led a Hachsharah institute in Steckelsdorf, and went to Danzig from where he and his wife came to Holland as refugees in 1938. He started as director in Gouda in January 1939. During the occupation, Sjosjana became involved with resistance activities; she arranged false papers for the students (van der Straaten, 1998) before they went into hiding.

---

55   Amsterdam, 21st April 1907-Sobibor, 16th April 1943.
56   Dossier.
57   Like the orphanage in Leiden, the opening of Catharinahoeve on 6th October 1937 was attended by dignitaries from other "pillars" of the Dutch society, such the mayor, three aldermen, and the municipal secretary.

Table 9.2   Hachsharah Institutions in the Netherlands c. 1942

	Deported/Hiding or Escape		Perished	Returned	Palestine[1]	Survived % A	B
Deventer	Deported:	102	80	21	1	22 %	48 %
	Hiding or Escape:	119	36	61	22	70 %	
Elden (Arnhem)	Deported:	36	9	21	6	75 %	78 %
	Hiding or Escape:	4	0	1	3	100 %	
Werkdorp	Deported:	218	181	35	2	37 %	36 %
Wieringermeer	Hiding or Escape:	81	10	50	21	88 %	
Mishrachi	Deported:	103	82	18	3	20 %	32 %
Hachsharah	Hiding or Escape:	26	6	19	1	77 %	
Agoedat	Deported:	29	16	8	5	45 %	47 %
Hachsharah	Hiding or Escape:	26	13	13	0	50 %	
Loosdrechtse	Deported:	0	-	-	-	-	71 %
Rade	Hiding or Escape:	48	14	23	11	71 %	
Gouda	Deported:	2	1	0	1	50 %	76 %
Catharinahoeve	Hiding or Escape:	19	4	11	4	79 %	
Total Hachs-	Deported:	490	369	103	18	25 %	
harah in The	Hiding or Escape:	323	83	178	62	68 %	
Netherlands	Unknown[2]:	(8)	?	?	?	?	
1942-43	Total:	8 + 813	452	[3]281	[4]80		44 %

1   With or without Palestine certificate, legally or illegally across borders, or by Austausch
2   All from Deventer. These eight are not included in the total numbers.
3   181 men and 100 women
4   52 men, 28 women

Summarized by I. Brasz, in Pinkhof 1998 p. 14.
Other sources (eg Schippers, 2015, Asscher, 1996) may quote different numbers. Figures may also be different depending on the exact date, since members frequently moved in and out, or between institutions. Some pre-war centres had been closed by the Germans, such as Mijnsheerenland, the children there were transferred to Loosdrecht.
There were close links between the Youth Aliyah and the refugee children described in Chapter 5.2.

From his letters to Hijme Stoffels[58] it is clear that Litten had enlisted the support of Hijme Stoffels in trying to change Bram's status in the Civil Registry to G1 (half-Jewish, see Ch. 9.2), making use of the fact that it was unclear who Bram's "natural" father was.

According to Stoffels, Bram and his mother had started a notarized procedure, claiming that a certain Mr. Pieter van Klaveren was his biological father. This was

58   The Stoffels archive, Courtesy Mr. P. de Jong, Noordwijk, who donated the archive to the author.

pure fantasy. They came up with the idea after seeing his name on a truck passing by. Stoffels intervened when he realized that the trick would never work just like that. He mentions this affair in his report to Yad Vashem (Stoffels & Stoffels-van Brussel, 1967) as *"a story, in all its tragedy almost amusing, and worth putting it in a book."* In 1972 Stoffels told Kerkvliet and Uitvlugt that they decided to contact this Mr. van Klaveren who knew nothing about it and who was quite upset being inadvertently accused of having parented a child with another woman than his wife. But Stoffels and Bram apparently convinced him to go along with the scam.

The documents show that he eventually succeeded in "legalizing" Bram as a "half-Jew" (G1), but only after considerable delay. In his letter of 6th April 1943, Litten expresses his gratitude for the Stoffels' efforts on behalf of Bram, but also reports that Bram is still waiting for a decision by the *Rijksinspectie* (National Civil Registry).[59] The procedure was started in November 1942, four months had passed and Litten was clearly worried. It is three weeks since the liquidation of the orphanage in Leiden. He asks Stoffels

Figure 9.28: Manfred Litten and Sjosjana Serlui and their son, Gideon, on a beach in Holland. From the Litten photo album, which one of his pupils brought to Palestine. Humboldt University website and Ghetto Fighters' House.

to go to The Hague to speak on behalf of Bram to the relevant civil servant. He also mentions that yet another notarized declaration from Pieter van Klaveren is required, on top of all the other documents which had been arranged already. Stoffels answers him the same day, and Litten thanks him for that on 8th April. He tells Stoffels that *"Bram's mother and his second father[60] have just last week been deported to Westerbork. If he [Stoffels] will be unable to get the* Rijksinspectie *to issue a G1 certificate maybe he can put Bram on the Calmeyer list in view of the fact that Bram was baptised."* Obviously Stoffels had confirmed that he would go to the *Rijksinspectie* as Litton requested. Not for the first time, one wonders how Hijme and Emilie were able to manage so many time-consuming "projects".

Litten had been alert enough to flee Germany when he still could, and he had no illusions about what the Germans were planning to do with the Jews in Holland. He

---

59   The Civil Registry was known to be slow to pass on a positive decision (by the *Entscheidungstelle* led by Calmeijer) to the people involved, with in some cases fatal consequences (van den Boomgaard, 2019).
60   That is: his mother's new husband, A. de Lange; they were both killed in Sobibor four days later.

Figure 9.29: Director Manfred Litten (front row, fourth from right) surrounded by staff and students of the Jewish Pioneer horticulture school in Gouda. Second right (in Bermuda) is Bram Degen. The photo must have taken between July 1942 and March 1943. Courtesy Ghetto Fighters' House.

and Sjosjana, who was also active in Joop Westerweel's resistance group, probably started preparing for *onderduik* by the end of 1942, if not before. By early 1943, there were probably some 20 students on the farm[61]; some members[62] had left earlier. On 22nd April 1943 they all had to report for transport to Camp Vught, and further deportation "to the East". The Litten's managed to get them all into *onderduik* with the help of a neighbour. He also arranged *onderduik* for his eight-year-old son, Gideon. He and Sjosjana went into hiding in different places, but they were caught, Sjosjana at a checkpoint on a railway station. Both perished. Seven of the students also perished, one of them by falling off a mountain during an attempt to cross the Pyrenees into Spain. Crossing the Pyrenees is part of Lodi Cohen's story (next chapter). At least fifteen of the students survived the war. Litten's son also survived, the only dark-haired boy in a gentile family with six kids of their own,

61   The list of Jewish residents of Gouda submitted to the *Zentralstelle* in April or early May 1942 lists 24 students plus three: Manfred Litten, his wife and son.
62   One of the youth leaders in Gouda, Rolf Schloss, had escaped to Switzerland in early 1942 (Ghetto Fighters' House, in Schippers, 2015).

all very blond[63]; he settled after the war in Israel as Gideon Laton. Manfred Litton may have had premonitions about his own fate, because he asked one of his boys who was going to try reach Palestine via Spain to take with him their family photo album, and to give it to Gideon after his bar mitzvah, in case Manfred did not survive the war. The album safely reached Gideon in Palestine.[64]

Figure 9.30: Bram Degen and Piet de Vries in Amsterdam, probably late 1943 (ref. Bram's letter to Stoffels).

Bram moved to Amsterdam after his G1 status was confirmed, wrote a letter to Stoffels, and had a ceremonial picture taken when Piet de Vries passed by after his release from Westerbork (Fig. 9.30). After the war, he settled in Australia. Having suffered from diabetes for many years, he was no longer able to participate in the efforts to reconstruct and preserve the history of the Leiden orphanage (L.P. Kasteleyn, personal communication).

A few of the Dutch pre-war Hachsharah farms, including Catharinahoeve, were revived after the war, but times had changed (Schippers, 2015), and survivors often had no interest in staying in Holland now that they were free to leave Europe, never mind British-controlled immigration hurdles in Palestine.

At least three other boys from the Leiden orphanage joined one of the Hachsharah farms: David Beem (Laag Keppel), Israel Wygoda (Beverwijk), and Lodi Cohen (Loosdrecht). Israel Wygoda moved to France, where he had family. He reputedly joined the resistance[65]. He spent a few years in Palestine after the war before returning to France. David Beem was killed in Sobibor on 9th July 1943. Lodi's escape story follows below.

9.7   Lodi Cohen escapes to Spain

The account of Lodi Cohen, who escaped to Palestine via Spain, is linked to the next, about Herman Stofkooper, who escaped to Switzerland. Although each story stands on its own, they have a common context: Dutch fugitives and the overland

---

63 See http://db.yadvashem.org/righteous/righteousName.html?language=en&itemId=4036731.

64 Gideon donated the album to the Ghetto Fighters' House (cat. no. 245); also see the story of Manfred, Humboldt University, https://www.hu-berlin.de/de/ueberblick/geschichte/stolpersteine/biographien/ManfredRalfLitten.

65 Courtesy Mrs. B. Bikker, Leiden, who contacted his family.

escape routes through Belgium, occupied France, and so-called "Free France", and then crossing the Swiss or the Spanish border, with or without valid papers.

Lodi (Lodewijk) was born in Leiden on 17th September 1917; his brother Ies (Izak Hertog) was born on 16th April 1920. Their father died on 6th January 1930, and in March the boys moved in with their uncle, Hartog Cohen. But Hartog died on 24th May 1930. He was presumably seriously ill, because Lodi and Ies were taken in by the Leiden orphanage on 14th April 1930 (i.e. some five weeks before he died). Lodi spent five and a half years in the orphanage, Ies eight and a half years (see Fig. 4.14 for a 1932 group photo; they are nos. 5 and 20). Lodi and Ies were cousins of Elizabeth Cohen, the second wife of Director Italie.

Lodi was one of the few orphanage pupils (Herman Stofkooper was another) who received a higher secondary education: he attended the *Gymnasium* (grammar or Latin school) in Leiden, but he may have left without a diploma. According to Mirjam Pinkhof (1998), he joined the Hachsharah/Youth Aliyah in Loosdrecht in 1939. Like Catharinahoeve, described in the previous chapter, this *Paviljoen Loosdrechtse Rade* was one of several places in Holland (Table 9.2) where youngsters were given agricultural training[66] in preparation for moving to Palestine.

There were close links between the Youth Aliyah and the refugee children described in Chapter 5. Interest in Zionist ideals was much greater in Central and Eastern Europe than in pre-war Holland, where the wish to integrate or assimilate was much stronger. By the outbreak of the Second World War in September 1939, Youth Aliyah had managed to transport some 5000 children from Germany to Palestine, and some 15,000 others to countries around Germany, especially to the UK and the Netherlands. The Hachsharah institutions also provided a convenient refuge for unaccompanied children arriving in Holland, and the professed aim to move on to Palestine, rather than become permanent citizens of the Netherlands, helped in assuaging the Dutch government. Consequently, the Dutch Hachsharah[67] institutions were home to a great number of refugee children from Germany, Austria and Poland. Many of them had arrived in the Netherlands without parents[68] before the war. Some were as young as thirteen when they arrived. During the first years of the German occupation, there were probably some 800 children and staff in these houses (Table 9.2), including those of the religious Mishrachi and Agudat movements, which rejected "political" Zionism but still considered themselves Palestine Pioneers. Deventer was the oldest, established in 1918. Most of the

66 The education included other vocations as well, modern Hebrew, culture, and – in some places – religion. But the idea of cultivating land in Palestine, including marshland and desert, had special significance.

67 I use the term in the broadest sense, to include all institutions training youngsters as "Palestine Pioneers".

68 See list of refugee children's homes (not only Hachsharah) at http://www.dokin.nl/refugee-homes-in-nl/.

Figure 9.31: Lodi Cohen at his desk in Loosdrecht, probably 1939. Photo M. Pinkhof, courtesy Ghetto Fighters Museum (GFH, Israel)

others were established after the Nazi takeover in Germany: *Werkdorp Wieringermeer* in 1934, Gouda (Catharinahoeve) in 1937, Loosdrecht (Paviljoen Loosdrechtse Rade) in 1939. *Werkdorp* was not officially part of Hachsharah, but it is commonly and logically included when discussing young unaccompanied refugees, Palestine Pioneers, from the East and how they were taken care of in the Netherlands.

From the opening in 1939, Jacov Zurawel was director of the Paviljoen; he was posted in Holland from kibbutz Givat Brenner to help set up and manage the Youth Aliyah. He and his wife held British passports, and they left Holland in a hurry during the invasion of May 1940. Lodi Cohen took over as director.

With his 22 years at the time he took over, Lodi was "old" compared to the adolescents, indeed many of them still children, whom he was looking after. Before he took over, he sat in a small corner office (*"in the shadow of overbearing Jacob Zurawel"*, according to Mirjam Pinkhof) looking after administration (Fig. 9.31). He also gave religious lessons a few times a week. Trained to become a rabbi before coming to Loosdrecht, he was, by all accounts, a big, forceful, and intelligent man and a good and knowledgeable teacher. Lodi was assisted by Channa de Leeuw, Betty Britz, and later by Menachem Pinkhof[69] and Joachim "Shushu" Simon. They would later become members of the Westerweel resistance group (Schippers, 2015).

Before the German invasion in May 1940, when the Dutch army considered flooding the area (a method which had worked well as defense against the Spaniards in the sixteenth century), the pioneers were evacuated to Alkmaar, where they slept on straw in the local synagogue. They considered it a pleasant excursion, and

---

69   Clara Asscher-Pinkhof (see Ch. 9.3) was a sister of his father.

in September 1940 featured the event in an operetta (in German, of course, since most of the children could not speak Dutch fluently):

Wir sind marchiert durch Alkmaar's Strassen
und haben Decken mitgebracht.
Lodi ging vorne an der Spitze
das hat uns viel Freud' gemacht

(We were marched through Alkmaar's streets,
and brought along our blankets.
Lodi walked in front and led the way,
which was really amusing)
(It sounds much better in German!) (Pinkhof, 1998, p. 19)

The Paviljoen was not a farm in itself: the pioneers worked on farms in the Loos-drecht area. Lodi arranged the individual farms to which each of them was assigned, with the help of a farmer named Schenk who lived close by. Later, Schenk also assisted in arranging *onderduik*. Pinkhof's book is remarkable in that it contains photographs and stories of the many people, the children, but also the farmers, and farmhouses which played a role in the employment and subsequent *onderduik* of the Paviljoen's residents. All 49 people on the 1940 photograph (Fig. 9.32) have been identified.

Everything changed on 10th May 1940. It was difficult for the leaders (themselves barely 25 years old) to address the inevitable disillusion of the youngsters, who quickly realized that they were now captives of the Germans, again, and had to fight not only to get into Palestine which had been virtually closed by the British, but also to escape from occupied Holland over a heavily guarded border with Belgium. Contrary to the Leiden orphanage, where the few (somewhat younger) German refugees such as Lotte and Henny Adler had been absorbed by the pre-existing relatively carefree, possibly even complacent Dutch community, the Loosdrecht youths were politically much more aware and astute. They were generally far more suspicious and cynical about German intentions, and far less prepared to follow the advice from Joodse Raad officials to obey the authorities, not to resist, and not to go into hiding. Shushu Simon and Menachem Pinkhof soon made it clear they were prepared to ignore the Joodse Raad's advice. Shushu could talk from experience: in 1938 he had been incarcerated in Buchenwald.

Nevertheless, there were intense discussions in Loosdrecht during 1941 and 1942 whether to go willingly to Westerbork, or to resist. They had even prepared rucksacks,

Figure 9.32: Palestine Pioneers, Loosdrecht, probably summer 1940. Lodi Cohen, then director, standing at far right, Juda Pinkhof standing third from right; Menachem Pinkhof sitting front row, third from right. Out of 49 people on this photo, 23 perished. Everybody on this photo has been identified. For names, see Pinkhof 1998, or dossier Lodi Cohen. Photo courtesy Ghetto Fighters' House.

survival kits for when they were sent to Westerbork,[70] just as the management of the Leiden orphanage had done. But the willingness to resist increased as one anti-Jewish decree was issued after another. *Werkdorp Wieringermeer* had been "inspected" by Willy Lages and Klaus Barbie in early 1941,[71] before it was virtually shut down on 20th March 1941. As part of razzias held in June 1941 some 60 *Werkdorp* pioneers were picked up and deported to Mauthausen on 22nd June 1941, where all of the youngsters were killed before the end of the year (the significance of these early deportations to Mauthausen is discussed in Ch. 8.1).

70   Testimony A. Heinrich, Ghetto Fighters' House Archives 84, 1955.
71   Photos of the roll call (NIOD Beeldbank 62312 or 138237) during that event belong to the saddest surviving pictures; note that this took place less than year into the German occupation of Holland.

Some pioneers[72] managed to escape to Switzerland in 1942. But for most others, in the first instance, to resist deportation meant going into hiding: *onderduik*. Pinkhof (1998, p. 67) states:

> Onderduik *at the beginning of 1942 was not yet an obvious thing to consider. Only very few people decided to go into hiding, and still fewer managed to find a suitable address. Organized assistance to* onderduikers *by the resistance movement had yet to be developed.*

Conditions in Loosdrecht were increasingly difficult. The Paviljoen was overcrowded, facilities were poor, there was no heating during the exceptionally cold winter of 1941/1942. The pressure to take action increased. They realized they needed help (and money) from non-Jewish sympathizers. Pinkhof (then still Mirjam Waterman, not yet married to Menachem Pinkhof), herself a teacher, had good contacts with colleagues at the *Werkplaats* in Bilthoven, a school run by Kees Boeke and his wife based on rather unconventional if not controversial educational principles. A former Bilthoven *Werkplaats* teacher, Joop Westerweel, was asked for assistance. Mirjam knew him because she had two younger sisters at the *Werkplaats* in 1939. Soon contact between the pioneers and non-Jewish sympathizers, all sharing compatible views with respect to authorities, whether German or Dutch, led to a more or less consolidated group of resistance fighters. Bouke Koning and others from the Bilthoven *Werkplaats* also became involved early. Koning knew both Mirjam Waterman and Menachem Pinkhof and had offered to let Menachem hide at his place (Schippers, 2015). Like Joop Westerweel, Koning was infused with anti-authoritarian ideas and principles.[73] He had served time in prison for refusing military conscription (ibidem, pp. 33, 63).

The year before, in March/May 1941, the Germans had two representatives of the Jewish community in Prague, R.I. Friedman and Jacob Edelstein, the *Judenältester* in occupied Prague and later in Theresienstadt, visit the Netherlands to advise David Cohen and Abraham Asscher how to set up and manage the Joodse Raad of Amsterdam. Edelstein had the opportunity to escape to Palestine before the war but decided to stay with the Jewish community of Czechoslovakia. He and his family were killed in Auschwitz in June 1944. By the time of his visit Edelstein had no illusions about the German intentions. Edelstein also visited the Loosdrecht Youth

---

72 Some of these early escapees left without discussing their plans with others (Schippers, 2005). Paul Siegel tells us (2001) that he arranged a substantial amount of Belgian, French and Swiss francs at the request of a Hachsharah youth leader from Gouda to enable them to escape together. He took the money, but never came back to Paul, who only found out about his escape when he received a postcard from Switzerland.

73 In this respect he resembled Wim (Johan) van Straten, who shielded Aron Wolff (Chs. 9.4 and 10.3).

Aliyah, he had been a Hachsharah member himself. According to both Menachem and Mirjam Pinkhof he was unambiguously pessimistic about what the Germans had in store for the Jews in occupied Europe. Jozeph Melkman (who had advised the mother of Aron Wolff to get him out of the orphanage and into hiding, Ch. 9.4), remembered that in at least one of the meetings he had in Holland Edelstein said *"that the Germans intend to kill us all"*. Although Edelstein's premonition did not change the position (about escaping or going into hiding) of Asscher and Cohen, or for that matter his own, it did not fall on deaf ears with the refugee leaders such as Menachem Pinkhof and Lodi Cohen. When the large-scale deportations from Amsterdam began in July 1942, to Westerbork and on to Auschwitz, the Loosdrecht leaders decided to let the entire group of 48 residents disappear before they could be deported. Westerweel came over to help them find *onderduik* addresses, with several other non-Jewish friends from the *Werkplaats* period. Soon the group, which later became known as the Westerweel Group, consisted of some ten to twelve Jewish and non-Jewish people, engaged in finding *onderduik* addresses at short notice. On the evening of 15th August 1942, the 44 Paviljoen residents and the four leaders were provided with false papers and delivered to addresses all over the Netherlands. When the Germans arrived at the Paviljoen a few days later the place was empty. A remarkable achievement in a densely populated country where all movements and every activity were watched by the authorities. Many were taken in by people in the Limburg village of Sevenum. None of these were caught during the remaining years of the occupation (van Rens, 2013). Lodi left a letter to Erica Blüth to thank her for her support and leaving her a few bills to pay:

Loosdrecht, 16th August 1942

Dear Mrs. Blüth,
When this letter reaches you, our Paviljoen will be an empty home. All residents will have gone. We would like to inform you and the entire [Youth Aliyah] committee by means of this letter which we address to you because whenever we encountered problems or difficulties, you were there to assist us.
We did not involve you in our last great concern here in Loosdrecht because we felt we should not make you co-responsible for actions for which only we ourselves must be accountable.
There remains one technical matter: a stack of unpaid bills and unanswered mail left on the table in Room 16. Thank you for everything, and until we meet again,
The residents of Paviljoen Loosdrechtse Rade.

Erica was on the leadership team of the Youth Aliyah, and her husband (Curt) held a senior position at the Joodse Raad. She warned Lodi and the others that the *ontruiming* of the Paviljoen was planned for 16th August, which, as mentioned above, triggered the immediate departure of all inhabitants into *onderduik* (Pinkhof, 1998, p. 74; see also Schippers, 2015). However, many hiding places were only available for a few days, some *onderduikers* had to leave again without knowing where to go; some host families were themselves in dire straits; there was little food and the *onderduikers* had no ration cards. There is no "wild nature" in Holland where people can hide for long periods (Paul Siegel tried, see below) and every nook and cranny of the country was under German control. Even the furthest outlying farmhouse could expect to be raided by the Dutch or German police at any time. Moreover, because of their looks and German accents the pioneers were a serious danger to whomever gave them shelter. The youngsters also suffered from loneliness, boredom, and desperation at their *onderduik* addresses. Westerweel and his comrades travelled the country to solve problems. The Jewish members of the Westerweel Group received *Sperre* from the Joodse Raad, allowing them more freedom of movement, at least temporarily. But the situation was becoming untenable, and alternatives had to be considered. Escaping by sea had become virtually impossible once the Germans started to control and fortify the coastline, leaving only one realistic option: going south to Switzerland or Spain.

For the young and generally adventurous *chalutzim*, an important advantage of such escape plans, compared to *onderduik*, was probably that boredom was not part of it. By 1942 overland escape involved tremendous difficulties and risks, conceivably even more so than going into hiding. Guides, so-called *passeurs*, were required to get across four controlled borders (Holland > Belgium > Occupied France > Vichy France > Switzerland or Spain), contacts to provide food, safe lodging in Antwerp, Brussels, Paris, Vichy France, cash in three different currencies, counterfeit identities and travel papers, and so on. How to start, and whom to contact? There was no telephone number to call, and Herman Stofkooper (Ch. 9.8) found his first *passeur* through a barber in Breda. In October 1942, eight pioneers left[74]. They were all seventeen years of age, except Juda Pinkhof (Menachem's brother) who was 21. It was a terrible scam. After crossing the border with Belgium, they were driven straight to Brussels and handed over to the German police. One of them smuggled a warning note to the others back home. After the war, it transpired that the eight boys were deported from Kazerne Dossin (Belgium, see Ch. 8.4) to Auschwitz on 31st October, where they were all killed on or around 3rd November 1942.

Possibly influenced by this disaster, the Westerweel Group decided to organize the escape routes themselves, by travelling the route, establishing their own contacts, and returning to Holland to send others on their way (Pinkhof, 1998). The decision to try and do as much as possible themselves may also explain why there was virtually

---

74   Sigi Adler, Bernard Aschheim, Robert Dürheim, Lili Kellner, Esra Jurovics, Fabian Schön, Jossel (Josef?) Waldman, and Juda Pinkhof (Menachem's brother). All eight are in Figure 9.32.

Figure 9.33: Lilo Spiegel and Lodi Cohen (front row first and second from left) amongst fellow Palestine Pioneers celebrating their escape across the Pyrenees, Barcelona, Spain, 10th September 1944. The small boy is Uri Durlacher (Dor). More names in dossier (also see Siegel, 2001, 2005). Photo courtesy Ghetto Fighters' House.

no contact with the other escape lines that became active between summer 1942 and 1944, such as the Dutch-Paris escape line (Koreman, 2016, 2018), or Dutch consular staff in southern France who provided assistance to refugees going to Spain or Switzerland (Plantinga, 1998).

Nevertheless, from October 1942 several of the pioneers (some after escaping from Westerbork) managed to cross the Pyrenees into Spain, while others were caught and deported to Auschwitz or other camps in the East. Mirjam Pinkhof estimated that the Westerweel Group cared for some 200 *onderduikers*, of which some 150 escaped over the Dutch border. Some 80 crossed the Pyrenees into Spain, of which 70 reached Palestine before the end of the war. Lodi Cohen and his wife, Lilo, were amongst them (Fig. 9.33). Lodi reported (in *Dawar Hachalutz* of September 1945, *fide* Pinkhof, 1998, p. 109):

> *Lilo and I tried three times to cross the Pyrenees but only by the fourth attempt did we succeed in reaching Spain. With us came Betty (Britz[75]), Ludi (?), Heinz*

75 Family names in brackets are assumed, based on the list of Loosdrecht pioneers.

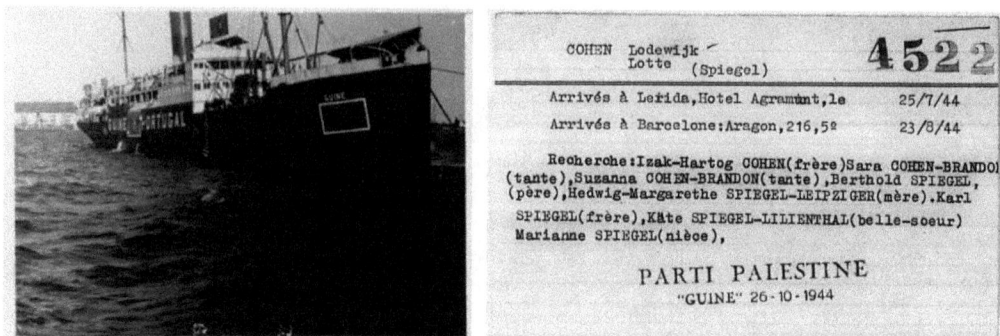

Figure 9.34: Left: SS *Guiné* in the port of Cadiz, June 1944. Right: the JDC registration card for Lodi and Lilo Cohen. Source: JDC Archives, Barcelona.

(Cosman), Ruth Durlacher, Lore Süsskind. Spain was like paradise. It was July 1944, I still remember, after five years of wartime food, the taste of the first banana we received in Andorra. [...] It was easy to get Palestine certificates in Spain; you just told them you wanted to go to Palestine and that was it. We were kept by the Joint [Distribution Committee] and had an easy life, which quickly became boring. Via Barcelona [Fig. 9.28] and Lerida we arrived in Cadiz to board a ship. And at last, on the 4th of November 1944, we arrived in Haifa. It is difficult to describe our emotions. We arrived in the middle of the war with 430 people who had just narrowly escaped Nazi Europe. Among them were 58 from Holland, including 11 from Loosdrecht.

According to records held by the JDC, the *"Joint"*, Lodi and Lilo arrived in Lerida 25th July 1944, and in Barcelona on 23rd August (Fig. 9.34). They left Cadiz on the *Guiné* on 26th October and arrived in Haifa on 4th November.[76] Upon arrival in Palestine they were quarantined in the Atlit Camp south of Haifa; the same camp where, three months earlier, the mother of Aron Wolff (Ch. 9.4) was interned, and where Mindel Färber (Ch. 9.3) had been collected by her mother.

Long after the war, as part of unrelated historical research in Israel in 1973, Hans Schippers interviewed pioneers who had survived the war with the help of the Westerweel Group:

Their stories about onderduik *activities, escapes from Westerbork, and treks across the Pyrenees Mountains into Spain, were fascinating, but not triumphant, and very conscious of the fact that so many of their comrades had yet fallen into the hands*

---

76 There was another Aliya ship that month, the SS *Niassa*, also carrying a number of pioneers from Holland.

of the Germans. Always, they mentioned the non-Jewish helpers with reverence: they were convinced that without them they would not have survived. (Schippers, 2015, p. 7)

Both Mirjam Pinkhof and Lilo Cohen-Spiegel have deposited stories from their journey to Spain and Palestine in the Ghetto Fighters' House museum in Israel. Lodi (and supposedly Lilo) settled in kibbutz Sde Nehemia in the Galilee.

Not much is known about how the Loosdrecht pioneers managed to cross Vichy France, which, as we will see in the next chapter, was becoming increasingly dangerous from the summer of 1942 onwards. Their reports do tell us, however, about the dangers of crossing the Pyrenees. Several attempts to reach Spain in the cold winter of 1943/1944 failed, until a successful convoy of 28th February 1944. One of the boys (Isi Tiefenbrunner) fell into a ravine close to the Spanish border. They had been abandoned by their *passeur*. His fellow travellers could not reach him and, being in dire straits themselves, they were forced to leave him there to die. The reports tell us little about any difficulties they had to face in Spain, or how many of the pioneers, if any, were arrested by the Guardia Civil after crossing the border without papers, or if any were interned in the concentration camp of Miranda de Ebro. Lodi's comment (above) about Spain feeling like paradise is certainly not representative for many other refugees who were arrested in Spain in 1942 and 1943 (Koreman, 2018; Huisman, 2018). But by the time of Lodi's crossing (July 1944), the regime in Spain had significantly softened (more information in Ch. 9.8).

A fascinating and very complete account of his escape to Palestine, from Hachsharah in Deventer to Westerbork and over the Pyrenees to Spain, is given by Paul Siegel (2001). He had gone into hiding in a forest, had to give it up, and ended up in Westerbork. After a period of self-reflection and deliberations, he escaped from Westerbork[77] a few weeks later. He travelled through Belgium and France aided by the Westerweel Group. The contrast with the (following) story of Herman Stofkooper is striking. The Westerweel escape line almost looks like a guided tour, except that it was deadly serious. Westerweel travelled to the last shelter at the foot of the mountains just to say goodbye and farewell to the group (ibidem) and then returned to Holland to pick up the next one.

The (Jewish and non-Jewish) members of the Westerweel Group paid a high price for trying to bring the youngsters to safety. Shushu Simon crossed the borders several times trying to establish the escape route to Switzerland, but in January 1943 he was caught trying to get back from Belgium into Holland. He managed to send a warning to his comrades and committed suicide two days later to prevent betraying

---

77 Escape was relatively easy, but it took time even for the daring ones to make that decision. Paul was given that time, thanks to the connections and the solidarity within Youth Aliya.

their identities. On 11th March 1944, Bouke Koning and Joop Westerweel, who had just returned to Holland after sending the group of 28th February on its way to Spain, were caught when trying to guide two Jewish girls across the Belgian border. As a result of a failed attempt to get Joop out of prison, both Mirjam and Menachem Pinkhof were arrested as well, and brought to Westerbork. They narrowly escaped deportation as *Häftlinge* to Auschwitz by intervention of Curt Blüth (Erika's husband), and both survived the war in Bergen Belsen. Westerweel was executed by the Germans on 11th August 1944, in the Vught concentration camp,[78] just weeks before allied forces liberated the southern part of the Netherlands. Bouke Koning survived the war, but he never recovered from his ordeal in Vught, Oranienburg, Buchenwald/Dora, Ravensbrück and Peltoff/Gross-Rosen (?) where he was freed by the Soviet army (Ghetto Fighters' House archives).

The *Westerweel Forest* was planted on the slopes of Mount Efraïm/Ramat Menashe, with a small monument for the members of the group in Kibbutz Gil'ad (Even Yitshak). The specific history of the Westerweel Group and its association with the Loosdrecht Hachsharah pioneers has been described by Schippers (2015; for other examples of Jewish/non-Jewish resistance, see Moore, 2010). The Dutch-Paris escape line is described by Koreman (2018).

Both Bram Degen (previous chapter) and Lodi seem to thank their survival to a significant extent to the much higher level of alertness, suspicion, and preparedness to resist the Germans in the Hachsharah of Gouda and Loosdrecht, under the influence of people such as Manfred Litten or Shushu Simon, and other refugees from Germany, but also to people like the Stoffels or the non-Jewish members of the Westerweel Group who decided – early during the occupation – to resist the Germans by helping them before it was too late. The contrast between Hijme Stoffels and Joop Westerweel (and to a degree Johan van Straten) could not have been greater than it was, in character, political belief, religiousness, or social status. In peacetime, they belonged to different "pillars", and they would conceivably not even have talked to each other. But during the war they shared values which made both stand up against the Germans and put their very life at risk in an early phase of the war, when it was not at all certain that Germany would be defeated.

The preference for trying to reach either Spain or Switzerland depended in part on the specific motivations of each individual escapee. Spain, itself under fascist and Nazi-sympathetic rule following the Spanish Civil War (1936-1939), was not an attractive destination for fugitives with leftish political backgrounds, but it offered the more likely route for those keen to join or rejoin the war from England. For those whose priority was to escape persecution, like the Jews, it did not matter so much, but Switzerland certainly appeared to be more neutral and in a better

---

78 This camp, near 's Hertogenbosch, was the only SS concentration camp outside the German Reich.

shape than Spain. Escape lines, such as Dutch-Paris, only developed gradually from summer 1942. It should also be recognized that conditions in Vichy France, as well as around clandestine entry into both Switzerland and Spain, changed significantly during 1942 and 1943, and most fugitives had no access to up-to-date information. The position of the Swiss government towards refugees hardened from mid-1942, while the position of the Spanish government softened from early 1943, when Franco replaced some of the most outspoken fascist members of his government. No doubt the German defeat by the Soviet army at Stalingrad in January 1943 and the increasing role of the USA in the war played a role in the changing attitude of the Spanish government.

In the end, many other factors, and some purely random events, determined their fate. The Loosdrecht pioneers originally thought about going to Switzerland but they ended up aiming for Spain. The following story is about Herman Stofkooper and his fiancé, who aimed to go to Spain, but ended up in Switzerland instead.

9.8 Herman Stofkooper escapes to Switzerland

Herman Stofkooper (Groningen, 29th May 1918) arrived in the orphanage in Leiden on 16th December 1929, less than half a year after the inauguration of the new building. When his parents divorced in 1922, Herman had stayed with his mother, Sophia Cohen. Contact with his father was lost, and financial difficulties[79] forced Sophia to send Herman to Leiden when he was eleven years old. In Leiden he was registered in grade 6[80] at the *bovenschool* at Langebrug: he appears on the school photograph taken that year (Fig. 4.10). Mimi Weiman remembered[81] that he was never really happy in Leiden, although he tried to make the best of it. We see Herman on more than one of Mimi's photographs, such as Figure 5.5 (1934), standing next to Lodi Cohen, and Figure 5.6, close to Jupie Pront, who was a special friend to both Herman and Mimi. He left after almost six years, on 30th September 1935, when he was seventeen. Jupie and Mimi left the same year. He moved to Tilburg in the south of the country, and took employment in the textile industry.

The following account is largely based on Herman's post-war report of his wartime experiences.[82] I have left much of the detail intact because it allows one to more vividly imagine what it implied to decide not to report for deportation, and instead

---

79 Information courtesy Mr. A. Stofkooper, 2019.
80 The highest grade in elementary school, nowadays grade 8.
81 Interviews with L.P. Kasteleyn.
82 The 23-page report (in Dutch) is in his dossier. He wrote the original report shortly after the war, but it was lost. He wrote it again many years later, which probably explains why some pertinent facts are missing.

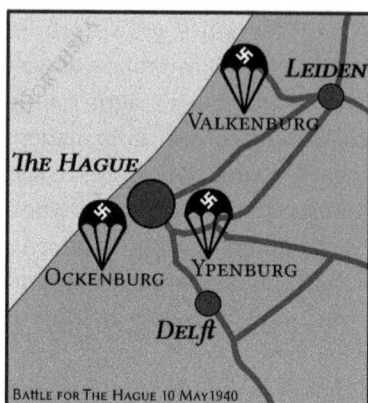

Figure 9.35: The battle for The Hague, 10th May 1940. The distance from Leiden to The Hague is about 16 km. Source: oSeveno, Wikipedia, https://en.wikipedia.org/wiki/Battle_for_The_Hague#/media/File:Aanval_op_Den_Haag_1940-en.svg.

try to travel illegally through occupied Europe, without a plan or an organization to support you, relying on total strangers for help. It also allows a comparison with the other escape stories included in this chapter, and the random events which caused Herman to end up in Switzerland, and not in Spain, as he had intended when he left Tilburg.

When Holland mobilized in August 1939 Herman was drafted into military service. He was garrisoned in Katwijk aan Zee when the Germans invaded on 10th May 1940. That same day German airborne troops tried to capture the three military airports surrounding The Hague, the seat of the Dutch government. Herman's unit was deployed around the Valkenburg airfield (Fig. 9.35), which was very close to Katwijk and Leiden. He took part in the very fierce fighting from 10th to 14th May during which the Germans failed to capture The Hague.[83] After capitulation, he tried to escape to England from Katwijk before being interned as a POW by the Germans.

He was released from captivity on 29th May 1940 and returned to Tilburg to work again in the textile (*"tricotage"*) factory. The plant was Jewish-owned and was soon dispossessed. Herman himself, also being Jewish, was dismissed by the German *Verwalter* who had taken control of the business. Being unemployed, he was given a part-time job with the local branch of the Joodse Raad in 1941, while teaching modern Hebrew in Tilburg and in Breda, where he met his future wife, Aaltje Henriette (Jet) Cohen. In March 1942, they were engaged, and Herman visited her by bicycle, since Jews were no longer allowed on the train. The distance between Tilburg and Breda is about 30 km, about two hours on a bicycle each way.

Then one day Herman's future father-in-law (Marcus Samuel Cohen) put the garbage bin on the curb in the morning, without first putting on his coat. The yellow star which all Jews had to visibly wear in public (from 29th April 1942) was attached to that coat. A Dutch Nazi sympathizer who saw him outside his house without his star reported him. He was taken to the police station and sent home after being told he would receive a fine. Other neighbours volunteered to put up the

---

83   This is the area through which Truus Wijsmuller travelled on her way to Amsterdam on 13th May (Ch. 9.1).

money, but instead Marcus was arrested again by the police[84] on 23rd May[85] 1942 and delivered to the police prison in Breda. He was never seen by his family again. After the war it transpired that he was taken to the SD prison at Haaren and from there to the infamous concentration camp of the German police in Amersfoort, where he was killed on 14th October that same year, but Herman and Jet did not know that at the time. Still, the disappearance of Marcus Cohen because of a trivial offense probably played a role in Herman's decision that it was time to escape, and that going south was the only realistic option available.

Herman still had his part-time job with the local branch of the Joodse Raad. In June 1942 he was instructed to create a list of names of Jews who would "qualify" for *werkverruiming* (German: *Arbeitseinsatz*). This was, as we know today, just another bogus step on the way of deporting *all* Jews to the East; the first mass transport from Westerbork would take place just weeks later, on 14th July 1942 (see Ch. 6). He refused and was dismissed from the job at the Joodse Raad.

I did not wish to be involved with selecting fellow Jews for these German labour camps. A few days later, when the list of Jews who had to report for medical examination to determine if they were fit enough for these 'labour camps' came out, I was not surprised to find my name near the top of the list.

He obtained a statement from his own doctor that he was not fit, and took it to the official examination doctor, who was a Nazi sympathizer. Although not prepared to believe the statement, he still gave Herman a three-month stay. *"This was the moment I decided to go to Breda and talk to my fiancé about fleeing from Holland."* He then talked to a barber who had mentioned possibilities to escape some months before.[86] From the beginning, the idea was to go through Belgium, France and Spain and Portugal to Britain. Herman considered himself as still under military duty and was keen to join the small Dutch colony of émigrés around the government in exile in London, and possibly join the military there. On 13th July 1942 the barber arranged for a *"passeur"*, a "professional" people smuggler, to talk to Herman the next day, and after agreeing on a payment (the man normally made a living by smuggling horses across the Belgian border), the time of departure was set for the next day at noon. Herman did not return to Tilburg, and a friend collected some clothes for

---

84 To determine whether it was the German police, or the Dutch police following German instructions, we would need to research the police archives of Breda to see if a record has been kept.

85 Herman gives the date as "Whitsun Saturday", which fell on 23rd May in 1942.

86 Not such a strange thing: like taxi drivers, barbers often talked about anything during their work, and moreover, they knew most of their clients personally. In addition, smuggling goods across the Belgian border was a popular sport and not seen as wrongdoing before the war in the border provinces of the Netherlands.

him, and informed his family that he would not come back. Saying goodbye to Jet's mother was difficult. She refused to come with them, nor did she want to go into hiding, because she still hoped her husband would return from captivity.

Herman and Jet met the *passeur* as agreed at the bus station in Ginneken (Breda). They took the bus to the South, and then crossed the border on bicycle through the farm fields. They were duly delivered to a café in a small Belgian border village, to meet another *passeur* who would bring them to Brussels (via Antwerp). It was the first day of experiencing the terrible anxiety which accompanied all illegal travellers in the German-occupied countries. They had no clue whether the first *passeur* was trustworthy, or the second, or any of the other strangers they would have to rely on during the journey, until they met the first local Dutchmen in Vichy France. Countless are the stories where the *passeur* took the money and then disappeared, or, worse, delivered his charges to the police. Indeed, the first *passeur* had accepted the payment to cover the entire trip out of Holland to Brussels. But the second *passeur* required another payment. *"So, what choice do you have? Your life is at stake, so as long as you have money left, you pay."* Herman does not mention how much he paid the first and second *passeur*. Sources quoted by Koreman (2018) report that "professional *passeurs*" in France charged 3000 to 5000 francs per person, a significant amount for most refugees. Other, less reputable *passeurs* could charge up to 20,000 francs, a small fortune.

They travelled by bus to Antwerp, where they acquired false papers, and by train to Brussels, where they were delivered to a café in an inconspicuous part of the city. They were given a room and told to wait until someone would contact them. With nothing to do they went for walks during the day, until Herman spotted two NSB men he knew from Tilburg. After that they did not dare to go outside. After a week, a certain Mr. Rubens dropped by, who had heard about Herman and Jet being in Brussels. Rubens was also waiting for further guidance on the way south, with his father and his brother. He told Herman about a Doctor Goor, from Tilburg, who was in Brussels and who was believed to know people able to arrange train transport from Brussels directly to the French/Swiss border. But he quoted a price way beyond the means of Mr. Rubens and Herman and Jet. They declined the offer.

Another week had passed, in Brussels, when they were contacted in the café by a woman, who said she could bring them to "Free France". She took them to another place, where they met about 30 Belgian officers, as well as Rubens and his father and brother. Together they took the train to the Belgian/French border (c. 30th July; dates are estimated based on his report). Remarkably, the woman did not ask for money, and Herman had no clue how he and Rubens had ended up with this company. But the fact that she looked after the Belgian officers gave him some confidence that she was a bona fide helper. Later, one of the officers told him she was a member of the

"Deuxième Bureau", the French contra-espionage department, and that her name was Mrs. Luisette. They left the train to pass the border on foot, and once in France took a train to Paris. The crossing was relaxed; the woman told them they could walk within sight of border officials without fear. This was very different compared to travelling by public transport in Holland, which had become very dangerous, with checkpoints at bus and railway stations and patrols in the trains themselves. She brought them to a hotel in Paris which was frequented by Germans and told them that the chances of identity checks were smaller for that reason. The following morning they went to the Paris South Station to take a train to the demarcation line: the border between occupied France and so-called "Free France", or "Vichy France" (Fig. 9.36), after the city which the government of Pétain choose as its seat upon signing the Armistice with Germany on 22nd June 1940. Note that the map shows, among other things, Holland having a *civil* Nazi administration, Belgium, northern France and the Atlantic coast having a German *military* government, and Vichy France as it existed until November 1942.

Herman and Jet did not know what the situation in Vichy France was, two years after the armistice, nor were they much concerned. To them, it was "Free" France. They were – understandably – focused on getting across the demarcation line, now just a few kilometres ahead of them, and thus escaping German control.

Mrs. Luisette took them from the station into the woods, where they stumbled into a group of some 50 Jewish refugees from Eastern Europe with crying children. They had been abandoned by their *passeur* and did not know what to do. Mrs. Luisette decided, after some discussion with the Belgian officers, that the refugees would be taken along by her as well. They had to cross the Le Cher River to get into Vichy territory.[87] The group, now uncomfortably large, waited in anxiety in the woods the rest of the day, while she was trying to arrange a crossing. Finally, during the night, they marched single file through the village, close to the buildings in absolute silence, without meeting a German patrol, to the river, where a long cable had been rigged from one bank to the other. They waded through the waist-deep water holding the line and keeping the luggage above their heads. The refugees carried the smaller children on their shoulders; some elderly people got stuck in mid-stream and were assisted by the officers.

No German patrol was in sight and we reached Free France without a glitch, thinking the worst of the journey was now past us. […] But that was not the case. The worst had yet to come. Mrs. Luisette informed us she could provide no further assistance.

---

87 Herman does not mention the name of the village. I could also not locate the village of Luchon, which they reached *after* the crossing. We should remember that he had to reconstruct his post-war report after losing the original.

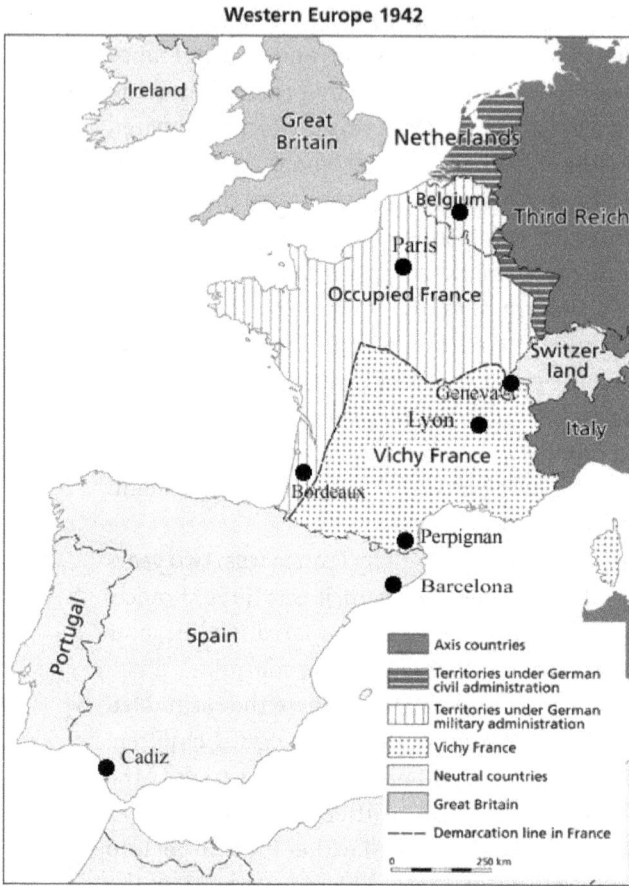

Figure 9.36: Western Europe, June 1940 to November 1942, showing Holland under direct Nazi civil control, Belgium and occupied France under German military control, and "Free" France under the Vichy puppet government. Fugitives travelling to Spain or Switzerland had to cross four borders, including the Demarcation Line between occupied and "Free" France. Source: Koreman, 2018, courtesy Oxford University Press (USA).

We had to make our own arrangements to get to the Spanish border. Something had gone wrong, but she would not tell us what. She advised us, and the refugees, to report to a refugee camp nearby. The Belgian officers went their own way, we did not see them again. Much later we heard that Mrs. Luisette was caught and summarily executed. We shared a taxi to bring us to the camp, but when we got there, we had a bad feeling about it. We had the taxi bring us to Luchon, where we took the night train to Lyon, as suggested by Mr. Rubens, who knew that there was a Dutch desk, representing the free Dutch government in London, with the Swedish consulate. The desk was run by Sally Noach and his two brothers. We had obtained false identity papers in Belgium but now that we had left German-occupied Europe, we felt safe to reassume our true identity. This turned out to be a serious mistake, but what did we know?

Indeed, it was a mistake to assume that by crossing the demarcation line, they had effectively escaped German occupation. They did not fully appreciate that "Vichy" was no more than a puppet or even a vassal government, which only existed at the pleasure of the Germans. It was increasingly willing to collaborate with the Nazis if the pretense of retaining French sovereignty could be preserved. Just three months after the arrival of Herman and Jet in France the situation would drastically change. Triggered by the allied landings in North Africa on 8th November, German (and Italian) troops occupied the remaining "free" area of France on 10th-11th November 1942. Annecy and the border area came under Italian control, but in Lyon the German police and security service could now operate without restraint.

At this time, Herman and Jet were still planning to get to England via Spain. But there was no immediate opportunity to move to Spain, and it seems that their contacts, who probably were suggested by Mrs. Luisette, were focused on moving people to Switzerland. Via Sally Noach, Herman and Jet met the family Hannie and Jaap de Jong, a party of five including Hannie's parents and her sister. The family Rubens went their own way from Lyon. Neither the party of Hannie and Jaap, nor Herman and Jet, had much money left, but Sally Noach suggested a cheap hotel. Hannie's parents and her sister had lost their spirits when they were abandoned near Bordeaux, after their *passeur* had taken almost all their money, and they decided to return to Holland. Hannie and Jaap decided not to give up and had moved on from Bordeaux (in the German-occupied zone) to Lyon. They also found a cheap restaurant to eat, and someone provided them with the required ration coupons.

After a few days in the hotel (probably around 12th August) they were woken up in the middle of the night by the French (Vichy) police, who took them, and all other refugees in the hotel to St. Jean Prison in the city, where they had to stand in the courtyard until the next day. Their anxiety was understandably high, even though nobody in the party knew that by this time the Vichy government was rounding up all Jews with foreign nationalities to deliver them to the Germans for deportation to (mainly) Auschwitz.[88] On the next day Sally Noach appeared at the prison, and he managed to get them released. Most likely he used his "Swedish" status and the fact that at this time the French police was focused on Eastern European Jews. This reduced their anxiety such that they simply returned to the hotel, until a few days later they were again arrested by the police. For a second time, Sally Noach managed to get them released, and this time Herman realized they should get out of Lyon. But they had no clue where to go to, and how, and had no choice but to return again to the hotel. A few days later (c. 20th August?) they were arrested for the third time. The police told them that picking up all foreigners was a precautionary measure related to a visit to Lyon[89] by Marshal Pétain, the head of the French "Vichy" state, and there was no need for anxiety *as long as they were not Jewish*. Next morning, they all had to report to a police officer to answer questions. Herman's name did

---

88 The infamous round-up of "Vel d'Hiv" had taken place just a few weeks earlier. The French police arrested some 13,000 Jews, including 4000 children, and imprisoned them in the Winter Velodrome before delivering them to the Drancy internment camp from where they were deported to Auschwitz. This action alone represented more than a quarter of the 42,000 French Jews sent to concentration camps in 1942, of whom only 811 (< 2%) would return after the end of the war.
89 Pétain made several well-publicized visits to Lyon in 1940-1943, but there seems to be no reference to such a visit in August 1942.

not trigger suspicion, but Jet's name (Cohen) was immediately recognized as Jewish. After Jet claimed that the name was also common among Dutch Protestants, the man let her pass. Nevertheless, they were not released, but interned in a fortress near the city. They were well treated. Four days later they were released with some of the other detainees, and they returned to Lyon and the Dutch Desk by tram. At the Dutch desk they were told to leave as quickly as possible, and that they were unable to provide any further assistance in reaching and crossing the border. The recommendation was to try the Swiss route, and at this point Herman abandoned his plan to reach England. He probably realized that chances to leave Switzerland, being a land-locked country surrounded by Nazi territory, to proceed to England, would be less than doing so from Spain. They were given the address of a Jewish family in Geneva, and the advice not to report to the Dutch consulate if they managed to reach Geneva, because the consulate would be obliged to report their arrival to the Swiss authorities, who would possibly return them to France. Herman observed that the French in the occupied zone had been more helpful than those in the Vichy area.

Now thoroughly nervous about being arrested again, the four of them (Herman and Jet, and Hannie and Jaap de Jong) managed to reach Annecy by train. They took a bus from Annecy to Abbé du Pommier right in the Jura Mountains, and started walking north. Jet's shoes were falling apart and walking in the mountainous terrain quickly became difficult. When they were hailed by two men on the way, they realized it would be useless to deny that they were fugitives, but the guys turned out to be friendly. They were given a meal and shelter for the night. The following day they were brought to a local café, where they were waiting, again in anxiety, for the whole day. At dusk, the two men appeared and gave them instruction how to proceed after reaching the border.

> When we came to a railway line, we were told to cross it quickly, not to respond if challenged, and walk straight into the woods at the other side. We thanked the guys for their help and ran across the tracks. Indeed, we were challenged, but got into the forest safely.
>
> When we emerged from the woods, and saw the lights of a village, we could not control our tears; at last we had escaped Nazi rule. It turned out we were in a Geneva suburb called Croix Rouge. We took a tram to the centre, hoping to locate the family Fischer. I cannot remember how we got Swiss money. Hannie and Jaap had been given another name to contact, so it was just Jet and I who – very reluctantly, it was after midnight – knocked on the door. The Fischers were sympathetic, and gave us something to eat and drink, but they wanted us to leave again because it was illegal to give refugees lodging. They suggested that we go to the railway station to spend the rest of the night in the waiting room, and then take a train to Bern next morning. When we explained our fear of being arrested by the Swiss police and being sent back

to France, they relented, and allowed us to stay in their house. Mr. Fischer put us on the train to Bern early next morning. When we arrived in Bern [on 15th September 1942] we met Hannie and Jaap again, and together we reported to the Dutch embassy.

At the embassy in Bern, Herman and Jet were cordially received by Jhr Quarles van Ufford, who asked them to tell him the whole story of their escape. Herman and Jet pretended to be married, which was not correct, for fear of being sent to separate internment camps. They hoped to get officially married in Switzerland as soon as possible. The embassy arranged a hotel in town and told them to wait there while they reported them to the Swiss authorities.[90] They were collected the next morning at the hotel to be interviewed at the police station, where they were asked to write down their story, each of them separately. They were again well treated and could return to the hotel later that day. They were also allowed to move around Bern freely, which they did.

A few days later we received sad news from Holland. Jet's mother [Regina Goudsmit] had been deported to the East. She had gone to Westerbork after the Joodse Raad *had assured her that she would be reunited with her husband there. [...] It was a terrible shock for Jet, who had not given up hope that her father would be released, so that they both could have gone into hiding. We left Holland without saying goodbye to her parents or her brother, not realizing we would not see any of them ever again.*

Herman's own mother [Sophia Cohen] was also deported to Westerbork and from there to Auschwitz[91] on 9th February 1943. Herman tried to arrange a Palestine certificate in Geneva to prevent her deportation from Westerbork, but the papers were returned to him with the annotation that she had already been "sent through" to the East.

Six weeks later [i.e. around 30th October?] all fugitives were told to leave Bern in view of an upcoming football match with Nazi Germany. Under police escort we went to

---

90 Once in Switzerland, much depended on whether the refugees were given legal (residence) status or not. The Dutch representatives were careful to openly support only the "legal" group. The complexity, the problems and frustrations associated with helping refugees (including Jews, resistance fighters, people keen to reach England to fight) who were threatened to be turned back to Vichy France, as well as those who reached Swiss soil, were innumerable (Koreman, 2018, and references therein; Plantinga, 1998). One support group succeeded in arranging legal papers before the refugees crossed the border, but it took time to arrange the documents, smuggle them back to France, arrange money for food, train tickets, and so on. Some refugees had to wait in a French prison, others waited in hiding in Lyon or Annecy. It also took time for refugees who did not have prior contacts in Switzerland, no doubt the majority, to find helpers through referral and hearsay. Herman and Jet were very fortunate indeed.

91 With her new husband, Levie Kapper.

Montreux by train, and by funicular to the mountain village of Glion [el. 800 m]. Glion had a Dutch school, to serve children of Dutch families living there. The school could also serve children of Dutch fugitives, but we were soon transferred to yet another village, Caux, at 1100 m elevation. We were again lodged in a hotel. Many hotels in the ski areas were closed because the war had damaged the tourist industry. The Dutch embassy had rented some hotels to lodge Dutch fugitives and provided food and clothing. [...] We would stay there for more than a year and regretted that we had nothing to do but hiking around Caux, or even to Montreux. [...] [In] late 1943 we were again transferred: to Mont Pellerin, a village some 1000 m above Vevey. The hotel was run by a Swiss couple, a housekeeper, and a cook, and here the 200 fugitives were given tasks to perform, mostly in the running of the hotel. We were put to work in the kitchen, which suited me well since I like cooking. [...] There were two kitchen crews of four men and four women each, supporting the Swiss cook. Feeding everybody was hard work, but we were happy that it finally brought an end to the terrible idleness of the year before.

The fugitives spent the remaining two years of the war in Caux, except that Herman and other men were sent to a camp for three months to do ground-moving work, in a period when Swiss men were called up for military or reserves duty. Herman and Jet were able to exchange letters with friends in Holland. When they inquired about some clothing they had left behind in Tilburg, not expecting a serious answer in view of the chaos in Europe, they were surprised to receive a package by mail a few weeks later. Herman found a travel permit issued by the Joodse Raad in a pocket and feared that Lenie (who sent the package) could have been arrested if the German censor had found it. This was around July 1944, after the allied landings in Normandy. After the liberation of Paris and then Brussels, hopes ran high that Holland would also soon be liberated. Herman joined a volunteer group led by Dr. Polak-Daniels, planning to provide aid to people returning from concentration camps in Eastern Europe. He then got an official appointment from the Dutch government in London. He was allowed to leave the hotel and live in Geneva on a small stipend. After getting officially married in spring 1945, Herman moved to Paris, while Jet had to wait (August 1945) in Geneva. The volunteer group did not get Soviet permission to go to Poland, and after two weeks in Paris without any news from Polak-Daniels, Herman managed to get back to Holland with help from the American forces. *"For three years we had lived in Switzerland, a country surrounded by countries at war, and using their resources while it was difficult enough for the Swiss to feed their own people as well as thousands of refugees. We were very grateful for that."*

Back home, Herman was confronted with an invoice from the Dutch government: to pay back support money he had received while in Switzerland. Herman and

Jet left Holland 15th July 1942; they arrived in Bern on 15th September, two months later. They had been well aware of the risks travelling through occupied Holland, Belgium and occupied France, but they had little notion about how dangerous Vichy France was in 1942, and how lucky they had been to get to Bern. Southern France had experienced years of incoming refugees, first from the south because of the Spanish Civil War, then from the north as a result of the German onslaught in May-June 1940. Dutch refugees received assistance from Dutch diplomatic staff in France and Switzerland. As early as May 1940, a special committee to support refugees was established in Paris.

After the Armistice of 22nd June 1940, consular staff (such as J. Kolkman and M. Jacquet) in Vichy, Lyon, Toulouse and other places continued to provide assistance (Plantinga, 1998), with financial support provided by the Dutch government in exile in London. So did local Dutch residents in southern France, businessmen such as Sally Noach who got Herman and Jet released by the Vichy police, or Jean Weidner, who was asked for help by a friend, and who proceeded to become the central figure of the Dutch-Paris escape line (Koreman, 2018). Given the fact that Vichy France was essentially a vassal state of Germany, the presence of Dutch consulates was of, course, peculiar. They were loyal to the Dutch government in exile in London, while Holland itself was occupied, and the Germans exerted serious pressure on Vichy to close them down. Vichy resisted, probably to maintain the appearance of French sovereignty, and when they gave in to the pressure in November 1940 they allowed many of the ex-consular staff to continue to operate from *"offices Néerlandais"* or under the aegis of the Swedish representation. It was a paradoxical situation. The same wish to retain some degree of sovereignty inevitably led to Vichy giving in to German pressure step by step. But at the same time, it allowed the Dutch presence in Vichy France to play a clever game by insisting that it was up to the French and not the Germans to decide how the Dutch refugees should be treated. When Vichy arrested foreign Jews, and began to deliver them to the Germans, who promptly deported most of them to Auschwitz via Drancy, they managed time and again to obtain special status for Dutch (and Belgian?) nationals, and get them out of prison, often more than once. At this time (mid-1942) crossing the Swiss border was also becoming riskier. As mass deportations of Jews from Western Europe were in full swing, the Swiss government became concerned with the increasing numbers of (Jewish) refugees seeking asylum.[92] It closed the border in August 1942, and instructed the police to arrest and return to France whomever tried to cross the border illegally. Herman and Jet had received excellent advice, to cross the border

---

92   Refugees were also trying to enter Switzerland from Germany/Austria and Italy; Estimates about the number of refugees who were arrested and returned to Vichy France vary widely (between 3000 and 25,000).

and walk as far inland as possible, and to move on to Geneva and Bern as quickly as possible. Herman's report describes at least 20 moments between leaving Breda and arriving in Bern when a single mishap could have meant disaster, incarceration, or even deportation to a death camp in Eastern Europe. There is no doubt that they were exceedingly lucky all through their two-month journey. Also beyond dispute are the many occasions where they received help from total strangers in Holland, Belgium and France in the crucial years 1942-1943. Many of those helpers remained anonymous, and many never sought or received recognition for what they did.

A documentary film, *"De Joodse Bruiloft"* (Huisman, 2018), about another Jewish couple from the Netherlands (Barend Boers and Mimi Dwinger) who successfully escaped to Spain in 1942 is informative, and it is relevant to understand the journey of Herman Stofkooper. The film includes an old interview with Sally Noach showing the prison in Lyon from which he managed to get Dutch refugees released in 1942, before they could be delivered to the Germans by Vichy France.

9.9   Elchanan Italie survives in Germany as "Johannes Bonnet"

Just like the family Klein (Ch. 7.12), Elchanan (12th February 1920), or Ernst as he was called in Holland, became part of the wartime history of the orphanage through the actions of Hijme and Emilie Stoffels (see also Ch. 10.3). He was the son of Arthur Italie, one of the four siblings of Nathan Italie, and thus Nathan's nephew. He got to know the Stoffels in early 1942 through his uncle, and he was more sensitive than Nathan at the Stoffels' insistence that he should not allow himself to be deported by the Germans. From October 1942, Elchanan was hiding in a hospital in The Hague. Around 18th March 1943, after the last razzia in Leiden, he fled from The Hague, and moved in with Stoffels. He was 23 years old at the time.

```
30. Bok,Pieter, geboren te Nijmegen, 25Jan13.            L16/68686
    arts; geb.datum gewijzigd; contact: Stoffels; niet gelegal.

31. Bonnet,Jozeph Johannes, geboren te Leiden, 25Jan14.  L16/69790
    Jood; gegevens valsch; echte naam: Italie; contact: Stoffels;
    in BR gelegaliseerd.

32.Boom,Cornelis, geboren te Apeldoorn, 1Apr12.          L16/69815
   ge illegaal werker; gegevens valsch; contact: Arthur; gelegal.
```

Figure 9.37: Entry no. 31 in the list prepared by Cor van Wijk (1946) provides the false persoonsbewijs (pb) number, the reason for issuing a false pb (*"Jood"*, Jewish), false biodata, the real name being Italie, the fact that the pb was arranged through Hijme Stoffels, and that it was "legalized" in the Civil Registry to reduce the chances that the forgery would be discovered. Entry no. 30, also arranged by Stoffels, is quite different: this pb is also a forgery, but all the data are correct except the birth date and the pb number. This pb was made to keep the person out of the age range whereby he would be drafted for forced labour in Germany (see also Ch. 10.3).

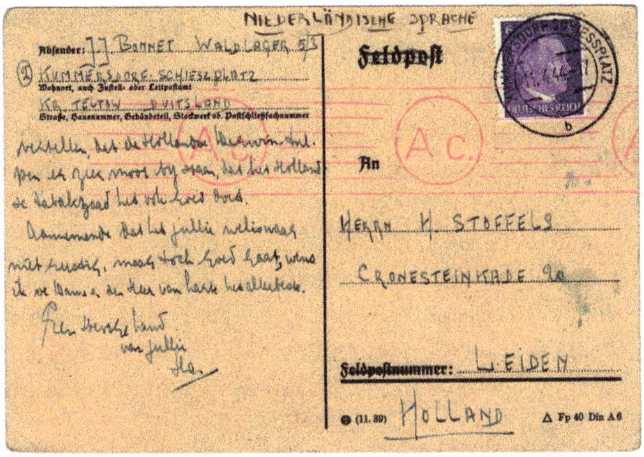

Figure 9.38: Postcard from Elchanan, writing as J.J. Bonnet, to Hijme and Emilie, 8th April 1944. He signs as "Hans" (Johannes). From the Stoffels' private archive. Private collection.

The Stoffels were also harbouring other *onderduikers* at the time (like Ingrid Klein) and the presence of Elchanan was another – risky – complication. Emilie found it difficult to oblige his request to cook kosher food, and Elchanan found it difficult to stay inside the house. On occasion he went outside without removing his *yarmulka*. Stoffels quickly arranged another hiding place for him: in a forestry

Figure 9.39: Marriage photograph of Elchanan Italie and Greet Salomons, 1947. From Stoffels photoalbum, courtesy Mrs. M. Vink. Private collection.

work camp, of all places in Germany: the *Waldlager Kummersdorf-Schieszplatz* just south of Berlin. He provided him with false identity papers in the name of Johannes Joseph Bonnet (Fig. 9.37). Bonnet was a real person, living in Oegstgeest (Leiden) and active in the local resistance, so Stoffels probably knew him. Whether Bonnet was informed that Stoffels used his identity for someone else, I don't know.

Elchanan kept Stoffels informed, sending at least one letter and a postcard (Fig. 9.38). In September 1944 he became seriously ill, and decided to return to Leiden, after obtaining a certificate from the Swedish mission in Berlin and a travel permit from the German authorities. In Leiden, Stoffels arranged for him to be hospitalized, and it seems that he remained in Leiden thereafter. A tricky situation because there were now two men called J.J. Bonnet walking around in Leiden, and the "real" Bonnet was well known in Leiden.

After liberation in May 1945, Stoffels was appointed director of the Nederlands Volks Herstel (National Rehabilitation Organization; Neij and Hueting,1988) in Leiden, which allowed him to sign the certificate which restored Elchanan to his true identity. The address on the document shows that Stoffels arranged for him to stay in the vacated building of the orphanage, around the corner.

Stoffels and van Wijk were also involved with legalizing the many false pbs they had issued, by confirming the true identities of the owners.

Elchanan married Gretha (Greet) Salomonson in 1947; a beautiful marriage photograph was included in the Stoffels' photo album (Fig. 9.39). The following year they emigrated to Palestine, where they became members of the religious kibbutz Yavne. Two years later, when the country was still in chaos following the war of independence, Hijme and Emilie went to Israel to visit all their wartime friends (Ch. 10.3).

References

Asscher-Pinkhof, Clara, 1966; *"Danseres zonder benen"* [Dancer without legs]. The Hague, Leopold, ISBN 9025800033. [This impressive autobiography has not been translated into English. She is known in the USA as Clara Pinkhof, the author of *"Star children"*, Detroit, Wayne State University Press, 1986.] See Ch. 9.3.

Beer, W. de, et al., 2015; *"Een veilig nest voor vervolgden. Verhalen over Joodse onderduikers in Rijnsburg"*. Genootschap Oud Rijnsburg. [A collection of stories about the many Jewish *onderduikers* (including Sara Philipson and Rita Klein) who found shelter in this small strictly reformed Christian village in the Leiden area. The stories are included as they were told, without being checked against other sources or documents.]

Boomgaard, Petra van den, 2019; *"Voor de nazi's geen Jood"*. Hilversum, Verbum, ISBN 9789493028043. [With English summary at the back; *"How more than 2500 Jews were able to escape deportation by evading racial regulations"*; certainly the most comprehensive study to date.]

Hodge, Deborah, 2012; *"Rescuing the children: The story of the Kindertransport"*. Toronto, Tundra Books, ISBN 9781770492561. [Contains a chapter on the SS *Bodegraven*.]

Huisman, Annet (dir.), 2018; *"De Joodse Bruiloft"*. Documentary film. Omrop Fryslân. [After the passing of Barend Boers and Mimi Dwinger, their three children opened a suitcase full of documents about their parents' escape from Holland through Vichy France and over the Pyrenees in 1942. The parents had never discussed this even with their children. In 2017, the children followed the route of their parents as closely as possible, while the documentary adds historical context.

Kasteleyn, L.P., unpublished A; *"Notities van gesprekken met Mimi de Wind-Weiman"*. Not available to the author in written form; B; *"Notities van gesprekken met Piet de Vries"*. Included in Dossier Piet de Vries. C; *"Brieven van Hans Kloosterman"*. Included in Dossier Hans Kloosterman.

Keesing, Miriam, 2013; *"Truus Wijsmuller-Meijer, a forgotten heroine"*. In: *"Celebrating 75 years of Kindertransport"*, pp. 32-33. https://www.dokin.nl/publications/celebrating-75-years-of-kindertransport-truus-wijmuller-a-forgotten-heroine/.

Koreman, Megan, 2016; *"Gewone helden. De Dutch-Paris ontsnappingslijn 1942-1945"*. Amsterdam, Boom, ISBN 9789058755568 (paperback). See also Plantinga, 1998.

Koreman, Megan, 2018; *"The escape line: How the ordinary heroes of Dutch-Paris resisted the Nazi occupation of Western Europe"*. New York, Oxford University Press, ISBN 9780190662271 (hardcover)/|9789461279606 (e-book).

Lang, Wally de, 2021; *"De razzia's van 22 en 23 februari 1941 in Amsterdam. Het lot van 389 Joodse mannen"*. Amsterdam, Uitgeverij Atlas Contact, ISBN 9789045042749. [This first comprehensive account of the razzias which preceded the February Strike, and the fate of the deportees to Buchenwald and Mauthausen was published just before the present book went to press.]

Lanzmann, Claude (dir.), 1997; *"Un vivant qui passe"* [A visitor from the living]. [A 65-minute documentary based on his interview with Maurice Rossel, the Swiss representative of the International Red Cross who visited Theresienstadt on 23rd June 1944, and who allowed himself to be utterly hoodwinked by the Nazis. Also filed as USHMM Film 2891.]

Maor, Roni, 2011; *"The finger in the dyke: The survival story of a Jewish child in Holland during the Holocaust"*. [The autobiography of Aron Wolff, in Hebrew; www.rimonim-publishing.com, 115 pp.] See also the private report by van Straten, 1992.

Melkman-de Paauw, Fré, 2002; *"Hoe het verder gaat weet niemand. Naoorlogse brieven uit Amstdam naar Palestina"*. Commentaries by J. and D. Michman. Amsterdam, Contact, ISBN 9025419626. [Relevant for the reuniting of *onderduik* children with surviving parents, and the story of Aron Wolff, Ch. 9.4.]

Michman, Jozeph & Bert Jan Flim (eds), 2004; *"The encyclopaedia of the righteous among the nations: Rescuers of Jew during the Holocaust. Volume: The Netherlands"*. Jerusalem, Yad Vashem.

Michman, Jozeph, Hartog Beem & Dan Michman, 1999; *"Pinkas. Geschiedenis van de joodse gemeenschap in Nederland"*. Incorporating research by Victor Brilleman. Amsterdam, Uitgeverij Contact & NIK, ISBN 9025495133. [The original text of this comprehensive history of the Jews in the Netherlands is also available in Hebrew, Yad Vashem, Holocaust Martyrs' and Heroes Remembrance Authority, Jerusalem, 1985.]

Moore, Bob, 2010; *"Survivors: Jewish self-help and rescue in Nazi-occupied Western Europe"*. Oxford, Oxford University Press, ISBN 9780199208234.

Neij, R. and E.V. Hueting, 1988; *"Nederlands Volksherstel 1944-1947. Een omstreden hulporganisatie in herrijzend Nederland"*. Culemborg, Lemma. ISBN9051890125

Pinkhof, Mirjam, 1998; *"De jeugdalijah van het Paviljoen Loosdrechtse Rade. 1939-1945"*. Historische Reeks Loosdrecht #4. Hilversum, Verloren. [A book (in Dutch) about the Palestine Pioneers in Loosdrecht, and the activities of the Westerweel resistance group; contains biographies of the resident children, mostly German and Polish refugees, as well as local farmers who sheltered them from the Germans. The book contains many photographs, with individuals identified, and is relevant for the story of Lodi Cohen (Ch. 9.7). More information is available in the Ghetto Fighters' House museum in Israel, Beit Lohamei Hagettaot North of Haifa.] See also Schippers, 2015, and van der Straaten, 1998. For an interview (1988) with Pinkhof by Ellen Land, see www.humboldt.edu/rescuers/book/Pinkhof/mpstory1.html.

Plantinga, Sierk, 1998; *"Joseph Willem Kolkman (1896-1944) en de Engelandvaarders: De hulp aan Nederlandse vluchtelingen in Vichy-Frankrijk"*. In: Aalders, G. (ed.), 1998; *"Oorlogsdocumentatie '40-'45*. Zutphen, Walburg Pers. pp. 10-36. [No footnotes; the annotated version is available in NIOD, or directly from the author of the article.]

Rens, H.A.V. van, 2013; *"Vervolgd in Limburg. Joden en Sinti in Nederlands-Limburg tijdens de Tweede Wereldoorlog"*. Maaslandse Monografieen 76. Hilversum, Verloren, ISBN 9789087043537.

Schippers, Hans L., 2015; *"De Westerweelgroep en de Palestinapioniers. Non-conformistisch verzet in de Tweede Wereldoorlog"*. Hilversum, Verloren, ISBN 9789087044978. *English edition:* Hans Schippers, 2019; *"Westerweel Group: Non-conformist resistance against Nazi Germany; A joint rescue effort of Dutch idealists and Dutch-German zionists"*. De Gruyter Oldenbourg: New perspectives on modern Jewish history, V.11; ISBN 9783110580006.

Siegel, Paul, 2001; *"Locomotieven trekken wagons, 1933-1945"*. Utrecht, Van Gruting, ISBN 9789075879100. The English translation (Siegel, Paul, 2005; *"Engines pull wagons: A personal story"*. Trans. by Gilda Gordon. Amsterdam, Olive Press, ISBN 9077787011/9789077787014) was not used in preparing this book.

Stoffels, H. & E. Stoffels-van Brussel, 1967; *"Unpublished"*, 22nd November. [A list of (some of) their activities in support of Jewish citizens of Leiden from February 1942, such as arranging *onderduik* addresses, false papers, etc. The list was written at the request of Elchanan Italie, in support of a proposal by him and the family Philipson-Armon to award the Yad Vashem award to Stoffels and his wife.

Straaten, Frans van der, 1998; *"Palestina-Pioniers in Nederland: herinneringen en belevenissen aan/van gedurende de oorlogsjaren 1939-1945: Om nooit te vergeten"*. Capelle a/d IJssel, MES Grafische Bedrijven, ISBN 9076061130. [This book contains a wealth of information, as well as listings of the refugees in the various Hachsharah institutions, but it has had limited circulation. One copy is available in the Joods Historisch Museum, Amsterdam, and another in the Koninklijke Bibliotheek in The Hague.] See also Pinkhof, 1998

Straten, J.W. van, 1992; *"Herinneringen aan de oorlog van de verzetsman J.W. van Straten over de jaren 1940-1945"*. 5 volumes. [An incomplete photocopy of parts II and III (1942-1944) is in the library of the Joods Historisch Museum, Amsterdam, catalog D7608. The author had access to the original report, courtesy Mr. B. van Straten.]

Sturhoofd, Pamela & Jessica van Tijn (dirs), 2020; *"De kinderen van Truus"* [The children of Truus Wijsmuller]. Documentary film. Amsterdam, Special Eyes Co. [Contains the testimony of Helga Gottschalk.] An English version is expected to be released on Netflix in June 2021. See https://www.truus-children.com/ or www.facebook.com/truuschildren. For more information: info@special-eyes.nl.

Sykes, Christopher, 1965; *"Cross roads to Israel: Palestine from Balfour to Bevin"*. London, Collins (also New English Library, Indiana University Press and others), ISBN 0253201659/9780253201652. [A fascinating description, from the British perspective, of the final stages of the British Mandate in Palestine.]

Vishniac, Roman, 1983; *"A vanished world"*. New York, Farrar, Straus & Giroux.

Wasserstein, Bernard, 2014; *"The ambiguity of virtue: Gertrude van Tijn and the fate of the Dutch Jews"*. Cambridge, MA, Harvard University Press, ISBN 9780674281387. [An earlier version of this book was published in Dutch in 2013: *"Gertrude van Tijn en het lot van de Nederlandse Joden"*, Amsterdam, Nieuw Amsterdam, ISBN 9789046814352.]

Wijsmuller-Meijer, Truus, 1961; *"Geen tijd voor tranen"*. Amsterdam, Querido, also Salamander. [Autobiography, recorded by L.G. Vrooland. Out of print, but text is available on the site of the Historische Vereniging Alkmaar.]

Zegveld, W.F. van, 1993; *"Joods Wees- en Doorgangshuis Leiden, bewoners 1890-1951"*. Originally in: *"De Joden van Leiden"*. Unpublished; 4 volumes. [Several copies were made, available (i.a.) at Erfgoed Leiden (ELO) and the Joods Historisch Museum, Amsterdam. The results of his painstaking research have served as a basis for subsequent investigations. Note that his report is an important source of information on children and staff in the Leiden orphanage who are not included in this book because they had left before the move to the new building in 1929, as well as Jewish citizens of the Leiden region who were not connected to the orphanage.]

10 After the war

Abstract

Upon liberation in May 1945, the priority for the very few Jewish survivors was to find out what had happened to their family and friends and those who did not return. For many, it took several years before they received official confirmation that they had to be assumed dead, that they had probably been murdered at a certain camp or place, on an assumed date. Many distressing stories are documented in the Red Cross War Archive. Hijme and Emilie Stoffels were honoured by the Yad Vashem award in 1968, Wim and Dien van Straten in 1971. So were many others who tried to save people from persecution and murder. The three Germans who were most directly involved with the liquidation of the orphanage served long prison terms after commuted death sentences. The commandant of Westerbork, Gemmeker, came off very lightly; he served less than six years. Of the three Dutch policemen who carried the heaviest responsibility for arresting Jews in Leiden and sending them to their death, Adrianus Biesheuvel served nine years in prison. De Groot was shot dead by the Dutch resistance in 1944. Their boss, Steven van Musscher, escaped to Germany and was never tried.

Keywords: Red Cross War Archive, displaced and missing persons, orphans, half-orphans, custody issues, Yad Vashem, Righteous among the Nations, post-war tribunals, Dutch police, collaboration, resistance

There were many regions and cities in Europe which were devastated by the war, including of course in Germany itself. The western part of the Netherlands, densely populated and the economic heartland with the cities of Amsterdam, The Hague, Rotterdam and Utrecht, was in particularly bad shape in May 1945. Following the invasion in Normandy on 6th June 1944, and the difficult breakout from the bridgeheads later that month, the Allies[1] made surprisingly rapid progress. Paris was liberated on 25th August 1944, Brussels on 4th September, a mere eleven and twelve and a half weeks after the landings in Normandy. Hope ran high in the Netherlands that the war would be over before Christmas 1944. But the northward

---

1   That is: the Western Allies, not to forget the advances made, at terrible cost, by the Soviet armies.

Focke, Jaap W., *Machseh Lajesoumim: A Jewish Orphanage in the City of Leiden, 1890-1943*.
Taylor & Francis Group, 2021
DOI: 10.5117/9789463726955_CH10

advance of the allies in September 1944 (Operation Market Garden), from Belgium into Holland across three rivers and several canals got stuck at Arnhem at the bridge across the Rhine. Thereafter, the allies pushed due east from liberated France and Belgium, into the industrial part of Germany and towards Berlin. The Netherlands north of the rivers entered a long period of eight months, with exceptionally cold conditions, serious shortages of food and fuel and widespread famine in the urban areas. German terror persisted and got worse. On 1st and 2nd October 1944 the German army took revenge for an attack on a car with Wehrmacht officers in the small village of Putten by executing seven people, burning houses, and carrying off 659 men and boys, almost the entire male population of Putten of sixteen years and older, to the Amersfoort concentration camp. From there, 601 were deported to concentration camps in Germany; 552 were killed by attrition. Hardly a day passed[2] without people being executed or just shot dead somewhere in the occupied part of the Netherlands, often in groups of 5 to 20, as reprisals for anti-German activity. On 8th March 1945 the Germans took revenge for an attack on an SD car which (unknown to the attackers) carried Hanns Albin Rauter, the chief of all German (and de facto Dutch) police forces in the Netherlands, who was injured. In total, the Germans executed 278 people that day: 177 men near the site of the attack, and 161 in different groups[3] throughout the country. Much of the infrastructure was destroyed, and whatever could be dismantled was carried off to Germany. Holland was liberated after the fall of Berlin (2nd May) and the surrender of the remaining German armies in Holland, Denmark and north-east Germany on 4th/5th May 1945. It took some fifteen years and significant assistance from the US Marshall Plan before it was to some degree back on its feet.

It is therefore not altogether surprising that during the first ten to fifteen years after 1945 the country was almost exclusively focused on the personal experiences of each individual, restoring one's livelihood, and economic recovery, with little attention (at least by today's standards) to the travails of the survivors of the death camps, or those coming back from concentration camps, prisons, or military operations. Interest in the war, or at least the willingness to talk about it, was low.

Ian Buruma, the author of *"Year zero: A history of 1945"* (2013), describes his father's post-war experiences, back in his fraternity at the University of Utrecht in September 1945:

> *There may have been Jewish students among [us] who had been hiding for years under the floorboards of houses belonging to brave gentiles prepared to risk their necks. But my father does not remember anyone being especially bothered about*

---

2   See list at https://nl.wikipedia.org/wiki/, search for: Originele_Lijst_van_geëxecuteerden_1945.
3   Ibidem, or search for *"aanslag Rauter"*.

such things; no one was interested in personal stories, Jewish or otherwise; they all
had personal stories, often unpleasant.

For liberated Europe, the year 1945 was the start of a new era amidst chaos and
confusion and dominated by *"trauma, revenge, regrets, the desire to forget, the need*
to remember" (ibidem: quote by D. Sassoon). People wanted to get back to normal, to
how it was before the war. But the world had changed and did not allow it, resulting
in new conflicts such as colonial wars or internal strife.

There was little coordinated effort from the Dutch government to go out and
bring the survivors home in 1944-1945. Jules Schelvis, one of the eighteen Dutch
survivors of Sobibor, describes how he got home via Vaihingen, by train and truck,
sleeping in cold cloister corridors, his elation standing on Dutch soil again at the
border, and the terrible anti-climax when he finally reached Amsterdam (Schelvis,
2007a). Non-Jewish surviving victims of the Nazis were not treated any better.
Pim Boellaard, an early resistance fighter who was caught and who survived
Natzweiler (Struthof)[4] and Dachau, also managed to get back to Holland on his
own. But he was a much stronger person than many of his fellow survivors, some
of whom could hardly stand on their feet. When he realized that the government
was making little effort to bring the remaining Dutch prisoners back from Dachau,
he organized his own private car column to bring them home (with the support of
Prince Bernhard) (Withuis, 2013). It has been considered a "scandal" (Bossenbroek,
2001, p. 112), given the fact that Belgian as well as French officers arrived at Dachau
within days of its liberation on 29th April 1945 to organize repatriation of their
countrymen. In 2000 the Dutch government apologized for the "cold reception"
for the survivors. But the massive "SOTO" study which had been commissioned
(ibidem) suggests that the extremely negative view about the post-war reception
requires some qualification. Views expressed by individual stories are not always
supported by archival documentation, and the notion that the Dutch government
displayed a callous disinterest is not sustained, even if there were serious lapses in
the organization. Bossenbroek and others also point out that the post-war society
cannot be judged against norms and standard of the 1980s, when Holland had
become a welfare state with government being held responsible for every "sorrow
and misery" of its citizens. The problems facing the returning survivors were seen
at the time as facing the society as a whole, while caring for individuals was left – as

---

4   Natzweiler or Strutthof, in the French Alsace (not to be confused with Stuthoff, near Danzig, where
Paula Jacobsohn was killed), was a *Nacht und Nebel* camp, where the Nazis kept resistance fighters whom
they wanted to disappear without trace. Boellaard found conditions in Natzweiler to be much worse than
in Dachau.

it was before the war – to each of the "pillars" or categories[5] involved. But the Jewish community which could have taken care of the few thousand survivors had been almost completely wiped out, while the government did not wish to single them out or discriminate between Jews and other victims of the war. It is easy to understand the disappointment, frustration, anger and bitterness of survivors who had to fight to retrieve their stolen property or the house they lived in before deportation, who were presented with outstanding property – and council tax bills for periods *after* their deportation or charged for assistance received during their escape.

Another, deeper problem facing the Jewish survivors was that they were considered *"the lucky ones"* who had little reason to complain. The wartime experiences were expected to wear off with time. Most people, initially including many survivors themselves, did not realize how intensely the trauma of the Holocaust and having lost entire families was going to affect them, and even their post-war children, in later years. Psychiatrists were among the first to warn that they needed help, and recognition, coining the concept of the concentration camp syndrome (or KZ syndrome, on account of the German term *Konzentrationslager*), which eventually also covered survivors who had not gone through the camps and their descendants. A few years after liberation, many Jewish survivors decided to leave Holland, indeed Europe, for good. They were not alone: between 1947 and 1970 half a million[6] Dutchmen (some 5% of the population) left Europe, motivated by economic duress or fear for a third world war, and encouraged by the Dutch government, to countries like the USA and Canada, South Africa, or Australia and New Zealand. For the few Jewish survivors, Israel was of course also an important destination. Emigration skyrocketed in 1948/1949.

Seminal books on the Holocaust in Holland were first published by Herzberg (1985), in 1950, and Presser, in 1965. But it was really Lou de Jong and his series *"De Bezetting"* (The Occupation) on television, then a brand-new medium, that people were confronted with the occupation outside their own immediate sphere of experience. The 21-part series, which ran from 1960 to 1965, attracted a very large audience and had a mesmerizing effect on the Dutch, who, for the first time, were presented with a coherent view of what really happened between 1940 and 1945, including, of course, the Holocaust (or Shoah). At the same time, the trial of Adolf Eichmann in Jerusalem (1961) opened the eyes of the world for the enormity of the Shoah. It was also during these years that the first post-war generation, including the present author, was confronted with the history of the war.

---

5   SOTO investigated Jews, Roma and Sinti, political prisoners, resistance fighters, POWs, workers returning from forced labour, military personnel and civilians repatriated from Indonesia (the former Dutch East Indies).

6   Government data. Not including some 200,000 people who emigrated to countries within Europe.

But, back in 1945, Jewish survivors were generally focused on one question only: *Where are our children, our parents, grandparents, uncles, nephews, cousins, friends, neighbours?*

10.1 Where are they? The intolerable uncertainty

"Upon liberation in May 1945, frenzied crowds were celebrating in the streets for months." Many photos and film fragments exist to support this statement.[7] But it did not apply to the few Dutch Jews who had returned from the camps, or those who had surfaced from *onderduik*. Rather, they were glued to a radio, or visiting Red Cross offices, to find out where their family member and friends were. Weekly radio broadcasts announced only the few people who were confirmed to be still alive. But there was, in general, no news about those – the overwhelming majority of deportees – who had *not* returned. It is difficult today to understand that many people still had no confirmation about the fate of their loved ones, years after the war. But the chaos in Europe was enormous in 1945, with millions of displaced persons, refugees, survivors, parents looking in vain for their children, and children who were never reunited with their parents or family, Jewish and gentiles, victors and foes. On the cover photo of Ian Buruma's book (2013) about the year 1945, a woman shows a photograph of (presumably) her son to laughing soldiers returning from the war on the remote chance that someone may recognize him and tell her what happened to him.

Legal considerations also caused delays before official statements could be issued about Jewish victims who had simply vanished from the face of the earth without leaving remains or records. For family members of persons who never returned from deportation it was of the utmost importance to receive some evidence-based confirmation of their death, and where and when they were killed, if only to relieve them from the uncertainty and allow them to deal with the loss.

Clara Adler-Braun, the mother of Lotte and Henny (Ch. 5.7), had sent letters from the USA to Leiden during the war, via the Red Cross, who probably forwarded them to the Joodse Raad until it stopped operating in 1943. As soon as she heard about the German surrender in Holland on 5th May 1945, she sent a letter to the Red Cross (Fig. 10.1), asking how she could get in touch with Lotte and Henny. In her letter (9th May 1945) Clara writes that she managed to get US entry visas for the girls in 1941, when it was too late to get them over. It is the first document of many[8] spanning the period May 1945 to 1959, in which Clara, and then her son Kurt, try to establish

---

7   From the (otherwise excellent) young persons' TV series *"13 in de oorlog"* (2009).

8   Dossier.

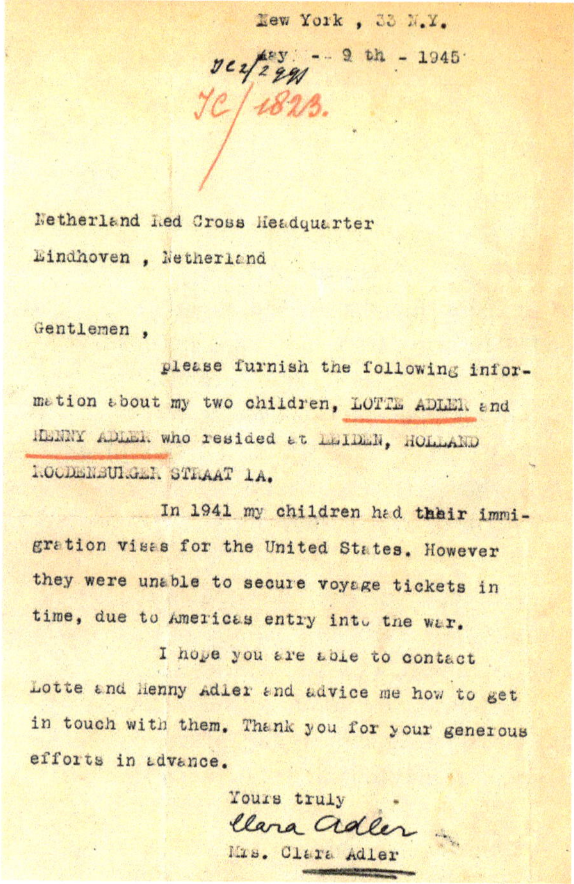

New York , 33 N.Y.

May - 9 th - 1945

JC/2291

JC/1823.

Netherland Red Cross Headquarter

Eindhoven , Netherland

Gentlemen ,

please furnish the following infor-
mation about my two children, LOTTE ADLER and
HENNY ADLER who resided at LEIDEN, HOLLAND
ROODENBURGER STRAAT 1A.

In 1941 my children had their immigration visas for the United States. However
they were unable to secure voyage tickets in
time, due to Americas entry into the war.

I hope you are able to contact
Lotte and Henny Adler and advice me how to get
in touch with them. Thank you for your generous
efforts in advance.

Yours truly

Clara Adler

Mrs. Clara Adler

Figure 10.1: Four days after the German surrender in the Netherlands, Clara Adler wrote to the Red Cross to find out the whereabouts of Lotte and Henny. Red Cross Archives, 2017.

what had happened to Lotte and Henny.

On 18th November 1945 it is still assumed that Lotte was deported to Auschwitz. On 30th November 1946, the Red Cross bureau in Westerbork reports to The Hague that she was deported *"to the East"* on 23rd March 1943, but that at this time (one and a half years after the war!) *"no further information on her is available"*. The Joint Distribution Committee requests the Red Cross on 18th May 1949 to *"expedite sending back the information requests [...] because family oversees are anxiously waiting for information"*. On 15th August 1949, for the first time, a formal declaration is issued (Fig. 10.2) by the Red Cross about Lotte Adler:

[She] *arrived in Westerbork on 19th March 1943, [and] was deported to Sobibor on 23rd March 1943. Taking into account the witness accounts by Sara Engel, Chaim Engel, and Ursula Stern, who survived deportation out of the more than 33,000 persons deported to this camp from Westerbork, that practically all deported people were killed by gas asphyxiation immediately upon arrival, [...] she must be assumed to have died on or around the 26th of March 1943.*

On 14th November 1957 the Red Cross Bureau in Germany issued a *"certificate of incarceration"* for Lotte to government officials in Wiesbaden, West Germany, but making the point that the document could not be used as a death certificate, and no such certificate was presented to the officials. The Red Cross in The Hague then confirms her death to the *Ambtsgericht* in Frankfurt. On 5th January 1959, a notary public in California writes a letter on behalf of Kurt Adler, asking for copies of the relevant documents and certificates. He writes about Kurt's sisters Lotte and Henny *"who were in hiding"*. The letter shows how little even close relatives know at

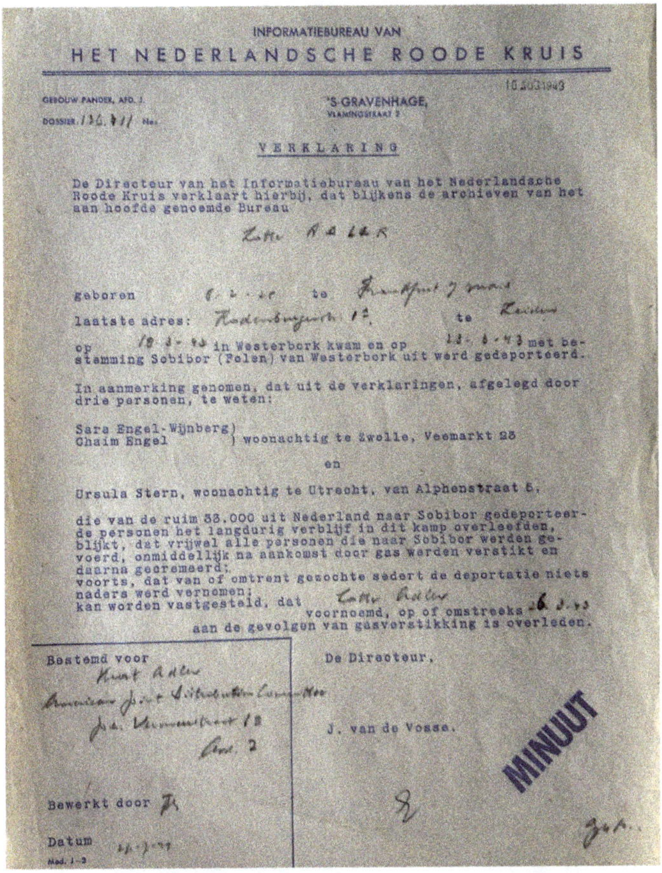

INFORMATIEBUREAU VAN

HET NEDERLANDSCHE ROODE KRUIS

GEBOUW PANDER, AFD. J. 'S-GRAVENHAGE, VLAMINGSTRAAT 2

DOSSIER 136.711 No.

VERKLARING

De Directeur van het Informatiebureau van het Nederlandsche Roode Kruis verklaart hierbij, dat blijkens de archieven van het aan hoofde genoemde Bureau

Lotte ADLER

geboren ... te Frankfurt a/Main

laatste adres: ... te ...

op ... in Westerbork kwam en op ... met bestemming Sobibor (Polen) van Westerbork uit werd gedeporteerd.

In aanmerking genomen, dat uit de verklaringen, afgelegd door drie personen, te weten:

Sara Engel-Wijnberg)
Chaim Engel) woonachtig te Zwolle, Veemarkt 23

en

Ursula Stern, woonachtig te Utrecht, van Alphenstraat 5,

die van de ruim 33.000 uit Nederland naar Sobibor gedeporteerde personen het langdurig verblijf in dit kamp overleefden, blijkt, dat vrijwel alle personen die naar Sobibor werden gevoerd, onmiddellijk na aankomst door gas werden verstikt en daarna gecremeerd;
voorts, dat van of omtrent gezochte sedert de deportatie niets naders werd vernomen;
kan worden vastgesteld, dat Lotte Adler voornoemd, op of omstreeks ... aan de gevolgen van gasverstikking is overleden.

Bestemd voor
Kurt Adler
American Joint Distribution Committee

De Directeur,

J. van de Vosse.

MINUUT

Bewerkt door

Datum

Mod. J-3

Figure 10.2: The formal death certificate for Lotte Adler, including the evidence that there was no doubt about her fate. Issued on 15th August 1949 and referring to three witness accounts. Courtesy Red Cross, The Hague, 2017. For documents not included in the book, see the Lotte & Henny Adler dossier.

that time about what really happened between 1940 and 1943. With respect to the millions of victims who were murdered in the Holocaust by premeditated plan, organized and executed as if it were an industrial enterprise, it is probably fair to say that it took 15 to 20 years to get enough facts together, and the documentary evidence, to document what had happened, and how it was done.

It took decades more to digest these facts and develop a comprehensive view of the enormity of the Holocaust; not to mention attempts to *understand* it. That process has not been concluded to this day.

10.2 Reunited, but without the father

There were 4138 children in *onderduik* at the end of the war (i.e. September 1944 for the southern provinces of Brabant and Limburg, May 1945 for the rest of the country), of which 3458 were Jewish (Michman et al., 1999, p. 209). Of those, 1417 children could be reunited with one or both parents, including Kurt and Helga Gottschalk, Aron Wolff, the five children Philipson (Fig. 10.3), the four children Klein (Fig. 10.4) and the children of Rebecca Franschman (the mother of Piet de Vries) and Barend Springer, for whom Stoffels had arranged *onderduik*.

It would seem totally self-evident today that all Jewish children who had one or two parents returning from the camps (preciously few in any case), or surfacing from *onderduik*, would be reunited with them at the earliest opportunity. And indeed, they all were reunited, without exception, but not without problems, fights, and sadness. Some young children had become strongly attached to their foster parents, while others never did. There were good and less-good foster parents, and the motivation of foster parents offering shelter to Jewish children varied. Aron Wolff (in 2017) could still perform the rituals which he learned when hiding (temporarily) with a Reformed Protestant family in Apeldoorn (Ch. 9.4); but it may have improved his safety, and the family as far as Ronnie remembers did not try to convert him. But some other Christian *onderduik* parents did. Some *onderduik* foster parents even argued, during the war when they probably still expected most parents to return

Figure 10.3: Jet Philipson-Simons with her children shortly before their emigration to Palestine, 1947. From left: Sara (19th September 1940), Elias (6th January 1937-6th March 2016), Jet (20th March 1911-2nd June 1992), Menachem (13th October 1942), Rika (4th November 1935), and Jacob (9th June 1938). From the Stoffels photo album. Private collection.

Figure 10.4: Rosa Klein-Mendel with her children, Rita, Ingrid and Ben, 1947. They moved to Florida, USA, in 1952. From the Stoffels' photo album. Private collection.

eventually, that they should not have to return the children to their parents. But ultimately all returning parents were reunited with surviving children.

The situation around the children who survived the war while their parents did not, the real orphans, was more complex, and subject to decisions by courts. Some people argued that the children should be returned to the Jewish community, small as it had become, even if the child had become fully integrated in their non-Jewish *onderduik* family. Others argued that the court should only consider what it believed to be the best interest of the child. Many are the heart-breaking stories where the foster parents did not want to let their *onderduik* child go, or the child did not want to be forcefully sent to a surviving family member they did not know.

Many children continued to visit their foster parents for many years even from Israel or the USA, including Aron Wolff and the children Klein and Philipson.

Other children experienced *onderduik* as a very difficult period. For many years Merlyn Frank has come to the memorial service at Leiden orphanage to talk to the students from the Erasmus College. She was only three years old when she was rescued from the train to Westerbork. She tells them how she was unable to show affection for her foster mother because she could not give up looking for her own mother, ever. Frank's book *"Koosje"* (1998) is not only a monument to her mother, who had the terrible courage to give her and her baby brother away to total strangers[9] in

---

9   Members of the Utrecht student group who were present on the platform of the Utrecht railway station, where the train stopped on the way to Westerbork. There were no guards, and the family stood close to the doors.

Figure 10.5: Emilie and Hijme, hitchhiking through Israel, 1949. Private collection.

a split-second decision, but probably also Merlyn's way of finally having found her.

Of those children in the Leiden orphanage who were still very young in 1943, only Mindel Färber survived the war. The other children who survived were old enough in 1945 to make their own decisions, such as Hans Kloosterman, who was thirteen in May 1940, but eighteen in May 1945. But even in his case, the reunion with his father following his release from Westerbork and the post-war period were far from easy. Hans went to Australia; as did Bram Degen. Elchanan Italie and his wife, Greet, and Jet Philipson and her children (Fig. 10.3) left for Israel. Rosie Klein and her children (Emilie's neighbours in 1941, Fig. 10.4) settled in Miami, Florida. Ben and Gerda Meijer, the other neighbours of Emilie *"from the Mariënpoelstraat"*[10] started a successful dairy farm in Beit Yitzhak, Israel (Kopuit, 1974).

Hijme and Emilie visited the families Italie, Philipson and Meijer in Israel in 1949, and left a report and photographs (Fig. 10.5) of their trip. The country was still in turmoil, having barely escaped being destroyed by four invading armies. Conditions were visibly very poor, with no adequate housing, no services, no public transport. Hijme writes that it took them a day to realize that the only way for them to move around was to do what everybody else was doing: stand along the road with their suitcase and hitch-hike (Fig. 10.5). It was a new experience for Hijme, who drove around Europe in his own car before the war.

10.3   Recognition for the righteous

Yad Vashem was created by the Israeli parliament in 1953. Its mission included *"paying tribute to the Righteous Among the Nations who risked themselves to save Jews during the Holocaust"*. During the first ten years, with budgetary and organizational

10   There were three families Meijer in Leiden, all originally cattle merchants from the village of Vlagtwedde, and all three had a son called Benjamin of about the same age.

Figure 10.6: Tree-planting ceremony at Yad Vashem for Hijme and Emilie Stoffels, 7th May 1968. In white shirt: Elchanan Italie; behind him with white headscarf: his wife, Greet. Right: The trees of Truus Wijsmuller (centre, in front) and Hijme and Emilie (behind, close to the low wall) in 2017. Photos from Stoffels' album, private collection

constraints, attention focused on data gathering, research, amassing the evidence, and – above all – recording the names of the victims (see Epilogue). The Yad Vashem website, describing the development of the "Righteous" programme,[11] mentions that

> the need to ceremoniously honour rescuers was raised again and again by survivors.
> They had not forgotten those who stood by their side during the Holocaust, main-
> tained contact with their rescuers after the war, sent them packages and money,
> invited them to come to Israel, and wrote to Israeli leaders and to Yad Vashem
> requesting to pay tribute to those that had saved their lives.

In 1962 the first trees were planted, and in 1963 the *Commission for the Designation of the Righteous* was inaugurated. From the beginning, the need for a rigorous process, based on agreed guidelines and criteria, was recognized, and the commission was staffed accordingly, to include senior members of the judiciary.

It did not take long for the families Italie, Philipson and Klein to start the procedure for Hijme and Emilie Stoffels. Elchanan Italie (Ch. 9.9) wrote to Hijme (probably in early 1966) for help in getting the necessary documentation together. Hijme and Emilie rarely talked about what they did during the war (Ab van Brussel, personal communication), and to the best of my knowledge never sought public or private recognition for their actions. Responding to Elchanan's request, Emilie wrote

11   See www.yadvashem.org/yv/en/exhibitions/righteous/milestone03.asp.

a shortlist of names, and Hijme put together a typed summary. On 7th May 1968 Hijme and Emilie were honoured at Yad Vashem. A tree was planted along the Lane of the Righteous that same day (Fig. 10.6).

Hijme's summary (Stoffels & Stoffels-van Brussel, 1967) is a rather modest account of their activities. The recovery of their private archive in 2004 revealed that Stoffels did much more during the war than what he wrote down in 1966. He provided new identities and papers to many people (Fig. 10.7), such as Sara Bromet, who received a *"new pb to replace her J-stamped original"* (lower part of Fig. 10.7). He added by hand the number of the counterfeit new pb: 06951. Sara's original pb (no. 06009 with J-stamp and *Sperre*) is shown in Figure 6.2.[12] Below "Bromet" are listed Leendert van den Heuvel and Tine Heskes, the new identities of the parents of Donald de Marcas (Ch. 7.3). The cases of Hugo van de Wal (the son of Inspector van de Wal, one of Stoffels' "good" contacts in the Leiden police force [see the first line on Fig. 10.7]) and the two other boys, Johannes and Willem Arie, are quite different: they all received new but false pbs, identical in every detail to the old ones, except their birth year, which was changed to make them one or two years *younger*, probably to extend their status as students. On the other hand, the birth years of Koumans, Snellen and van Deenen (Fig. 10.7) were changed to make them a few years *older*, to prevent them being arrested and sent to Germany to do forced labour (*Arbeitseinsatz*). The Germans called up men based on their age. Hijme also made a false pb for himself, indicating he was five years older than he actually was.

It was virtually impossible to produce a perfect counterfeit Dutch pb; it contained too many sophisticated security elements (Ch. 6.2). But Stoffels had access to blank originals thanks to two contacts at the Leiden Civil Registry: Cor van Wijk and Kees Montanus. They were also able to make changes in the registries to make sure there were no discrepancies between the forged document and the records in the Town Hall. But duplicates, including a photograph, signature and fingerprint, were also stored by the National Registry, in The Hague at the *Villa Kleykamp* and out of reach of the resistance, so dangers remained. The records in the *Villa Kleykamp* were partially destroyed during a precision bombing by the Royal Air Force on 11th April 1944. Hijme had a list of names which could be used for falsifications safely after the bombardment, but for many people it was too late.

On one of the work notes (Fig. 10.8), Hijme replies to Bep Bedak (later Bep Schaap), discussing with her details of counterfeit *persoonsbewijzen* in the making, using code numbers to indicate who the receiver is, and advising her to *"use a real Leiden*

---

12   Sara did not eventually need the false pb: she escaped deportation by her marriage to a non-Jewish partner. But that escape route was not yet known to exist at the time when Stoffels provided her with a new identity.

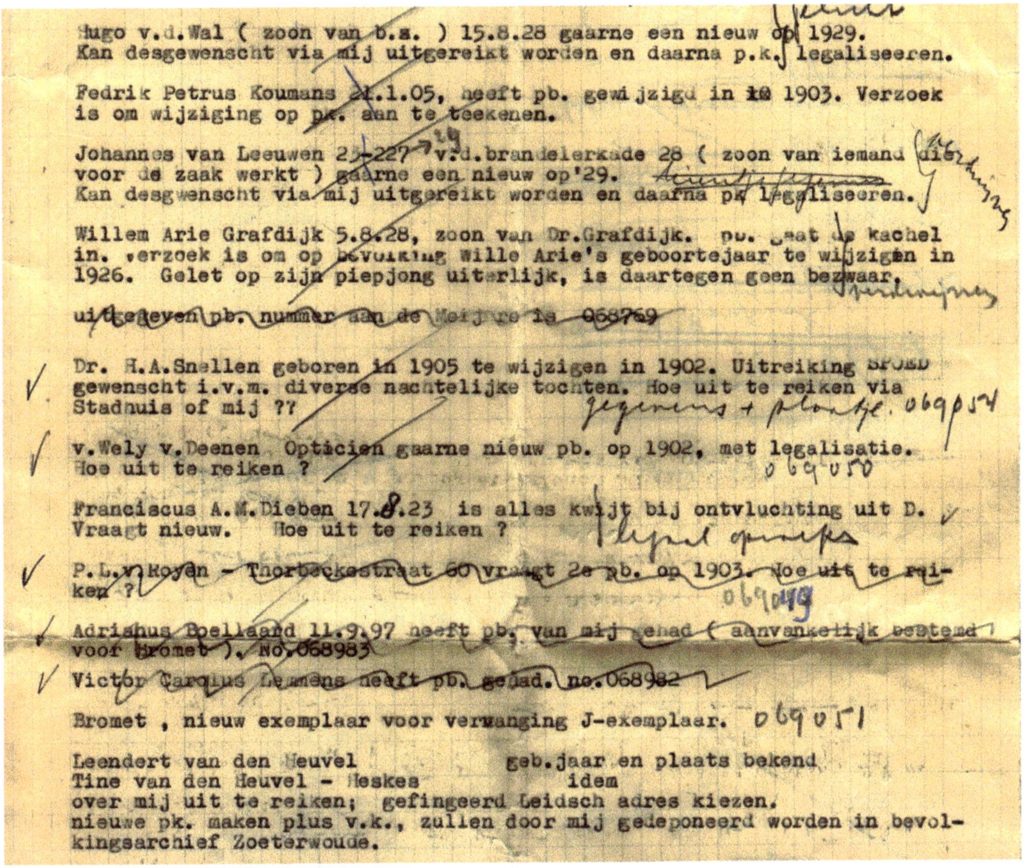

Hugo v.d.Wal (zoon van b.s.) 15.8.28 gaarne een nieuw op 1929.
Kan desgewenscht via mij uitgereikt worden en daarna p.k. legaliseeren.

Fedrik Petrus Koumans 21.1.05, heeft pb. gewijzigd in 1903. Verzoek is om wijziging op pk. aan te teekenen.

Johannes van Leeuwen 2?-227 v.d.brandelerkade 28 (zoon van iemand die voor de zaak werkt) gaarne een nieuw op'29.
Kan desgwenscht via mij uitgereikt worden en daarna pk legaliseeren.

Willem Arie Grafdijk 5.8.28, zoon van Dr.Grafdijk. pb. gaat de kachel in. verzoek is om op bevolking Wille Arie's geboortejaar te wijzigen in 1926. Gelet op zijn piepjong uiterlijk, is daartegen geen bezwaar.

uitgegeven pb. nummer aan de Meij..re is 068769

Dr. H.A.Snellen geboren in 1905 te wijzigen in 1902. Uitreiking spoed gewenscht i.v.m. diverse nachtelijke tochten. Hoe uit te reiken via Stadhuis of mij ??

v.Wely v.Deenen Opticien gaarne nieuw pb. op 1902, met legalisatie. Hoe uit te reiken ?

Franciscus A.M.Dieben 17.8.23 is alles kwijt bij ontvluchting uit D. Vraagt nieuw. Hoe uit te reiken ?

P.L.v.Royen - Thorbeckestraat 60 vraagt 2e pb. op 1903. Hoe uit te reiken ?

Adrianus Boellaard 11.9.97 heeft pb. van mij gehad (aanvankelijk bestemd voor Bromet). No.068983

Victor Carquis Lemmens heeft pb. gehad. no.068982

Bromet , nieuw exemplaar voor vervanging J-exemplaar.

Leendert van den Heuvel geb.jaar en plaats bekend
Tine van den Heuvel - Heskes idem
over mij uit te reiken; gefingeerd Leidsch adres kiezen.
nieuwe pk. maken plus v.k., zullen door mij gedeponeerd worden in bevolkingsarchief Zoeterwoude.

Figure 10.7: Part of a work note (probably between van Wijk and Stoffels) listing active cases of providing people with counterfeit identity papers. From the Stoffels' private archive. The handwriting is by the Stoffels. Private collection.

street name, but a non-existing house number. [...] *Use a typewriter and copy the initial of the civil servant by taking any other pb issued in Leiden."* He warns her not to let anybody travel; the day before the *Feldgendarmerie* (German police) was active in the trains, checking the pb of travellers against lists which they carried with them. If in doubt, they could arrest the person and check the papers against the above-mentioned central records.

In the same note Hijme asks Bep to give him a call first before visiting his house, because on her previous visit *"Hans [Kloosterman], who knows you, has seen you and now knows you are involved; Daan [Piet] de Vries is also staying in our house. Did he see you as well?"* Bep replies she will be more discreet in the future, and that Piet has not seen her that day.

Van Wijk kept track of what they did and prepared a list after the war with details of all the forgeries (van Wijk, 1946). He listed some 400 persons who received false

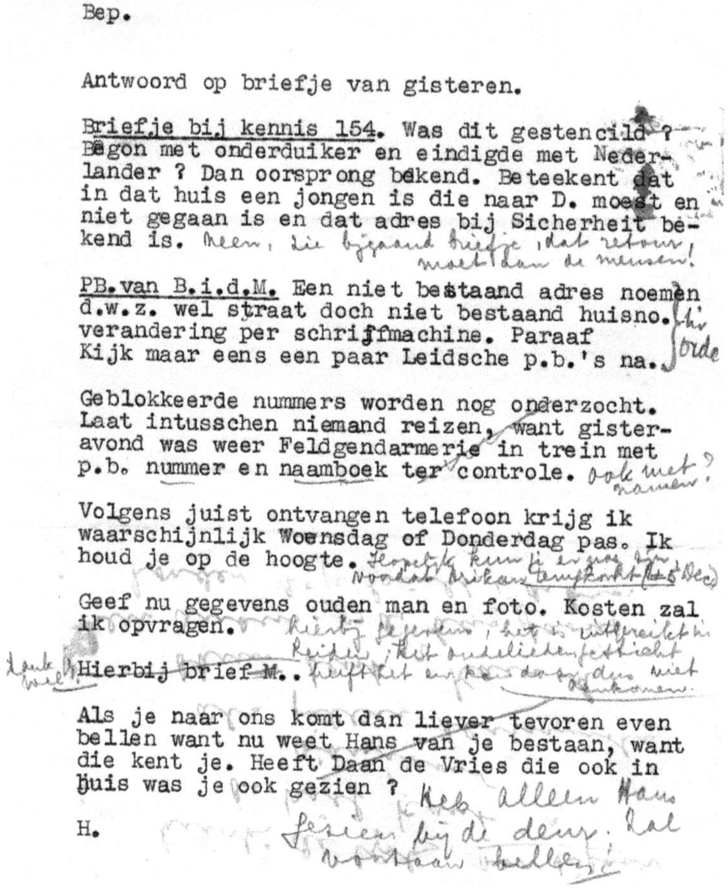

Bep.

Antwoord op briefje van gisteren.

Briefje bij kennis 154. Was dit gestencild ?
Begon met onderduiker en eindigde met Neder-
lander ? Dan oorsprong bekend. Beteekent dat
in dat huis een jongen is die naar D. moest en
niet gegaan is en dat adres bij Sicherheit bekend is. *neen, zie bijgaand briefje, dat retour,
moet dan de menschen!*

PB. van B.i.d.M. Een niet bestaand adres noemen
d.w.z. wel straat doch niet bestaand huisno.
verandering per schrijfmachine. Paraaf
Kijk maar eens een paar Leidsche p.b.'s na. *hr orde*

Geblokkeerde nummers worden nog onderzocht.
Laat intusschen niemand reizen, want gister-
avond was weer Feldgendarmerie in trein met
p.b. nummer en naamboek ter controle. *ook met namen?*

Volgens juist ontvangen telefoon krijg ik
waarschijnlijk Woensdag of Donderdag pas. Ik
houd je op de hoogte. *heroptk kun ji en jas ... Noodat Arikan ... (±5 Dec)*

Geef nu gegevens ouden man en foto. Kosten zal
ik opvragen. *hierbij ... ; het is uitgeraakt in Leiden; het oudelieden ... niet ... komen*

dank wel Hierbij brief M.. ... *en ... den niet ...*

Als je naar ons komt dan liever tevoren even
bellen want nu weet Hans van je bestaan, want
die kent je. Heeft Daan de Vries die ook in
huis was je ook gezien ? *heb alleen Hans*

H. *... by de deur. Zal voortaan ...*

Figure 10.8: Another work note from Hijme to Bep Bedak about providing false identity
papers to various people (see text). Handwritten comments are from Bep, probably
late 1943. Private collection.

identity papers through himself and his colleague at the Leiden Civil Registry,
Montanus, of which 124 were arranged through Stoffels. Elchanan Italie is included
as no. 31 (Fig. 9.37). Cor gave Hijme the materials to fabricate the pbs himself; much
of it was found in the boxes of their private archive, which was made available by
the family of Emilie van Brussel in 2004 (courtesy Mr. P. de Jong). Apart from van
Wijk, Montanus and Stoffels, a surprisingly large number of people were involved
in the identity scam: other well-known members of the resistance such as Lex
Bernard, Bep Bedak and Gerda Meijer, the people in need of help, people who knew
where they should go for help, and so on. Stoffels and his wife were well known
in Leiden through their respective Protestant and Catholic congregations. The
parents and siblings of Emilie van Brussel were very worried at the time that they

were taking too many risks. Work notes in their private archive such as Fig. 10.8 show that Stoffels was well aware of the risks.

The owners of these counterfeit pbs, if only the birth date was false, often continued to "walk around" in public. This type of hiding for the Germans contrasts with the classic idea of people hiding in dark spaces and never coming out, but they were *onderduikers* nevertheless (Siebelt, 2015).

Among the 72 Jews included in van Wijk's list is Leesha Rose, at that time Leesha Bornstein. She received the false identity Elizabeth (Lies) Bos, and subsequently became an active member of the group by arranging false papers for eighteen others. She secured Yad Vashem recognition for both van Wijk and Montanus in 1983. Her book *"The tulips are red"* (Rose, 1978, 1980) contains much detail about the activities around van Wijk, as well as his photograph (ibidem p. 233).

As said, the Stoffels were both recognized by Yad Vashem on 28th April 1968. Their tree stands proudly along the Avenue of the Righteous, next to the tree for Truus Wijsmuller (Fig. 10.6). The family Philipson presented them with a photo album. Hijme died in Noordwijk on 2nd May 1975, 67 years old. Emilie died on 5th February 1995. Ingrid Klein flew in from the USA on the next day for the funeral, which was also attended by Elchanan Italie, Piet Krans and others who had all found a hiding place at the Stoffels' house between 1943 and 1945, or elsewhere, through their facilitation.

Dien and Wim ("Johan") van Straten were recognized by Yad Vashem[13] on 22nd June 1971 for sheltering Aron Wolff (Ch. 9.4) and at least three other Jewish *onderduikers*. They made several visits to Israel (Fig. 10.9), and Ronnie returned to Huizen on several occasions.

The families who sheltered the children Klein and Philipson were also recognized (details in Michman & Flim, 2004, or the Yad Vashem website).

The Yad Vashem award is awarded on behalf of the Jewish people or the Jewish nation to non-Jewish people who contributed to the survival of Jews during the Holocaust. Beyond doubt the programme has proven itself over the decades. But it leaves unrecognized the many *Jewish* Dutchmen who helped to save people from persecution and those who performed other acts of resistance. Within the "small-scale history" of the Leiden orphanage I have mentioned Leesha Bornstein (Rose) in this chapter, Ralph and Jansje Litten-Serlui in Chapter 9.6, and Mirjam and Menachem Pinkhof-Waterman, Shushu Simon and others associated with Lodi Cohen in Chapter 9.7. In Leiden itself, Gerda Meijer and Bep Bedak (Schaap) were active co-workers of Stoffels before they became active outside Leiden. Last but not least, those who had the courage to go into hiding, like the families Philipson

13   See https://righteous.yadvashem.org/?search=van%20straten&searchType=righteous_only&langu age=en&itemId=4022534&ind=1.

Figure 10.9: Visiting Ronnie's family in Israel, 20th July 1971. From right: Amir (Ronnie's son), Wim ("Johan") and Dien van Straten, Mr. Alban and his daughter, Bert van Straten, Mrs. Alban, and Serlina de Paauw in the left corner. Photo, taken by Ronnie, from van Straten's report.

and Klein, and the family of Donald de Marcas, also performed important acts of resistance.

10.4   The perpetrators: Was justice done?

The most senior Nazis obviously carried the heaviest responsibility for the planning and execution of the Holocaust in the Netherlands, people like Seyss-Inquart (executed), Rauter (executed), SS Major General Wilhelm Harster (twelve years' imprisonment, but released in 1953), SS Major Wilhelm Zöpf (who escaped justice in the Netherlands[14]) in The Hague, or their bosses in Berlin, such as Himmler (suicide) and Eichmann (executed in Israel in 1962), to name just a few. The people shown in Figure 10.10 were the "hands-on" perpetrators in planning, coordinating,

---

14   Zöpf represented Eichmann's Office IV B4, the Jewish affairs and deportation bureau of the RSHA in Berlin. He was seconded to the SS in The Hague in 1941, to work under Harster. The two had known each other for a long time. Zöpf coordinated the deportation of Jews to the concentration camps in the East. He fled in 1945, but was identified in 1959 in West Germany. Germany, however, refused to extradite him. In 1967 the mood in Germany had begun to change. Both Harster and Zöpf were tried in München, convicted and sentenced to prison terms.

Figure 10.10: The main German perpetrators in the context of this book. Photos: NIOD and various other sources.

Franz Fischer (1901-1989)
Death > Life; released 1989

Ferdinand aus der Fünten (1909-1989)
Death > Life, released 1989

Willy Lages (1901-1971)
Death > Life, Released 1966

Albert K. Gemmeker (1907-1982)
Ten years, released 1951

and executing the systematic hunting down and deportation of the Dutch Jews. Fischer, Aus der Fünten, and Lages became the focus of public attention after the war when they were imprisoned in Holland.

Franz Fischer was a *(Waffen)-SS-Sturmscharführer* (sergeant major). He fanatically hunted down Jews in The Hague and surrounding region and was responsible for the deportation of some 13,000 Jews from The Hague. Some 12,000 of those were killed, mainly in Auschwitz and Sobibor. He was present in person in Leiden on 17th March 1943, the day of the razzia and the *ontruiming* of the orphanage (Kasteleyn, 2003). His death sentence in 1950 was commuted by Queen Juliana of the Netherlands, after which he spent the rest of his life in prison in Breda. He was released in January 1989 and died the same year in his birth town of Bigge (Germany).

Ferdinand aus der Fünten was a *SS-Hauptsturmführer* (captain) and an executive officer in the *Zentralstelle*. He was the key figure in the deportation of some 50,000 Jews from Amsterdam. He personally led the brutal deportation to Auschwitz of 1000 patients from the Jewish Mental Institute in Apeldoorn on 22nd January 1943. He was sentenced to death in 1950 but, like Fischer, he was pardoned by Queen Juliana, after which he spent the rest of his life in prison in Breda. He was released in January 1989 together with Franz Fischer and died in April of that year in Duisburg, Germany.

Willy Lages was a *SS-Sturmbannführer* (major); he was Aus der Fünten's superior, as head of the *Zentralstelle* in Amsterdam and as such responsible for the deportation and murder of more than 100,000 Jewish Dutchmen. He "visited" *Werkdorp Wieringermeer* in early 1941 together with Klaus Barbie, the "Butcher of Lyon", as a preliminary to the deportation and murder of the Werkdorp Palestine Pioneers. He was also responsible for the capture, torture and execution of Dutch resistance

Figure 10.11: Public protests in 1952 and 1966 against the leniency shown to Lages and, by implication, Fischer and Aus der Fünten. Wikipedia.

Amsterdam, 12th October 1952
Public protest against the pardoning of Willy Lages by Queen Juliana.

Amsterdam, 18th September 1966
Public protest against the release of Willy Lages by Justice Minister Samkalden (PvdA); *"Terug in zijn cel"* ("Back in his cell").

fighters. He personally attended the execution of Johannes Post of the Rijnsburg resistance group on 16th July 1944 (see the story of Sara Philipson and the death of de Groot, below). He was sentenced to death in 1949, and again in the Court of Appeal in 1950. He was pardoned by Queen Juliana against the express wishes of the cabinet. Although the war had not yet received much public attention at this time, the pardon resulted in public protests (Fig. 10.11, left). He was also incarcerated in Breda. He was released in 1966 because he was assumed to be terminally ill, but he recovered while in Germany, where he lived for another five years. His release by Minister of Justice Ivo Samkalden (Labour Party, *Partij van de Arbeid*) caused public outcry yet again (Fig. 10.11, right). Years later the proposal (1972) by Minister of Justice Dries van Agt, of the Catholic People's Party, to release the three remaining German prisoners (Fischer, Aus der Fünten, and Joseph Kotälla, the "butcher" of Camp Amersfoort) again caused such a public uproar that the proposal was withdrawn. Kotälla died in prison in 1979. The other two were released in 1989, when it was certain that they were on the brink of death. Together, the four and after the release of Lages, the *"Breda Three"* (Piersma, 2005) dominated public discussion for many years.[15]

Albert Konrad Gemmeker was *Kommandant* of Camp Westerbork from 12th October 1942 to April 1945. He must have been known to everybody on the list at the back of this book who passed through Camp Westerbork after 12th October 1942

---

15   From many post-war interviews it is clear that Minister of Justice van Agt never understood why there was such extraordinary opposition against his 1972 proposal to release them. The Dutch refusal to release them caused protests in Germany during Queen Juliana's state visit in November 1971. The protesters generally refused to accept that they were war criminals of the worst kind, calling them *"prisoners of war"* instead.

when he took command. Compared to the brutality of his two German predecessors, his regime seemed to be a relief. He realized that behaving as a "gentleman" was a much more clever and effective way to preserve the deception about the "labour camps" and keep the prisoners hushed. He maintained a relatively polite and sometimes courteous attitude to the inmates; he did not show any violence or brutality such as was normally ingrained in the SS. He allowed all necessary social services (hospital, dentists, a school, kindergarten, library, sports activities) to be organized by those inmates who were not immediately sent "through" to the East. Most impressive was the regular performance of a cabaret (rather a "revue"). Gemmeker always attended, laughed abundantly, but never applauded (van Liempt, 2019). It was a highly successful and very hideous tactic: under his command more than 80,000 Jews were exported from Holland to various death camps without any significant disturbance. Behind the gentlemanlike façade lurked a compulsory urge to please his superiors, and, above all, meet the weekly target number of Jews to be deported. He was super-sensitive to any real or perceived lack of respect from his prisoners. For an offense like not removing a hat in a timely fashion when Gemmeker passed by, or not applying a garden rake energetically enough, a prisoner could find himself on the list for the next transport: a death sentence.

After the war, Gemmeker claimed that he never knew what was happening with the people he put on the trains, and he maintained that claim until his death in 1989. It is impossible to believe that he, a senior SS officer, getting his instructions from Eichmann in Berlin via Zöpf and Harster in The Hague, would not have known what was being done to the Jews when they arrived in the East. He was also personally present in Apeldoorn on 22nd January 1943 when more than a thousand mental patients were brutally thrown into a train, which went straight to Auschwitz to prevent unrest in Westerbork, and surely, he knew that the patients were not going to any "labour camp". But post-war prosecution was, so it seems, unable to find enough documentary evidence to convict Gemmeker, and no doubt his non-brutal behaviour in Westerbork also helped him to dodge the death penalty. He was convicted in 1949 and sentenced to ten years imprisonment, but he was released on 20th April 1951, about two years later, pardoned by Queen Juliana on the recommendation of Minister of Justice Johan van Maarseveen, of the Catholic People's Party. Thus, he spent six years in prison, including the pre-conviction period, about 40 minutes for each man, women and child who perished after being deported from Westerbork under his direction. The post-war German Justice Office investigated the possibility of putting Gemmeker on trial again, following the trials of Harster and Zöpf, without success. Gemmeker successfully escaped justice again, but not without an exceptional degree of good luck (van Liempt, 2019).

Figure 10.12: The main Dutch perpetrators in the context of this book. Photos courtesy Nationaal Archief/ CABR, The Hague.

Steven van Musscher as Dutch police officer and in uniform of the Waffen-SS. Fled in April 1945 to Germany, which refused to extradite him. Died 2003.	Adrianus Biesheuvel (1909-1986) Served c. 9 years.	Willem de Groot Shot dead by Dutch resistance 1944 at the *onderduik* address of Sara Philipson in Rijnsburg.

Like the four Germans in Figure 10.10, the three Dutchmen in Figure 10.12 were most actively involved with the deportation of the Jewish inhabitants of Leiden, including the inhabitants of the orphanage.

Steven van Musscher was in charge of the Leiden police squad which arrested 59 people in the orphanage on 17th March 1973 and despatched them by train to Westerbork. He was a former naval officer who sympathized with the Germans and became a member of the NSB in October 1940. Later, he joined the Waffen-SS and followed the Nazi indoctrination course in Avegoor (Fig. 10.12). He was appointed to the Leiden police force on 15th August 1941, ostensibly to replace people who were considered disloyal to the German authorities. He was well educated, completed higher secondary education (HBS-B) and a merchant naval college before receiving his commission as a navy officer in 1937. He had no patience for unprofessional behaviour, irrespective of any political affiliation. He wrote a damning "character" report (21st January 1944) about commissioner Ulrich Hoffmann, who had been his superior officer in Leiden, and who was a fellow NSB member.[16]

---

16 Van Musscher was asked by his superiors in the Nazi organization to comment on Hoffmann's application to be admitted as *"begunstigend lid"* of the *"Germaanse SS"*. Van Musscher advised against it. He thought Hoffmann was an entirely unreliable character, prepared to do anything in his own interest. He quotes examples: *Hoffmann infiltrated successfully into a student resistance group by giving his word that his informant would not be harmed. He had him arrested nevertheless. He entertained an amorous relation with another student, and had her arrested as well after she became pregnant.* He also used his position for personal gain. I suspect that his education at the naval academy shaped his belief in a code of honour. Nevertheless, he faithfully executed orders from the German and Dutch authorities to arrest and deport Jews. Letter in Dossier van Musscher.

He was promoted to chief of police in Gouda on 1ˢᵗ April 1944 and received a commission as *Oberleutnant* with the *Ordnungspolizei* in Rotterdam.[17] In line with his behaviour in Leiden, he proved to be a zealous administrator who demanded strict and proper behaviour and discipline from his subordinates, and he was used to exercising authority. He put an end to the practice of municipal civil servants in Gouda of giving direct instructions to police officers. He was afraid that the Gouda police station would be raided by the resistance. In May 1944 he instructed his staff to keep the station entrance locked at all times and to ensure that whoever opened the door was covered from behind by a colleague with a drawn loaded handgun. During Operation Market Garden in September 1944 (the attempt of the allies to cross the major rivers and canals between liberated Belgium and Arnhem), when people expected the whole of the Netherlands to be freed from the Germans, van Musscher told his wife and daughter to move to Germany, while he stayed in Gouda. He wrote to her about his transfer to Rotterdam and to a training camp near Munich, which he attended. In February 1945 he told her that he might be transferred to the Eastern Front.

On 10ᵗʰ May 1945, four days after liberation, van Musscher was suspended from his police commission on suspicion of collaboration with the Germans. No address was given on the document: he had escaped to Germany weeks earlier, realizing how his wartime activities would be judged after the war. He probably knew that his membership of the Waffen-SS entitled him to German nationality. He would not have known, but probably counted on, any future German government not being willing to extradite German nationals. Indeed, several attempts by the Dutch Justice Department to have him extradited failed. Twenty years after the war, the public prosecutor in Rotterdam instructed the police commissioner in Gouda (van Musscher's last domicile in Holland) to maintain him on the wanted list (police records, Gouda, 23ʳᵈ March 1965). But the (West) German government continued to protect him until his death in 2003.

Adrianus Biesheuvel and Willem de Groot probably formed the most notorious duo of Jew hunters in the Leiden police force. They worked in a special unit, the *Documentatiedienst*, within the police force, dedicated to political and sensitive tasks. They were dedicated "Jew hunters" in the sense of van Liempt (2005). Biesheuvel was present at the liquidation of the orphanage on 17ᵗʰ March 1943. It is not known if de Groot (the duo operated mostly together) was also at the orphanage or whether he was hunting Jews elsewhere in Leiden that day. In this period the duo was engaged full-time with arresting Jews (some still lived at their official addresses) and hunting those who had gone into hiding. After spending one or more nights in a police cell in Leiden, most of them were delivered to

---

17   There is also a report about a promotion to *Hauptmann* in September 1944.

the SiPo in The Hague. They duly reported their successful arrests in the police records, often signing their report by name, or "Documentatie Dienst". Analysis of these archives (Kasteleyn, 2003, and personal communication) shows that the two men arrested 76 Jews without doubt, and probably 127 all together in the ten months they worked together.[18] On Wednesday, 23rd June 1943, just before midnight, they arrested five people at Oude Rijn no. 48, including Jacob Philipson, his parents-in-law[19] and the man who gave them shelter. Five days later the "catch of the week", some fifteen people (including at least four men who had sheltered the *onderduikers*) were delivered to the German police (presumably in The Hague or Rotterdam).

The duo made many more arrests, as a duo or on an individual basis, and not only in Leiden and its surrounding villages, but also in other places. On 31st July 1943 Biesheuvel records the arrest that day, in Amsterdam, of Robert I. de Groot. He also arrests Frederik Kerkhoven, who harboured Robert at his home. He duly records the "legal" basis for these arrests: Robert for having moved to a new address as a Jew without permission, and Kerkhoven for having provided shelter to a Jew who had committed a criminal offense. Both spent six nights in a cell in the Leiden police station before being handed over to the Germans. I don't know (yet) what happened to Kerkhoven.[20] Robert de Groot, "Robbie", was killed in Auschwitz on 6th November 1943. He was six years old.

Willem de Groot was shot by a member of the Johannes Post resistance group on Monday, 17th January 1944, during their raid on the house of Piet "Sik" van Egmond in Rijnsburg, the *onderduik* address of Sarah Philipson. It has been assumed that she was betrayed, but no specific evidence for that has yet come to light. Rijnsburg was a tight community with a large number of Jewish *onderduikers* (de Beer, 2015). A few "unreliable" characters, including one NSB member, were warned that they would be killed if they spoke a word to the police or the Germans. De Groot and Biesheuvel must have had suspicions about this village but had not been able to make any arrests. It is possible that they were attracted to this house by the underground activities of van Egmond and his many co-workers. Rita Klein was also in hiding in Rijnsburg, delivered by Emilie Stoffels. She stayed with another Van Egmond family.

The above-mentioned police reports were available to the courts after the war. But as time passed the sentences became less severe. Biesheuvel was sentenced in December 1948 to thirteen years in prison. A request for pardoning by his parents

---

18   Between Biesheuvel's arrival at the Leiden police force on 1st March 1943 and de Groot being killed on 17th January 1944.
19   Jacob Simons and Sara Simons-Soosman.
20   He is not listed in databases in Holland or Yad Vashem

was declined in August 1951. He was released in 1954, after serving seven years. De Groot was posthumously stripped of his pension rights in February 1948, leaving his wife, who was in poor health, and her two children in destitution. She wrote a letter to (then Crown Princess) Juliana acknowledging her husband's role in hunting Jews but asking her not to punish her and the children for his acts. She had been openly supportive of the Nazi regime and her request was denied. Later, the children's pension rights as orphans were restored.

There were more members of the Leiden police force who collaborated with the Germans to varying degrees. Stoffels wanted some 20 of them to be prosecuted or at least investigated in 1945. No part of the research underlying this book was more depressing than reading the dossiers of the Special Tribunals (CABR[21]) in the National Archives (see van Liempt & Kompagnie, 2013). The cool, matter-of-fact reports in the archives of the Leiden police force (Kasteleyn, 2003) about arresting people and handing them over to the Germans are equally depressing.

Yet this study has also bought to light small but significant acts of defiance by people who never sought recognition for what they did. Van Musscher himself reports that two of his colleagues in the police force visited De Sitterlaan 94 early in the morning of 17th March 1943 to warn the Jews in hiding there that they would be arrested later that day. I do not know who the *onderduikers* were (the address is not listed by Siebelt 2011b) or the police officers.

There can be little doubt that the few selected people in Chapter 10.3 were heroes, and those in this chapter (10.4) were not, but evaluating the behaviour of the vast majority of people who were neither, the "bystanders", remains controversial to this day. The German occupation has had a formidable and lasting impact on Dutch society. The question of "good and bad" dominated post-war historiography (Herzberg, 1985; Presser, 1965; de Jong, 1969-1994). It was hardly possible to do historical research without causing emotional and politically charged debates and personal attacks on authors. In the 1980s, Blom argued that the time had come to analyze the history of the occupation with a little more "distance", looking for possible alternative methods of research which would not be controlled and restrained by the moralizing framework of "good and bad" (Blom, 1986). Some 20 years later he concluded that academic research had indeed made significant progress in this direction, but that the public debate remained within the good vs bad framework as strongly as ever before (Blom, 2007).

---

21   Some 130,000 individuals were investigated by these post-war tribunals for possible collaborations with the Germans (not only with respect to the persecution of Jews).

Figure 10.13: 14th November 2007; Students of the Erasmus College in Zoetermeer held a first memorial service at the erstwhile orphanage. A new group of students came over to Leiden every year to read out the names, until Corona halted the tradition in 2020.

10.5   The next generation

The text from Deuteronomy quoted at the beginning of this book admonishes us not just to remember "what our eyes have seen" but to pass it on to our children and grandchildren. Indeed, to retrieve and preserve the names and the memory of the murdered children would be rather futile if we cannot pass on the memory to next generations.

Every year, on or around 17th March, students from a secondary school in Zoetermeer hold a memorial service at the orphanage (Fig. 10.13). To date thirteen "generations" of students have taken part in the ceremony. After visiting the Leiden synagogue for an introduction[22] to Jewish religion and culture, the story of Esther is told, since the ceremony takes place around mid-March, close to Purim, and in memory of the fact that the group from Leiden celebrated Purim three days after their arrival in Westerbork, and just before the first group was deported to Sobibor. After listening to Merlyn Frank's lecture (Ch. 10.2), they walk to the former orphanage along the route shown in Figure 4.9. After a short introduction about what happened on 17th March, the students read out the names of the 55 children and staff who were forcefully removed from the building that night (Table 7.1) and who did not return from deportation.

The Jewish orphanage in Leiden never reopened. In fact, most orphanages, and many other Jewish social institutions in Holland (van der Eerden, 2014; Staal, 2008, 2015) had been destroyed beyond recovery: the communities they were meant to serve no longer existed. Some institutions, such as the boys' orphanage (Megadlé

---

22   Usually given by Mrs. Malka Polak.

Jethomim) on the Amstel (in 1947 it moved to Emmalaan 7 in Amsterdam[23]), and the Bergstichting in Laren, served as a home for children who survived the Holocaust for a limited time. Jacob Brilleman reports (postcard to Hijme Stoffels, 25th July 1945) that they had 90 children in Laren. The Bergstichting (van der Eerden, 2014) closed its doors in the 1960s. The orphanage on the Amstel was demolished in 1977, with practically all the remaining derelict houses of the former Jewish Quarter. But the orphanage building in Leiden still stands. The Leiden synagogue was ransacked inside, but it was restored after the war. However, the pre-war Jewish community never recovered and regular services cannot be held anymore.

The fact that the two buildings have survived has been important to the successful holding of the ceremony over the years. So has the fact that the names of the children who lived there are known, and that there are photographs to show and stories to tell. The Holocaust does not lend itself to romanticized fantasy stories or theatre films. The students always ask whether what we tell them *has actually happened*. According to Mr. Hans Wolf, who was their history teacher for most of these years, it is the reading aloud of the names of the individuals and knowing something about each of them what makes the strongest impression on the students. That is a moving observation.

The orphanage building in Leiden was sold to the government after the war and the proceeds were used in part to build Beth Juliana in Israel. It had many different occupants after the war. Seemingly Elchanan Italie was one of the first after liberation (Ch. 9.9). It served as a temporary *"openbare"* (public) school with eleven classrooms until new buildings were ready in 1959,[24] after which the GG&GD (municipal health service) moved in. The building currently serves as a medical centre.

I hope that the building, which externally is still in its original shape, might someday become a municipal monument, because of its historical and its architectural significance. But not before the horrid post-war extensions along the Cronesteinkade have been removed, and the unique back side of the building (Fig. 3.6) can be seen again from the street. Any such plan could also consider including the houses on the opposite side of the Roodenburgerstraat at the corner with the Cronesteinkade, which were built in the same style as the orphanage.

---

23 Niek van Zutphen, *"Het Joodse Jongensweeshuis in de Emmalaan, 1947-1965"*, in *Ons Amsterdam*, 18th May 2014, https://onsamsterdam.nl/. It closed in 1965

24 The new school was built on Oppenheimerstraat, as was the Catholic St. Joseph School. Both schools were inaugurated at the same time (*Leids Dagblad*, 13th June 1959).

References

Beer, W. de, et al., 2015; *"Een veilig nest voor vervolgden. Verhalen over Joodse onderduikers in Rijnsburg"*. Genootschap Oud Rijnsburg. [A collection of stories about the many Jewish *onderduikers* (including Sara Philipson and Rita Klein) who found shelter in this small strictly reformed Christian village in the Leiden area. The stories are included as they were told, without being checked against other sources or documents.]

Blom, J.C.H., 1986; *"In de ban van goed en fout? Wetenschappelijke geschiedschrijving over de bezettingstijd in Nederland"*. In: Abma et al., 1986 , pp. 30-52.

Blom, J.C.H., 2007; *"In de ban van goed en fout. Geschiedschrijving over de bezettingstijd in Nederland"*. Amsterdam, Boom, ISBN 9789085064633.

Bossenbroek, Martin, 2001; *"De meelstreep. Terugkeer en opvang na de Tweede Wereldoorlog"*. Amsterdam, Bert Bakker, ISBN 905123697.

Buruma, Ian, 2013; *"Year zero: A history of 1945"*. London, Atlantic Books, ISBN 9781848879379/373.

Eerden, E. van der, 2014; *"De Berg-Stichting: 'oase in harde en desillusioneerende maatschappij'"*. Contactblad '40-'45, pp. 4-7. ISSN 1569-1209.

Frank, Merlyn, 1998; *"Koosje. Een dinsdagkind"*. Schoorl, Conserve, ISBN 9054290927.

Herzberg, A.J., 1985; *"Kroniek der Jodenvervolging, 1940-1945"*. Amsterdam, Querido, ISBN 9021465779. First published in 1950.

Jong, L. de, 1969-1994; *"Het Koninkrijk der Nederlanden in de Tweede Wereldoorlog"*. http://www.dbnl.org or http://www.loedejongdigitaal.nl/. [The standard (contemporary) history of the Netherlands during the war. The entire text is available online (with search facility). For more recent interpretations, see Blom et al., 2021.]

Kasteleyn, L.P., 2003; *"Vervolging en bescherming, joden in Leiden 1933-1945"*. Leiden, Museum de Lakenhal.

Kopuit, M., 1974; *"Groot boeren- en kaasbedrijf van oud-Leidenaars in Beth Jitschak"* [Dairy farm of Ben Meijer and family]. *Nieuw Israëlitisch Weekblad*, 11 January, p .7.

Liempt, A. van, 2005; *"Hitler's bounty hunters: The betrayal of the Jews"*. New York, Berg, ISBN 1845202031/9781845202033.

Liempt, A. van, 2019; *"Gemmeker. Commandant van Kamp Westerbork"*. Amsterdam, Balans, ISBN 9789460039782 (hardcover)/9789460039799 (ebook).

Liempt, A. van & J. Kompagnie (eds), 2013; *"Jodenjacht: de onthutsende rol van de Nederlandse politie in de Tweede Wereldoorlog"* [Hunting down Jews: The shocking role of the local Dutch police during the German occupation], 5th ed. Amsterdam, Balans, ISBN 9789460037221.

Michman, Jozeph & Bert Jan Flim (eds), 2004; *"The encyclopaedia of the righteous among the nations: Rescuers of Jew during the Holocaust. Volume: The Netherlands"*. Jerusalem, Yad Vashem.

Michman, Jozeph, Hartog Beem & Dan Michman, 1999; *"Pinkas. Geschiedenis van de joodse gemeenschap in Nederland"*. Incorporating research by Victor Brilleman. Amsterdam, Uitgeverij Contact & NIK, ISBN 9025495133. [The original text of this comprehensive history of the Jews in the Netherlands is also available in Hebrew, Yad Vashem, Holocaust Martyrs' and Heroes Remembrance Authority, Jerusalem, 1985.]

Piersma, Hinke, 2005; *"De drie van Breda. Duitse oorlogsmisdadigers in Nederlandse gevangenschap 1945-1989"*. Amsterdam, Balans, ISBN 9050186610/9789050186612.

Presser, J., 1965; *"Ondergang. De vervolging en verdelging van het Nederlandse Jodendom, 1940-1945"*. 's-Gravenhage, Staatsuitgeverij/Martinus Nijhoff. [The entire Dutch text is available online (with search facility) at http://www.dbnl.org. Although written more than half a century ago, the book is still very readable and impressive today.] An English translation was published by E.P. Dutton & Co. in 1969 (ASIN B000LD8D7S), and again in 1988 under the title *"Ashes in the wind: The destruction of Dutch Jewry"* by Wayne State University Press; re-issued in 2010, ISBN 9780285638136.

Rose, Leesha, 1978; *"The tulips are red"*. South Brunswick, Barnes & Co., ISBN 0498021769. [Leesha Rose (Bornstein during the war) collaborated in the resistance with van Wijk and Stoffels.]

Schelvis, Jules, 2007a; *"Binnen de poorten. Een verslag van twee jaar Duitse vernietigings- en concentratiekampen"*. Amsterdam, De Bataafse Leeuw, ISBN 978906707626. [Schelvis is one of the 18 survivors of the 34,314 people deported from Westerbork to Sobibor. This is his own account of his deportation and survival.]

Siebelt, Alphons, 2011b; *"Gids voor Leiden in de Tweede Wereldoorlog. Beschreven in 650 adressen"* [Guide to Leiden in the Second World War, described in 650 addresses]. Leiden, Ginkgo.

Siebelt, Alphons, 2015; *"Hij zit bij de onderduikersbond. Hulp aan Leidse onderduikers in de Tweede Wereldoorlog"*. Leiden, Primavera Press. [A study of the organized assistance to *onderduikers* in Leiden, arguably the most important form of resistance during the occupation of the Netherlands, where armed resistance was virtually impossible for the lack of wilderness areas where partisans could hide.]

Staal, Philip, 2008; *"Roestvrijstaal. Speurtocht naar de erfenis van Joodse oorlogswezen"*. Delft, Eburon, ISBN 9789059722712. English edition: Staal, 2015.

Staal, Philip, 2015; *"Settling the account (Mijn erfenis)"*. Bloomington, iUniverse, ISBN 9781491751664/51657.

Stoffels, H. & E. Stoffels-van Brussel, 1967; *"Unpublished"*, 22nd November. [A list of (some of) their activities in support of Jewish citizens of Leiden from February 1942, such as arranging *onderduik* addresses, false papers, etc. The list was written at the request of Elchanan Italie, in support of a proposal by him and the family Philipson-Armon to award the Yad Vashem award to Stoffels and his wife.

Wijk, Cor van, 1946; *"Mijn werk in de Nederlandse Verzetsorganisatie 'Strijdend Nederland'"*. Typescript, Regionaal Archief Leiden (now Erfgoed Leiden & Omgeving). [An account of his wartime activities, including the provision of (at least) 420 blank but genuine pb's to the Leiden underground movement. No less than 124 of these were used by Stoffels.]

Withuis, Jolande, 2013; *"Weest manlijk, zijt sterk. Pim Boellaard (1903-2001) Het leven van een verzetsheld"*. Amsterdam, De Bezige Bij, ISBN 9789023478430.

Epilogue

I have been conscious of the danger that this book would become "unreadable", if only because the reader would be overwhelmed by far too many names. Indeed, looking at the Index, the number of names is very large. The reader was advised (in the Preface) not to try and remember all the names, but to focus on a limited number of persons, and let them take you through the stories. To what extent this approach has been successful remains an open question, but I could not leave the names out. The basis for this intransigence goes back to my very first visit to Yad Vashem in 1974.

I was not immediately impressed with the museum as it was at the time, until I came upon a dark room in a corner halfway up a staircase and closed off by a heavy door like those used in prisons. Looking through the bars, the room was painted pitch black and the walls were lined with boxes with thousands upon thousands of index cards, filled in by hand or by using a typewriter. It was the core of the *Names Project*, a courageous attempt, started in 1953, to retrieve and preserve the names of the victims of the Holocaust and the evidence that they ever existed. Slowly it dawned upon me that we knew for certain that millions of Jewish men, women and children had been swept off the face of the earth within just a few years, but that for most of them we did not even know their names. That realization left a deep impression. In 1974 the database contained the names of some 950,000 victims, based on national records and witness reports.

Visiting Yad Vashem in 2017 for a second time, the museum had been totally revamped into a newly built and architectonically very impressive complex. It plays an active role in historical research, Holocaust education, documentation, and commemoration. But it is still the "Names Room" with its black boxes which arguably forms the essential core of Yad Vashem. An article by Cynthia Wroclawski, *"Unto every person there is a name"*, published in the *Yad Vashem Quarterly Magazine* special edition of December 2013, contained a graph showing the status of the project. The graph (Fig. 11.1, reworked by the author to a linear time scale and updated based on advice of Mr. Alexander Avram, director of the Hall of Names, February 2020) highlights the dramatic increases related to archives in Eastern Europe becoming accessible in the late 1990s.

Focke, Jaap W., *Machseh Lajesoumim: A Jewish Orphanage in the City of Leiden, 1890-1943*.
Taylor & Francis Group, 2021
DOI: 10.5117/9789463726955_EPILOGUE

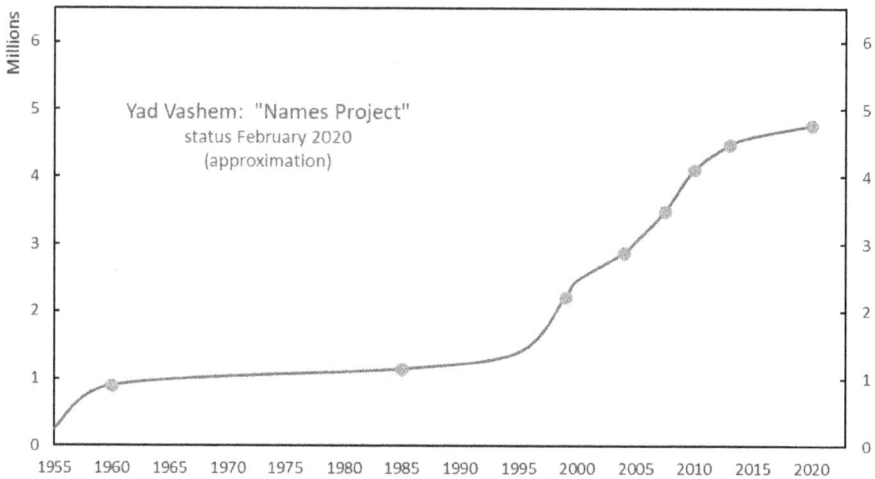

Figure 11.1: Yad Vashem's Names Project; recovered names against time. An approximation, hand-drawn by the author based on data points in Wroclawski (2013) and advice by Mr. Alexander Avram (Yad Vashem, February 2020).

Yad Vashem means: *"a Hand (Monument) and a Name"*. The law passed in 1953 by the Israeli parliament to establish Yad Vashem stipulates the following in Section 2:

> The task of Yad Vashem is to gather into the homeland material regarding all those members of the Jewish people who laid down their lives, who fought and rebelled against the Nazi enemy and his collaborators, and to perpetuate their names and those of the communities, organizations and institutions which were destroyed because they were Jewish.

The statement is printed on every "Page of Testimony" used to create the database.

The wish to be remembered, and the idea that people are only really dead if they are not remembered anymore by anyone, is a pervasive thought in human culture. Thus, retrieving and including all the names, and *"adding a face to every name"* by including photographs and stories became the primary objective of this book.

To retrieve and preserve hard evidence based on documents in archives and multiple witness accounts became an important secondary objective. It is disconcerting to observe how often false and incorrect statements were found during this investigation. Once repeated and uncritically copied from one website to another, they become "facts" in their own right.

Preserving the (documentary) evidence is also important because as time goes by it becomes more difficult for people to believe that the events described in this book really happened, particularly in non-Western countries. This should not be a surprise; the Holocaust is, I think, beyond understanding. As a German judge once remarked in a post-war Nazi trial, it is *"only after studying the extensive and detailed documentary evidence that one can accept that the incomprehensible has indeed become reality"*.

I tried to stay away from discussing controversial issues as much as possible because it would have drawn attention away from describing the history of this orphanage and the people who lived there. But inevitably the stories in this book raise difficult questions which often do not allow easy, black-and-white answers, or judgements.

I began these investigations in a despondent mood, as a flurry of publications had just become available documenting how many people in various professions, the police, or the civil service, notaries, estate agents and others, or individuals, had collaborated or profited from the near total destruction of Dutch Jewry during or immediately after the war. The despondency will not go away as new depressing information continues to come to light. But I also came across many instances where people did the right thing, sometimes taking serious risks: the civil servant in Den Ham, the unknown *onderduik* parents in Apeldoorn, and so on. Many never asked or received recognition for what they did. Even the often-quoted reproach that so many people, the "bystanders", *"did nothing"* to prevent the deportations, is not so simple as it sounds. In some cases, the reproach seems justified without much doubt, for example, when the Dutch civil service classified half-Jews as J2, without raising the possibility to classify them as G1 (Ch. 6.2). On the other hand, many *onderduik* children, like Ronnie and Marietje (Ch. 9.4), and Rita "Roelofs" Klein, played in the streets and went to school, and many locals must have wondered where they had come from and suspected the truth. But they were not betrayed. Van Straten and Stoffels, despite their rather obvious activities, were not betrayed. Maybe we have no right to expect more from "bystanders" who had their own children and families to look after. Moreover, it is impossible to know how we ourselves would have behaved under circumstances which today are virtually unimaginable to most of us.

Even more controversial is the question of what people knew at the time about the fate of the deportees. If one defines carefully what "knowing" means, a convincing case can be made (van der Boom, 2012) that apart from a few top Nazis, neither the bystanders, nor the victims themselves, knew in 1942-1943 that practically all deportees were killed on the day of arrival in the so-called labour camps. But that is not the end of the story. Hijme and Emilie Stoffels "knew" when they risked their own life to shelter Jews; Rebbe de Hond "knew" when he called out *"Hineni"* when boarding the train to Sobibor; the mothers of Nicky Hakker and Merlyn Frank "knew" when they gave their children away to total strangers, possibly never to see them again. No parent would do that unless under duress of mortal danger.

Numbers become less impressive the bigger they are. The death of someone you know tends to have a bigger impact than large numbers of fatalities far away. When I began this project, I was under the impression that I had a reasonable knowledge of the Holocaust. But it was only by *"getting to know"* individuals such as Sally Montezinos and finding out (Ch. 8.5) that not a single family member survived the war to remember him, that I began to grasp the significance of the Holocaust and its final stage of genocide, and the importance of preserving the names and memory of the victims. I hope this book will contribute to that purpose.

References

Boom, B. van der, 2012; *"Wij weten niets van hun lot"*. Amsterdam, Boom, ISBN 9789461054777. [A study of contemporary sources to determine what people knew at the time about the fate of the Jewish deportees.]

List of abbreviations and acronyms

AJDC	See JDC.
ANWB	Koninklijke Nederlandse Toeristenbond ANWB (Royal Dutch Touring Club ANWB).
AOS	Archief Oorlogsslachtoffers (War Victims Archives of Belgium), Brussels.
ARA	Algemeen Rijksarchief (National Archives of Belgium), Brussels.
CABR	Centraal Archief Bijzondere Rechtspleging (Central Archives for Special Criminal Jurisdiction), National Archives, The Hague. CABR contains thousands of dossiers on people who were investigated, and sometimes charged and convicted, of war crimes or collaboration with the Germans. Very depressing to read.
CBJB	Comité voor Bijzondere Joodsche Belangen (Committee for Special Jewish Interests); est. March 1933. Abraham Asscher, later co-chairman of the Joodse Raad, chaired the CBJB. David Cohen was secretary; see also CJV. See extensive article on https://en.wikipedia.org/wiki/Committee_for_Jewish_Refugees_(Netherlands).
CJV	Comité voor Joodsche Vluchtelingen (Committee for Jewish Refugees), part of CBJB, est. April 1933. David Cohen, later co-chairman of the Joodse Raad, was chairman of the CJV. Executive members Gertrude van Tijn-Cohn and Raphael Eitje managed the actual work of the CJV, which in its heyday employed more than a hundred paid and volunteer staff. See: https://en.wikipedia.org/wiki/Committee_for_Jewish_Refugees_(Netherlands).
ELO	Erfgoed Leiden en Omgeving (The Regional Archive in Leiden).
GFH	Ghetto Fighters' House. A holocaust museum north of Haifa with an extensive Dutch section, originally set up by Miriam Pinkhof. GFHA = GFH Archives
HBS	Hogere Burgerschool. The most common form of higher secondary education, giving access to higher academic and technical institutions.
ITS	International Tracing Service (Bad Arolsen, Germany). Covering some 17.5 million people, one of the biggest archives on victims and survivors of Nazi persecution.
IWC	Israëlietische Weezen-Corporatie. Established in Leiden in 1879 "to care for [Jewish] orphans of any age, and to support families after the death of the breadwinner [i.e. usually the father]."
JDC	American Joint Distribution Committee. Colloquially known as "the Joint". It had a post-war office in The Hague. Also AJDC.
JHM	Joods Historisch Museum (Jewish Historical Museum), Amsterdam, www.jck.nl.
JVvVV	See J4V.
J4V	Joodse Vereniging voor Verpleging en Verzorging (Jewish Association for Nursing and Care). The Nazis liquidated most Jewish organizations, foundations and institutions in the course of 1942, but not those providing care. Instead, on 4th

November 1942, they forced them all into one single care organization, the J4V. Included were eight Jewish hospitals, thirteen old-age homes and eight orphanages. This gave the Nazis control over the institutions, but it also allowed the institutions to be left alone during the second half of 1942, when deportations were in full swing. The J4V preserved the notion that the sick, the old, or the very young would not be deported to "labour camps" in the East, which convinced some to bring their children to the Leiden orphanage in this period (Ch. 6.8). Also JVvVV.

JR	Joodse Raad (Jewish Council [of Elders])
KNAW	Koninklijke Nederlandse Academie van Wetenschappen (Royal Netherlands Academy of Arts and Sciences).
KZ (or KL)	*Konzentrationslager* (concentration camp); colloquial use. In official Nazi documents the abbreviation KL is used (Kogon, 1974).
LC	*Leidse Courant* (*Leidsche Courant*). A regional newspaper (1909-1992) with Catholic affiliations. tracing its origins back to 1688. It continued to publish during the war and was not allowed to resume operations in May 1945 (Siebelt, 2011a. See also NLC.
LD	*Leids Dagblad* (*Leidsch Dagblad*). The leading newspaper in Leiden and environs, est. in 1860. Before the war, more so than later, it had national stature and featured local items in addition to national and international news. It was forced to accept pro-German articles from October 1941, but refused to accept an NSB chief editor, leading to its prohibition as per 1st January 1944.
Liro	Lippmann, Rosenthal & Co. A bank used by the Germans to collect all confiscated Jewish properties, funds, capital, valuables during the Second World War.
NA	Nationaal Archief (National Archives), The Hague.
NIOD	Nederlands Instituut voor Oorlogs Documentatie (Netherlands Institute for War Documentation), Amsterdam. The main depository of knowledge about the Second World War in the Netherlands. Formerly RIOD.
NLC	*Nieuwe Leidse Courant* (*Nieuwe Leidsche Courant*). A regional newspaper with Protestant affiliations derived from *De Rotterdammer*, with local news added. It was closed down by the Germans on 16th October 1941 for refusing to print pro-German articles. It resumed publication on 7th May 1945. See also LC and LD.
NS	Nederlandse Spoorwegen (Dutch National Railways).
NSB	Nationaal-Socialistische Beweging in Nederland (National Socialist Movement in the Netherlands). The Dutch fascist party, led by Anton Mussert. He was executed after the war.
OD	Ordedienst. The internal (Jewish) "auxiliary police force" in Westerbork (van Riet, 2016).
OPK	Oorlogs Pleeg Kinderen. Commission to resolve custody issues for children who had survived the war in *onderduik*. See Chapters 9.4 and 10.2.
pb	Short for *persoonsbewijs*, the national identity card introduced during the war by the Dutch Civil Registry. It was very difficult to produce a counterfeit pb unless one

	had access to blank originals.
POW	Prisoner of war.
RIOD	Rijksinstituut voor Oorlogs Documentatie (National Institute for War Documentation). The institute of Loe de Jong and his base of operations when writing the official Dutch war history (de Jong, 1969-1994). RIOD was transformed into NIOD in 1999.
RSHA (G)	*Reichssicherheitshauptamt* (Reich Main Security Office). Created by Himmler in September 1939 to combine all German police, intelligence and security forces under his own control. Being at the core of the SS state, the RSHA was a huge bureaucratic organization which also harboured Adolf Eichmann's *Referat IV B4*, which coordinated the logistics of the deportations across occupied Europe.
SiPo/SD (G)	*Sicherheits Polizei/Sicherheits Dienst* (Security Police/Intelligence Service). A German police and security force that gave instructions directly to the police force of the Netherlands.
T4	Acronym for the Nazi euthanasia programme. Tiergarten no. 4 was the location of its nerve centre in Berlin. Using gas for mass-killing purposes was developed as part of T4, and many perpetrators of Aktion Reinhard had previous T4 "experience"; see Chapters 7.6 and 8.1.
ULO	*Uitgebreid lager onderwijs* (extended lower education). A common form of secondary education in the Netherlands, usually from age twelve to sixteen.
USHMM	US Holocaust Museum, Washington, DC, https://www.ushmm.org.
WA	Weerbaarheidsafdeling (Resistance Department). The paramilitary arm of the NSB, the Dutch Nazi party. Before the war, the WA was banned by the government, but it was reinstated during the occupation.

Dutch or German words used in the text

Arbeidsinzet	Deployment of nationals of the Netherlands and other occupied countries in German factories, farms, etc., to fill gaps in the workforce resulting from military conscription; initially voluntary, later obligatory depending on age.
Anschluss	(G) The incorporation of Austria, the land of Hitler's birth, into the German Reich on 13th March 1938. A large proportion of the population welcomed the *Anschluss*.
Antragstelle	(G) Literally: office to submit a request, i.e. not to be deported. Part of the Jewish self-administration in Westerbork subject to German approval.
Ariërverklaring	On 5th October 1940 all Dutch citizens employed in public service (at any level of government, and including publicly funded institutions such as Leiden University) had to submit a signed declaration to the effect that they had no Jewish ancestors. Subsequently, Jewish Dutchmen in public service were first suspended, and then dismissed.
Austausch	(G) Exchange (of prisoners). In the Bergen-Belsen concentration camp, groups of prisoners with special passports or Palestine certificates were held separately, in case they could be exchanged for national or ethnic Germans held by the allies. One of the children in the orphanage escaped to freedom through the Palestine transport of June 1944 (Ch. 9.3).
Berufsverbot	(G) Exclusion order. A prohibition to practice in certain professions, based on one's religion, race, political affiliation, etc.
de Bezetter	Literally "the occupier". A colloquial word indicating the collective German occupation authority, whether civil or military. A very useful term since the individuals were not necessarily Nazis.
Dienstbode	Domestic staff, house maids. The orphanage employed 116 such staff on a temporary basis between 1890 and 1943.
Dienstleiter	(G) Department head in the Westerbork internal (Jewish) organization. An *Oberdienstleiter* supervised them all. Originally set up by the Dutch commandant when Westerbork was still only a refugee camp, the Germans made good use of these functionaries, who were not only fluent in German, but who (mostly) also knew how to adapt to their German overlords. The role of these Jewish functionaries in Westerbork remains controversial to this day.
Durchgangslager	(G) Transit camp from where Jews were deported to death camps in Eastern Europe. Westerbork was the primary transit camp in the Netherlands, like Kazerne Dossin in Belgium, and Drancy in France.
Einsatzgruppen	(G) Special SS "deployment units". Mobile death squads which followed the Wehrmacht into newly conquered areas in Poland and into the

	Soviet Union and the Baltic states to implement the "Final Solution". See Chapter 7.6.
Engelandvaarders	People who tried to reach England from occupied Holland. For many of them the primary aim was to continue the fight against Germany. Although the word *"vaarder"* suggests escape by ship across the North Sea, many came overland, mostly through Belgium and France to Spain.
Entscheidungsstelle	(G) Literally: the office where decisions were taken. The German office supervising the Civil Registry as to approving or rejecting requests to change the registration as full-, half-, or quarter-Jew. The head of the *Entscheidungsstelle* was the German Hans Calmeyer. He is credited with having saved numerous Dutch Jews by approving their change in status as Jews or half-Jews, often on flimsy grounds. See Chapters 6.2, 7.3, 7.7 9.2.
Häftling	(G) Literally: prisoner. In Westerbork, it applied to those who were caught in hiding (*onderduik*) or other "illegal" activities. Most *Häftlinge* (also called *"strafgevallen"*) were put on the first available transport to the East.
Illegaliteit	Literally: the "illegality", meaning the resistance movement. A strange and yet very meaningful word for what is called "the resistance" in other countries. The Nazis took care, certainly in the beginning, to underpin their actions by official, pseudo-lawful, promulgations, edicts, etc. In a country where people (before the war) were used to being respectful and obedient towards authority and the law, it was apparently logical to regard resistance as unlawful, hence illegal, even if done with great pride.
Joodse Raad	Jewish Council (of elders). Created by order of the German authorities, initially for Amsterdam (where some 60% of Dutch Jews were domiciled) but soon for the entire country. The Joodse Raad was co-chaired by A. Asscher and D. Cohen (see also CBJB and CJV). It became defunct in September 1943 when the deportation of Jews from Holland was virtually completed.
Kweekschool	Vocational institute, teacher training college.
Mediene	Jewish communities which existed outside Amsterdam, in cities like The Hague and Rotterdam or Leiden, usually in the small towns and villages of the provinces.
Onderduiker	Literary: *"someone who has dived under (the surface)"*, a person in hiding from the authorities. Initially predominantly Dutch Jews and members of the resistance, joined later in the war by men who were trying to escape forced labour in Germany (or other occupied territories), i.e. the *arbeidsinzet*.
Ontruiming	Literally: emptying a room or a building. This seemingly innocuous word, in the context of this book, has terrible overtones as it applies to forcefully taking people out of their homes with lethal intentions.

Persoonsbewijs	Abbreviated as "pb". A special identity card designed for use within the (occupied!) Netherlands by the head of the Civil Registry, J.L. Lentz, a civil servant in the Dutch Home Office. It was introduced in April 1941 for all citizens aged fifteen and above (Ch. 6.2). The Germans were pleased with the Dutch pb, which was very difficult to falsify, more difficult even than the model being used in Germany itself. Lentz was convicted for collaboration after the war. The ID card used in France and Belgium was "a joke" compared to the Dutch pb. Hijme Stoffels could provide people with good false pbs only because he had access to genuine blanks from two friends at the Registry Office of the Leiden municipality (Chs. 9.3 and 10.3).
Razzia	Coordinated action by police and/or military to round up victims of persecution, by the closing of streets or whole neighbourhoods and systematically doing house searches.
Sperre	(G) A temporary reprieve from deportation, with a stamp in the *persoonsbewijs*. Everybody with a J stamped in the pb wanted to get such a reprieve, which initially were allocated by the Joodse Raad, but of course it was just another German ruse. Once most Jews without a *Sperre* were deported, they started to cancel the *Sperre* one after another.
Sperrgebiet	(G) Area from which civilians are banned for military and/or political reasons.
Umschlagplatz	(G) Literally, place of transfer. Term used in the first place for the collection point adjacent to the Warsaw Ghetto, from where some 260,000 Polish Jews were transported to the Treblinka death camp. There were many such collection points all over occupied Europe. In Amsterdam, the Hollandsche Schouwburg (now part of the Holocaust Museum) served the same purpose, and so did Loods 22 in Rotterdam.
Verwalter	(G) Administrator, custodian. Following registration in October 1940, Jewish shop and business owners were dispossessed and a *Verwalter* was appointed by the occupation authorities.
Verzuiling	*Zuil* means "column" or "pillar". *Verzuiling* indicates a society which is strongly based on religious and/or socio-political denominations, each having their own networks, political party, newspapers, radio stations, schools and even cemeteries. Terms like compartmentalization or segregation may be used, but this may be misleading. The "columns" suggest that together, they support, indeed carry, the society as a whole, and *verzuiling* did not exclude close cooperation between them.
Weggehaald	"Taken away", deported. Also used: *opgehaald*, which means "collected". Seemingly innocuous words, but in the context of the occupation these words have become very sinister euphemisms, implying people were taken out of their homes, often by Dutch policemen, handed over to the Germans,

	taken to Westerbork, deported to Eastern Europe, and killed upon arrival.
Wehrmacht	(G) The German army. It played a subordinate role in occupied Holland,
	because the Germans installed a civilian Nazi government on 18th May 1940,
	the Dutch government having moved itself to London.
Zentralstelle	(G) Stands for *Zentralstelle für Jüdische Auswanderung* (Central Office for
	Jewish Emigration). Established in Holland on 31st March 1941. Until 1941
	Jews in Germany could still leave the Reich (albeit with difficulty, and
	only after abandoning everything they possessed). In the Netherlands,
	however, leaving "legally" became effectively impossible from the start
	of the occupation in May 1940. By 1941 the *Zentralstelle* had developed
	into the main German office coordinating the registration, isolation, and
	deportation of the Dutch Jewry to the death camps. By mid-1942 the word
	Auswanderung (emigration) had become no more than a euphemism for
	deportation and mass murder.

In line with most international literature, the terms 'the Netherlands' and 'Holland' are used as synonyms, although strictly speaking they are not.

List of 168 children and 9 staff who lived in the orphanage (1929-1943)

The following pages contain the basic list as it underpins all the stories in this book. The list includes 168 children who lived for at least some 2 months in the new Orphanage in Leiden from its inauguration in august 1929, including the children of director Italie, and including the 25 children (Table 2.1) who moved from the old to the new building during the summer of 1929. It is based on the investigation of primary sources and archives by C.W. van Zegveld, L.P. Kasteleyn, the present author, and recently Mrs. B. Bikker and colleagues of Stichting Herdenking Jodenvervolging Leiden, spanning a period of more than 30 years. Yet the list is certainly not "definitive". It remains perfectly possible that future research results will require the list to be amended or corrected.

The date of death as given in the list is the *officially recorded* date. These dates were set, sometimes long after the war, for legal reasons; see Chapter 10. Only very few of these dates can be confirmed with exact certainty. In Buchenwald and Mauthausen, prisoners were registered upon arrival, and their death was also recorded. But both the date and the cause of death (as transmitted to the families) were often falsified to hide the fact that groups of prisoners were killed on the same day, see Chapter 8.1.

In Auschwitz, deportees who were selected for labour were registered, and their death was recorded in *Sterbebücher* and other documents, but the Dutch authorities did not take these data into account when the legal date of death was determined (Schütz, 2011).

In Sobibor, it was assumed that the journey from Westerbork took three days, and practically all the deportees were gassed immediately upon arrival. For those very few who were selected for work in Sobibor, they will not have survived the uprising of 14th October 1943. Those who were sent to one of the Sobibor satellite camps (such as Sally Montezinos) may have survived until 8th November, when all these satellite camps were liquidated (witness accounts recorded by the Red Cross, second edition February 1947; in NIOD library (EVDO02_NIOD05_7880.pdf[1]). For Sally Montezinos the official date is 4th November 1943, he will almost certainly not have survived the liquidation of Dorohucza on 8th November, and in fact he may well have died long *before* that date.

The arrival date in Westerbork is based on the date of registration as recorded by the Joodse Raad, in some cases one or two days after their arrival. The 59 people

---

1   Also on https://www.herdenkingleiden.nl/wp-content/uploads/2020/12/EVDO02_NIOD05_7880.pdf.

who were taken from orphanage on 17th March 1943 arrived in Westerbork in the morning of 18th March, so that date is given in the list even if they were registered a day later.

Twelve children lived in the orphanage during two separate periods. On the printed list you will only find the first entry date, and the last exit date. The columns containing the interruption period are part of the spreadsheet but not shown to keep the printed list manageable. The days of absence have of course been deducted to calculate the total time each child lived in the orphanage. Broken years are quoted in decimals based on days, not months: one year and six months is given as 1.5 years.

Children who lived in the Jewish orphanage in Leiden from 1929 (by name)

last updated on 6-6-2021

n.a. = not applicable

Name (Family, Given)	Place of birth	Date of Birth	Orphanage in:	Orphanage out:	Days	Years decimal	Deported to Westerbork or other	Dep. From Westerbork or other	Barak No.	official DoD Date of Death	Place of death	Age reached	Comments
Adler, Lotte	Frankfurt a/M	8-2-1925	22-11-1938	17-3-1943	1576	4,3	17-3-1943	23-3-1943	66	26-3-1943	Sobibor	18,1	
Adler, Henny Henriëtte	Frankfurt a/M	23-7-1930	22-11-1938	17-3-1943	1576	4,3	17-3-1943	23-3-1943	66	26-3-1943	Sobibor	12,7	Th-BB 16-5-1944
Appel, Esther	Amsterdam	22-5-1918	10-12-1929	1-9-1936	2457	6,7	8-4-1943	18-1-1944	62	12-4-1945	Bergen-Belsen	26,9	Not in Shoah Databases
Arndt, Rita	Berlin	4-1-1928	10-8-1935	21-5-1939	1380	3,8					prob. survived		
Auerhaan, Leman (Leo)	Amsterdam	24-11-1922	7-10-1929	25-11-1940	4067	11,1	5-10-1942	3-3-1944	1A-2	31-7-1944	Auschwitz	21,7	In WBK Sperrkartotheek; brief uit Monowitz
Beem, Hermina Juliana (Mien)	Rotterdam	9-6-1918	12-9-1929	17-11-1937	2944	8,1	11-2-1943	2-3-1943	66	5-3-1943	Sobibor	24,7	Not in Orph. 29-7 to 11-9-1937
Beem, Juliana Hermina (Juultje)	Rotterdam	26-1-1920	12-9-1929	2-5-1938	3112	8,5	13-7-1942	21-7-1942	66	30-9-1942	Auschwitz	22,7	Not in Orph. 27-9 to 8-11-'37. St.B. DoD 19-8
Beem, Jozef David	Rotterdam	4-7-1926	12-9-1929	17-3-1943	4934	13,5	17-3-1943	23-3-1943	66	26-3-1943	Sobibor	16,7	
Beem, David Jozef	Rotterdam	17-6-1922	12-9-1929	1-8-1941	4341	11,9	3-7-1943	6-7-1943	57	9-7-1943	Sobibor	21,1	
Beer, Abraham (Bram) de	Amsterdam	10-8-1939	28-7-1942	17-3-1943	232	0,6	16-11-1943	16-11-1943	66	19-11-1943	Auschwitz	4,3	Father barak 65
Bekker, Golderiesje (Golda)	Den Haag	2-4-1915	10-6-1929	16-12-1929	189	0,5	31-3-1943	15-11-1943		10-12-1943	Auschwitz	28,7	married Mozes F. Wachtmann
Bekker, Betsy	Den Haag	27-11-1916	10-6-1929	16-12-1929	189	0,5	20-1-1943	9-2-1943		12-2-1943	Auschwitz	26,2	married Abr. Schuyer
Berg, Henriëtte van den	Amsterdam	5-8-1925	13-2-1934	5-8-1935	538	1,5		16-7-1942	Vught	30-9-1942	Auschwitz	17,2	peculiar: diff. Transport/same DoD as Marie
Berg, Marie (Maria) van den	Den Haag	1-6-1927	12-2-1934	5-8-1935	538	1,5		31-7-1942		30-9-1942	Auschwitz	15,3	source DoD?
Bilk, Nathan	Den Haag	9-2-1924	12-2-1934	10-5-1939	1914	5,2	6-3-1943	10-3-1943	66	13-3-1943	Sobibor	19,1	
Blog, Wilhelmina (Willy)	Apeldoorn	1-1-1934	23-7-1936	17-3-1943	2428	6,7	17-3-1943	23-3-1943	66	26-3-1943	Sobibor	9,2	
Bobbe, Jetje (Jetty)	Den Haag	25-4-1924	24-5-1928	17-3-1943	5410	14,8	17-3-1943	23-3-1943	66	26-3-1943	Sobibor	18,9	
Bobbe, Benjamin	Rotterdam	11-2-1939	7-11-1942	17-3-1943	130	0,4	17-3-1943	4-5-1943	66	7-5-1943	Sobibor	4,2	
Bobbe, Louis	Den Haag	7-3-1941	7-11-1942	17-3-1943	130	0,4	17-3-1943	4-5-1943	66	7-5-1943	Sobibor	2,2	
Brink, Ihno ten	Lingen	22-9-1932	2-3-1936	9-7-1942	2320	6,4	9-7-1942	4-9-1944	66	6-10-1944	Auschwitz	12,0	>Th.st.>Au 4-10-1944. RK list 239/72 1972
Cohen, Lodewijk (Lodi)	Leiden	25-9-1917	14-4-1930	14-10-1935	2009	5,5	n.a.				survived	23,1	Escaped > Pyrenees> Palestina 1944
Cohen, Izak Hartog (Ies)	Leiden	16-4-1920	14-4-1930	24-10-1938	3115	8,5	18-5-1943		65	21-5-1943	Auschwitz		
Cohen, Andries	Amsterdam	18-11-1923	23-10-1930	17-6-1932	603	1,7	15-7-1942	21-7-1942		30-9-1942	Auschwitz	18,9	
Cohen, Hijman	Amsterdam	26-3-1927	23-10-1930	19-6-1934	1335	3,7	18-10-1943	25-1-1944		31-5-1944	Auschwitz	17,2	AMS Orph ;Vught>18-10-43WBK; dob 28/3 on JR
Cohen, Sara	Amsterdam	14-7-1935	7-12-1938	7-2-1939	62	0,2	11-9-1942	14-9-1942		17-9-1942	Auschwitz	7,2	
Dagloonder, Mietje (Mieke)	Amsterdam	29-11-1927	18-12-1929	20-5-1931	708	1,9	27-2-1943	2-3-1943	66	26-3-1943	Sobibor	15,3	
Dam, Samuel van (Hemerik)	Amsterdam	15-8-1924	11-6-1929	10-7-1939	81	0,2	n.a.			14-7-1990	survived	65,9	Kamp Vught NIOD M.68; DoD 14-7-1990
David, Bermann	Köln	27-10-1926	20-4-1939	13-7-1942	4420	12,1	n.a.			27-10-2017	survived	91,0	JR: Oude Kampbewoners
Degen, Abraham Cordanus (Bram)	Leiden	16-12-1925	6-6-1930	30-5-1940	1410	3,9	Vu 3-7-43				survived		Hachsharah Gouda. G1 Not deported
Engelschman, Samuel	Amsterdam	24-8-1927	13-11-1929	6-6-1930	203	0,6	28-11-1942		4	9-7-1943	Sobibor	17,6	Not in Orph. 6-6-1937 to 10-2-1937
Engelschman, Barend	Amsterdam	29-8-1938	15-11-1929	20-1-1941	786	2,2				18-6-2012	survived	84,8	Dec. Woerden (Geni)
Ensel, Izak	Rotterdam	8-12-1929	20-1-1941	17-3-1943	170	0,5	17-3-1943	23-3-1943	66	26-3-1943	Sobibor	4,6	Brother Jacob 8-1-1932
Familier, Ruth Ellen	Köln	8-12-1929	1-8-1939	18-1-1940	798	2,2					survived		Not in any Shoah Database
Färber, Mindel	Düsseldorf	9-4-1928	8-1-1941	17-3-1943	1239	3,4					survived	15,0	Bergen Belsen > Palestina 30-6 / 10-7-1944
Feniger, Herszel (Harry)	Amsterdam	12-9-1930	14-10-1935	6-3-1939	2367	6,5	30-3-1943	30-3-1943	51	2-4-1943	Sobibor	12,6	Deported to Liebenau 9-3-1943
Feniger, Hendrina (Henny)	Amsterdam	14-10-1935	14-10-1935	7-4-1942	1374	3,8	30-3-1943	30-3-1943	51	2-4-1943	Sobibor	64,0	Deported to Liebenau 9-3-1943
Fleurima, Louis	Rotterdam	21-5-1936	18-2-1939	23-11-1942	1374	3,8	9-3-1943	9-3-1943		30-5-2000	survived	57,7	Ex Orph. R'dam; return R'dam 1941
Fleurima, Melna	Rotterdam	21-5-1936	18-2-1939	23-11-1942	3729	10,2	9-3-1943	9-3-1943		18-1-1994	survived	20,6	
Frenkel, Marianne(Mirjam)	Rotterdam	29-7-1922	31-12-1930	17-3-1943	4459	12,2	27-2-1943	2-3-1943	85	5-3-1943	Sobibor	18,9	
Frenkel, Cornelia (Corry)	Rotterdam	25-4-1924	31-12-1930	17-3-1943	4459	12,2	17-3-1943	23-3-1943	66	26-3-1943	Sobibor	18,9	
Goldenberg, Greta	Amsterdam	24-1-1936	4-12-1939	6-3-1942	823	2,3	11-2-1943	2-3-1943	66	5-3-1943	Sobibor	7,1	

last updated on 6-6-2021

n.a. = not applicable

Children who lived in the Jewish orphanage in Leiden from 1929 (by name)

Name (Family, Given)	Place of birth	Date of Birth	Orphanage in:	Orphanage out:	Days	Years decimal	Deported to Westerbork or other	Dep. From Westerbork or other	Barak No.	Date of Death (official DoD)	Place of death	Age reached	Comments
Gottschalk, Helga Sara	Geilenkirchen	18-11-1932	20-4-1939	10-7-1939	81	0,2	n.a.	n.a.			survived		Escaped on SS Bodegraven 14-5-1940
Gottschalk, Kurt Adolf Israel	Geilenkirchen	15-7-1937	20-4-1939	10-7-1939	81	0,2	n.a.	n.a.			survived		Escaped on SS Bodegraven Died USA Feb. 2021
Goudsmit, Bertha	Den Haag	14-8-1924	6-8-1942	17-3-1943	223	0,6	17-3-1943	23-3-1943	66	26-3-1943	Sobibor	18,6	
Grosswachs, Esthera (Esther)	Den Haag	27-7-1931	19-12-1939	18-4-1940	121	0,3	8-12-1942	12-12-1942		15-12-1942	Auschwitz	11,4	
Grosswachs, Malka	Den Haag	10-8-1932	19-12-1939	18-4-1940	121	0,3	8-12-1942	12-12-1942		15-12-1942	Auschwitz	10,3	
Grosswachs, Sarah	Den Haag	10-8-1936	19-12-1939	18-4-1940	121	0,3	8-12-1942	12-12-1942		15-12-1942	Auschwitz	6,3	
Günsberg, Fanny Susanne	Gelsenkirchen	25-1-1927	5-1-1938	17-3-1943	1897	5,2	17-3-1943	23-3-1943	66	26-3-1943	Sobibor	16,2	
Günsberg, Lothar	Gelsenkirchen	22-4-1928	24-10-1938	17-3-1943	1605	4,4	17-3-1943	23-3-1943	66	26-3-1943	Sobibor	14,9	
Gurfinkel, Rudi	Hanau	4-6-1919	6-4-1933	23-6-1933	78	0,2	n.a.	n.a.			Z. Yaakov	93	Emigr. Palestine 24-12-1934;
Gurfinkel, Make	Köln	3-9-1920	6-4-1933	23-6-1933	78	0,2	n.a.	n.a.	66				Emigrated to Palestine 1934
Gurfinkel, Benjamin	Köln	26-10-1921	6-4-1933	23-6-1933	78	0,2	n.a.	n.a.	66		USA	67	Emigr. Palestine 1934; later USA
Gurfinkel, Esther	Köln	1-5-1923	16-4-1933	23-6-1933	68	0,2	n.a.	n.a.					Emigrated to Palestine 1934
Gurfinkel, Ida	Köln	28-8-1925	16-4-1933	23-6-1933	68	0,2	n.a.	n.a.					Emigrated to Palestine 1934
Gurfinkel, Marga	Köln	28-1-1930	16-4-1933	23-6-1933	68	0,2	n.a.	n.a.					Emigrated to Palestine 1934
Hakker, Maurits	Den Haag	29-3-1929	15-2-1943	17-3-1943	30	0,1	17-3-1943	18-5-1943	66	21-5-1943	Sobibor	14,1	
Hakker, Simon	Den Haag	24-2-1933	15-2-1943	17-3-1943	30	0,1	17-3-1943	18-5-1943	66	21-5-1943	Sobibor	10,2	
Hamerslag, Enny	Amsterdam	27-12-1935	6-11-1941	1-3-1943	480	1,3	8-4-1943	18-5-1943	58	21-5-1943	Sobibor	7,4	Left before 17-3; 1-3 is assumed
Hamerslag, Judith	Amsterdam	10-12-1937	6-11-1941	1-3-1943	480	1,3	8-4-1943	18-5-1943	58	21-5-1943	Sobibor	5,4	Left before 17-3; 1-3 is assumed
Hamerslag, David	Amsterdam	23-11-1939	6-11-1941	1-3-1943	480	1,3	8-4-1943	18-5-1943	58	21-5-1943	Sobibor	3,5	Left before 17-3; 1-3 is assumed
Heerma van Voss, Etty	Amsterdam	16-6-1931	28-8-1942	17-3-1943	201	0,6	17-3-1943	13-4-1943		16-4-1943	Sobibor	11,8	Left before 17-3; 1-3 is assumed
Hekster, Sylvain	Amsterdam	7-6-1931	21-12-1937	15-2-1943	786	2,2	20-6-1943	6-7-1943	83	9-7-1943	Sobibor	12,1	
Herskovits, Eva	Hannover	8-3-1928	18-6-1941	7-11-1941	142	0,4	n.a.			12-7-1973	survived	45,3	1941>Hannover>1944>Th>Auschw>USA NJ. mother's name (van Dijk) also used
Heuman, Emanuel Victor	Sittard	25-6-1932	11-3-1939	5-10-1940	574	1,6		28-8-1942		31-8-1942	Auschwitz	10,2	
Italie, Hanna Sara	Leiden	11-5-1935	11-5-1935	17-3-1943	2867	7,9	17-3-1943	18-5-1943	66	26-3-1943	Sobibor	7,9	Daughter of director Italie
Italie, Elchanan Tsewie	Leiden	8-2-1937	8-2-1937	17-3-1943	2228	6,1	17-3-1943	23-3-1943	66	26-3-1943	Sobibor	6,1	Son of director Italie
Jacobsohn, Paula	Hamburg	3-4-1925	17-5-1934	3-11-1936	901	2,5	12-2-1942	18-1-1944	11	28-2-1945	Stutthof	19,9	Th>Auschw. 16-5-1944>Stutthof (Danzig)
Jansen, Henderina (Henny)	Amsterdam	1-6-1917	15-2-1932	3-5-1935	1173	3,2				7-1-2009	survived	91,6	Not dep. aka Henny Behr
Jong, Hetty Maud Ellen de	Palembang	8-8-1919	6-9-1932	30-9-1936	1485	4,1	30-10-1943	19-5-1944	67	22-5-1944	Auschwitz	24,8	Edward Frankenhuis born 24-2-1944 in WBK
Kam, Marianne (Mary) van	Rotterdam	16-1-1931	4-4-1940	17-3-1943	716	2,0	17-3-1943	23-3-1943	66	26-3-1943	Sobibor	12,2	Not in Orph. 21-7-1941 to 17-7-1942
Kam, Heiman van	Rotterdam	15-3-1933	4-4-1940	17-3-1943	716	2,0	17-3-1943	23-3-1943	66	26-3-1943	Sobibor	10,0	Not in Orph. 21-7-1941 to 17-7-1942
Kam, Herman van	Rijswijk	18-1-1935	4-4-1940	17-3-1943	716	2,0	17-3-1943	23-3-1943	66	26-3-1943	Sobibor	8,2	Not in Orph. 21-7-1941 to 17-7-1942
Kam, Arthur van	Rijswijk	23-8-1937	17-7-1942	17-3-1943	243	0,7	17-3-1943	23-3-1943	66	26-3-1943	Sobibor	5,6	
Kirschenbaum, Chaim (Charles)	Belfort	2-9-1926	17-11-1930	17-3-1943	4503	12,3	17-3-1943	23-3-1943	66	26-3-1943	Sobibor	16,6	> barak 35; arrival orph. uncertain
Klausner, Regine (René)	Den Haag	22-7-1940	30-4-1942	17-3-1943	321	0,9	17-3-1943	4-5-1943	66-35	7-5-1943	Sobibor	2,8	> barak 35;
Klein, Didia	Parijs	12-5-1925	10-2-1930	17-3-1943	4783	13,1	17-3-1943	21-9-1943	66-71	6-5-2001	survived	76,0	Deported to Auschwitz. died in Bergen (N.H.)
Kloos, Ludwig	Düsseldorf	14-6-1916	16-10-1920	17-11-1932	4415	12,1	19-7-1942	24-7-1942		30-9-1942	Auschwitz	26,3	DOB 16-6 on JR card
Kloosterman, Anthonius H. (Hans)	Amsterdam	19-2-1927	2-12-1929	17-3-1943	4853	13,3	17-3-1943	27-5 release'd	66-64	3-5-2005	survived	78,2	G1; Released from Westerbork
Kloots, Sientje	Rotterdam	22-6-1938	21-12-1942	31-12-1942	10		220-1-1943	9-2-1943		12-2-1943	Auschwitz	4,6	source: list De Tombe
Konijn, Mary	Amsterdam	13-11-1928	14-1-1935	5-3-1943	1845	8,1	29-6-1943			2-7-1943	Sobibor	14,6	Not in Orph. 5-3-1941 to 5-3-1943
Konijn, Marcus (Max)	Amsterdam	9-4-1930	14-1-1935	5-3-1943	1845	8,1	29-6-1943			2-7-1943	Sobibor	13,2	Not in Orph. 5-3-1941 to 5-3-1943
Konijn, Betty	Amsterdam	6-5-1931	14-1-1935	5-3-1943	1845	8,1	29-6-1943			2-7-1943	Sobibor	12,2	Not in Orph. 5-3-1941 to 5-3-1943
Konijn, Lia	Amsterdam	20-9-1932	14-1-1935	5-3-1943	1845	8,1	29-6-1943			2-7-1943	Sobibor	10,8	Not in Orph. 5-3-1941 to 5-3-1943

last updated on 6-6-2021

n.a. = not applicable

Children who lived in the Jewish orphanage in Leiden from 1929 (by name)

Name (Family, Given)	Place of birth	Date of Birth	Orphanage in:	Orphanage out:	Days	Years decimal	Deported to Westerbork or other	Dep. From Westerbork or other	Barak No.	official DoD Date of Death	Place of death	Age reached	Comments
Kool, Barend Bora	Amsterdam	4-8-1928	16-1-1931	30-5-1932	500	1,4	ex Apeldoorn	22-1-1943		25-1-1943	Auschwitz	14,5	No trp date on JR card; but on A.Bos lijst
Korper, Simon	Amsterdam	22-4-1937	17-10-1941	3-3-1943	502	1,4	6-4-1943	18-5-1943		21-5-1943	Sobibor	6,1	WBK 6-4-43
Kzernitzky, Daniel	Amsterdam	1-8-1933	8-7-1937	1-8-1940	1120	3,1					prob. survived		Not in Shoah databases
Landau, Bernhard Leon	Wenen (Au)	2-5-1926	16-5-1931	30-11-1931	198	0,5					prob. perished		Not in Shoah databases; 1940 in Krakau
Lapidas, Egon	Treuburg	13-1-1924	15-11-1933	13-2-1934	90	0,2	ex Berlin>	24-10-1941		5-12-1942	Łódź	18,9	"Litzmannstadt"
Leeda, Rachel (Chelly)	Amsterdam	21-1-1922	25-9-1924	6-9-1933	3268	8,9	8-4-1943	11-1-1944	55	26-7-1959	survived	37,5	>B.Belsen> 17-11-1944 Liebenau
Levie, Sara (Selma)	Raamsdonk	14-2-1926	2-11-1932	6-9-1933	308	0,8				8-7-2011	survived	85,4	Died in Vught 2011
Levie, Maurits	Raamsdonk	14-2-1926	2-11-1932	16-6-1936	1322	3,6	10-4-1943	27-4-1943	65	30-4-1943	Sobibor	17,2	> Rudelsheim
Lichtenbaum, Frieda Itta	Ginneken	17-10-1927	18-8-1932	17-3-1943	3863	10,6	17-3-1943	4-5-1943	66	7-5-1943	Sobibor	15,6	
Liffmann, Ruth	Düsseldorf	16-11-1934	20-4-1939	13-6-1939	54	0,1					survived		>Belgium 13-6-1939. >>USA
Liebfreund, Gemmi	Den Haag	7-10-1933	6-3-1936	30-9-1938	938	2,6	6-3-1943	10-3-1943	66	13-3-1943	Sobibor	9,4	>Orph. The Hague 1938
Limburg, Levie (Louis)	Amsterdam	27-2-1923	25-7-1932	22-4-1941	3193	8,7	5-10-1942	12-10-1942		13-11-1943	Auschwitz	19,9	
Lipschits, Alexander Jacob	Bergen o/Zoom	24-8-1926	15-5-1930	13-10-1930	151	0,4	ex Dossin	31-7-1943		2-8-1943	Auschwitz	16,9	Deported with parents from Mechelen
Maarssen, Henriette (Jet)	Amsterdam	31-8-1925	6-8-1942	9-3-1943	215	0,6	20-6-1943	20-7-1943		23-7-1943	Sobibor	17,9	
Meijers, Salomon	Den Haag	4-4-1937	nov-42	13-1-1943	73	ca 0,2	18-3-1944	23-3-1944	58	26-3-1944	Auschwitz	7,0	caught in onderduik in Limburg
Meijers, Bernard	Den Haag	16-12-1939	nov-42	13-1-1943	73	ca 0,2	18-3-1944	23-3-1944	67	26-3-1944	Auschwitz	4,3	caught in onderduik in Limburg
Mogendorff, Henriette (Jetty)	Amsterdam	23-11-1925	28-7-1942	17-3-1943	232	0,6	17-3-1943	27-4-1943	66	30-4-1943	Sobibor	17,4	Deported with parents
Mogendorff, Cecilia	Amsterdam	5-11-1926	28-7-1942	17-3-1943	232	0,6	17-3-1943	27-4-1943	66	30-4-1943	Sobibor	16,5	Deported with parents
Mogendorff, Roza	Amsterdam	1-12-1932	4-11-1942	17-3-1943	133	0,4	17-3-1943	27-4-1943	66	30-4-1943	Sobibor	10,4	Deported with parents
Montezinos, Salomon Levie (Sally)	Den Haag	6-5-1924	21-12-1926	17-3-1943	5930	16,2	17-3-1943	27-4-1943	66-64	4-11-1943	Dorohucza	19,5	DoD before 8-11-43
Muller, Frits	Wormerveer	8-2-1912	10-2-1917	14-2-1930	4752	13,0				23-1-1998	survived	86,0	Not deported. Died in Arnhem
Muller, Marianne (Jannie)	Wormerveer	22-1-1914	31-5-1917	4-9-1930	4844	13,3					survived		Not deported (mixed marriage)
Overste, Jacques	Amsterdam	7-10-1923	9-11-1929	16-6-1930	219	0,6	4-10-1942	5-10-1942		8-5-1945	Central Europe	21,6	Buchenwald
Overste, Adolf Maurits	Amsterdam	28-7-1926	9-11-1929	16-6-1930	219	0,6				4-10-2004	survived	78,2	Not deported
Pool, Mozes (Max) van der	Wildervank	29-2-1916	27-9-1922	13-10-1930	2938	8,0					survived		
Poons, Philip	Den Haag	6-12-1930	ca jan. 1943	17-3-1943			17-3-1943	4-5-1943	66	7-5-1943	Sobibor	12,4	18/3/43 WBK; deported 4/5/43 +parents?
Poons, Harry	Den Haag	13-7-1940	ca jan. 1943	17-3-1943			17-3-1943	4-5-1943	66	7-5-1943	Sobibor	2,8	18/3/43 WBK; deported 4/5/43 +parents?
Porcelijn, Salomon Elias (Sal)	Amsterdam	7-8-1919	13-12-1930	3-2-1937	2244	6,1					survived		Not deported; died 3/1987 Paterson NJ
Porcelijn, Johan (Hans)	Amsterdam	21-1-1924	31-12-1930	11-12-1941	3998	10,9				30-9-1942	Auschwitz	18,7	
Preuss, Inge	Berlin	26-2-1928	4-10-1933	7-9-1934	338	0,9				29-12-2012	survived		Geni/Inge-Preuss
Pront, Judith (Jupie)	Amsterdam	23-3-1916	11-9-1924	11-11-1935	4078	11,2	26-5-1943	1-6-1943		4-6-1943	Sobibor	27,2	
Protter, Ralph Heinz	Köln	10-5-1930	12-4-1937	17-3-1943	2165	5,9	17-3-1943	23-3-1943	66	26-3-1943	Sobibor	12,9	
Redisch, Benno	Amsterdam	13-7-1939	24-6-1940	13-7-1942	749	2,1	26-5-1943	1-6-1943	55	4-6-1943	Sobibor	3,9	refugee ex Poland>Germany
Reeder, Hartog Samuel (Harry) de	Rotterdam	11-8-1914	25-9-1918	9-8-1932	5067	13,9					survived		Not deported
Ritmeester, Salomon	Amsterdam	16-3-1928	9-9-1932	17-3-1943	3841	10,5	18-5-1943	18-5-1943	66	21-5-1943	Sobibor	15,2	
Ritmeester, Barend	Amsterdam	24-4-1930	9-9-1932	6-3-1939	2369	6,5	26-5-1943	1-6-1943	58	4-6-1943	Sobibor	13,1	> Rudelsheim
Rotstein, Salomon	Amsterdam	20-7-1937	25-9-1939	17-3-1943	1269	3,5	17-3-1943	23-3-1943		26-3-1943	Sobibor	5,7	
Rozeveld, Herman Bert	Leiden	25-12-1930	5-1-1933	17-3-1943	3723	10,2	17-3-1943	23-3-1943	66	26-3-1943	Sobibor	12,3	
Sanders, Debora	Den Haag	12-6-1934	13-4-1939	18-8-1941	858	2,3	?	5-4-1944		25-10-1944	Auschwitz	10,4	>Th.stadt 5/4/44; >Auschw. 23/10/44
Santen, Jansje (Jenny) van	Amsterdam	15-3-1914	16-6-1924	25-4-1932	2870	7,9				9-9-1962	survived	48,5	Died in New York
Santen, Karel van	Amsterdam	16-9-1918	21-12-1926	2-7-1940	4942	13,5	Schoorl			10-9-1941	Mauthausen	23,0	22-2 Arrested>*Buchenwald>**Mauthausen
Santen, Esther (Esje) van	Amsterdam	20-5-1920	5-2-1923	3-2-1943	6029	16,5				3-3-2016	survived	95,8	Not in Orph. 31-3-1939 to 25-9-1942

last updated on 6-6-2021

n.a. = not applicable

Children who lived in the Jewish orphanage in Leiden from 1929 (by name)

Name (Family, Given)	Place of birth	Date of Birth	Orphanage in:	Orphanage out:	Days	Years decimal	Deported to Westerbork or other	Dep. From Westerbork or other	Barak No.	official DoD Date of Death	Place of death	Age reached	Comments
Schipper, Heinrich	Vienna	30-3-1921	8-4-1933	22-6-1933	75	0,2	ex K.Dossin	12-9-1942		15-9-1942	Auschwitz	21,5	Transport IX/472 Kazerne Dossin
Schipper, Klara	Köln	9-1-1925	8-4-1933	22-6-1933	75	0,2				3-1-2018	survived	93,0	>USA Claire Kleeman
Schipper, Leon	Köln	20-10-1928	8-4-1933	22-6-1933	75	0,2				16-1-2015	survived	86,2	Belgium > USA
Schlesinger, Anni	Wenen (Au)	5-2-1934	20-4-1939	10-7-1939	81	0,2	15-4-1940	18-1-1944		6-10-1944	Auschwitz	10,7	>Th>4-10-44Auschw
Segal, Reina	Amsterdam	5-1-1925	28-12-1927	17-3-1943	5558	15,2	17-3-1943	23-3-1943	66	26-3-1943	Sobibor	18,2	
Simons, Annie	?	?	?	?									Not found in any database.
Slap, Isaac	Amsterdam	26-11-1935	23-3-1939	23-6-1939	92	0,3	25-5-1943	25-5-1943	65	28-5-1943	Sobibor	7,5	
Slier, Henriëtte (Henny)	Rotterdam	26-2-1930	25-8-1941	17-3-1943	569	1,6	17-3-1943	4-5-1943	66	7-5-1943	Sobibor	13,2	
Spier, Henny (Harry)	Den Haag	7-6-1925	24-5-1928	17-3-1943	5410	14,8	17-3-1943	4-5-1943	66>64	7-5-1943	Sobibor	17,9	Unsuccessful G1 attempt
Spiro, Sientje	Den Haag	27-3-1916	4-3-1926	24-9-1935	3491	9,6	18-10-1943	19-10-1943		22-10-1943	Auschwitz	27,6	
Spiro, Abraham (Bram)	Den Haag	29-5-1917	4-3-1926	3-3-1936	3500	10,0		25-1-1944		26-3-1944	Auschwitz	26,8	Not in Orph 5-8-35 to 4-1-36 ∞ H Cosman
Stofkooper, Herman	Groningen	29-5-1918	16-12-1929	30-9-1935	2114	5,8	n.a.	n.a.	n.a.	15-10-1990	survived	72,4	Escaped to Switzerland 1942 *Onderduik*
Straten, Louise Dora (Lies) van	Den Haag	18-11-1928	15-1-1943	16-3-1943	60	0,2	n.a.	n.a.	n.a.		survived		Arrival date uncertain. *Onderduik*
Stratum, Abraham (Bram) van	Groningen	27-11-1924	7-11-1935	17-11-1941	2202	6,0				30-9-1942	Auschwitz	17,8	
Stratum, Mozes (Max) van	Groningen	3-3-1917	7-11-1935	17-3-1943	2687	7,4	17-3-1943	23-3-1943	66	26-3-1943	Sobibor	16,1	
Strauss, Edith	Buchen	3-6-1930	22-11-1938	27-10-1939	339	0,9					survived		Joined mother in USA 1939
Vega, Rika Alvares	Amsterdam	17-9-1932	6-11-1941	17-3-1943	496	1,4	17-3-1943	18-5-1943	66	21-5-1943	Sobibor	10,7	
Vega, Isaac Alvares	Amsterdam	19-6-1934	22-7-1942	17-3-1943	238	0,7	17-3-1943	18-5-1943	66	21-5-1943	Sobibor	8,9	
Vega, Maurits Alvares	Amsterdam	23-4-1937	6-11-1941	29-4-1942	174	0,5	Apeldoorn	22-1-1943	n.a.	25-2-1943	Auschwitz	5,8	Apeldoorn>Auschwitz not via WBK
Vega, Henriëtte	Amsterdam	1-9-1938	6-11-1941	17-3-1943	496	1,4	17-3-1943	18-5-1943	66	21-5-1943	Sobibor	4,7	
Vega, Willem Alvares	Amsterdam	5-8-1939	6-11-1941	17-3-1943	496	1,4	17-3-1943	18-5-1943	66	21-5-1943	Sobibor	3,8	
Velleman, Margarita Henriette	Rotterdam	4-3-1925	14-8-1942	17-3-1943	215	0,6	17-3-1943	23-3-1943	66	26-3-1943	Sobibor	18,1	
Velleman, Marianna Rosa	Rotterdam	6-9-1926	14-8-1942	17-3-1943	215	0,6	17-3-1943	23-3-1943	66	26-3-1943	Sobibor	16,6	
Veltein, Hijman	Bussum	22-4-1916	19-5-1923	15-7-1930	2614	7,2		31-7-1942		30-9-1942	Auschwitz	26,4	
Vries, Harry de	Haarlem	18-6-1913	30-3-1921	9-8-1932	4150	11,4	27-5-1943	1-6-1943	60	4-6-1943	Sobibor	30,0	
Vries, Jacob (Jaap) de	Haarlem	5-5-1917	30-3-1921	30-8-1935	5266	14,4	ex Drancy	27-9-1942	n.a.	1-10-1942	Auschwitz	25,4	
Vries, Pieter (Daniël) de	Amsterdam	12-3-1925	11-10-1935	17-3-1943	2714	7,4	17-3-1943	27-5 releas'd	66>64	18-3-2011	survived	86,0	G1. Released WBK
Vries, Jozef (Joop) de	Amsterdam	25-7-1929	11-10-1935	18-9-1939	1438	3,9	23-8-1942				survived		ref. Barend Springer
Wahrhaftig, Gusta	Den Haag	31-10-1940	12-1-1943	28-2-1943	47	0,1		27-4-1943	68	30-4-1943	Sobibor	2,5	Left before 17/3/43 Deported with parents
Weddingen, Francina van	Den Haag	22-3-1932	8-8-1935	21-8-1936	379	1,0					survived		1936>Belgium; not in Shoah databases
Weddingen, Willem Frederik van	Den Haag	22-3-1932	6-9-1935	21-8-1936	350	1,0					survived		1936>Belgium; not in Shoah databases
Wegloop, Isidoor (Davidson)	Amsterdam	13-8-1926	16-4-1930	7-8-1933	1209	3,3	9-4-1943	13-4-1943	58	16-4-1943	Sobibor	16,7	> Rudelsheim
Weiman, Mietje (Mimi)	Rotterdam	10-7-1917	14-1-1927	30-4-1935	3028	8,3				30-5-2015	survived	97,9	Not deported. Died in Scheveningen
Weiman, Samuel Salomon (Sal)	Rotterdam	14-2-1919	11-2-1929	29-4-1936	2634	7,2	4-10-1942	5-10-1942		31-8-1943	Centr. Europe	24,5	Deported 5-10-1942
West, Hartog (Harry) van	Amsterdam	7-5-1920	27-7-1932	27-7-1932	182	0,5	17-5-1943	18-5-1943	70	30-11-1943	Sobibor	23,6	Arr'd 14-5-1943. DoD before 8-11-43
West, Anna Bertha van	Amsterdam	1-9-1923	27-6-1931	28-7-1932	397	1,1	17-5-1943	18-5-1943	70	30-11-1943	Sobibor	20,2	Arr'd 14-5-41 DoD before 8-11-43
West, Adriana van	Rotterdam	8-1-1921	28-12-1926	27-11-1929	1065	2,9	n.a.	n.a.	n.a.	29-7-2008	survived	87,6	Not deported
Witteboon, Jacques Maurice	Amsterdam	26-4-1918	28-12-1927	10-11-1936	3240	8,9	Pithiviers	17-7-1942		2-9-1942	Auschwitz	24,4	Pithiviers>Kosel>Auschwitz
Wittenburg, Victor Emanuel	Amsterdam	1-8-1930	29-11-1933	2-3-1936	824	2,3	25-7-1942	31-7-1942		2-8-1942	Auschwitz	12,0	11/1933 > N.I Orph. Amsterdam
Wolff, Aron (de Paauw) van	Amsterdam	27-7-1938	13-9-1940	12-11-1942	790	2,2	n.a.	n.a.			survived		Onderd.'42; >Palestine'46.
Wolff, Betje Jacoba (Betsie)	Den Ham	13-7-1924	11-1-1932	11-3-1943	4077	11,2	n.a.	n.a.			survived		G1 (Stoffels)

Children who lived in the Jewish orphanage in Leiden from 1929 (by name)

last updated on 6-6-2021

n.a. = not applicable

Name (Family, Given)	Place of birth	Date of Birth	Orphanage in:	Orphanage out:	Days	Years decimal	Deported to Westerbork or other	Dep. From Westerbork or other	Barak No.	official DoD Date of Death	Place of death	Age reached	Comments
Worms, Jozeph (Joop)	Amsterdam	26-2-1920	16-1-1923	29-4-1940	6313	17,3	24-7-1942	31-7-1942		30-9-1942	Auschwitz	22,6	Check DoD
Wygoda, Israel	Fulda	25-10-1922	13-9-1936	2-3-1941	1631	4,5	n.a.	n.a.		5-4-1993	survived	70,4	>1942France > 1958Palestine>1967France
168 children (incl. H&E Italie)										perished		71,4%	
										(prob) survived		28,6%	
Staff: (present on 17-3-1943)													
Attenberg, Floortje	Amsterdam	23-3-1904	7-2-1929	17-3-1943	5151	14,1	17-3-1943	23-3-1943	66	26-3-1943	Sobibor	39,0	child carer, seamstress
Bierschenk, Rachel	Amsterdam	1-11-1894	29-7-1924	17-3-1943	6805	18,6	17-3-1943	23-3-1943	66	26-3-1943	Sobibor	48,4	child carer, seamstress, superv. linen room
Gobes, Mietje (Mien)	Amsterdam	21-12-1899	15-3-1923	17-3-1943	7307	20,0	17-3-1943	23-3-1943	66	26-3-1943	Sobibor	43,3	child carer
Italie, Nathan	Leeuwarden	10-04-1890	4-1-1922	17-3-1943	7742	21,2	17-3-1943	23-3-1943	66	26-3-1943	Sobibor	53,0	director of the orphanage
Italie-Cohen, Lies	Leiden	2-3-1902	23-7-1934	17-3-1943	3159	8,7	17-3-1943	23-3-1943	66	26-3-1943	Sobibor	41,1	
Klein, Esther	Oldenzaal	17-8-1909	14-9-1939	17-3-1943	1280	3,5	17-3-1943	23-3-1943	66	26-3-1943	Sobibor	33,6	religious teacher, maid ("dienstbode")
Leeuw, Jet de	Barneveld	29-12-1888	10-11-1925	17-3-1943	6336	17,4	17-3-1943	23-3-1943	66	26-3-1943	Sobibor	54,2	housekeeper, deputy director
Vries, Barend de	Leiden	20-6-1922	9-12-1942	17-3-1943	98	0,3	17-3-1942	23-3-1943		26-3-1943	Sobibor	20,8	PE trainer
Blitz, Alice	Leiden	18-7-1923	20-10-1941	17-3-1943	513	1,4	17-3-1943	23-3-1943	66	26-3-1943	Sobibor	19,7	took refuge in orphanage

NB: Date of Death is the officially recorded DoD; the actual DoD may be different in may cases, see text.
Twelve children spent two periods in the orphanage: the interruption period is quoted in the comments column. This period is taken into account when calculation the residence period in days and years.

Bibliography

Many of the references are in Dutch, but if available, a reference to an English translation is provided, or an English-language alternative suggested. In a few cases an English comment is added to the reference to explain its significance in the context of this book; in that case try the first part of the reference and search the site, or use a search engine.

Dutch composite family names are referred to in the Dutch tradition: F. van der Straaten as Straaten, F. van der; Joyce van de Bildt, as Bildt, Joyce van de, Piet de Vries as Vries, Piet de, etcetera. This deviates from what is customary in the USA. Double family names are commonly, but not always, indexed on the second name: Alvares Vega as Vega.

Internet references (URLs) are provided in some cases for convenience, particularly if it allows direct access to relevant text without retrieving the book or article. URLs may also be quoted in the footnotes of the text, if no proper reference was available. Although they were all "live" by the time this book went to press (February 2021), some may change in the future. If any of the URLs become defunct, entering only the first term of the URL will often bring you to the home page of the website, then search from there, or use a general search engine.

Reference is also made to individual dossiers which were created by the author during the investigations, such as "dossier of Betsy Wolff". They contain information and documentary evidence which could not be included in the book. Please contact the author if you need access for further research.

Aalders, G., 1999; *"Roof. De ontvreemding van joods bezit tijdens de Tweede Wereldoorlog".* Den Haag, SFU Uitgevers, BSN 9012087473. An English translation was published in 2005: *"Nazi looting: The plunder of Dutch Jewry during the Second World War".* Bloomsbury, ISBN 9781859737279. [The addition of the word "Nazi" in the translated title is misleading, since the more shocking aspect of this book is the complicity of "ordinary" Dutchmen, who were not necessarily "Nazis".]

Aalders, G. (ed.), 1998; *"Oorlogsdocumentatie '40-'45.* Zutphen, Walburg Pers.

Abma, G. et al. (eds), 1986; *"Tussen goed en fout: nieuwe gezichtspunten in de geschiedschrijving 1940-1945".* Franeker, Wever, ISBN 9061354072.

Abraham, Daniel, 2009-2020; *"The Dora".* http://danielabraham.net/tree/related/dora/. [An ongoing internet project about the Dora, by the son of one of her passengers.]

Abuys, G. & D. Mulder, 2006; *"Genezen verklaard voor ... : Een ziekenhuis in kamp Westerbork, 1939-1945".* Hooghalen Herinneringscentrum, Kamp Westerbork, ISBN 9789023242475.

Appel, Lea, 1982; *"Het brood der doden. Geschiedenis en ondergang van een joods meisjes-weeshuis"*. Baarn, Bosch & Keuning, ISBN 9024644275. [An illustrated history of the Ashkenazi girls' home in Amsterdam. For a description of the Ashkenazi boys' home in Amsterdam, See Choekat, 1986, and references in Ch. 1.]

Asscher, Berrie (Jissachar), 1996; *"Van Mokum naar Jeruzalem (1924-1944)"*. Beersheva, private publication. [Pioneer of the Catharinahoeve in Gouda who escaped over the Pyrenees with the *Hachalutz* and Westerweel underground.] See also Siegel, 2001, and Benjamin, 1990.

Asscher, E., Ph. Coppenhagen, B.P. Gomperts & J.M. Lob, 1938; *"Gedenkboek ter gelegen-heid van het 200-jarig bestaan van het Nederlandsch Israëlitisch Jongensweeshuis Megadlé Jethomim te Amsterdam"* [Commemorative book on the occasion of the 200th anniversary of the Dutch Israelite Boys' Orphanage Megadlé Jethomim in Amsterdam (in Dutch)]. Published by the Board of Governors. See also Choekat, 1986, and Appel, 1982.

Asscher-Pinkhof, Clara, 1966; *"Danseres zonder benen"* [Dancer without legs]. The Hague, Leopold, ISBN 9025800033. [This impressive autobiography has not been translated into English. She is known in the USA as Clara Pinkhof, the author of *"Star children"*, Detroit, Wayne State University Press, 1986.] See Ch. 9.3.

Beer, W. de, et al., 2015; *"Een veilig nest voor vervolgden. Verhalen over Joodse onderduikers in Rijnsburg"*. Genootschap Oud Rijnsburg. [A collection of stories about the many Jewish *onderduikers* (including Sara Philipson and Rita Klein) who found shelter in this small strictly reformed Christian village in the Leiden area. The stories are included as they were told, without being checked against other sources or documents.]

Benjamin, Yigael, 1990; *"They were our friends: A memorial for the members of the Hachsharot and the Hehalutz underground in Holland murdered in the Holocaust"*. Jerusalem, As-sociation of Former Members of the Hachsharot and the Hehalutz Underground in Holland. See http://www.westerweel-hechaluz-group.com/.

Bildt, Joyce van de, 2017; *"The memory of the Joop Westerweel resistance movement in Israel and the Netherlands"*. In: Finnay, 2017, pp. 175-194.

Blom, J.C.H., 1986; *"In de ban van goed en fout? Wetenschappelijke geschiedschrijving over de bezettingstijd in Nederland"*. In: Abma et al., 1986 , pp. 30-52.

Blom, J.C.H., 1989a; *"Crisis, bezetting en herstel. Tien studies over Nederland 1930-1950"*. The Hague, Universitaire Pers Rotterdam.

Blom, J.C.H., 1989b; *"Nederland in de jaren dertig: een 'burgerlijk-verzuilde' maatschappij in een crisisperiode"*. In: Blom, 1989a, pp. 1-27.

Blom, J.C.H., 1989c; *"The persecution of the Jews in the Netherlands: A comparative Western European perspective"*, European History Quarterly 19, 333-351. See also Griffioen & Zeller, 2011.

Blom, J.C.H., 2007; *"In de ban van goed en fout. Geschiedschrijving over de bezettingstijd in Nederland"*. Amsterdam, Boom, ISBN 9789085064633.

Blom, J.C.H. & J.J. Cahen, 2017; *"Joodse Nederlanders, Nederlandse joden en joden in Nederland (1870-1940)"*. In: Blom et al., 2017, pp. 275-359.

Blom, J.C.H., D.J. Wertheim, H. Berg & B.T. Wallet (eds), 2021; *"Reappraising the history of the Jews in the Netherlands"*. Trans. by David McKay. London, Littman Library of Jewish Civilization, ISBN 9781786941879. [In press.]

Blom, J.C.H., H. Berg, B. Wallet & D. Wertheim (eds), 2017; *"Geschiedenis van de Joden in Nederland"*. Balans, ISBN 9789460034374. [The English edition, not used in preparing this book, is in press with Littmann Library, see Blom et al., 2021.]

Blom, J.C.H., R.G. Fuks-Mansfeld & I. Schöffer (eds), 2002; *"The history of the Jews in the Netherlands"*. Oxford, The Littman Library of Jewish Civilization, ISBN 9781904113553 or 9781874774518.

Boellaard, Pim. See Withuis, Jolande, 2013.

Bolle, Mirjam, 2003; *"Ik zal je beschrijven hoe een dag er hier uitziet. Dagboekbrieven uit Amsterdam, Westerbork en Bergen Belsen"*. Amsterdam, Contact, ISBN 9025417027.

Boom, B. van der, 2012; *"Wij weten niets van hun lot"*. Amsterdam, Boom, ISBN 9789461054777. [A study of contemporary sources to determine what people knew at the time about the fate of the Jewish deportees.]

Boomgaard, Petra van den, 2019; *"Voor de nazi's geen Jood"*. Hilversum, Verbum, ISBN 9789493028043. [With English summary at the back; *"How more than 2500 Jews were able to escape deportation by evading racial regulations"*; probably the most comprehensive study to date.]

Bossenbroek, Martin, 2001; *"De meelstreep. Terugkeer en opvang na de Tweede Wereldoorlog"*. Amsterdam, Bert Bakker, ISBN 905123697.

Boterman, F., 2015; *"Duitse daders. De jodenvervolging en de nazificatie van Nederland (1940-1945)"*. Arbeiderspers, ISBN 9789029504867. [While acknowledging the complicity of a significant part of the Dutch population, whether willing or passive, this book reminds the reader that none of this would have happened without the German Nazification during the occupation.]

Braber, Ben, 2013; *"This cannot happen here: Integration and Jewish resistance in the Netherlands 1940-1945"*. Amsterdam, Amsterdam University Press, ISBN 9789089645838. Available online at www.oapen.org. [This book answers the question whether and how the integration of Jews into Dutch society influenced their resistance to persecution during the German occupation of the Netherlands in the Second World War.]

Brasz, Chaya, 1993; *"Dodenschip Dora. Een oude kolenboot redde honderden Joden ondanks Nederlandse tegenwerking"*. Vrij Nederland, 1 May. See also Abraham, Daniel.

Brasz, Chaya & Yosef Kaplan (eds), 2001; *"Dutch Jews as perceived by themselves and by others: The proceedings of the eighth International Symposium on the History of the Jews in the Netherlands"*. Leiden, Brill, ISBN 9004120386. [This volume contains English-language articles on many aspects of Jewish life and history in the Netherlands.] See also Kaplan, 2008.

Buruma, Ian, 2013; *"Year zero: A history of 1945"*. London, Atlantic Books, ISBN 9781848879379/373.

Census (the Netherlands), 1930 and other years. Available at www.volkstellingen.nl.

Choekat, Daan, 1986; *"Daantjes jeugdjaren in het Joodse Jongensweeshuis"*. Bne Brak, Daan Choekat & Sons, ISBN 9652220841. [An insider's view of the Ashkenazi boys' home on the Amstel, Amsterdam]. See also Asscher et al., 1938, and Appel, 1982.

Cohen, E.A., 1979; *"De negentien treinen naar Sobibor"*. Amsterdam, Elsevier, ISBN 9010025136.

Creveld, I.B. van, 2001; *"Het wezen van wezen. Joodse wezen in Den Haag 1850-1943. Een monument"*. De Nieuwe Haagsche, ISBN 9077032096. [Describes the history of the Jewish orphanage in The Hague and its liquidation in 1943.]

Creveld, I.B. van, 2004; *"Hulp aan wezen in oorlogstijd"*. De Nieuwe Haagsche, ISBN 9077032711. [Reports on new information about the orphanage in The Hague based on the orphanage's archives, upon their recovery and return from Russia.]

Croes, M., 2006; *"The Holocaust in the Netherlands and the rate of Jewish survival"*. Holocaust and Genocide Studies 20 (3), 474-499.

Croes, M., 2011; *"Verschillen in deportatiecijfers verklaard?"*. In: Völker, 2011, pp. 257-278. [A critical review of Griffioen & Zeller, 2011. See www.researchgate.net, publication 282662196; for rebuttal, see https://www.academia.edu/22663238/.]

Croes, M. & P. Tammes, 2004; *"Gif laten wij niet voortbestaan. Een onderzoek naar de overlevingskansen van joden in de Nederlandse Gemeenten"*. Rijksuniversiteit Groningen. [Dutch text; for an (abbreviated) English summary, see Croes, 2006.]

Crone, F., 2005; *"Voorbijgaand verblijf. Joodse weeskinderen in oorlogstijd"*. Amsterdam, De Prom, ISBN 9068011162. [Focused on refugees from Germany and the Jewish orphanage in Utrecht.]

Duin, Th. van & K. van Ommen, 2000; *"Van stadspolder tot beschermd stadsgezicht. Het ontstaan en de groei van de Professoren- en Burgemeesterswijk en Rijndijkbuurt"*. Leiden, Vereniging Professoren- en Burgemeesterswijk, ISBN 909014174X.

Eerden, E. van der, 2014; *"De Berg-Stichting: 'oase in harde en desillusioneerende maatschappij'"*. Contactblad '40-'45, pp. 4-7. ISSN 1569-1209.

Evers-Emden, Bloeme, 1994; *"Geleende kinderen. Ervaringen van onderduikouders en hun joodse beschermelingen in de jaren 1942-1945"*. Kampen, Kok, ISBN 9024262232. [*Geleend* is a bi-directional word: its meaning includes "borrowed from" as well as "lent to".]

Fast, Vera, 2011; *"Children's exodus: A history of the Kindertransport"*. London, Tauris, ISBN 9781848855373. See also Harris & Oppenheimer, 2000.

Finnay, P. (ed.), 2017; *"Remembering the Second World War"*. Basingstoke, Taylor & Francis, ISBN 9781138808140.

Flim, B.J., 1996; *"Omdat hun hart sprak. Geschiedenis van de georganiseerde hulp aan Joodse kinderen in Nederland, 1942-1945"*. Kampen, Kok, ISBN 9024260264. [An extensive study of the organized support (i.e. to find and maintain hiding places) for Jewish children in the Netherlands.] English text: Flim, 2001.

Flim, B.J., 2001; *"Opportunities for Dutch Jews to hide from the Nazis, 1942-1945"*. In: Brasz & Kaplan, 2001, pp. 289-305.

Frank, Merlyn, 1998; *"Koosje. Een dinsdagkind"*. Schoorl, Conserve, ISBN 9054290927.

Gessel, Ruud van, 2015; *"De Joodse Raad/The Jewish Council"*. Amsterdam, Brooklyn Producties. [A television documentary made with journalist Hans Knoop about the tragic dilemma of the two chairmen of the Joodsche Raad.] Available on YouTube, with English subtitles.

Gigliotti, Simone & Hilary Earl (eds), 2020; *"A companion to the Holocaust"*. Hoboken, Wiley & Sons, ISBN 9781118970522.

Griffioen, P. & R. Zeller, 2011; *"Jodenvervolging in Nederland, Frankrijk en België, 1940-1945. Overeenkomsten, verschillen, oorzaken"*. Amsterdam, Boom, ISBN 0789085068112. [Comparison of Jewish victimization rates in the Netherlands, Belgium and France.] An English summary of the dissertation which preceded (2008) the book is available from the University of Amsterdam at https://pure.uva.nl/ws/files/4255606/58120_12. pdf. See also P. Griffioen & R. Zeller, 2006; *"Anti-Jewish policy and organization of the deportations in France and the Netherlands, 1940-1944: A comparative study"*, Holocaust and Genocide Studies 20 (3), 437-473, and a similar comparative study with respect to Belgium: P. Griffioen & R. Zeller, 1998; *"The persecution of the Jews: Comparing Belgium and the Netherlands"*, Netherlands J. Social Sciences 34 (2), 126-164.

Grüter, Regina, 2017; *"Kwesties van leven en dood. Het Nederlandse Rode Kruis in de Tweede Wereldoorlog"*. Amsterdam, Balans, ISBN 9789460036538. [A critical investigation of the perceived failings of the Dutch Red Cross during the German occupation, including war victims in the Far East.]

Gutmann, Ruth, 2013; *"A final reckoning: A Hannover family's life and death in the Shoah"*. Tuscaloosa, University of Alabama Press, ISBN 9780817387181. Available on Scribd.com. Original German edition: Herskovits-Gutmann, 2002.

Hammel, A. & B. Lewkowicz (eds), (2012); *"The Kindertransport to Britain 1938/39: New perspectives"*. Amsterdam, Brill/Rodopi, ISBN 9789042036154. [This book offers different or complementary views compared to Harris & Oppenheimer, 2000, or Fast, 2011.]

Happe, Katja, 2017; *"Viele falsche Hoffnungen: Judenverfolgung in den Niederlanden 1940-1945"*. Paderborn, Ferdinand Schöningh Verlag, ISBN-13 9783506784247. [A Dutch translation was published in 2018: *"Veel valse hoop. De jodenvervolging in Nederland 1940-1945"*. Atlas Contact, ISBN 9789045035888.]

Harris, M.J. & D. Oppenheimer, 2000; *"Into the arms of strangers: Stories of the Kindertransport"*. London, Bloomsbury, ISBN 158234101X. http://www.kindertransport.org/history.htm. See also: Fast, 2011, and Hammel & Lewkowicz, 2012.

Heijden, C. van der, 2001; *"Grijs verleden. Nederland en de Tweede Wereldoorlog"* [Grey history: The Netherlands and the Second World War]. Amsterdam, Contact, ISBN 9789025496944; reprinted in 2009, ISBN 9789025431808. [A somewhat controversial book suggesting that between the heroes and the traitors a black-and-white judgement is often impossible.]

Heitink, K. & A. Nooij, 2012; *"Bennekom Joods Toevluchtsoord 1940-1944"*. Bennekom, Historische Vereniging Oud-Bennekom, ISBN 9789078592037. [Only this second edition contains the story of Sara Philipson after her flight from Rijnsburg.]

Herskovits-Gutmann, Ruth, 2002; *"Auswanderung vorläufig nicht möglich. Die Geschichte der Familie Herskovits aus Hannover"*. Göttingen, Wallstein, ISBN 3892445079. English edition: Gutmann, 2013.

Herzberg, A.J., 1985; *"Kroniek der Jodenvervolging, 1940-1945"*. Amsterdam, Querido, ISBN 9021465779. First published in 1950.

Hillesum, Etty, 2002; *"Etty: The letters and diaries of Etty Hillesum, 1941-1943"*. Ed. by Klaas A.D. Smelik. Grand Rapids, Wm. B. Eerdmans Publishing Company, ISBN 0802839592. Originally published in Dutch in 1986 by Uitgeverij Balans, Amsterdam.

Hodge, Deborah, 2012; *"Rescuing the children: The story of the Kindertransport"*. Toronto, Tundra Books, ISBN 9781770492561. [Contains a chapter on the SS *Bodegraven*.]

Houwink ten Cate, J.Th.M., 1993; *"Heydrich's security police and the Amsterdam Jewish Council (February 1941-October 1942)"*. In: Michman, 1993, pp. 381-393.

Houwink ten Cate, J.Th.M, with W. Lindwer, 1995; *"De Joodsche Raad voor Amsterdam 1941-1943"*. In: Lindwer & Houwink ten Cate, 1995, pp. 13-32.

Hovingh, G.C., 1995; *"Johannes Post. Exponent van het verzet. Een biografie"*. Kampen, Kok, ISBN 9024264626. 2nd ed., 1999.

Huisman, Annet (dir.), 2018; *"De Joodse Bruiloft"*. Documentary film. Omrop Fryslân. [After the passing of Barend Boers and Mimi Dwinger, their three children opened a suitcase full of documents about their parents' escape from Holland through Vichy France and over the Pyrenees in 1942. The parents had never discussed this even with their children. In 2017, the children followed the route of their parents as closely as possible, while the documentary adds historical context. Based on Zeldenrust, 2018. [Relevant to understand Herman Stofkooper's escape, Ch. 9.8.]

Israel, Jonathan I., 1998; *"The Dutch Republic: Its rise, greatness, and fall, 1477-1806"*. Oxford, Clarendon Press, ISBN 0198730721/8207344.

Italie, Gabriel, 2009; *"Het oorlogsdagboek van dr. G. Italie. Den Haag, Barneveld, Westerbork, Theresienstadt, Den Haag 1940-1945"*. Ed. by Wally M. de Lang. Amsterdam, Contact, ISBN

9789025427917. [The war diary of Gabriel Italie, one of the brothers of Nathan Italie, the director of the Jewish orphanage in Leiden.]

Jacobs, Luise, 2000; *"De verborgen massamoorden in Schloss Hartheim"*. In: Keulen-Woudstra, 2000, pp. 31-42. [Relevant to understand the false death details of Philip van Santen (Ch. 8.1) recorded in Holland.]

Jong, L. de, 1969-1994; *"Het Koninkrijk der Nederlanden in de Tweede Wereldoorlog"*. http://www.dbnl.org or http://www.loedejongdigitaal.nl/. [The standard (contemporary) history of the Netherlands during the war. The entire text is available online (with search facility). For more recent interpretations, see Blom et al., 2021.]

Jonkers-Stroink, P. & A. de Bruin, 2016; *"Familiekroniek Heerma van Voss. Deel 7b"*. Private publication.

Kaplan, Yosef (ed.), 2008; *"The Dutch intersection: The Jews and the Netherlands in modern history"*. Leiden, Brill. Available online (from some universities) at EBSCOhost Academic Collection – World Wide. [This volume contains English-language articles on many aspects of Jewish life and history in the Netherlands.] See also Brasz & Kaplan, 2001.

Kasteleyn, L.P., 2003; *"Vervolging en bescherming, joden in Leiden 1933-1945"*. Leiden, Museum de Lakenhal.

Kasteleyn, L.P., unpublished A; *"Notities van gesprekken met Mimi de Wind-Weiman"*. Not available to the author in written form; B; *"Notities van gesprekken met Piet de Vries"*. Included in Dossier Piet de Vries. C; *"Brieven van Hans Kloosterman"*. Included in Dossier Hans Kloosterman.

Keesing, Miriam, 2013; *"Truus Wijsmuller-Meijer, a forgotten heroine"*. In: *"Celebrating 75 years of Kindertransport"*, pp. 32-33. https://www.dokin.nl/publications/celebrating-75-years-of-kindertransport-truus-wijmuller-a-forgotten-heroine/.

Keesing, M., P. Tammes & A.J. Simpkin, 2019; *"Jewish refugee children in the Netherlands during World War II: Migration, settlement, and survival"*. Social Science History 43 (4), 785-811.

Kerkvliet, G. & M. Uitvlugt, 1973; *"Een pot picalilly voor Westerbork. Journalistiek verslag over de vernietiging van het joodse weeshuis in Leiden"*. Den Haag, Q-Producties. Author's collection. [The original stencilled report, containing verbatim quotes from interviews with the Stoffels, Geertje Gebert, and Piet de Vries.] See also Kerkvliet & Uitvlugt, 1974.

Kerkvliet, G. & M. Uitvlugt, 1974; *"De vernietiging van het Joodse Weeshuis te Leiden tijdens de Duitse bezetting"*. Studia Rosenthaliana 8, 268-299. [An abbreviated version was published as G. Kerkvliet & M. Uitvlugt, 1988; *"Een pot piccalilly voor Westerbork. Verslag van de vernietiging van het Joodse weeshuis te Leiden"*. Jaarboekje voor Geschiedenis en Oudheidkunde van Leiden en omstreken 80, 147-180.]

Keulen-Woudstra, Alice B. van (ed.), 2000; *"Mauthausen, 1938-1998"*. Utrecht, Van Gruting, ISBN 9075879067/9789075879063.

Klein-Roskin, Ingrid, 1995; *"Observations on the end of an era"*. Private report. Author's collection. [Contains the wartime memories and history of Ingrid, Rita and Benjamin Klein.]

Knoop, Hans, 1983; *"De Joodsche Raad. Het drama van Abraham Asscher en David Cohen"*. Amsterdam, Elsevier, ISBN 9010046567. See also van Gessel, 2015 (an updated documentary available on YouTube, with English subtitles) and Somers, 2010.

Kogon, Eugen, 1974; *"Der SS-Staat. Das System der deutschen Konzentrationslager"*. München, Kindler Verlag. [Kogon was a Christian opponent to the Nazi regime who survived 6 years in Buchenwald.]. Dutch edition: Kogon, Eugen, 1976; *"De SS-staat"*. Amsterdam, Amsterdam Boek, no ISBN. English and Dutch translations exist in several editions.

Kogon, Eugen, 1983; *"Nationalsozialistische Massentötungen durch Giftgas. Eine Documentation"*. Frankfurt a/M, S. Fischer Verlag, ISBN 3100404025.

Kopuit, M., 1974; *"Groot boeren- en kaasbedrijf van oud-Leidenaars in Beth Jitschak"* [Dairy farm of Ben Meijer and family]. *Nieuw Israëlitisch Weekblad*, 11 January, p .7.

Koreman, Megan, 2016; *"Gewone helden. De Dutch-Paris ontsnappingslijn 1942-1945"*. Amsterdam, Boom, ISBN 9789058755568 (paperback). See also Plantinga, 1998.

Koreman, Megan, 2018; *"The escape line: How the ordinary heroes of Dutch-Paris resisted the Nazi occupation of Western Europe"*. New York, Oxford University Press, ISBN 9780190662271 (hardcover)/|9789461279606 (e-book).

Lang, Hans-Joachim, 2011; *"Die Frauen von Block 10. Medizinische Versuche in Auschwitz"*. Hamburg, Hoffmann und Campe, ISBN 9783455502220.

Lang, Wally de, 2021; *"De razzia's van 22 en 23 februari 1941 in Amsterdam. Het lot van 389 Joodse mannen"*. Amsterdam, Uitgeverij Atlas Contact, ISBN 9789045042749. [This first comprehensive account of the razzias which preceded the February Strike, and the fate of the deportees to Buchenwald and Mauthausen was published just before the present book went to press.]

Lanzmann, Claude (dir.), 1985; *"Shoah"*. [A nine-hour documentary masterpiece. Available on DVD from various sources. This film is virtually devoid of archive material. Instead, Lanzmann extensively interviewed perpetrators as well as bystanders. He succeeds in making many of them talk relatively freely and uninhibited about the past by using a seemingly innocuous interview technique. He also interviewed surviving victims, using a different, but equally effective, technique to overcome their reluctance to talk. One of the most moving, and disturbing, such interviews is with Abraham "Abe" Bomba, one of the barbers in Treblinka who had to cut off the hair of the women before they were gassed. This interview, and some other parts of the documentary, can be found on YouTube.]

Lanzmann, Claude (dir.), 1997; *"Un vivant qui passe"* [A visitor from the living]. [A 65-minute documentary based on his interview with Maurice Rossel, the Swiss representative of the International Red Cross who visited Theresienstadt on 23rd June 1944, and who allowed himself to be utterly hoodwinked by the Nazis. Also filed as USHMM Film 2891.]

Lanzmann, Claude (dir.), 2001; *"Sobibor: 14th October 1943, 16:00".* [A 95-minute documentary containing a detailed witness account by Yehuda Lerner of the revolt in Sobibor, which caused the Germans to close down the camp and its subsidiary camps and kill all the remaining prisoners.] See also Schelvis, 2007/2008.

Leman, IS, (5689) 1929; *"Het Centraal Israelitisch Wees- en Doorgangshuis te Leiden in woord en beeld (1890-1929)".* Title on the cover: *"Uit de geschiedenis van een nuttige instelling".* Den Haag, Drukkerij Levisson, with contributions by J.L Palache.

Liempt, A. van, 2005; *"Hitler's bounty hunters: The betrayal of the Jews".* New York, Berg, ISBN 1845202031/9781845202033.

Liempt, A. van, 2019; *"Gemmeker. Commandant van Kamp Westerbork".* Amsterdam, Balans, ISBN 9789460039782 (hardcover)/9789460039799 (ebook).

Liempt, A. van & J. Kompagnie (eds), 2013; *"Jodenjacht: de onthutsende rol van de Neder-landse politie in de Tweede Wereldoorlog"* [Hunting down Jews: The shocking role of the local Dutch police during the German occupation], 5th ed. Amsterdam, Balans, ISBN 9789460037221.

Ligtenberg, L., 2017; *"Mij krijgen ze niet levend. De zelfmoorden van mei 1940".* Amsterdam, Balans, ISBN 9789460038457. [About the sharp increase in suicides immediately upon the German invasion in May 1940.]

Lindwer, Willy, 1990; *"Kamp van hoop en wanhoop. Getuigen van Westerbork, 1939-1945"* [Camp of hope and despair: Witness account from Westerbork]. Amsterdam, Balans, ISBN 9050180981.

Lindwer, W. & J.Th.M. Houwink ten Cate, 1995; *"Het fatale dilemma: De Joodsche Raad voor Amsterdam, 1941-1943".* Den Haag, Sdu Uitgeverij Koninginnegracht.

Luijters, Guus, Raymund Schütz & Marten Jongman, 2017; *"De deportaties uit Nederland 1940-1945. Portretten uit de archieven".* Amsterdam, Nieuw Amsterdam, ISBN 9789046822456.

Maor, Roni, 2011; *"The finger in the dyke: The survival story of a Jewish child in Holland during the Holocaust".* [The autobiography of Aron Wolff, in Hebrew; www.rimonim-publishing.com, 115 pp.]

Mazower, Mark, 2005; *"Salonica – City of ghosts: Christians, Muslims and Jews, 1450-1950".* London, Harper Collins, ISBN 9780007120222.

Mechanicus, Philip, 1964; *"In dépôt: dagboek uit Westerbork"* [Diary from Westerbork]. Amsterdam, Polak & van Gennep.

Meijer-Wijler, Gerda, 1993; *"A personal history, 1923-1945".* [Unpublished document (in English), written for her children and grandchildren. Gerda was neighbour to both Emilie van Brussel (before she married Hijme Stoffels) and the family Klein. She played an active role in the Dutch resistance. She emigrated to Israel with other surviving members of her family, building a successful dairy farm in Beth Jitschak (Kopuit, 1974). She also deposited an (English language) report of her activities between September 1944 and May 1945 at NIOD, also available at www.weggum.com.]

Melkman, Jozeph, 1974; *"De briefwisseling tussen Mr. L.E. Visser en Prof. Dr. D. Cohen". Studia Rosenthaliana* 8, 107-130.

Melkman-de Paauw, Fré, 2002; *"Hoe het verder gaat weet niemand. Naoorlogse brieven uit Amstardam naar Palestina".* Commentaries by J. and D. Michman. Amsterdam, Contact, ISBN 9025419626. [Relevant for the reuniting of *onderduik* children with surviving parents, and the story of Aron Wolff, Ch. 9.4.]

Mendes da Costa, Joseph, 1934; *"Het Portugeesch-Israëlitisch Meisjesweeshuis 'Mazon Habanoth' Amsterdam 5495 (1734) 6 Sebath, 5694 (1934): uitgegeven ter gelegenheid van zijn tweehonderdjarig bestaan".* [Memorial book, 200 years of the Sephardic girls' orphanage in Amsterdam; rare copy in JHM (JCK), Amsterdam.]

Metz, Daniël, 2005; *"Een historisch overzicht van acht joodse weeshuizen in Nederland". Misjpoge, tijdschrift van de Nederlandse Kring voor Joodse Genealogie* 2005-2.

Michman, Dan, 1989; *"Migration versus 'Species Hollandia Judaica': The role of migration in the nineteenth and twentieth centuries in preserving ties between Dutch and World Jewry". Studia Rosenthaliana* 23, 54-76.

Michman, Dan, 2017; *"Adolf Hitler, the decision-making process leading to the 'Final Solution of the Jewish Question', and the Grand Mufti of Jerusalem Hajj Amin al-Hussayni: The current state of research".* Jerusalem, Yad Vashem Publications.

Michman, Dan, 2020; *"Characteristics of Holocaust historiography and their contexts since 1990: Emphases, perceptions, developments, debates".* In: Gigliotti & Earl, 2020, pp. 211-232.

Michman, Jozeph, 1987; *"Met voorbedachten rade. Ideologie en uitvoering van de Endlösung der Judenfrage".* Amsterdam, Meulenhoff, ISBN 9029098473. [An analysis of the ideology which gave rise to the Holocaust and how it developed from the moment Hitler declared his intention to remove all Jews from Europe.]

Michman, Jozeph, 2001; *"Ideological historiography".* In: Brasz & Kaplan, 2001, pp. 205-214.

Michman, Jozeph (ed.), 1993; *"Dutch Jewish history: Proceedings of the fifth Symposium on the History of the Jews in the Netherlands, vol. 3".* Jerusalem, Institute for Research on Dutch Jewry.

Michman, Jozeph & Bert Jan Flim (eds), 2004; *"The encyclopaedia of the righteous among the nations: Rescuers of Jew during the Holocaust. Volume: The Netherlands".* Jerusalem, Yad Vashem.

Michman, Jozeph, Hartog Beem & Dan Michman, 1999; *"Pinkas. Geschiedenis van de joodse gemeenschap in Nederland".* Incorporating research by Victor Brilleman. Amsterdam, Uitgeverij Contact & NIK, ISBN 9025495133. [The original text of this comprehensive history of the Jews in the Netherlands is also available in Hebrew, Yad Vashem, Holocaust Martyrs' and Heroes Remembrance Authority, Jerusalem, 1985.]

Moore, Bob, 1997; *"Victims and survivors: The Nazi persecution of the Jews in the Netherlands 1940-1945"*. London, Arnold, ISBN 0340691573/0340495634.

Moore, Bob, 2001; *"The Dutch churches, Christians and the rescue of Jews in the Netherlands"*. In: Brasz & Kaplan, 2001, pp. 277-288.

Moore, Bob, 2010; *"Survivors: Jewish self-help and rescue in Nazi-occupied Western Europe"*. Oxford, Oxford University Press, ISBN 9780199208234.

Moore, Bob, 2011; *"Jewish self-help and rescue in the Netherlands"*. Tijdschrift voor Geschiedenis 124 (4), 492-505.

Nachama, Andreas. See Stiftung Topographie des Terrors, 2018.

Neij, R. and E.V. Hueting, 1988; *"Nederlands Volksherstel 1944-1947. Een omstreden hulporganisatie in herrijzend Nederland"*. Culemborg, Lemma. ISBN9051890125

NMG Productions, 2010; *"Bagage van Leiden. Een Joods weeshuis in oorlogstijd"*. [A video documentary (50 minutes) about the Jewish orphanage in Leiden. The film can be viewed at https://www.nmgproductions.nl/portfolio?lang=nl.]

Piersma, Hinke, 2005; *"De drie van Breda. Duitse oorlogsmisdadigers in Nederlandse gevangenschap 1945-1989"*. Amsterdam, Balans, ISBN 9050186610/9789050186612.

Piersma, Hinke, 2019; *"Op eigen gezag: Politieverzet in oorlogstijd"*. Amsterdam, Singel Uitg., ISBN 978902141684.

Pinkhof, Clara. See Asscher-Pinkhof, 1966.

Pinkhof, Mirjam, 1979; *"Menachem"*. Published in Haifa in Dutch as well as in Hebrew. [A monument for her husband (1920-1969) with many stories about the Palestine Pioneers from Loosdrecht.]

Pinkhof, Mirjam, 1998; *"De jeugdalijah van het Paviljoen Loosdrechtse Rade. 1939-1945"*. Historische Reeks Loosdrecht #4. Hilversum, Verloren. [A book (in Dutch) about the Palestine Pioneers in Loosdrecht, and the activities of the Westerweel resistance group; contains biographies of the resident children, mostly German and Polish refugees, as well as local farmers who sheltered them from the Germans. The book contains many photographs, with individuals identified, and is relevant for the story of Lodi Cohen (Ch. 9.7). More information is available in the Ghetto Fighters' House museum in Israel, Beit Lohamei Hagettaot, North of Haifa.] See also Schippers, 2015, and van der Straaten, 1998. For an interview (1988) with Pinkhof by Ellen Land, see www.humboldt.edu/rescuers/book/Pinkhof/mpstory1.html.

Plantinga, Sierk, 1998; *"Joseph Willem Kolkman (1896-1944) en de Engelandvaarders: De hulp aan Nederlandse vluchtelingen in Vichy-Frankrijk"*. In: Aalders, 1998, pp. 10-36. [No footnotes; the annotated version is available in NIOD, or directly from the author of the article.]

Plicht, Elias van der, 2001; *"Geld"*. In: van Liempt & Kompagnie, 2001, pp. 151-190. [This author reviewed the CABR dossiers relevant for Leiden, including the role played by Adrianus Biesheuvel and Willem de Groot.]

Presser, J., 1965; *"Ondergang. De vervolging en verdelging van het Nederlandse Jodendom, 1940-1945"*. 's-Gravenhage, Staatsuitgeverij/Martinus Nijhoff. [The entire Dutch text is available online (with search facility) at http://www.dbnl.org. Although written more than half a century ago, the book is still very readable and impressive today.] An English translation was published by E.P. Dutton & Co. in 1969 (ASIN B000LD8D7S), and again in 1988 under the title *"Ashes in the wind: The destruction of Dutch Jewry"* by Wayne State University Press; re-issued in 2010, ISBN 9780285638136.

Rens, H.A.V. van, 2013; *"Vervolgd in Limburg. Joden en Sinti in Nederlands-Limburg tijdens de Tweede Wereldoorlog"*. Maaslandse Monografieen 76. Hilversum, Verloren, ISBN 9789087043537.

Rens, H.A.V. van, et al., 1994; *"Een voetnoot bij de wereldgeschiedenis. Beek tijdens de Tweede Wereldoorlog"*. Wat Baek os bud #17. Beek, Stichting Herdenking Oorlogsslachtoffers. [For correct dates, see Rens, 2013.]

Riet, Frank van, 2016; *"De bewakers van Westerbork"*. Amsterdam, Boom, ISBN 9789058756077. [A re-evaluation of the role of the OD (*Ordedienst*), the internal Jewish Police force in Camp Westerbork.]

Rose, Leesha, 1978; *"The tulips are red"*. South Brunswick, Barnes & Co., ISBN 0498021769. [Leesha Rose (Bornstein during the war) collaborated in the resistance with van Wijk and Stoffels.]

Rose, Leesha, 1980; *"De tulpen zijn rood. Het aktieve verzet van een Joods meisje"*. Katwijk, Servire, ISBN 90632512203.

Rutten, Stefan, 2014; *"Joods Gouda: geschiedenis van de joden in Gouda"*. Gouda, Gouds Metaheerhuis & Verzetsmuseum Zuid-Holland, ISBN 9789090281506.

Salemink, Theo, 2001; *"Strangers in a strange country: Catholic views of Jews in the Netherlands, 1918-1945"*. In: Brasz & Kaplan, 2001, pp. 107-123.

Schelvis, Jules, 2001; *"Vernietigingskamp Sobibor. De transportlijsten"*. Amsterdam, De Bataafse Leeuw, ISBN 906707516. [A most important document, it published the deportation lists made, and secretly copied, in Camp Westerbork. It contains the names and date of birth of 34,313 people deported in 19 train transports from Westerbork to Sobibor, a journey which took 3 days. Only 18 people (including Schelvis) survived.]

Schelvis, Jules, 2007a; *"Binnen de poorten. Een verslag van twee jaar Duitse vernietigings- en concentratiekampen"*. Amsterdam, De Bataafse Leeuw, ISBN 978906707626. [Schelvis is one of the 18 survivors of the 34,314 people deported from Westerbork to Sobibor. This is his own account of his deportation and survival.]

Schelvis, Jules, 2007b; *"Sobibor: A history a Nazi death camp"*. Oxford, Berg, in association with USHM, ISBN 978184520418. Republished in 2014 by Bloomsbury, ISBN 1472589068.

Schelvis, Jules, 2008; *"Vernietigingskamp Sobibor"*. De Bataafse Leeuw, ISBN 9789067076296. For the English translation, see Schelvis 2007b.

Schippers, Hans L., 2015; *"De Westerweelgroep en de Palestinapioniers. Non-conformistisch verzet in de Tweede Wereldoorlog"*. Hilversum, Verloren, ISBN 9789087044978. *English edition:* Hans Schippers, 2019; *"Westerweel Group: Non-conformist resistance against Nazi Germany; A joint rescue effort of Dutch idealists and Dutch-German zionists"*. De Gruyter Oldenbourg: New perspectives on modern Jewish history, V.11; ISBN 9783110580006.

Schram, Laurence, 2018; *"Dossin. Wachtkamer van Auschwitz"*. Tielt, Lannoo, ISBN 9782390250395. [One of the first comprehensive studies about the transit camp Kazerne Dossin in Mechelen (Belgium), through which 25,484 Jews and 352 Roma and Sinti were deported to Auschwitz, including Alexander Lipschitz and his family. Only 1222 survived the deportations.]

Schute, Ivar, 2020; *"In de schaduw van de nachtvlinder"*. Amsterdam, Prometheus, ISBN 9789044642438. [A recent publication by a member of the Sobibor archaeology team.]

Schütz, Raymund, 2011; *"Vermoedelijk op transport. De Joodsche Raad Cartotheek als infor-matiesysteem binnen sterk veranderende kaders: repressie, opsporing en herinnering. Een archiefwetenschappelijk onderzoek naar de herkomst, het gebruik en het beheer van een bijzondere historische bron"*. MA thesis, Free University of Amsterdam. [An indispensable report when interpreting the index cards kept by the Joodse Raad of Amsterdam on all people who were to be deported from the Netherlands. The cards were kept by the Red Cross (War Documentation) in The Hague until February 2018; now in the Holocaust Museum, Amsterdam. Dutch text available at https://www.joodsebibliotheek.nl.]

Schütz, Raymund, 2016; *"Kille mist"*. PhD thesis, Free University of Amsterdam. [This study, sponsored by the Dutch Notary Professional Association, brought to light, more than 70 years after the war, the dismal role of Dutch public notaries in registering new ownership of stolen Jewish assets (such as real estate), while hiding the original Jewish ownership.]

Schütz, R., 2017; *"Het dossier van het Oorlogsarchief"* [The Red Cross War Archive in The Hague]. In: Luijters, 2017, pp. 19-32.

Siebelt, Alphons, 2011a; *"Een Burcht van papier"*. *Leids Jaarboekje 2011*, 166-189. Historische Vereniging Oud Leiden, ISSN 0922-6699.

Siebelt, Alphons, 2011b; *"Gids voor Leiden in de Tweede Wereldoorlog. Beschreven in 650 adressen"* [Guide to Leiden in the Second World War, described in 650 addresses]. Leiden, Ginkgo.

Siebelt, Alphons, 2015; *"Hij zit bij de onderduikersbond. Hulp aan Leidse onderduikers in de Tweede Wereldoorlog"*. Leiden, Primavera Press. [A study of the organized assistance to *onderduikers* in Leiden, arguably the most important form of resistance during the occupation of the Netherlands, where armed resistance was virtually impossible for the lack of wilderness areas where partisans could hide.]

Siegel, Paul, 2001; *"Locomotieven trekken wagons, 1933-1945"*. Utrecht, Van Gruting, ISBN 9789075879100. The English translation (Siegel, Paul, 2005; *"Engines pull wagons: A personal story*". Trans. by Gilda Gordon. Amsterdam, Olive Press, ISBN 9077787011/9789077787014) was not used in preparing this book.

Somers, E., 2010; *"Voorzitter van de Joodse Raad. De herinneringen van David Cohen (1941-1943)"*. Zutphen, Walburg Press, ISBN 9789057305368. [Annotated edition of the memoires of David Cohen, which he dictated in 1955 in defence of his wartime actions as co-chairman of the Joodsche Raad. For a critical review, see Edwin Rabbie, 2010; *"Over de moraliteit"*. *Textualscholarship.nl.* https://www.textualscholarship.nl/?p=3936.]

Staal, Philip, 2008; *"Roestvrijstaal. Speurtocht naar de erfenis van Joodse oorlogswezen"*. Delft, Eburon, ISBN 9789059722712. English edition: Staal, 2015.

Staal, Philip, 2015; *"Settling the account (Mijn erfenis)"*. Bloomington, iUniverse, ISBN 9781491751664/51657.

Stam-van der Staay, Mien, 2003; *"Lotte. 'Ik zing terwijl het binnen in mij huilt'. Lotte Adler, 1925-1943"*. Leiden, Museum De Lakenhal, ISBN 9071655172.

Stiftung Topographie des Terrors (represented by Nachama, Andreas), 2018; *"Topography of terror: Gestapo, SS and Reich Security Main Office on Wilhelm- and Prinz-Albrecht-Straße: A documentation"*. 9th revised edition. Berlin, ISBN 9783941772175.

Stoffels, H. & E. Stoffels-van Brussel, 1967; *"Unpublished"*, 22nd November. [A list of (some of) their activities in support of Jewish citizens of Leiden from February 1942, such as arranging *onderduik* addresses, false papers, etc. The list was written at the request of Elchanan Italie, in support of a proposal by him]

Stoop, P., 1988; *"De geheime rapporten van H.J. Noordewier. Berlijn, 1933-1935"*. Amsterdam, Sijthof, ISBN 9021839954.

Straaten, Frans van der, 1998; *"Palestina-Pioniers in Nederland: herinneringen en belevenissen aan/van gedurende de oorlogsjaren 1939-1945: Om nooit te vergeten"*. Capelle a/d IJssel, MES Grafische Bedrijven, ISBN 9076061130. [This book contains a wealth of information, as well as listings of the refugees in the various Hachsharah institutions, but it has had limited circulation. One copy is available in the Joods Historisch Museum, Amsterdam, and another in the Koninklijke Bibliotheek in The Hague.] See also Pinkhof, 1998

Straten, J.W. van, 1992; *"Herinneringen aan de oorlog van de verzetsman J.W. van Straten over de jaren 1940-1945"*. 5 volumes. [An incomplete photocopy of parts II and III (1942-1944) is in the library of the Joods Historisch Museum, Amsterdam, catalog D7608. The author had access to the original report, courtesy Mr. B. van Straten.]

Sturhoofd, Pamela & Jessica van Tijn (dirs), 2020; *"De kinderen van Truus"* [The children of Truus Wijsmuller]. Documentary film. Amsterdam, Special Eyes Co. [Contains the testimony of Helga Gottschalk.] An English version is expected to be released in June 2021. See https://www.truus-children.com/ or www.facebook.com/truuschildren. For more information: info@special-eyes.nl.

Sykes, Christopher, 1965; *"Cross roads to Israel: Palestine from Balfour to Bevin"*. London, Collins (also New English Library, Indiana University Press and others), ISBN

0253201659/9780253201652. [A fascinating description, from the British perspective, of the final stages of the British Mandate in Palestine.]

Szur, Grigori, 1997; *"De Joden van Wilno. Een kroniek 1941-1944"*. Amsterdam, Jan Mets, ISBN 9053301879. [A succinct report on the destruction of the ghetto of Wilno (Vilnius), based on manuscripts in Russian, delivered by Vladimir Poroedominski and published by Jan Mets. Apart from the original manuscript (in Russian), this Dutch edition (2019) is the only publication in existence to date.]

Vishniac, Roman, 1983; *"A vanished world"*. New York, Farrar, Straus & Giroux.

Völker, B. (ed.), 2011; *"Over gaten, bruggen en witte paters – sociaal kapitaal in sociologisch onderzoek. Liber Amicorum voor Henk Flap"*. Amsterdam, Rozenberg.

Vries, Hans de, 2000; *"Sie starben wie Fliegen im Herbst"*. In: Keulen-Woudstra, 2000, pp. 7-18.

Vries, Hans de, 2011; *"Mauthausen. Een geval apart"*. https://pure.knaw.nl/ws/files/6338408/2011 and search for Vries_MauthausenEenGevalApart.pdf. [In Dutch, summarizing the special significance of Mauthausen in Dutch wartime history.]

Vries, H. de, B. Perz, L. Jacobs, A. Baumgartner & D. Wingeate Pike (eds), 2000; *"Mauthausen, 1938-1998"*. Utracht, Van Gruting, ISBN 9075879067 and 9789075879063.

Vries, Piet de, 2000; *"Herinneringen"*. Notes from several interviews with Piet, recorded by Leonard Kasteleyn.

Wallet, B.T., 2017; *"Tussen marge en centrum. Joden in naoorlogs Nederland"*. In: Blom et al., 2017, pp. 407-485. [English translation in press.] See Blom et al., 2021.

Wasserstein, Bernard, 2014; *"The ambiguity of virtue: Gertrude van Tijn and the fate of the Dutch Jews"*. Cambridge, MA, Harvard University Press, ISBN 9780674281387. [An earlier version of this book was published in Dutch in 2013: *"Gertrude van Tijn en het lot van de Nederlandse Joden"*, Amsterdam, Nieuw Amsterdam, ISBN 9789046814352.]

Wijk, Cor van, 1946; *"Mijn werk in de Nederlandse Verzetsorganisatie 'Strijdend Nederland'"*. Typescript, Regionaal Archief Leiden (now Erfgoed Leiden & Omgeving). [An account of his wartime activities, including the provision of (at least) 420 blank but genuine pbs to the Leiden underground movement. No less than 124 of these were used by Stoffels.]

Wijsenbeek, S.S., 1933; *"Gedenkboek 100 jaar Joods Weeshuis Rotterdam"* [Memorial book: 100 years of the Jewish orphanage in Rotterdam]. [A rare copy at Rotterdam Gemeentearchief, no. 1174.]

Wijsmuller-Meijer, Truus, 1961; *"Geen tijd voor tranen"*. Amsterdam, Querido, also Salamander. [Autobiography, recorded by L.G. Vrooland. Out of print, but text is available on the site of the Historische Vereniging Alkmaar.]

Withuis, Jolande, 2013; *"Weest manlijk, zijt sterk. Pim Boellaard (1903-2001) Het leven van een verzetsheld"*. Amsterdam, De Bezige Bij, ISBN 9789023478430.

Wolff, Aron. See Maor, 2011.

Wroclawski, Cynthia, 2013; *"Unto every person there is a name"*. *Yad Vashem Quarterly Magazine*, special edition, December.

Zee, Sytze van der, 2010; *"Vogelvrij. De jacht op de Joodse onderduiker"* [Outlawed: The hunt for Jews in hiding]. Amsterdam, Bezige Bij, ISBN 9789023454328.

Zegveld, W.F. van, 1993; *"Joods Wees- en Doorgangshuis Leiden, bewoners 1890-1951"*. Originally in: *"De Joden van Leiden"*. Unpublished; 4 volumes. [Several copies were made, available (i.a.) at Erfgoed Leiden (ELO) and the Joods Historisch Museum, Amsterdam. The results of his painstaking research have served as a basis for subsequent investigations. Note that his report is an important source of information on children and staff in the Leiden orphanage who are not included in this book because they had left before the move to the new building in 1929, as well as Jewish citizens of the Leiden region who were not connected to the orphanage.]

Zeldenrust, Auke, 2018; *"De Joodse Bruiloft. Een koffer vol oorlogsgeheimen"*. Amsterdam, Boom, ISBN 9789024420551.

Persons index

Numbers in brackets indicate Figure numbers, and photographs on which that individual has been identified. Thus: "Person, name (1.12) 15, 152" means the person is shown in Figure 1.12 and is mentioned on pages 15 and 152.

Subjects index

For Product Safety Concerns and Information please contact our EU
representative GPSR@taylorandfrancis.com
Taylor & Francis Verlag GmbH, Kaufingerstraße 24, 80331 München, Germany